North Dakota State University Libraries
GIFT FROM

Stephen Fischer-Galati, editor
East European Monographs

Also in the Variorum Collected Studies Series

C.A. MACARTNEY
Studies on Early Hungarian and Pontic History

FRANCIS J. THOMSON
The Reception of Byzantine Culture in Medieval Russia

ERIK FÜGEDI
Kings, Bishops, Nobles and Burghers in Medieval Hungary

NIKOLAI TODOROV
Society, the City, and Industry in the Balkans, 15th–19th Centuries

ZSIGMOND PÁL PACH
Hungary and the European Economy in Early Modern Times

PÉTER GUNST
Agrarian Development and Social Change in Eastern Europe, 14th–19th Centuries

JERZY TOPOLSKI
The Manorial Economy in Early-Modern East-Central Europe: Origins, Development and Consequences

ANTONI MACZAK
Money, Prices and Power in Poland, 16th–17th Centuries

GUSTAVE ALEF
Rulers and Nobles in 15th-Century Muscovy

SAMUEL H. BARON
Explorations in Muscovite History

THOMAS S. NOONAN
The Islamic World, Russia and the Vikings, 750–900

JERZY KLOCZOWSKI
La Pologne dans l'Eglise médiévale

WLADIMIR VODOFF
Princes et principautés russes, Xe–XIIe siècle

ALAIN DUCELLIER
L'Albanie entre Byzance et Venise (Xe–XVe s.)

VARIORUM COLLECTED STUDIES SERIES
Studies in East–Central Europe
General Editor: Ivan T. Berend

East European Nationalism,
Politics and Religion

Professor Peter F. Sugar

Peter F. Sugar

East European Nationalism, Politics and Religion

VARIORUM

Aldershot · Brookfield USA · Singapore · Sydney

This edition copyright 1999 by Peter F. Sugar.

Published in the Variorum Collected Studies Series by

Ashgate Publishing Limited
Gower House, Croft Road
Aldershot, Hampshire, GU11 3HR
Great Britain

Ashgate Publishing Company
Old Post Road
Brookfield, Vermont 05036–9704
USA

Ashgate website: http://www.ashgate.com

ISBN 0–86078–806–7

British Library CIP data
Sugar, Peter F.
  East European Nationalism, Politics and Religion —
  (Variorum Collected Studies Series: CS667).
  1. Nationalism—Europe, Eastern. 2. Nationalism—Europe, Eastern—
  History. 3. Ethnicity—Europe, Eastern. 4. Europe, Eastern—Politics
  and government. I. Title
  320.5'4'0947

US Library of Congress CIP data
Sugar, Peter F.
  East European Nationalism, Politics and Religion / Peter F. Sugar.
      p.   cm. — (Variorum Collected Studies Series: CS667)
  Includes bibliographical references (hbk: alk. paper)
  1. Nationalism—Europe, Eastern—History—20th century. 2. Europe,
  Eastern—Ethnic relations. 3. Europe, Eastern—Politics and
  government—20th century. 4. Religion and politics—Europe, Eastern—
  History—20th century. I. Title. II. Series: Variorum
  Collected Studies Series: CS667
  DJK42.S78   1999   99–30100
  320.54'0943–dc21   CIP

The paper used in this publication meets the minimum requirements of the
  American National Standard for Information Sciences – Permanence of Paper for
  Printed Library Materials, ANSI Z39.48–1984. ∞ ™

Printed by TJ International Ltd, Padstow, Cornwall

VARIORUM COLLECTED STUDIES SERIES CS667

CONTENTS

Introduction   vii–xi

Acknowledgements   xii

NATIONALISM AND ETHNICITY

Introduction

I   From Ethnicity to Nationalism and Back Again   67–84
    Nationalism: Essays in Honor of Louis L. Snyder,
    eds M. Palumbo and W.O. Shanahan. Westport, CT:
    Greenwood Press, 1981

II Ethnicity in Eastern Europe   1–16
    Ethnic Diversity and Conflict in Eastern Europe,
    ed. Peter Sugar, Santa Barbara – Oxford: ABC-Clio,
    1980, pp. 419–444

NINETEENTH-CENTURY MANIFESTATIONS

Introduction

III The Problems of Nationalism in Eastern Europe:
    Past and Present   1–20
    East European Program Occasional Paper 13.
    Washington DC: The Wilson Center, 1988

IV Government and Minorities in Austria–Hungary
    Different Policies with the Same Result   1–52
    Der Donauraum 1–2. Vienna: Böhlau Verlag, 1997

V   Austria–Hungary and the Balkan Crisis:
    An Ingenious Improvisation   66–85
    Insurrections, Wars, and the Eastern Crisis in the 1870s,
    East European Monographs 197, eds B. Kiraly and
    G. Stokes. New York: Colombia University Press, 1985

INTERACTION WITH POLITICS AND RELIGION

Introduction

VI	Continuity and Change in Eastern European Authoritarianism: Autocracy, Fascism and Communism *East European Quarterly 18. Boulder, CO: University of Colorado, 1984*	1–23
VII	Fascism in Interwar Eastern Europe: The Dichotomy of Power and Influence *Eastern Europe in the 1970s, eds S. Sinanian, I. Deak, P.C. Ludz. New York – London: Praeger Publishers, Inc., 1972*	13–32
VIII	The Historical Role of Religious Institutions in Eastern Europe and their Place in the Communist Party-State *Religion and Nationalism in Soviet and East European Politics, Duke Press Policy Studies, ed. P. Ramet. Durham, NC: Duke University Press, 1989*	42–58
IX	Nationalism and Religion in the Balkans since the Nineteenth Century *The Donald W. Treadgold Papers 8. University of Washington, 1996*	7–50
X	Religion, Nationalism and Politics in East-Central Europe *Working Papers 2, Center for European and Russian Studies, Los Angeles: UCLA, 1995*	1–17
XI	Eastern European Nationalism in the Twentieth Century *Suna Kili'ye Armağan: Cumhuriyete Adanmış bir Yaşan. Istanbul: Boğaziçi University Press, 1998*	347–363
Index		1–16

This volume contains xiv + 288 pages

INTRODUCTION

A considerable part of my publications deal with nationalism in general and its Eastern European manifestations in particular. A selection of these is gathered in this volume. They resulted from a life-long professional interest in the manifestations of this social phenomenon. Looking back, this wish to study and, hopefully, to understand the nature of and the role played by nationalism appears to have been inevitable.

I was born in Hungary during the short months of Count Mihály Károlyi's government (31 October 1918 – 19 January 1919) and grew up during the years that followed the signing of the Trianon Peace Treaty (19 June 1919). These were the years of 'revisionism', the demand that this treaty be revised and that Hungary be treated justly (*igazságot Magyarországnag*). This slogan meant different things to different people. The modest revisionists asked for the return to Hungary of those territories in which roughly three million Magyars lived. The more extreme revisionists felt that justice demanded the re-establishment of the borders of 'historic Hungary'. All revisionists were hostile to the neighbouring states and their message was repeated endlessly, in the strongest possible nationalistic terms, by textbooks, the media, and the speeches and statements of politicians.

This language reached nearly ridiculous extremes when addressed to the troops stationed on the borders of Hungary with Czechoslovakia prior to the first Vienna Arbitration (2 November 1938). Serving my obligatory military service with these units, I listened to these daily tirades with growing unease because I could not but become aware of the exaggerations and propaganda they presented.

As soon as I was demobilized, I left Hungary and was very fortunate to spend the years of the Second World War in a neutral country. There I was subjected to the daily communiqués of all belligerents and the declarations and speeches of their leaders. I had my choice. The western Allies spoke the language of nationalism, the Axis preached racism, and the Soviets a mixture of Bolshevism and and a corrupt version of nationalism. It was easy to reject the latter two, and the wish to understand the first was born.

When I began my university studies at the City College of New York, my interest in nationalism was reinforced by two professors then teaching at this institution. One of these was Hans Kohn whose works, together with those of Carlton J.H. Hayes, were among the few available dealing with the topic of nationalism.[1] The other, Louis L. Snyder, was then working on a relevant volume which we discussed in seminars.[2] By the time I was ready to begin graduate studies my interests in nationalism and Eastern Europe were well established. Fortunately, new books continued to be published dealing with nationalism,[3] and my major advisor, Professor Cyril E. Black, one of America's leading Eastern European experts, shared and encouraged my interest.

In spite of the growing number of articles, essays and volumes discussing nationalism, I found practically none dealing with its Eastern European variants. I began to look for answers to the many questions that came to mind. One of the first results of this search was the essay: 'External and Domestic Roots of Eastern European Nationalism'[4] and the last: 'Eastern European Nationalism in the Twentieth Century' included in this volume as chapter XI.[5] I felt deeply honoured when my colleagues, the members of the American Association for the Advancement of Slavic Studies, recognized my work as that of 'one of the first American scholars to promote the study of Eastern Europe in America'.

While the readers of this volume will find most of my ideas presented in the pieces included in it, a few topics remain to which I would like to direct their attention. They have intrigued most scholars studying Eastern Europe and, as far as I can see, still remain without a fully convincing and generally accepted resolution of the issues they raise.

When Scandinavia, the Iberian Peninsula, the Lowlands, the Baltic States or Western Europe as a whole are mentioned, everybody knows what regions of the continent are covered by these eponyms. The same is true of Russia (with or without Belorussia and Ukraine). What lies between these two well-defined regions? Is it Central Europe (with or without Germany), Eastern

---

1 Hayes, Carlton J.H., *Essays on Nationalism* (New York; Macmillan, 1926) and *The Historical Evolution of Modern Nationalism* (2nd ed., New York; Macmillan, 1949). Kohn, Hans, *Prophets and People; Studies in Nineteenth Century Nationalism* (New York; Macmillan, 1947). *The Idea of Nationalism; A Study in its Origins and Background* (New York; Macmillan, 1948)
2 Snyder, Louis L., *The Meaning of Nationalism* (New Brunswick, NJ; Rutgers Press, 1954)
3 The other works that influenced me the most during my graduate student days were: Shafer, Boyd C., *Nationalism, Myth and Reality* (New York; Harcourt, Brace & World, 1955), and Deutsch, Karl W., *Nationalism and Social Communications* (Cambridge, Mass.; M.I.T. Press, 1953)
4 First published in Peter F. Sugar and Ivo J. Lederer (eds), *Nationalism in Eastern Europe* (Seattle & London; University of Washington Press, 1969) and reprinted in Peter F. Sugar, *Nationality and Society in Habsburg and Ottoman Europe* (Aldershot, Hampshire; Variorum, 1997)
5 First published in *Suna Kili'ye armağan. Cumhuriyete adanmış bir yaşam* (Istanbul Boğaziçi Üniversitesi Yayinevi, 1998)

Europe, East-Central Europe, Southeastern Europe? Does the last mentioned of these simply serve as a synonym for the Balkans or does it also include Romania (with or without Transylvania and Bessarabia-Moldova)? Two scholars tried to evade answering these questions by selecting well-chosen titles for their works. Alan Palmer wrote about *The Lands Between* and Hugh Seton-Watson entitled a series of lectures, published subsequently, *The Sick Heart of Modern Europe*.[6] These titles and the multiplicity of regional labels raise two fundamental questions for which nobody has yet given a definitive answer.

Are these lands between East and West part of Europe and should they, therefore, simply be included in the study of Europe, or were their sicknesses serious and long-lasting enough to have produced endemic alterations requiring special treatment? This question might appear to be raised only to allow a simple and self-evident answer. This is not the case. Prior to 1989 I have repeatedly heard, even from academic and political decision makers: 'It is useless to study Eastern Europe, the region is and always was an appendix of Russia (Soviet Union)'. At an important meeting in 1990 a representative of a federal agency told us that we should give up Eastern European studies because 'with the fall of Communism European normalcy returned to the region'. The statements in the media and, much worse, those of decision makers almost always show a sad ignorance of crises shaping events in Eastern Europe which they attempt to understand and possibly solve by applying theories and practices that fitted Western European or American situations. They diagnose and prescribe remedies knowing the sicknesses, but ignoring the lasting changes produced by the centuries.

No specialist can prescribe the proper medication – to continue with my medical figure of speech – if he is not familiar with the basic illness. Without a thorough knowledge of Europe, the study of Eastern Europe makes no sense. This statement is self-explanatory, but does not invalidate raising the question which it answers because it is still repeatedly asked and not everybody answers it the way I just did.

People interested in Eastern Europe can turn to several very good textbooks dealing with its modern history. During the last few decades several good national histories have also appeared covering the entire story of a given nation's past. Nobody is qualified to deal with the entire region's past and present. This requires a joint effort by area specialists.[7] Nobody has

---

6 Palmer, Alan, *The Lands Between. A History of East-Central Europe since the Congress of Vienna* (New York; Macmillan, 1970). Seton-Watson, Hugh, *The Sick Heart of Modern Europe. The Problem of the Danubian Lands* (Seattle & London; University of Washington Press, 1975).

7 Sugar, Peter F. and Donald W. Treadgold (eds), *A History of East Central Europe* (Seattle & London; University of Washington Press). Of the planned ten volumes seven are available. The eighth is in production.

argued as forcefully as Maria Todorova to prove that Eastern Europe and especially the Balkans are an integral part of Europe. She is a first-rate area specialist, but she would not claim to know as much about Poland and Hungary as she does about Bulgaria or Turkey.[8] It is not only the great diversity of languages that makes it practically impossible to achieve 'complete area specialization'. Eastern Europe has many dividing lines, not only linguistic ones. These are well known to the expert, but I feel that they should be mentioned with potential general readers in mind. The latest excellent short summary of these 'Fault Lines' was published by Gale Stokes.[9] Some of them are discussed also in the following essays. These must be kept in mind all the time when an attempt is made to understand events in Eastern Europe. For this reason, I would like to give a short list of some of them in this introduction to the various essays.

The most important 'Fault Lines' running through the region are those separating Western Christianity from Eastern Christianity and the latter from Islam. These denote not only religious differences which by themselves were of great importance for centuries, but, just as importantly, different world views. Contact between them also left its mark. Romanian Orthodoxy is different from Russian Orthodoxy in its approach to everyday life, just as Balkan Islam is very different from that of the fundamentalists in the Near East. Next in importance for the historic development of the people of Eastern Europe is the difference between those societies who were dominated traditionally by strong nobilities and those, all in the Balkans, who lacked this social stratum for several hundred years. The length of foreign rule and the behaviour of these rulers also indicates important and differing influences imposed by the German, Russian and Turkish speaking lords. The level and extent of industrialization, the presence or absence of neo-serfdom, and the different degrees of urban–rural dichotomy created other borders separating Eastern from Western Europe and the various eastern lands from each other. Eastern Europe as a whole is different enough from the western sections of the continent to require special attention, but it would be a great mistake to think of it as a monolith. it would be equally erroneous to equate the 'Fault Lines' with national or political borders. Very often these do not coincide as the tragic developments following the disintegration of Yugoslavia have drastically shown.

In almost all of the following studies, I indicate that no generally accepted definitions exist for even such basic concepts as ethnic group, nation or

---

8 Todorova, Maria, Imagining the Balkans (New York & Oxford; Oxford University Press, 1997)
9 Stokes, Gale, "Eastern Europe's Defining Fault Lines", in Sabrina P. Ramet (ed.), *Eastern Europe. Politics, Culture and Society since 1939* (Bloomington, IN; Indiana University Press, 1998), pp. 15–31

nationalism. In spite of this fact, we use these terms constantly and expect that those whom we address either orally or in print will know exactly what they mean. I cannot produce these missing definitions in this introduction, but feel that I must give some indications of what these terms denote in most instances when they appear in my writings.

In the already mentioned chapter of *Nationalism in Eastern Europe* I differentiated between the 'natural' and 'acquired' characteristics of individuals living in any given social group. The natural included a preference for the same foods, a common religion, the acceptance of a given social stratification, the belief in a real or mythical common history and ancestry, an attachment to a given region, common artistic styles, the almost instinctive belief that the way of life that results from these and other basic facets of life produce the best possible or the 'correct' form of existence and that those who live differently are wrong, possibly even bad enough to hate. These features and beliefs are absorbed by each member of each social group from the moment of birth and are dictated by the environment in which they grow up. These 'natural' characteristics indicate a preference for the 'known' and the rejection of everything unknown, strange, threatening and possibly hostile, and is true of every social group be it a clan, tribe, sept, horde or nation without defining or differentiating between them. All of these smaller or larger units of people think of themselves as the 'we' and label all others as the 'they'. The beliefs of the 'we' are the elements of ethnicity defining any given ethnic group.

While everybody is born a member of an ethnic group, nobody is born as a member of a nation. All humans are biological equals, but because they must live in communities or perish, they must belong to ethnic groups. Additional loyalties, the 'acquired' characteristics, turn any given individual into a member of a nation. What this nation is depends on what these acquired values are and on those who are able to present them forcefully enough to make the people accept them. This acceptance demands a certain psychological adjustment, especially if members of several ethnic groups are to be included in a given nation. The psychological aspect involved in this transformation is changeable and makes belonging to a nationality to a considerable extent a question of feeling. When this feeling is politically expressed and state directed it produces nationalism

Not everybody would agree with these explanations. They are not definitions. Hopefully, they will help the readers of this volume understand the meaning of these terms when I use them.

ACKNOWLEDGEMENTS

The author and publisher would like to acknowledge copyright and express their appreciation for permission to reproduce the articles in this volume to the following: Greenwood Publishing Group, Inc., Westport, CT (I and VII); ABC-Clio, Santa Barbara, CA (II); Böhlau Verlag, Vienna (IV); East European Monographs, Atlantic Research and Publications, Inc., New York (V); East European Quarterly, Boulder, CO (VI); Duke University Press, Durham, NC (VIII); The Henry M. Jackson School of International Studies, University of Washington (IX); Boğaziçi University Press, Istanbul (XI).

PUBLISHER'S NOTE

The articles in this volume, as in all the others in the Variorum Collected Studies Series, have not been given a new, continuous pagination. In order to avoid confusion, and to facilitate their use where these same studies have been referred to elsewhere, the original pagination has been maintained wherever possible.

Each article has been given a Roman numeral in order of appearance, as listed in the Contents. This number is repeated on each page and quoted in the index entries.

To SALLY gratefully for 45 great years.

NATIONALISM AND ETHNICITY

Nationalism is the ideology that justifies the beliefs and actions of any given nation. These actions can be military, economic, cultural, and so on, and can change over time as the aims of a given nation change in accordance with successes, failures, numerous innovations and the shifting relations of the states. Nationalism will alter its teachings accordingly, but will continue to demand the continuing primary loyalty of the nation whose wishes it claims to express. The nation was built on the likes, dislikes, beliefs and feelings of an ethnic or several cooperating ethnic groups, adding additional features to their basic values without supplanting them. When the population of a national unit, usually a state, begins to believe that it is exploited or mistreated, that the obligations heavily outweigh the advantages in belonging to this unit, it will seek security in something else and will retreat to the creed and customs of the ethnic group or groups that were never forgotten.

The first of the following two selections describes both the creation of nation-oriented loyalties and the circumstances that make people shift these loyalties back to their ethnic groups. I wrote this essay twenty years ago. The events of the last decade, the disintegrations of the Soviet Union, Czechoslovakia and Yugoslavia, have shown that the argument presented in this piece is still valid although the motivations for the loss of state-oriented loyalties are different from the ones I saw twenty years ago.

It is self-evident that the environment, with the advantages and disadvantages it offers, as well as the geographic location in which an ethnic group coalesces and creates its value system influence what this will be. The Greeks became seamen, the Arabs have a long vocabulary dealing with the camel, the Mongols built a horse-oriented society. The second essay in this section attempts to show what forces shaped the ethnicity of the people of Eastern Europe.

I

From Ethnicity to Nationalism and Back Again

NOBODY WHO, LIKE ME, GREW UP IN THE 1920s AND 30s IN EAST CENTRAL Europe could avoid getting deeply involved in nationalism. It dominated the region, poisoned the thinking of many people by its extreme manifestations, and prepared the terrain for the Second World War. When I moved to the United States and entered college, the man this volume honors, Professor Louis L. Snyder, whose scholarly involvement in nationalism needs no stressing, placed this phenomenon in its proper historical context for me in his classroom. After I became a historian myself, I continued to study nationalism in its various forms.

* * *

We have as many definitions of nationalism as we have scholars who wrote about it, irrespective of their academic disciplines. Yet, in spite of this endless diversity in definitions, agreement on a few salient features of nationalism has by now been reached. It is generally accepted that nationalism is a modern phenomenon that developed first in Europe and spread to other continents after the Industrial Revolution and the Enlightenment transformed societies and their values enough to weaken the hold of previous ideologies on the masses of people and demanded the emergence of new ones. We know from the Bible that men live not "by bread alone" and need an overriding group loyalty that keeps the great majority of any given society moving in the same direction, loyal to the same fundamental beliefs. For numerous centuries religion supplied this integrating force. In the period of early modern history religion lost this role slowly but surely, suffering from the Great Schism, the Reformation, numerous religious wars, heretical strife, and a certain dogmatic conservatism that did not adjust rapidly enough to the growing rate of change in society. For a while the monarch's personality served, if not as an embodiment of a set of fundamental beliefs, then at least as a symbol of the common interests and ambitions of some people. But the monarch's days were also passing. The development of a modern centralized state and, within its framework, the emergence of new social forces with special interests of their own ended the

Nationalism: Essays in Honor of Louis L. Snyder, eds M. Palumbo and W.O. Shanahan. Copyright © 1981 by Michael Palumbo and William O. Shanahan. Reproduced with permission of Greenwood Publishing Group, Inc, Westport, CT.

I

usefulness of the ruler as an acceptable symbol of unity. In a sense the so-called enlightened despots of the second half of the eighteenth century can be viewed as men and women who attempted to reshape the image of monarchy to make it acceptable to the new states and societies over which they ruled. In this sense their efforts ended in total failure. The new society, dominated by the emergence of the gradually more and more powerful urban middle classes operating within the strict framework of the modern centralized state, needed a new set of fundamental dogmas that served their interests and were, at the same time, acceptable to all other inhabitants of the state. The result of this attempt, first by the middle class and then by people coming from all walks of life, was what Professor R. R. Palmer so aptly called "the advent of the isms."[1] Most of the isms during roughly the last two centuries were nothing more than passing fads. These stillborn ideologies suffered from the fact that they were neither built on preexistent loyalties whose extension and transformation they represented nor did they offer solutions to real or imaginary problems which they promised to solve. The two most pervasive isms that made their appearance on the stage of world history during the last two hundred years are nationalism and Marxism. No wonder, then, that the latter, appearing after the first was already a force, Marxism, in its various forms, became an implacable enemy of its successful young predecessor, nationalism, which it derided as the weapon of the middle class serving to divert the interest of the workers from the "real" problems of society. This hostility and the resulting argumentation would not have been required had nationalism not captured the imagination and loyalty of those people, the workers, to whom Marxism appealed. A contemporary scholar, Professor Ernest Gellner, even went so far as to call Marxism "arrested nationalism."[2] It takes only a cursory look at present-day Eastern Europe and even certain regions of the Soviet Union where these two ideologies, nationalism and Marxism, coexist today to discover that nationalism is the stronger of the two forces and that Professor Gellner's argument might, indeed, turn out to be correct during the next few decades.

Nationalism, then, is the oldest and the most successful of the modern beliefs that offered people living in the modern state a set of values that succeeded in capturing their primary loyalty. From what was just said, it follows that a precondition of its success was the fact that it was built on the solid foundation of preexisting values. What nationalism did was to generalize these values and make them valid and acceptable for the inhabitants of that area whose leaders, the propagators of nationalism, wanted to convince their fellow men that they had common interests. In most cases the areas involved were the modern states, but in many cases these political units existed only in embryonic form (e.g. Greece after 1830) or simply as an ideal (e.g. Germany prior to 1870). Whatever the goal of the leaders was, the defense and maintenance of a state, its future growth, or its creation, nationalism served as its justification.

Nationalism could serve all these purposes because it was the extension of old loyalties such as localism, patriotism, common tradition, shared culture, mutually understandable language, and many others. In a previous essay dealing with nationalism I stressed the importance of the difference between these pre-nationalistic common denominators and the attempt of nationalism to replace them. I referred to the former as the "natural" and to the latter as the "acquired" characteristics of people.[3] The manner in which nationalism was acquired, propagated, and maintained is more than satisfactorily explained, in, among many other works, Karl W. Deutsch's well-known work on the subject.[4] Quite recently another important volume studied similar developments relating to nationalism and the modern state in a worldwide setting.[5] These authors mentioned, and all others who ever wrote on nationalism agreed, that irrespective of the form in which nationalism manifests itself anywhere in the world it is a modern, acquired belief that has to be maintained in the forefront of the peoples' minds and constantly reinforced by all the institutions of the modern state.

There can be no doubt that nationalism was, and is, probably the most successful belief ever presented to mankind. Even the loftiest religion or philosophy failed in gaining universal acceptance, but there is no corner on our globe today where the leaders of the most significant or the most insignificant state do not constantly use all the means of communications (in the widest sense) at their disposal to foster nationalism, the state-supporting loyalty. It does not matter if these states are the home of "old continuous nations" or regions in which "new states" are inhabited by "new nations," to borrow terms used by Professor Hugh Seton-Watson in the above-mentioned work, the leaders' emphasis on nationalism, and in the "new states" on building "new nations" is present everywhere. It is my contention that in spite of its tremendous success and its present-day omnipresence, nationalism has passed the peak of its effectiveness and has begun to lose its appeal. On the remaining pages I will argue that people all over the world are either reverting fully or partially from their "acquired" to their "natural" loyalties, or are refusing to give up their "natural" self-identity in order to "acquire" the characteristic of "new nations."

* * *

Practically all authors who wrote about nationalism agree that nationalism "politicized" those features of the old group's loyalties that could be extended from the narrowly regional to the statewide area in which the "nation" lived.

I

This seemingly simple statement contains some very important assumptions that were fundamental to the thinking and action of early, conscious nationalists. The first of these assumptions is that the state, in its effective or desired extension, is a basic unit, not only a political-legal concept, because its territory was inhabited by a "nation." This argument is circular. A state is a state because it is inhabited by a nation; yet the nation is the group of people who can have or wish to extend a state. From this argumentation derived the principle of "self-determination of nations" with its loaded political implications. What is even worse is that the statement assumes the existence of nations. At least the early nationalist knew that this assumption was at best defensible in the case of "old continuous nations," but certainly lacked universal validity. They set out to create nations. They produced institutions like academies of science and charged them with collecting native traditions and artifacts, with creating unified literary languages, and with producing "scientific" national histories. To show the uniformity of the discovered traditions, the "national patrimony," they fought for centralized school systems that became the basic propaganda tool at their disposal. The two concepts, nation and state, one political and the other demographic, became so closely interwoven that they became synonyms for all practical purposes. The relationship between the two was even more confused than that between the proverbial chicken and egg, because the primacy of neither could ever be established. France, for example, was certainly a state before a unified French nation existed.[6] The same is true of practically every so-called Third World state that came into being after World War II. On the other hand, there was certainly a Romanian nation living in the lands of the Regat before 1862 when the first united Romanian state came into being. Finally we have cases in which it is difficult to determine which of the two, nation or state, was the chicken or the egg. Did all Germans really desire a unified state on the eve of the Franco-Prussian War in 1870 when they knew that under the circumstances unity involved Prussian supremacy? There can be no doubt that culturally a German nation existed at the time, but did it exist politically? This is a crucial question if one accepts the verdict of most experts that nationalism is the political expression of group self-identity.

Finally, the definition of nationalism offered at the beginning of the previous paragraph also assumes that the nation is a united demographic unit whose political goals are uniform. If this had indeed been the case, the early nationalists would not have been forced into the role of propagandists, a role which the leaders of nations and states play constantly to the present day. Because the leaders of the various political units in existence today still are forced to "preach" nationalism, the appeal of this ideology must be considered as something artficial, "acquired," needing continuous and constant reinforcement. This is another reason why nationalism could not have become a force prior to modern times when modern technology and the institutions of the all-powerful centralized, modern state made available the cradle-to-grave propaganda tools used by nationalists.

Nationalism may be artificial as an ideology, yet it has been extremely successful because it was based, as already indicated, on preexistent loyalties. People everywhere prefer the known to the unknown. This is especially true when they have to choose between those with whom they want to associate and those whom they want to exclude from their midst. Furthermore, once they make this choice, they wish to live with their own "kind" according to their own customs and traditions without being told by "outsiders" that they can or cannot act according to their preferences. These preferences are the "natural" characteristics of any given group. Traditionally groups with these "natural" binding forces are small — clans, tribes, inhabitants of a village or a group of villages cut off from other regions by geographic barriers, religious sects, closely knit dialectical units, etc. — and have great difficulties in keeping their "purity" intact. They must turn to larger "units" to defend themselves. Related clans, the speakers of mutually understandable dialects, inhabitants of easily defendable areas, people with vague but traditional, common "histories," etc., form these somewhat larger units. Some of them were even further along the way to becoming nations by the time modern nationalism became a force and identified themselves as nations — Bavarians, Scots, Bretons, Boers, Serbs, Herreros, Kurds — to mention only a few. This trend was easily reinforced by the determination of goal-oriented early nationalists. These were the people who built on a "natural" basis and tried to extend it. A Hungarian in Transylvania surrounded by Romanian masses might have had nothing in common with the Hungarian in Slovakia except the fact that the latter too feared a non-Hungarian group among which he lived. The creators of modern Hungarian nationalism could bring these two groups together by showing them that their "Hungarian-ness" was something they had in common and that by working together they could keep others in check in both Transylvania and Slovakia. When the group that could be linked in this manner still felt too weak to succeed, the net was extended further and Panslavism in its numerous forms, Pangermanism, and Panturanism were born. Nothing shows better how "artificial" these movements were than the well-known fact that delegates to the first Panslav Congress in Prague had to use German as their language of discussion in 1848. Yet, in its slightly less ambitious forms, Panslavism created two states, Czechoslovakia and Yugoslavia. On the other hand, the history of these two states shows that state-building does not equal nation-building. Czechs and Slovaks are different nations to the present as are Serbs, Croats, Slovenes, and other inhabitants of Yugoslavia.

I

Even if state-building does not equal nation-building, nationalism was a dynamic force all through the nineteenth century and, until recently, in the twentieth century. There were enough groups around that realized they had more in common with one another than with others to accept, at least tentatively, the idea that they were a nation. They could be convinced of this within already-existing states or as the "majority" population of future states. As a matter of fact, in the nineteenth and early twentieth centuries the emphasis was one of creating or re-creating nations which, claiming the right of self-determination, set out to build or rebuild their states. It was only during roughly the last forty years that state-building began to precede nation-building. We had states before nations in the earlier period (for example most Latin American states), and we have had nations before states since World War I (e.g. Ireland), but, all in all, the pattern just indicated holds true. It is also worth noticing that if we think of the rather numerous "new states and new nations" category, the state always came first and the nation's existence is often questionable. Will nations be created to correspond to these new states, or will the "national" unity's strength decline even in the "old continuous nations?" Is there still an irresistible force operating in the world, the force of nationalism, or are newer forces, that are in fact much older, beginning to manifest themselves?

Let us look at some events that took place or continued to unfold in various parts of the world during the spring of 1979. In Chad a civil war continued to be fought between the forces of the president and the prime minister of the state. Chad is a political unit whose institutions are modeled on those of the "advanced, modern, politically mature" states, and is inhabited by members of the Chad nations (or potential nation). Yet, its two highest ranking public officials, living and going to their offices in the same capital city, N'Djamena, fought each other for several years. In the neighboring state of Cameroon the situation is tense and civil war, a confrontation between North and South, is a distinct possibility. In Great Britain the Welsh rejected "devolution" and the Scots approved it by such a narrow margin that the legislation could not be validated. In Uganda the remnants of Idi Amin's army continue to execute their enemies in the eastern provinces even after "the conqueror of the British Empire" disappeared from the scene and chances for victory faded completely. Great Britain is an "old" state in which the common-identity label of "British" has been used for many years. The famous Empire drew more administrators from Britons of Scottish origin than from those who were sons of England. Chad, Cameroon, and Uganda are "new" states. Other examples could have been cited, and I have used these countries only as examples.

All these, and many other possible cases, show either difficulties in creating nations and/or in keeping them together. The negative votes in Scotland and

Wales were not votes for British "nationalism," but simply rejections of bills that the voters considered either to be badly worded or not going far enough. While it would be easy to blame the unrest in Chad and Uganda on Lybian, Nigerian, or Tanzanian interference, the fact remains that "foreigners" can fish only in waters that are troubled by the local people. The issues over which the inhabitants of any given country disagree are not new. The problems in Québec were not "created" when General DeGaulle made his famous "vive le Québec libre" announcement.[7] He was just as much a "foreigner" in Canada as the Lybians are in either Chad or Uganda. The Quebequois would not be able to live in greater harmony with the French, who would ridicule their language, than they are ready to coexist with their English-speaking co-nationals. Scots, Welsh, and Croats had never fully accepted membership in "larger nations," and the various African people had neither enough time nor the inclination to accept inclusion into "nations" whose only reason for existence is that their borders were drawn — without any consideration of local factors — by colonial powers.

The various examples listed suggest to me that people all over the world, irrespective of their size or history, are reasserting or defending an identity that differs sharply from the one which the ruling elements of states proclaim as the one to which they owe primary loyalty. This phenomenon is observable in every corner of our planet irrespective of the nature of the regime. It is present in western democracies and in communist states, it can be observed in highly industrial and in so-called developing or backward regions on every continent. The obvious questions that must be asked are: What caused the emergence of this trend and where does it lead? In order to answer, however tentatively, these queries — especially the second one — it appears necessary to elaborate further on the concept of "old established" and "new" states.

What is involved in this differentiation has very little to do with the time span for which any given state was in existence. The United States and modern Germany are recent political creations, but for the purpose of what follows they will be considered "old established" states. This expression will be reserved for those political units whose inhabitants accepted, even if not unanimously and without reservation, the existence of the state practically from its emergence as an independent governing unit. The next group will consist of the "accepted" states whose populations had serious reservations when they were incorporated into any given political unit, but accepted it because all other alternatives looked even worse. Belgium, Yugoslavia, Czechoslovakia, Pakistan before the secession of Bangladesh, and Indonesia would be good examples. The group of "new" states becomes a very small one when using the grouping I now suggest. I propose to reserve this label for those states which came into being, usually by secession, when those who created them became

I

conscious of a new "national identity" for which they discovered an old "ethnic patrimony" as justification. Bangladesh is a good example and so is, to some extent, the development taking place in Greenland. If Quebec became independent she would be a "new" state in this sense of the word. It could even be argued that most Latin American states gained their independence by this process. Most of those states which Professor Seton-Watson considered new ones belong, according to my classification, in the group of "potential" states or states "in the making." Most of the African states fall into this category. They are those political units that came into being before a nation, whose home they claim to be, existed. They are "potential" states because, in the long run, no state can survive without the loyalty of its inhabitants and their future depends on the success or failure of their attempt at "nation-making."

These categories might not be scientific or acceptable, but they will help when an attempt is made to answer the second of the two basic questions: What caused the emergence of the trend so far discussed and where does it lead?

* * *

Any and every social unit, from the smallest family to the largest state, serves basically one purpose: to maximize the benefits and minimize the risks of those who belong to it. Members of these units always understand that they have to pay a certain price for membership. This well-known and often-repeated fact lies at the bottom of the eternal and unsolved problem of each social unit to find the most acceptable and simultaneously most expedient balance between freedom and security.

This search for a social unit that serves the needs of its members is the basic "natural" development to which I alluded at the beginning of this chapter. Up to a certain point in time and magnitude the resulting unit also remained "natural." Irrespective of what we call it — clan, tribe, caste, sect, etc. — the unit was based on blood ties, even if only the vaguest: common language, habits, traditions, taboos, religious beliefs, legends, and many other components. Geographic features and often the sheer problem of numbers set limits to this form of unit creation. It resulted in the emergence of ethnic groups whose members did not question their membership in the unit, who identified themselves by various totemic or other symbols as sharers of the same patrimony, who felt like kinsmen, and resented "outsiders." These units did not live in eternal peace and harmony, but they considered their problems and difficulties to be "internal" affairs and resented the attempt of "foreigners" to solve them. This developmental process is not simply ancient history; it occurs in our day too.

I

Not only is the attempt to create an independent Quebec the result of such a natural process of "ethnogenesis," but so is the emergence of the "black ethnic group" in the United States. In both cases the process took about the same amount of time and was identical. The Quebequois had to forget their home districts in France, which were often at odds with each other, and find a new identity amidst people who spoke another language, belonged to another church, and who, in spite of democratic institutions, practiced real or imaginary discrimination against them. The result was the transformation of Frenchmen first into French Canadians and then into Quebequois.

The case of the black population in our country is even clearer. They are descendants of numerous African people who, on that continent, are more likely to consider each other enemies or at least foreigners than brothers, and whom the masters of today's African states attempt to weld together into nations. Unlike the French in Canada, our blacks lost everything when they were forcibly transported to America; they lost their languages, religion, freedom, and dignity as human beings. In their case discrimination was only very seldom imaginary even after slavery was abolished. Furthermore, unlike the ex-slave in antiquity and in the middle ages, the American slave could not — within a generation or two — forget his unfree past and integrate into society because his past could never be denied, it was enshrined in his color. Consequently the American black made his color into the "natural" criterion of his ethnicity. This process is not too dissimilar from what occurred in India slightly earlier. Here religion, Islam, played the same role blackness played in America. It was the one undeniable feature that made it impossible for the future citizens of Pakistan to become full-fledged and equal citizens of a united and unified free Indian nation. (This has nothing to do with the fact that it is certainly exaggerated to speak of a united and unified Indian nation.) Even in these modern and special cases we witness a "natural" development, the creation of a social unit, large enough to be an ethnic unit, whose identity-feeling is strong and real and whose common aim is to maximize group benefits and minimize group risks.

Population growth and its relation to technological advancement, individual ambition and group greed, blood feuds, and many other factors which cannot be surveyed on a few pages took this "group creation" beyond the strict limits set by "natural" ethnicity. This process occurred, in Europe, from late antiquity to the early modern period. The first steps were relatively easy to take. The various early kingdoms on Europe's westernmost island could be united into England; Athenians, Spartans, Thebans, and all others who spoke a similar language could become Greeks; the seven tribes who crossed the Carpathians around 896 could merge into Hungarians; the various tribes on the Eurasian steppe finally emerged as Russians. Yet this second fu-

I

sion was never as "natural" and complete as the first one had been. This is why the echoes of feudalism have still not disappeared and why, to use only one example, it is still questionable to whom a Bavarian owes his first loyalty, to Munich or to Bonn.

The real problem emerged in the middle of the eighteenth century. The emergence of the modern, centralized state coincided with the birth of modern nationalism without which the modern state could not exist. Yet, at the same time, the Enlightenment placed great stress on the rights of the individual, including his freedom to associate freely with people of his own choice. The last-mentioned factor reinforced, in contradiction to the demands of the modern state, the freedom of individuals to seek the company and to protect the interest of those to whom they felt "naturally" drawn. Finally, roughly around the same time, a new development began with the Industrial Revolution that left most individuals far behind — the phenomenon known as the cultural lag — and bewildered enough to be grateful if somebody else took care of problems they could not understand, let alone master. This somebody was not an individual, but the new state. Once again, but now in a new, "modern" context, the old creation of social groups began.

The state, a political unit defined by a geographic demarcation line within which it was able to make itself obeyed, a capricious artificial structure if compared to earlier criteria determining belonging, promised maximum benefits and minimum risks (including the regulation of problems created by the more and more rapidly advancing technology) in exchange for loyalty of the "nation" defined as those people — irrespective of their previous loyalties — who lived within its borders. It is important not to forget that the state, regardless of what form it took, consciously or unconsciously saw the justification of its own existence not in the power factors that brought it into being, but in the eons-old justification of all social groupings: it claimed to be not a political structure, but a "natural," social unit — the national state. Nations supposedly were entitled to self-determination which, in this modern age, meant the right to life in their own state. The inherent *circulus viciosus* is obvious: nations have a right to their own state, but states have the right to lay claim to loyalties of those who inhabit it and this common loyalty makes them into a nation. In certain cases this contradiction produced curious concepts. A multinational state like Austria-Hungary had to admit that it was inhabited by more than one nation. This produced problems. A Frenchman could be loyal to France, but to what could the inhabitants of Austria-Hungary be loyal?[8] The answer was: to the *Gesamtmonarchie* (the totality of the monarchy). This is curious nationalism indeed, but is it so very different from the request that Scots, Welsh, Irish, and English all be loyal to Great Britain?

In spite of all these difficulties the states achieved their goals in the

I

nineteenth century. Although centralization advanced apace and the demands of the state on its citizens increased steadily, the individual still felt that he or she had "a life of his/her own" and that the benefits of citizenship outweighed its burdens. The roots of the phenomenon we witness today, and to which this chapter is devoted, lie in the First World War. This gargantuan struggle, justified by nationalism, demanded total involvement from everybody and brought the state into every facet of every individual's life. The end of the war did not bring back the "good old days," but the contrary. For reasons that cannot be discussed here, the state continued to increase its role and importance at the expense of that of the individual. World War II finally made the state the supreme arbiter of everybody's every move. In those states that I chose to call "old," "accepted," or "new," a turning point had been reached. What is ironic is that the "potential" states chose this very moment to imitate the others, not realizing that they had reached a stage of crisis affecting their very existence.

The problem created by the growth of the state's influence since 1914 is extremely complex. The description that follows is a gross oversimplification attempting to capture only the very essence of the problem.

The First World War was fought to make the world "safe for democracy," but within a few years Bolshevism and the numerous forms of Fascism emerged and flourished. This contradiction between the war's aims and the reality was paralleled by an economy that was less reliable and predictable than it had ever been before; by a series of international crises; by the further growth of the cultural and technological lag; by numerous scandals in high governmental circles; and by the growing demands of the states on their citizens, citing the numerous problems as justification for requesting new sacrifices to permit those in power to solve the problems. After the Great Depression the average man's belief in the ability of the statesmen and politicians to solve problems disappeared for all practical purposes. The economic and political events of the 1930s were certainly not designed to revive this confidence.

Compared to the second, even the First World War looked tame. Its aftermath brought the loss of empire to those who had previously had one; a diminution of the prestige of all states — with the exception of the Soviet Union and our country — which do not belong in my "potential" category; and a bipolarization of power that made the claim of states of being independent, powerful problem solvers ridiculous. The years since 1945 increased the technological and cultural gap even further, produced economic problems to which neither politicians nor economists could supply answers, and was rich in scandals of petty significance like the British Profumo case and some of true magnitude like Watergate. The world was never at peace, and tension was con-

I

stant. The last thirty-five years have been years of constant tension, rapidly multiplying laws and regulations affecting every aspect of life. In these years doubt in the efficiency of the state was transformed into skepticism, ironic attitudes, and finally, in some cases, into outright hostility. Even the most loyal and law-abiding citizen lost his faith in "Big Brother," the all-powerful, all-permeating state. When the state, as the major national-social unit, asked more and more from those whom it was supposed to protect and help and was not able to keep its promises, the majority of the people began to doubt its ability to maximize benefits and minimize risks for them. In other words, the state failed either in fact or in the view of the people to perform the duties that justified its existence.[9]

This was the moment when, more unconsciously than consciously, people looked for other units that might satisfy their basic needs. The first possible alternative, if for no other reason than because constant propaganda for numerous decades had made it evident, was the nation. Could the nation take back from the authorities the power it had delegated to them and restructure the state to fit its purpose? The answer was given in the negative. Such a restructuring needed an ideology as a guideline that was acceptable to the great majority of a given nation and was not found wanting previously. More importantly, once such a gigantic and fundamental task had to be entrusted to the "nation," the very concept of the nation had to be investigated. Without going into details, it turned out that every large social unit, called a nation, revealed so many internal divisions along so many different lines that it proved not only impossible to devise a generally acceptable national policy that could become the basis for the restructuring of the state, but that the concept of nation itself as the basic social unit became questionable.[10]

It was at this juncture that people began to "regress" from the large and relatively new and artificial "unit," the nation, to find security (often only imaginary) in smaller social entities that gave comfort if by nothing other than their familiarity.[11] This search for the comfortable, familiar, and secure does not mean that we are seeing a trend toward dissolving nations and states. This is impossible in the modern world in which at least the economically optimum size of social units is too large to permit a return from the nation to the tribe or some other smaller, "natural" unit. Furthermore, centuries of development have transformed these smaller units internally and have changed their place in larger society so completely that such a return is impossible. Québec, looking ahead to independence, wants to maintain its economic ties with Canada, and devolution in Britain does not involve the dissolution of Great Britain. What the advocates of these and numerous similar trends demand are miniature "common markets." They are certainly aware that the model Common Market of Western Europe has proven that ties have to go beyond the purely local to be effective. Seen from another perspective, the trend I see developing aims at transforming all but the "potential" states from centralized to federal states or making federalism and the units of the federation stronger where this form of state already exists. The model could easily be Switzerland. In this confederation even the question of citizenship is decided by the various cantons and not by the central government. Each Swiss is the citizen of a canton, although he has Swiss *Staatsangehörigkeit*.

The German expression just used, usually translated as citizenship, cannot be translated into English. Citizen translates into German as Staatsbürger. *Bürger* has its equivalents in the French *bourgeois* and the English *bourger* and in the Middle Ages simply meant inhabitant of a city. Citizenship originally denoted the rights an individual had because he shared in the privileges extended by some feudal authority, usually the king, to his city. With the emergence of the modern state and nationalism the meaning of this expression was broadened and began to connote belonging to a nation and its state. This usage is not quite correct and becomes even less so when we think of applying it to states that do not claim to be based on representing the interests of a nation — Soviet citizenship. The German word *Staatsangehöriger* is more precise because its translation reads: "appertainer of the state." Every Swiss is the citizen of his canton, while at the same time he is also a Swiss *Staatsangehöriger*. While the Quebequois want to go beyond this model and retain relations with the rest of Canada, not going beyond those of the common market, the advocates of devolution in Great Britain and the inhabitants of such states as Czechoslovakia and Yugoslavia would be satisfied with the Swiss model. The same can be said of the various newly emerging or reemerging "ethnic" groups all over the world and of all those social groups and units that in the so-called Third World resist their incorporation into nations. These smaller "ethnic" units see, rightly or wrongly, security in their groupings, whose identity they protect and through which they hope to secure their interests in dealing with the state.

Loss of faith in the state brought about the reemergence of ethnicity and the concomitant weakening of nationalism in all but the "potential" states, and in these the ethnic groups resist the states' attempts at nation-building. Yet, there are also clear indications that these ethnic groups realize that in the contemporary modern world socio-political units of a certain size — usually larger than their communities — are needed for survival in both the economic and political sense. The resulting compromise produces the previously discussed trend that apparently favors confederations as political solutions. While confederate states are possible, this cannot be said of nations. What, then, can replace the nation as the group of people who inhabit a confederate or any other type of state?

I

Several years ago Walker Connor gave us the by now generally accepted term of "ethnonationalism."[12] To him this term meant identity with and loyalty to the nation. I have recently used this expression to mean a developmental stage on the road from ethnicity to nationalism and applied it to those people who had left ethnic loyalties behind without fully accepting their belonging to a nation.[13] What I am discussing today is the reversal of this development, the loosening of national loyalties and the strengthening of ethnic feelings. Is this a return to "ethnonationalism" in the sense in which I used it previously? I do not think so for various reasons.

First of all history does not repeat itself and even less does it reverse itself. More importantly, people who moved from ethnicity to nationalism moved in a direction that led to an end which was not clearly perceived by them. People retreating from nationalism move away from something known to something else they believe they know, although they admit that it has changed during the years of national supremacy. The ideal that moves them is, therefore, not "ethnonationalism." I propose to reverse Professor Connor's expression because the direction in which people move today is the reverse of that which he has investigated, and call the phenomenon we are seeing today "natioethnism." It retains the nation — Swiss, British, etc. — but transfers primary loyalty and concomitant political power to its constituent smaller units — cantons or lands like Scotland, Wales, England. The emergence of "natioethnism" was what I had in mind when I ended the title of this study with the words: "and back again."

* * *

I would like to end this discussion with a short look at two extremes: the weakest, the "potential" states, and the strongest, our country. Neither of these seems to fit into the "natioethnic" trend discussed in the preceding pages.

The case of the "potential" states is in many ways disheartening. They emerged from longer or shorter periods of colonial domination either as a result of violent confrontation or of peaceful evolution, but were always both economically and politically weak. Their borders, in most cases, were not long established and historical, but relatively new and colonial. They rejected colonialism and everything for which their colonial masters stood, but had no native traditions to which they could turn to serve as the ideological justification of their existence as a "state" in the post-World War II period. Obviously, these "potential" Third-World states had numerous and multifaceted problems to face with little financial means, a minuscule group of people with adequate education, and few if any true friends. These problems do not fall within the limits of this study. What does is the problem of state- and nation-building.

I

At first sight we witness nothing new. States have existed before nations came into being elsewhere in the world in earlier periods. Yet, those earlier cases were very different from what goes on in our "potential" states today. The earlier states were not highly centralized and their rulers did not have at their disposal all the weapons of modern technology like the rulers of our highly centralized, contemporary "potential" states have. Furthermore, the states that came into being before the creation of nations had within their borders a rather homogeneous, although in some cases small, highly influential group of "state-makers" recruited usually from the ranks of the region's most influential people. This cannot be said of the leadership of the states "in the making." It emerged either by the accident of relatively high education, often coupled with positions in the colonial regimes, or resulted from positions of prestige tied to regional, tribal, or religious distinction. As a result, these states have really no "state-makers" but rather individuals in conflict. The complete artificiality of borders, once again different from earlier cases, has already been stressed repeatedly. Finally, the slow transformation from small, regional, "ethnic" loyalties to larger basic units had progressed much further in the earlier examples of "state-before-nation" developmental sequences than is the case in today's "potential" states. Yet, the leaders, divided as they may be, agree on one thing: their first task is the making of a nation. The result is tragic, involving large scale coercion, civil war, fratricide, and often even genocide. If the leaders' efforts can be understood as attempts to create carbon copies of successful states which claim to be nation-states, they certainly disregard the numerous differences surrounding the creation of both nation and state in the cases of their models and their own countries. The actions of these leaders are counterproductive. The more pressure they put on people not yet ready to give up their basic, "natural" loyalties, the more stubbornly they cling to them and the less they are inclined to see in the state the institution that maximizes their advantages and minimizes their risks. If it is true that a state needs the support of the majority of its inhabitants, the nation, then the efforts of the leadership in the "potential" states is designed to diminish their potential for creating a state. These efforts can result in ruthless dictatorships that might appear to be stable and efficient, but they will not create states, let alone nations. If the arguments presented in this study are valid, the road from potential to real state would be one that recognizes the "ethnic" individuality of peoples and attempts to fit them first into a loose confederation. With time and good treatment people living in these confederations might begin to move out of their ethnic shells, develop closer ties with each other and, in the end, consent to a transformation of their confederation into a federation and maybe even into a centralized state. There are very few signs that would indicate that this road is being taken anywhere. The longer the leaders insist on

I

creating nations by force, the weaker will be their chances of success. Their "potential" states will remain, at best, just that.

The one state that appears to be the least affected by the trend discussed in this paper is our own country. The federal structure of our government and even more the civil rights legislations of the post-World War II years are certainly important factors in making our life relatively immune to the centrifugal tendencies that "natioethnism" created all over the world. Yet, in my opinion, the most crucial factor is the nature of American nationalism. That we speak of American nationalism is in itself significant. This term is vague, much vaguer than United States nationalism would be; it is not tied as closely to the state as most other similar expressions are in other states. If one goes beyond that rather superficial observation into the history of the American nation, more important elements become obvious.

While English is our official language, and the dominant WASP element hoped that a uniform nation would emerge out of the American "melting pot," the pressure to relinquish habits, customs, beliefs, language, and religious affiliations was never unbearable in spite of obvious biases and discriminatory practices. The existence of "ethnic" groups was always recognized and was finally extended to our one large, true minority when the transformation of Negroes into blacks was accepted. When a serious crisis developed in our country and the population's faith in the government reached a low point as a result of Vietnam and Watergate, antidiscriminatory laws (certainly not passed just at this moment on purpose) that even made multilingual instruction in schools mandatory (to cite only one example) reestablished some belief in the government and directed attention in new directions. Our authorities, and to some extent even our society, favor "natioethnic" identification and action today. We recognize the multiethnic composition of the nation and do not insist that this is detrimental to national security and the survival of the United States. We might be on the brink of discovering something new: the multiethnic nation that is a federation of ethnic groups to the same extent to which our state is the federation of fifty smaller ones. Multi-national states have proven and are today proving that they are prone to grave difficulties. The present-day trend in the United States appears to indicate that multi-ethnic national states whose population is composed of "natioethnic" units are viable. While this favorable development might be the result of accidental developments made possible by the fact that our population (except our Indians) is made up of a multiplicity of immigrants, it does not follow that this solution is not possible in states whose inhabitants are all autochthonous. Our model, so different from all others, might be the solution for the above-discussed problems of the "potential" states.

* * *

In the last 200 years the movement from ethnicity to nationalism has occurred. Nation and state became — erroneously — practically synonyms. My argument is simply that this erroneous usage has to be given up not only because it was always wrong, but because the concept of nation and nationalism are changing. People are moving away from the extreme, centralistic interpretations of nationalism; they have discovered or rediscovered their "natioethnism" and are willing to be loyal only to nations that recognize the right to the existence of their "natioethnic" components. Because of the close connection in modern times between nation and state, the state too has to retreat from extreme centralization (in both its Marxist and non-Marxist forms) to federative and in some cases confederative structures. At present we see only the beginning of this development, and it is impossible to predict what its results will be. Nevertheless, I am convinced that what is emerging is not one of the many still-born "isms" of the last 200 years, but a serious new trend that will influence the history of mankind.

NOTES

[1] R. R. Palmer and Joel Colton, *A History of the Modern World*, 3rd ed. (New York, 1965), pp. 430-431.

[2] Ernest Gellner, "Ethnicity between Culture, Class and Power," in Peter F. Sugar ed., *Ethnicity in Eastern Europe* (Santa Barbara, forthcoming.)

[3] Peter F. Sugar, "External and Domestic Roots of Eastern European Nationalism," in Peter F. Sugar and Ivo J. Lederer eds., *Nationalism in Eastern Europe* (Seattle and London, 1969), pp. 3-9.

[4] Karl W. Deutsch, *Nationalism and Social Communications; An Inquiry into the Foundation of Nationality* (Cambridge, Mass. and New York, 1953).

[5] Hugh Seton-Watson, *Nations and States: An Enquiry into the Origin of Nations and the Politics of Nationalism* (Boulder, Colo., 1977).

[6] For an interesting study on the origin of a unified French nation see Eugen J. Weber, *Peasants into Frenchmen: The Modernization of Rural France* (Stanford, 1976).

[7] President de Gaulle's visit to Canada occurred in the summer of 1967.

[8] In fact Austria-Hungary did not exist. Hungary was a political unit after 1867, but it was associated not with Austria but with "die im Reichsrat vertretenen Kronen und Länder" (the crowns and lands represented in the imperial council) for which Austria was used as a convenient, short appellation.

[9] Nathan Glazer and Daniel P. Moynihan eds., in their "Introduction" to their

volume *Ethnicity: Theory and Experience* (Cambridge, Mass., 1975), came to the same conclusion: The state failed and people looked for new "primary loyalties." Their reasoning differs from my arguments, but our judgments concerning the problem under discussion are the same.

[10] The failure of the "class" concept in the socialist states is similar and for identical reasons so is the failure of the "nation" concept in nation-states.

[11] Glazer and Moynihan, in their above-cited introduction, quote from Daniel Bell's chapter in their volume ("Ethnicity and Social Change," pp. 141-174): "Ethnicity has become more salient [than class] because it can combine interest with an affective." The same can be said when ethnicity and its appeal is compared to nationalism. Both class and nationalism were proposed by their supporters as affectives, but failed because — in my terms — they were not "natural."

[12] See Walker Connor, "The Politics of Ethnonationalism," in *Journal of International Affairs,* 27 January 1973, pp. 1-21.

[13] Peter F. Sugar, "Ethnicity; The Case of Eastern Europe," in Sugar ed., *Ethnicity in Eastern Europe.*

II

ETHNICITY IN EASTERN EUROPE*

The last chapter of any study written by several scholars can take several forms. It might briefly recapitulate the major points and original contributions of the authors; it might contribute a conclusion; or it might add to the treatment of the topic. Each of these alternatives is appealing yet this volume will be ended differently. The approach taken grew out of the discussions held during the three day conference.[1] When theoretical issues were debated during that meeting, some area specialists prefaced their remarks by saying, "but in Eastern Europe ..." and others who were not East European specialists asked, "why in Eastern Europe...?" The participants tried to bring together theory, worldwide observation, and the East European experience, yet were repeatedly faced with East European peculiarities that made this attempt very difficult. One participant even suggested that the theoretical introduction, *Chapter I*,[2] should be paralleled by a short historical introduction explaining the peculiarities of Eastern Europe. These remarks and suggestions gave impetus to this attempt to present the "Case of Eastern Europe," for those interested in the problem of ethnicity.

Rereading the original and the reworked chapters several times confirmed the need to devote the last chapter to the "peculiar" features of ethnicity in Eastern Europe. These "peculiarities" are in no way "abnormal, atypical, sui generis," or so unique they cannot be found elsewhere, too; there is no need to present a picture of East European ethnicity as something special. The goal is to focus on several historical features and developments—all of which have also been observed outside of Eastern Europe—that created a matrix for the birth, growth, and persistence of ethnicity in Eastern Europe giving it characteristics that led to this inquiry.

Several authors have noted that states are not nations, nations are not ethnic groups, and that ethnicity is different from nationalism. They have paid more attention to the process that transforms an ethnic group into a nation than to any other topic. This chapter will focus on ethnicity.

II

There is no universally accepted definition of ethnicity. Yet, the concept is clear judging by the general agreement reached by the contributors to this volume. Professor Enloe stated that "... there is growing agreement that [ethnicity] is both objective and subjective.... [It] involves cultural attributes that can be observed, but those attributes must be assigned conscious value by a collection of people in order to amount to ethnicity.... Ethnicity is a social phenomenon, requiring a sense of belonging and an awareness of boundaries between members and nonmembers however vague...."[3] This definition takes into consideration the "objective attributes, subjective feelings, and behavioral patterns," often manifested by the use of numerous symbols, that result in a sense of ethnic identity by "a group of people ... in order to differentiate themselves from other groups,"[4] to quote Professor Brass. Professor Fishman stressed the same thing, in different terms, when he insisted on the importance of "experiencing ethnicity from the inside,"[5]—the subjective feeling—before it can be understood. Dr. Hofer's approach to the problem is that of a scholar looking at ethnicity from the inside. This same approach reappears in Dr. Conner's analysis when, following Max Weber, he writes about the *myth* without which no ethnic feeling of solidarity can develop.[6]

The problem, then, is not to define what ethnicity is, but what forces bring it into being and make it the common belief of an "ethnic category" or an "ethnic group." This crucial question presents a difficulty.

There seems to be agreement when this problem is approached "chronologically." According to Professor Fishman ethnicity developed in the premodern, preindustrial period produces "pre-mobilizational ethnicity ... the untutored and largely unconscious ethnicity of everyday life."[7] Professors Gellner and Brass address "ethnicity in industrial, or industrializing" societies during and after the eighteenth century. Their version of ethnogenesis suggests that it is important to recognize problems of economic competition, class distinction, and the numerous cultural and social boundaries that Professor Gellner schematizes with such remarkable skill. But by dealing with national and not ethnic conflict situations, he provides a good, first indication of where to look for important boundaries separating ethnicity from nationalism. He notes:

> Nationalism is, essentially, the transfer of the focus of man's identity to a culture which is mediated by literacy and an extensive, formal educational system. It is not the mother tongue that matters, but the language of the *école maternelle*.[8]

Each chapter in this book touched on the problem of schools and Professor Rezler provides some important statistical details. The use of scholars as a major propaganda weapon available to the state to teach and enforce conformity is nothing new. Those who fight for private schools that teach in a multiplicity of languages strive to maintain their "nationality" or national minority rights because the state dominated, modern school system belongs to a modern, industrialized world. The Poles made the organization and maintenance of a private school system a fundamental goal of "organic work" in the mid-1820s to defend their nationality, not simply to preserve their language or ethnicity. By then the Poles had acquired the "activated consciousness of ethnicity" that transformed it into nationalism. This transformation had occurred more slowly among the other people of Eastern Europe by 1820. The Poles were ahead of everybody else and their advanced status was due to the early attempts at modernization and industrialization following the partitions of Poland in 1772 and later in 1793 and 1795.

The Poles retained, with their nationalism, features of their ethnic identification, "those socio-cultural behaviors and values that derive from and define membership in communities of putative common ancestry."[9] Those features are perceived in Professor Petrovich's discussion of the Poles.[10]

The Poles of the 1820s were ethnically and nationally conscious. The relevant literature on that subject has never seriously considered the existence of that dual consciousness since nationalism is traditionally considered to be a "modernized," politicized form of ethnicity. Economic modernization and political nation building in Eastern Europe and several other regions occurred simultaneously under difficult circumstances amidst linguistically, religiously, and culturally heterogenous peoples. That does not involve the "orderly" development of ethnicity first and a transformation into nationalism, rather it is an emergence of the phenomenon that Dr. Conner calls "ethnonationalism."[11] "Ethnonationalism" differs from premodern ethnicity and postmodern nationalism. It develops under circumstances with the same characteristics under which ethnicity develops "organically" in the premodern setting, and those of nationalism developed "artificially" and rapidly by government pressure, modern communications, and schools in a "modern" surrounding. "Ethnonationalism" did not mature over centuries and then change like the ethnic, later national, values of the organically developing value systems, and it was not subjected to the pressure exercised by all-powerful modern governments. In other words, it is a kind of ethnicity to which all our theories and experiences apply either partially or with reservations because it did not emerge in a liberal or command society in the premodern or modern period. "Ethnonationalism" developed in modernizing societies that remained basically agricultural and politically medieval under theoretically powerful, but extremely inefficient, imperial governments. Those governments were replaced and the economic transformation accelerated in Eastern Europe beginning in 1945—by then ethnonationalism was a well-established "experience of rooted, intimate, and eternal belonging" that had to be protected against "foreigners" who proposed to change it overnight from the "outside." Ethnonationalism is still alive, but it is impossible to predict whether it will live or be replaced by a form of nationalism that will fit preconceived models of western scholarship.

The next few pages deal with "ethnonationalism" as a social phenomenon "in limbo" between the premodern and modern worlds. The philosophies which governed those worlds were not *laissez faire*; "modernization" never managed to eradicate agrarianism: urbanization often meant the creation of large "villages"; competition between "haves" and "have nots" speaking different languages and belonging to different churches was the reality. Under these circumstances development differed from the usual model. Ethnonationalism was an East European phenomenon that appeared elsewhere but not in émigré communities that left this region. That phenomenon will serve future scholars by helping them to understand societies that are neither "premodern" nor "modern," but almost eternally "semimodern."

Before the features of East European ethnonationalism can be analyzed, the "semimodern" society, polity, or state needs to be defined as a community consciously embarked on changing a traditional way of life. Such communities may move away from tradition, even alter it drastically, but they never succeed in fully emulating, let alone in "catching up" with the model that they propose to substitute for the system they wish to abandon. Thus a "semimodern" society resembles an acrobat suspended by his toes and fingertips between two chairs continually being pulled further and further apart. When that circus act is performed by an unwilling star, and most people in any society undergoing change are unwilling acrobats, they naturally tend to recall the prestress situation with longing; they see it as a peaceful ideal, and hope to land in its midst again, not between two, but on the older chair, when the stress becomes unbearable.

Yet, even though modernization might not succeed, states might fail or disappear, the community continues to exist. The act never fails! Furthermore, in spite of its innate conservatism, the surviving community adjusts to pressures and change. This often imperceptible change makes landing on the old chair as impossible as taking refuge on a new one never fully built. The community suspended between two chairs or unable to accept either a premodern ethnic or modern-national role, comprises the ethnonationalism of semimodernity.

Eastern Europe was in a state of semimodernity beginning with the first movements to change its social-political-economic structure in the second half of the eighteenth century until 1948. The development since then is inconclusive and impossible to evaluate. Yet, during the last thirty years the changes introduced were dictated by forces located outside the ethnic-national-state boundaries. Those changes were resisted by local forces which relied upon self-identifying values developed during the preceding two hundred years—those of East European ethnonationalism. Those years encompass the crucial developments.

First, the modernizing forces need to be examined to explain why they did not achieve their goals; then it is easier to explain how ethnonationalism developed in reaction to modernization. The major modernizing forces in Eastern Europe were the Romanov, Habsburg and Ottoman Empires. The need for change became apparent when the power of the western states became evident in comparison. Any attempt to "westernize" and "modernize" those Empires had to fail because the rulers were reluctant or incapable of giving up old values, they lacked the power and skills to affect thorough change, and the people lacked primary loyalty to the monarchy or state directed government.

The reluctance or inability to break with the past was most apparent in the Ottoman Empire. Its major reform movement was called *Tanzimat* (meaning purification) and its aim was to purify the state, get rid of corruption and forces that perverted the old, perfect system that was to be reestablished. In Russia, modernization began with either Alexander I or Nicholas I, and the twin pillars of the old order, orthodoxy and autocracy, were to be the foundations on which the new was to be built. Maria Theresa, the originator of reform in the Habsburg Empire, considered loyalty to the dynasty (later called *Kaisertreue*) and Roman Catholicism to be the unchangeable rocks on which her realm stood. Her son, Joseph II, rejected her approach, but subsequent Habsburgs returned to it in one form or another. Russians never forsook their pillars of wisdom and the government attempted to return to them even after 1905. Modernization based on those premodern principles resulted, at best, in semimodernity.

The lack of power and political and technological skills in the three empires hardly requires explanation. All three states lacked financial strength and were frequently bankrupt for all practical purposes. Individuals were often forced into playing the roles of modernizers and industrial entrepreneurs against their will, and financial problems precluded the development of military forces commensurate with the power position coveted by the three empires. All three however developed large political units in the course of the nineteenth century, "modern" bureaucracies in which the members never became true civil or state servants in a western sense. Those bureaucrats played the self-serving game played by Djilas's *New Class* in the communist states by advancing the aims of the state only when they coincided with their own advantages. They successfully avoided performing their duties by barricading themselves behind mountains of red tape or through delaying tactics that became known as *Schlamperei* in the Habsburg Empire and as "Balkan conditions" in Southeastern Europe.

The bureaucrats failed because they did not acquire the mentality of their colleagues in the West, and because of an appalling absence of technical skills. All sectors of the economy—finances, banking, industry, agriculture and services—in the three empires were unable to educate and recruit experts. Consequently, they remained more often than not fully dependent on the western states for investments, expertise and economic aid.

The three modernizing empires ruled over multiethnic, multi-religious, multilingual populations without commanding sufficient loyalty to ensure support of their governments' efforts. The Ottoman Empire failed to recognize ethnic differences when it embarked on modernization and the concept of nationhood was unknown in that state. Ottomanism, Turanism and Turkism appeared at the end of the nineteenth century too late to support the creation of a state-supporting nation. The Habsburg state was a conglomeration of political entities with traditional, mainly medieval, rights and a degree of self-government. When these rights fell into disuse they were reestablished by the Pragmatic Sanction of Emperor Charles VI that assured the right of inheritance of the throne through Maria Theresa and the female line of the Habsburg family. Since only a small minority, the "natio" or political nation, profited from these rights the government was faced with ruling in cooperation with the political nation or governing "unconstitutionally." The first alternative hamstrung the government either through the "natio's" conservatism or its egotism and when it tried to rule without having the cooperation of local authorities its efforts were faced with practically universal resistance. The Habsburg situation does not fit neatly in any of Professor Gellner's categories because there is no clear division between those who had power and those who did not. The masses, who clearly had no power, and the government, which theoretically had it all, were separated by the "natio" that could make common cause with either. When the "natio" allied with the government the government's power was diluted and could not be fully utilized; when it identified with the masses the "natio" became the main force creating ethnonationalism.

Russia experienced neither the Ottoman nor the Habsburg problem. The tsar-autocrat and his government possessed power and the rest of the nation, including the nobility, its wealth notwithstanding, had none. Yet, the Russian nobility that manned the military and civil offices was, in a sense, an equivalent of the Habsburg "natio." Within the limits of their military, civil, and legal jurisdictions and on their estates they enjoyed the same alternative as those who possessed local privileges in the Habsburg lands. The masses viewed the nobility as "the authority" who had a relative latitude in exercising it. The Russian peasant in Kazan was as far removed from the direct jurisdiction of the Tsar as the Romanian farmer in Transylvania was from the Emperor-Kings. The Tsar and the Emperor were quasi-mythical personalities who ranked just below God and, though good by definition, were unapproachable by the common people. In everyday life the local power holder was the reality.

These circumstances and the lack of effective communications created a chasm between the "modernizers" and those who had to accept change and under those conditions the western model of nation building was inoperative. Yet, despite these handicaps, governments reached even the lowest levels. Taxes were increased and collected, military service and the quartering of troops was enforced, land was expropriated to build roads, railroads and government buildings, and the law courts functioned. The authorities increasingly interfered in the everyday life of practically everybody in proportion to the governments' desire to modernize. Demands for change and additional sacrifice were made in the name of the state and nation; yet both were alien concepts. The need to sharpen and heighten existing feelings of self-identification developed in reaction to those demands and out of this need grew ethnonationalism to distinguish the community lacking a state orientation from other groups within the boundaries of semimodernity.

Ethnonationalism developed almost unconsciously and it was based on religion, ethnic collectivity, and language based on a "putative common ancestry." Religion played an interesting role, but not religion defined as a belief in the dogmas and mysteries of an organized church. That kind of belief is unknown among illiterate people who have lived for centuries in practical isolation. Religion for those people involved a localized and superstitious folk-religion—a major symbol of self, identity to differentiate "us" from "them." "Our belief" in God made "us" what "we" were; and "we" are the "chosen people." In this sense Professor Fishman is correct, "ethnicity ... was God-given." The "chosen-people" had common ancestors and a common past making the group an entity on its own without a state. Yet belief was not enough since belonging needs spiritual as well as palpable symbols. The symbols are supplied by the physical artifacts found in any house of worship: the Ka'aba in Mecca, the Wailing Wall in Jerusalem, and include the icons and statues of the Christian denominations. Those kinds of symbols, venerated as they are, are remote and insufficiently identified with the local self—"they do nothing for us." The people need living symbols that will act for the good of the self—the ethnic hierarch discussed by Professor Petrovich.

Every group had an ethnarch. The sultan was Khalif; Hungary had an Apostolic King and a Bishop-Primate; Poland a Bishop-Primate; the Greeks had the Patriarch in Istanbul and later the Archbishop of Athens; the Montenegrins had the Prince-bishop; the Serbs looked to the apostolic authority of Ipek and Sremski Karlovci; the Bulgarians to Ohrid; the Regateni Romanians to Bucharest; the Orthodox Transylvanian Romanians had an ethnarch in Sibiu and the Uniates had the Bishop in Cluj. It really did not matter if the sees were occupied or empty or if the incumbents were interested in the ethnic welfare of their flock; however the symbol of these religious offices to the various communities was important. The ill-timed radio address delivered by Cardinal József Mindszenty of Hungary on November 3, 1956, can only be explained by his belief that he was still Hungary's ethnarch and her only true representative. In this sense religion is one of three boundary setters between ethnic categories in Eastern Europe, part of the triad on which the region's ethnonationalism rests.

In any ethnic collectivity, ethnicity is "God-given" and it parallels religiosity. A "chosen people" must first have a feeling of being a people and the various groups of Eastern Europe that desired to establish an ethnic identity turned as far into their past as they possibly could in their search for roots. The belief systems of people are strikingly similar and the legends include such ancient characters reminiscent of Romulus and Remus, magic animals, fanciful raids and stories that cannot be verified but which survive in folklore. These subjective and fanciful stories establish a common origin and those who claim such common origin become "brothers" and "sisters" in the way that contemporary American blacks use those expressions. The South Slavic villager community (zadruga) and the Russian mirs are narrowly delimited survivals of such "brotherhood" feelings. The monotheistic religions and cultural orientation of these collectivities influenced the old stories to some extent. The cross of St. Hubertus appeared over the heads of mythical animals important in the stories of ancestors, but "sanctification" did not change the role played by these beasts. Their role was that of friends or enemies of forefathers whose descendants made up a specific in-group. Monotheism added the quality of "God-giveness" as understood by those whose faith was expressed by folk-religion, thus God became a partner or friend of the mythical ancestors.

The third aspect of ethnicity, language, is in a narrow sense a basic, indispensable means of communication. In the broad sense it is the major element of communications required to tie a group together. In the broadest sense language includes gestures, feelings expressed by dress, rituals, dietary habits and taboos, and other social manifestations that differ from one ethnic region to another. Numerous signals and symbols of that kind survive in Eastern Europe.

The basic importance of language is apparent. None of the ideas and beliefs mentioned here could carry feelings of identity without a language to express them, and Professor Fishman and Dr. Hofer have verified the importance of language in that context. It is equally important to note that language is used to unify and to differentiate ethnic groups. Obviously the creation of the Serbo-Croatian language did not result in the birth of a Yugoslav nation. Yet, it is reasonable to suggest that language unifies the Croats and that dialectical differences, representing various past historical experiences, still reflect primary loyalties among them. The Macedonians had to wait until their idiom was officially recognized as a language before they could insist on nationhood. Dialectology is therefore of interest to philologists, linguists, anthropologists, and ethnographers, and it is of primary importance to students of ethnicity interested in creating or advancing ethnic awareness among a given group of people. This was true during the "national movements" that emerged in Europe during the eighteenth and nineteenth centuries and is true today in the Third World and in the Celtic revival movement.

Yet, the emphasis on language assumed a special form in Eastern Europe and Chapter III[12] deals with that problem almost exclusively. Ethnic consciousness and language reform are directly related to an interest in the East European peasant, the unspoiled carrier of ethnic characteristics, and the basic features of ethnic identity have often been applied to all processes of its formation. The peasant orientation involved in the study of language as a factor in developing ethnonationalism introduces yet another difficulty. Since any phenomenon comprised of several components becomes different from all similar ones when one component is altered, we must assume that the linguistic component provides an explanation of ethnonationalism.

Feelings of ethnic belonging and nationalism developed naturally during the premodern, preindustrial period. In modern times, irrespective of the political system and the state of the economy at the time of a given state's "take-off" moment, the locus of such development is the urban, industrial society with no use for peasants. Modern attempts to pull populations together and create state-supporting communities will skip the ethnic identity phase and try to create a nationalist awareness coincidental with political borders. They will often try to eradicate existing ethnic loyalties to achieve their goals. Professor Gellner treated the alternatives that determine governmental success or failure under these circumstances. If his analysis is correct then those nations that emerged in the premodern period and those formulated in the modern period felt the need to find within a broad group of people a specific core with characteristics that could be expanded to cover an entire "nation" and legitimize its existence. That need arises under "semimodern" circumstances when the institutions that dominate everyday life and those interested in creating "nations" lack both the means to enforce their policies and an understanding of "modernity." Those "nation-builders" rely on remnants of the past—the unspoiled segment of their would-be "nation" (the peasantry in Eastern Europe)—to create a future that has no relationship with the values and lifestyles of those who represent the basis for the new identity. Without a past, a common heritage, no future is possible—it is impossible to make a silk purse from a sow's ear. What will eventually emerge from this effort will not be ethnicity or nationalism, it will be ethnonationalism.

Nobody in the three empires, from the rulers down to the lowliest subject, really knew the goals of the reforms contemplated when the attempt at change began. Those who believed that the future should reflect the interests and will of the "people," had to find, and sometimes create, a people first. Advocates of the people's interest could not model their reforms on the people who made up the state apparatus since that apparatus was comprised of "foreigners" who advocated an alien future. Yet, those advocates were part of the apparatus because their level of education and sophistication made it easier to communicate with the "oppressors" than it was to identify with the people. Before they could create a power base, they needed an identity that differed from that of the establishment. Members of the "political nation" and the clergy legally had such a base, but it was too narrow, and most importantly, it was not ideologically and emotionally appealing. These would-be leaders turned to the teachings of the West to find a broader political ideology and found it mostly incomprehensible or, worse, irrelevant. The only western thinker applicable to their need was Herder. Professor Fishman's words are relevant in that context:

> Herder's words constituted a return to and an intensification of the ancient Hebraic and Greek vision of ethno-linguistic sanctity. God's glory was recognizable in the ethnic diversity which He had created and each ethnicity was quintessentially represented by its language, its folklore, its glorious past, its ancestral traditions, its vision of greatness and its unique destiny mission.... These beauties deserved protection, preservation, and cultivation, and whatever political and economic realities tended to weaken or disregard them deserved to be altered.[13]

These words clearly indicated what had to be saved, cultivated, and developed and what had to be weakened and opposed. The beautiful things were with the people who had to be made aware; reformers had to become part and parcel of the basic ethnic community. Unfortunately the absence of a domestic middle class, an aristocracy or an "alienated" upper class left only the peasantry as such a basic community. This realization turned the ethnic awakening of East Europeans into its specific direction.

Ethnonationalism begins with the peasant fixation of East European reformers and the survival of this specific form of self-identification needs to be explained, and "semi-modernity" becomes a crucial factor in rationalizing the persistence of ethnonationalism in Eastern Europe. Ethnonationalism does not fit neatly into the existing models or concepts of ethnicity and nationalism. Furthermore, it was a static experience in that area for two hundred years. In most other cases, ethnicity was transformed into a nationalistic ideology which had its own history, varieties and transformational patterns. The history of Eastern Europe was not static and the tremendous changes which occurred there, even disregarding the last thirty years, suggest that the modification of ethnonationalism paralleled them. Yet ethnonationalism was a constant phenomenon in spite of its different manifestations.

This apparent paradox can be explained since no nation or state exists in a vacuum. They are all influenced by their relative economic and political positions on the international scene and their internal affairs, those that influence the development of local movements, reflect their international position. The position of East Europe measured in terms of economic and political-military power never changed. Eastern Europe was "ahead" of the non-European world at the end of the eighteenth century but "behind" those states that were considered "modern" at that time. Today's situation is similar since Eastern Europe has always been in the middle between "backward" and "modern." This position entailed certain disadvantages such as a dependence on foreign capital and "know-how," but it did not prevent "progress."

The empires first had to concede more "rights" to the population, they then became constitutional states, and finally disappeared. Their successor states were constitutional monarchies or republics and several even introduced universal male suffrage. Political parties, some of them ideological, appeared and by 1900 they began acting like the western parties. More and more cities became self-governing and the political structure changed drastically.

Similar economic changes occurred. Capital starved, local banks appeared and a larger proportion of gross national income was generated by industry. The city populations grew, at least in the capitals, and so did the rate of literacy. A native middle class developed, and, under its influence, cultural manifestations—theater, opera, concerts, exhibitions—supported by this segment of society materialized and flourished. Western European tourists who visited the major cities of Eastern Europe around 1900 felt at home. Yet the conditions that prevailed in Eastern Europe were markedly different than in earlier times.

Hugh Seton-Watson, a westerner with a deep understanding of Eastern Europe, wrote that the late 1930s witnessed numerous manifestations of the "peasant cult" in the cities:

... if the foreign visitor stays a little longer in the country, if he leaves the capital ... and keeps his eyes open ... he will see mud hovels, adorned by no rugs or pottery, housing families of seven or eight.... He will notice how the young peasant labourers ... look at the officials who examine their labour permits.[14]

Quite clearly, "modernization" had not reached the countryside and the authorities were still all powerful, intimidating the population. The population resented the authorities who demanded a lot from them but gave them very little. Obviously, the state had failed to legitimize the nation and the actions of its representatives. By the late 1930s all the governments of Eastern Europe except that of Czechoslovakia were dictatorships with access to developed tools of power greater than those wielded by the three empires. All the governments were stricter than those of the previous regimes. Yet, the occupants of these mud huts knew who they were and who were their "brothers" and "sisters." The peasants could identify those who endangered their existence. Ethnonationalism was very much alive.

The conditions observed by Seton-Watson were the result of much more than an urban-rural, industrial-agrarian cleavage. They were the result of "semi-modernity." All the East European states from the moment they gained their independence to when dictatorships were introduced, experienced a similar history. They all had legislative assemblies which represented only those in power. Governments lost elections as a result of foreign influence or when Prime Ministers decided that it was in their interest to lose. They all had self-serving bureaucracies recruited from a narrow segment of the population out of touch with the rest of the "nation." They were all intolerant, and persecuted minorities. They all had negative trade balances and most of their national incomes were produced by agriculture. They shared a faulty understanding of economic realities, or denied reality by hiding behind noneconomic excuses. The old "political nations" expanded, but the states were run solely in the interests of those who belonged to them. They uniformly lacked power in international politics and when they united (e.g., the Little Entente and Balkan League) they misused those alliances and failed to utilize them to maximize their common power. The East European states were unable to compete on the world market and remained economically "backward." The major cities were inhabited by people mostly unfamiliar with the countryside who nonetheless indulged in peasant cults in an imaginary world. The states thus had "modern," and "pre-modern" components.

They were houses divided and most of the rooms were still single unit mud huts.

As the ruling segments of the population became more modern, educated, and ambitious they understood most of their countrymen even less and became convinced that drastic measures were needed to remedy the situation. The drastic measures they took furthered their own narrow advantages or those perceived to be in the "national" interest. Unfortunately, their view of the common good did not coincide with that of the majority. As a result, the gap between those in power and the rest of the people grew. Draconic police measures soon followed. Governments became authoritarian, self-centered, and self-contained and under those conditions distrust became general so that the masses rejected even those ideologies proclaimed to work in their interests. The rejection of Austromarxism prior to the First World War illustrates the response of the people to anything that did not originate in their midst. They listened to priests and popes rather than to political agitators because religious figures had a place in their ethnonationalism and politicians did not. In short, Eastern Europe never became "modern." It copied the institutions but not the spirit that made modernization work elsewhere; it built cities but failed to integrate them into the country as a whole; it became industrialized, but relied on agriculture for most of its income; its educational systems were modernized in the cities yet there were never enough technocrats to embark on real economic reform; it claimed sovereignty and remained dependent; its leaders spoke for the people, but the people and their leaders were further apart than their grandfathers used to be. In other words, the states of Eastern Europe moved away from their traditional societies without moving the bulk of their people away from their traditions. Events moved too fast and started from a base too high to permit the development of ethnicity first and a transformation into nationalism. The resulting halfway house of "semi-modernity" was something between ethnicity and nationalism, ethnonationalism and the politicians lacked the power to transform it into a true nationalism.

Professor Gellner explained nationalism stating that "class conflict is a national one which failed to take off, for lack of deep cultural and symbolic differentiae." That conclusion is valid and so is his underlying assumption that all conflicts result from differences between various groups of people. Without differences there would be no class, no ethnic consciousness, no nationalism and since Eastern Europe certainly had more differences than any other region of comparable size those differences resulted in ethnonationalism. Ethnonationalism is nationalism that has failed to take off because it lacked sufficient growth to take it beyond the stage of semimodernity.

Notes

* - This study was the last chapter of Peter F. Sugar (ed.), *Ethnic Diversity and Conflict in Eastern Europe* (Santa Barbara - Oxford; ABC-Clio, 1980). The footnotes were added for this publication and, with the exception of n. 14, refer to essays published in this volume. - Numbers appearing in [ ] after page numbers refer to the original pagination.

1 - The Conference sponsored by the American Council of Learned Societies took place in Seattle, June 11-13, 1976.

2 - Paul Brass, "Groups and Nationalities. The Formation, Persistence and Transformation of Ethnic Identities."

3 - Cynthia H. Enloe, "Religion and Ethnicity. Some General Considerations."

4 - Brass, p. 3.

5 - Joshua A. Fishman, "Social Theory and Ethnography. Neglected Perspectives on Language and Ethnicity in Eastern Europe," p. 87.

6 - Tamás Hofer, "The Ethnic Model of Peasant Culture. A Contribution to the Ethnic Symbol building on Linguistic Foundations by East European peoples" and Conner, Walker, "The Ethno-political Challenge and Governmental Responses." See also Fishman, p. 79.

7 - Fishman, p. 84.

8 - Ernest Gellner, "Ethnicity between Culture, Class and Power," p. 244.

9 - Fishman, p. 71.

10 - Michael B. Petrovich, "Religion and Ethnicity in Eastern Europe," pp. 281-82.

11 - Conner, pp. 147-48, 168-70, 182-83.

12 - Hofer, see n. 6.

13 - Fishman, p. 75.

14 - Hugh Seton-Watson, *Eastern Europe between the Wars, 1918-1941* (London; Cambridge University Press, 1945), p. 76.

NINETEENTH-CENTURY MANIFESTATIONS

The political history of the twentieth century could be presented in terms of the struggle of three ideologies: nationalism, Fascism and the various versions of Marxism ranging from Christian Socialism to Marxism-Leninism-Stalinism. By the last year of this century only nationalism has remained as an important set of beliefs influencing the actions of politicians and the feelings of most people.

While this tripartite struggle occurred in the twentieth century, it cannot be understood without looking back to earlier periods, at least to the preceding hundred years. The three studies in this section try to supply background information for the understanding of the manifestations of nationalism in Eastern Europe.

The first essay, originally a lecture, was designed to discuss contemporary manifestation of Eastern European nationalism just prior to the drastic changes that occurred in 1989. In order to do this I was obliged to deal not only with the earlier period of the twentieth century, but had to move back to the nineteenth as well to make this survey comprehensible. Hopefully, it will prove to be a good introduction to the study and understanding of the subject to which this volume is devoted.

The next two selections attempt to show the strength of nationalism in the second half of the 1800s. Austria-Hungary, the multinational state *par excellence*, is the best example to present not only the power of national feelings, but also their gradual development. The dual monarchy that came into existence in 1867 had two governments, the Austrian and the Hungarian, each of which had to deal with a great variety of national groups. In their attempts to gain the loyalties of these groups for their halves of the state, the Austrian government became more and more lenient and liberal, while the Hungarian moved from relative liberalism to uncompromising authoritarianism. In spite of this fundamental difference, the reaction of the various 'minorities' to the actions and behaviour of the authorities was the same: they became more and more hostile to Habsburg rule, making the survival of that state less and less likely. Multinationality, possible in 1867, had to yield to the demands of numerous specific nationalisms by 1914. It is my opinion that even without a war Austria-Hungary, in the form in which the *Ausgleich* created it, would have died with the Emperor Franz Joseph in 1916.

The second of the two studies dealing with Austria-Hungary turns from internal problems to the state's foreign policy and shows the extent to which, less than ten years after its creation, the realm's multi-ethnicity already dictated foreign policy. Each move that the Common Minister of Foreign Affairs made in the years of 1875 to 1878 was dictated by his assessment of the reaction of the various nations living in the state he represented and not by his evaluation of the international situation.

III

THE PROBLEMS OF NATIONALISM IN EASTERN EUROPE PAST AND PRESENT

Defying the proclaimed ideological similarity of the various governments of Eastern Europe (except Greece) during the last 40 years, nationalism is the strongest single motivating force today in that region. Nationalism has forced those in power to make certain ideological concessions giving birth to a basic contradiction even in terminology, national communism. Still, a major issue for the leaders of the various parties and states remains unresolved: the people's primary loyalty has little if anything to do with the world view which they are supposed to accept as the sole valid motivating force for their behavior.

Obviously, the manifestations of nationalism in Eastern Europe today are different from those visible at the end of the Second World War, and deviate even more markedly from still earlier versions. Nationalism in Eastern Europe has its own history which must be understood when its present day varieties are analyzed. Therefore, a summary of this history will precede the discussion of today's problems.

For the purpose of this paper, Eastern Europe is defined as that part of the continent which lies east of the German and Italian speaking people and west of what were/are the borders of Russia/Soviet Union. This definition, which I have used for thirty years, is justified by the fact that it deals with people whose nationalism developed first after that of those living west of them; they were the first who had to adjust this new idea to local conditions and circumstances. This fact alone makes the study of nationalism in Eastern Europe important. Non-Europeans, as well as Europeans and Americans dealing with non-European lands and people, usually compare the nationalism and institutions of the so-called Third World to those of West European nations and states, in most cases with unsatisfactory results. A better knowledge of the East European varieties would make the comparisons much more fruitful because the East Europeans and all non-Europeans did not simply imitate the West Europeans, but everywhere created their own variations on the basic imported themes. More can be learned by people all over the world from the East Europeans' successes and failures than from those of the West Europeans.

III

Defining Nationalism

If the definition of Eastern Europe is fairly easy to present and justify, the same cannot be said about the definition of nationalism. As we all know, nobody has, so far, produced a definition of nationalism which has gained universal acceptance. It is relatively easy to fix a time frame for the existence of modern nationalism which is different from patriotism and all other feelings uniting people that go beyond the limits of the family. Boyd C. Shafer was only one of the many scholars to emphasize that "any use of the word nationalism to describe historical happenings before the eighteenth century is probably anachronistic."1 He was referring to eighteenth-century West European events. Why Shafer believed this is indicated by Ernest Gellner's clear statement that "nationalism as a phenomenon, not as a doctrine presented by the nationalists, is inherent in a certain set of social conditions; and these conditions...are the conditions of our time."2 Gellner's statement has timeless and universal validity because under the conditions of our time he understands the urbanized, industrialized societies whose daily life is regulated by a powerful central administration (democratic or undemocratic) irrespective of when and where a given political unit reaches this stage in its development.

Gellner refers to nationalism as a doctrine and as a phenomenon. As a phenomenon, he ties it to the industrial revolution, but he also indicates that for some people, the nationalists, it has been a doctrine. Some scholars agree with him, and try to define the concept. For example, Elie Kedourie writes that "nationalism is a doctrine invented in Europe at the beginning of the nineteenth century. It pretends to supply a criterion for the determination of the unit of population proper to enjoy a government exclusively its own."3 Others see nationalism as a "historical process,"4 "a state of mind,"5 or "a product of political, economic, social, and intellectual factors at a certain stage in history,...a condition of mind, feeling and sentiment."6 The one thing all these definitions have in common is the historical moment at which nationalism was born in Western Europe.

Nations, of course, existed before nationalism and can exist without it.7 Nations are brought together by what I, among others, have called the "natural," practically "inborn" feelings that everyone has for those fellow humans with whom he or she associates all his or her life and to whom, therefore, he or she feels attracted.8 Nationalism is "not something original or natural to man, like his physique or family,"9 according to Anthony D. Smith. It is "inscribed neither in the nature of things, nor in the hearts of men," agrees Gellner. Nationalism, I have argued in another study, is "acquired" by people, and each generation has to learn it anew.11 What is learned depends to a considerable extent on the teacher. Thus nationalism can and does mean different things in different countries at the same moment in history, or it can and does change its focus in a given country through time.

Somebody had to be the first teacher. This teacher or rather teachers were members of the emerging industrial bourgeoisie in what Hugh Seton-Watson described as the Old Continuous Nations.12 These are the same nations, those of Western Europe, that shaped what Gellner calls the "conditions of our time." The story is too well known to require repetition. What might be worth stressing is this new social force, the bourgeoisie, did not try to replace the old ruling class, the nobility, but instead wanted to eliminate its privileges and create equal opportunities for itself to gain the same prominence politically that they had already acquired economically. The bourgeoisie could not claim equal opportunity just for itself, as this would have simply increased the number and kinds of the very privileges it attacked. On the other hand, it could not claim equal political rights for everybody, a universalist approach that first appeared in the Declaration of Rights of Man and Citizens issued by the revolutionary French National Assembly on August 26, 1789. The group for which the emerging middle class claimed to speak, for whom it wanted equality, were the members of their "old continuous nations" which had developed over centuries and to them were "natural," well known entities. When they claimed liberties for the nation, they politicized that nation by claiming equal political, social, and economic rights for its members. In fact they tried to conquer government in the name of the nations. When they did this, they invented nationalism, popular sovereignty, modern democracy, classical liberalism, the concepts of human and civil rights -- to mention only the most important results of their gradually successful struggle. What they tried to create were the preconditions favorable for the development of the "conditions of our time." In this sense the Marxists are correct when they say that nationalism appeared when the industrial bourgeoisie acquired an increasing role in government. Yet, even this short summary of their actions proves that the Marxist interpretation of the bourgeoisie's motives is historically incorrect. Bourgeois nationalism, Lenin wrote, "drugs the minds of the workers, stultifies and disunites them in order that the bourgeoisie may lead them by the halter."13 Stalin agreed with this interpretation when he wrote that the bourgeoisie "appeals to its 'native folk' and begins to shout about the 'fatherland' claiming that its own cause is the cause of the nation as a whole. It recruits itself an army from among its 'countrymen'...."14 Both present nationalism as something invented by the middle class simply as a tool to dominate the workers, as a modern opiate for the masses to join the old one, religion, in keeping the lower classes in bondage. This interpretation could possibly deserve serious consideration had nationalism appeared on the political scene of the "old continuous" or any other nation after the

III

bourgeoisie's achievement of political power and after the emergence of consciously class-related differences between various segments of society. This was not the case. In another study, Ernest Gellner stresses this point very sharply when he states that "nationalism is not class conflict that has failed to reach consciousness, but class conflict is national conflict that has failed to take off for lack of deep cultural, symbolic differentiae."15 He sees class conflict, maybe even Marxism, as nothing more than frustrated nationalism!

The preceding remarks contain nothing unfamiliar to any, even superficial, student of nationalism. But I thought that making those remarks was necessary because their application to Eastern Europe demands that they be clearly kept in mind.

If nationalism must be inculcated into each new generation, if its acquisition by individuals as a doctrine, guide to action, or feeling, and so on, is the result of education, then much attention must be paid to the educator. Today, he or she is usually the teacher, on all levels of formal education, sharing with students something in which he or she usually believes often without knowing that it is the approved version of nationalism serving to legitimate the current regime. More will be said later about this role of formal education in propagating accepted forms of nationalism. The first propagators, teachers, of nationalist views were not formal, trained educators. In the lands inhabited by the "old continuous nations" they were the politically active educated members of the new industrial middle class, the first group of people fitting our present-day definition of the intelligentsia.

The Beginnings

In Eastern Europe around 1800 there was no industrial middle class, no intelligentsia. There were no national governments of states with which "nations" could identify and which, therefore, could be taken over by them. In many cases even national self-awareness was just beginning. Nations did, indeed, exist, but to what extent the people belonging to them were cognizant of their existence can be debated. With the exception of some relatively small areas in Bohemia and Silesia, even rudimentary beginnings of industrialization were lacking. Yet everywhere in Eastern Europe there were people who were dissatisfied with their position in society, who wanted to alter the rules and regulations which kept them in these positions, and who were looking for new arguments to bring about the desired changes. These people imported nationalism to Eastern Europe. It was a "new tool" which had proved effective in Western Europe and which they could use to build the social order of their dreams. These importers of nationalism had to be educated to read the literature in English, French, and German and to learn about events in the West. They also had to be ready to become politically active; they were the first to act as the East

III

European intelligentsia. They came from practically all social and professional strata, but not from the practically nonexistent middle class. Therefore, their goals, methods, aims, and philosophy had to be and were very different from those of the nationalists whose works they read and whose teachings they wished to apply to their own people and homelands. Nationalism, therefore, could not be adopted, it had to be adapted.

Who the adaptors were determined not only the immediate, original definitions of what was demanded by whom and for whom, but it also set a "tone," for the various emerging East European nationalisms, sometimes for decades, sometimes for more than a century. Nearly twenty years ago, I differentiated between four types of East European nationalism basing my definitions on the single criterion of the origin, programs, and lasting effects of these early East European nationalists.16 I will not repeat my arguments and descriptions, but will simply list the labels I used because, at least to some extent, they are self-explanatory. These were bourgeois, aristocratic, popular, and bureaucratic nationalism. In the first of these four varieties I placed only the Czechs; the Poles and Hungarians were my examples of the second; the Serbs and Bulgars illustrated the third variety; while the bureaucratic nationalists were found among the Turks, Greeks, and Romanians. I believe that what I did two decades ago still makes sense and will use some of these labels later, but today I wish to look at East European nationalism from a different point of view.

Irrespective of the time when the first East European nationalists became active -- the time lag between the earliest in one country and the latest in another can be as much as a century using certain criteria -- and, irrespective of the type of nationalism, 1848 roughly marked the end of the first period of nationalist activity in Eastern Europe. Disregarding numerous and important local variations, the East European nationalism in this first period of its existence was ideologically adaptive, romantic, nation- and myth-building, historical, and optimistic. Language reformers, historians, poets, and occasionally clergymen were the main propagators of this nationalism. Their aim was to make their respective nations conscious of their existence, proud of their past, and confident that the unsatisfactory present could and would be transformed into a future as glorious as the past. If the language was too backward to express these feelings using the modern vocabulary of nationalism and similar imported concepts, it had to be altered. If the past had not been glorious enough to justify the belief in a great future, it had to be recreated. In the Balkans hajduks, martalose, and so on -- whatever the label -- had to be recast as nationalistic freedom fighters.17 When national heroes of the required number or stature were missing, they had to be created.18 Where historical figures could be endowed with actions or ideas that suited the early nationalists, this too was done.19 Even historians of major

III

stature made "errors" consciously to serve the nationalist cause.20

The combination of the activities just listed with the type of person who undertook them produced an almost endless variety of early East European nationalisms. All of them were, obviously, different from the "model" which, at least in theory, the East Europeans were introducing in their lands. I used the rather neutral word, lands, on purpose because to speak of countries, let alone governments, would be misleading. The West European nationalists of the old continuous nations had not only nations, but also states of their own whose governments they wanted to take over, or at least reform, preaching popular sovereignty. The East Europeans not only had to create conscious nations, but also had to revive and/or create from scratch states in territories which, around 1800, were parts of the dynastic empires of the Romanovs, Ottomans, and Habsburgs. The Poles could also list the Hohenzollerns among their masters. Speaking of who should govern, how, and in the name of whom was secondary when first nations and then states had to be created.

During this first phase when all nations faced identical tasks though not necessarily at the same time, East European nationalism was more historical in its approach than what Herder or Rousseau had preached in the West, but it was, nevertheless, mainly cultural nationalism which did not see other nationals as enemies. The second period, roughly 1848 to 1914, moved away from this approach. This first variant of East European nationalism was basically nation- and myth-building.

The revolutionary year of 1848 has been studied repeatedly and in great detail as an all-European phenomenon and by various nations as an important event in their histories.21 Its importance for the history of East European nationalism, although it has been recognized, still awaits a good detailed study. What happened is the easiest to demonstrate in the lands of the Habsburgs. The 1846 events in Galicia created a sharp distinction between Poles and Ukrainians. This distinction was not solved by the Viennese government's establishment of the province of Bukovina as an independent Crownland three years later, and continued to deteriorate practically to the present day. In 1848 not only did the Croats, Slovaks, Serbs, and Romanians living in the lands of the Crown of St. Steven fight against the Hungarians, but their struggle created divisions which became worse and worse as time passed and before long also involved the Romanian and Serb states. While before 1848 serfs agreed at least on their common grievances, the free peasants of the post-revolutionary period remembered that they had fought each other in 1848 and were unable to work together to solve their remaining, by no means unimportant, common problems. Let us note also that the first Pan-Slav Congress was held in 1848 in Prague, that it was the first of the numerous Pan- movements, and that it represented the realization of several small nations that they were not strong enough to fight successfully for a state of their own and, therefore, they tried to do it as a group, a new super-nation.22 Finally, 1848 marked the defeat of classical liberalism and the emergence of a hard-nosed, power-grabbing approach to politics which we today label Realpolitik. To amass enough power for the next round of the struggle became more important than to justify the struggle ideologically.

The Watershed of 1848
Not surprisingly, all these important changes altered the nature of East European nationalism also. The leadership did not change too drastically and still represented the four approaches I described twenty years ago, but their aims and -- most important -- their methods had little in common with those of earlier periods. If nothing else, then the months of fighting concluded the phase of conscious nation-building. The actions of the Habsburgs and Romanovs made it clear that absolutism had to be ended and replaced by constitutional, national governments representing the will of the nations. In short, with some delay in relation to the West, the East European nationalists were now ready to fight for governments which would express the will of the sovereign people. They could not simply take over the running of affairs in Vienna or St. Petersburg because these cities were not capitals of old continuous nations like London, Paris, and, in a sense, even Berlin.

The nationalists' first task was to gain recognition for their nation's claim to sovereignty over a well-defined territory. Every nation had its claims and could justify them on historic, cultural, or ethnographic grounds. The problem was -- as is well known -- that these claims, justified or imaginary, overlapped in practically every respect. Was Bohemia a German or a Czech land? Was Transylvania Hungarian or Romanian? Was the Ukraine historically Polish, Russian, or Ukrainian? What were the borders of the Croatian Triune Kingdom? What lands were Bulgarian, which were Serb or Greek? These and many similar questions were given a great variety of answers based on all kinds of arguments and evidence. Of course, arguments presented by a group favoring them were considered to be "irrefutably" correct; those which presented different interpretations were just as "obviously" not only false but designed to rob those who had the truth of territory and independence.

Thus, between 1848 and 1914 nationalists faced two enemies: the dynastic empires from which they wanted to obtain at least autonomous self-rule and all the other people who shared their goals but also claimed some of the same territories, and the same determination to be recognized as sovereign over them. What emerged was something like a quod licet Jovi non licet bovi attitude of denying others the rights, privileges, and even the validity of dreams perfectly justified for one's own nation. It

III

took for granted that one's own nation was "the chosen people," the most talented and able, and therefore the one destined for regional leadership. This attitude can be seen in the writings of politicians in power, for example Ilija Garasanin; of those who had lost power, men like Lajos Kossuth; and even of those who hoped to come to power one day, as did Roman Dmowski. The Serbian statesman's well-known Nacertanije, Kossuth's plans of 1850 and 1862 for the creation of a Danubian Federation, and the young Pole's early thoughts recognized the multinationality of the region and proposed cooperation. Yet each of these men -- as well as others -- reserved for the Serbs, Hungarians, and Poles respectively the position of leadership and even the right to exclude from the hoped-for state those whom they considered undesirables.23

This exclusionary attitude created steadily sharpening hostilities and xenophobia, and also lead to the emergence of modern, political anti-Semitism. The nationalism of this second period became gradually more and more chauvinistic-jingoistic, state-building, present- and future-oriented, ahistorical, pugnacious, and exclusionary. Irrespective of the four groups of tone-givers repeatedly mentioned already, all nationalisms changed to this type from the one described for the first period of East European nationalism. The overall label for this second type of East European nationalism would be state-building although in the cases of Czechoslovakia and Yugoslavia, it was also nation-building.

Between the Wars

The third, shortest but by no means unimportant, period is the one between the two world wars. The well-known and always repeated result of the First World War was the elimination of empires and the creation, recreation, or drastic transformation of the states of East Central and Southeastern Europe. Equally well-known is the fact that most of these states, except Bulgaria and Hungary, were as multinational as the old empires had been, and that they either were satisfied and hoped to maintain the status quo or were revisionists who aspired to change it in accordance with their gains or losses following the war.24 These changes do not need detailed discussion since they have received it repeatedly in the past. While keeping them in mind, other factors have to be stressed because they drastically influenced the nature of nationalism in the region.

The first of these factors was the emergence of important middle and working classes as well as the growth of political consciousness among the peasantry. This change was caused in part by the war economy and in part by the various governments' goals to "modernize," "industrialize," and "urbanize." Consequently, victors and vanquished alike wrote new, democratic constitutions and paid lip service to democracy, school, and land reforms, to mention only the most important issues. These new constitutions and plans could not work. The post-1920 leaderships -- except for the short-lived Bêla Kun regime in Hungary and the longer Stamboliski government in Bulgaria -- were identical with those of the pre-1914 years. They usually did not want change, and even when they did, they did not know how to bring it about. They failed to see that the new system, parliamentary democracy, was based on something which could not be legislated or defined: democracy as a way of life which grew slowly and "organically" in the old continuous nations and their direct successors, the United States, Canada, or Australia, and was understood in these places without needing explanation or definition. Democratic institutions do not work without democracy, especially not in multinational states needing drastic economic readjustment.

The resulting confusion not only brought dictatorships to the East European countries but also drastic changes in their nationalisms. By 1920 all states, whatever the ideology of the ruling party, were ostensibly nation-states or rather people's states irrespective of nationality, in which the people were sovereign and the government legitimate because it carried out the people's will. In short, the goal of the early nationalists, first in Western Europe and then increasingly in Eastern Europe, to capture the government for the nationals had been theoretically achieved. In practice, faced with the changes brought about by the war and following peace settlements and the new social and economic conditions, the still ruling old leadership did not represent the people's will. Now the game plan was reversed. It was not the nationalists who tried to conquer government, it was the government that used nationalism to win the backing of the population. Experts dealing with nationalism in the post-World War II period, concentrating mainly on the so-called Third World, have stressed this new direction as a basic characteristic of nationalism.[25] It is considered to be the nation-building tool used by governments to convince the population that they deserve its support. We must realize that this reversal of roles first occurred in East Europe between the wars. The argument used by the governments went roughly like this: We know what you (the population) want; we want the same things and promise honestly and in the best of faiths to deliver them to you. After all, we are your government. We realize that our promises have, so far, remained unfulfilled. This is not our fault, but that of the dirty revisionists who want to reverse the just settlements of the peace treaties, or (in the case of the losers) the fault of our dirty neighbors who not only took our land but are now oppressing our brothers. As long as they do not change their policies, we must concentrate on defense and cannot afford major changes because countries are the weakest in periods of transition. As members of "our nation" we must stick together, support the government, and work for a better future for our fellow nationals. You must suppress, or at least

III

postpone, your desires for higher living standards, better working conditions, etc., in the name of the national goal, and of the future. The good of the nation, which the government understands and represents perfectly, is the most important consideration.

If Ernest Gellner was right -- and I believe that he was -- when he wrote about "nationalism as a phenomenon...inherent ...[in] the conditions of our time," in the urbanized, industrialized, highly centralized society, then what happened in Eastern Europe in the interwar period is simply the artificial introduction of state-sponsored nationalism before the "conditions of our time" warranted and justified it.

Under these circumstances, interwar nationalism retained some of the features of the preceding period. It certainly continued to be chauvinistic, pugnacious, and exclusionary, but it gained some new features becoming strongly propagandistic, state-centered, self-righteous, and directed against specific enemies. Who these enemies were -- neighbors, minorities, Jews, Communists, etc., -- was something the governments believed themselves justified to determine. While echoes of the earlier period could still be heard in statements such as "the unspoiled peasant is the best representative of our national purity and character" or "the backbone of the nation through the centuries were the nobles," these were, at best, nostalgic mementoes of what seemed to some to have been the better days of the past. When populists or village explorers took such beliefs seriously, the governments moved against them labelling them unpatriotic agitators. There could be only one nation, one nationalism, one interpretation of the past, present, and future -- and it was the government that knew what it was. Therefore, one more characteristic must be added to describe the East European nationalism of this interwar period: it was not only state-centered but also officially determined.

While these features were valid for all East European versions of nationalism in the interwar period, we must recognize two different types of nationalism. The status quo nations' assertiveness was mixed with self-satisfaction and a certain amount of fear that the revisionists' challenge might find supporters.

These nations had to place the results of the peace conference beyond the debatable, and thus their nationalism became presumptively indefeasible in addition to the other characteristics already mentioned. On the other hand, the defeated nations faced the general interwar problems but in more difficult circumstances than their "enemies." They also had to combat the inferiority complex or at least the self-doubt brought on by defeat. The incessant domestic and international propaganda harping on the crimes of the Paris peace makers served this purpose, but also increased the regimes' totalitarian tendencies. When this was reflected in their nationalisms it added to them revanchism and protofascism.

As the attempts of the East European governments to bring their countries up to the "conditions of our time" failed, as their anxieties increased, the sharpness of their attacks on all those who could be used as scapegoats increased and their definition of nation and nationalism narrowed until it shaded over into totalitarianism. In the interwar period its right-wing varieties were preferred, but once this approach to running societies was accepted, the door to all types of totalitarianism, including those of the left, was opened wide.

Under Communist Rule

The years of the Second World War, the first impression made by the behavior of the Soviet armies, and the differing experiences after 1945 (by 1948 at the latest) resulting everywhere in the establishment of Communist governments were demoralizing. I will disregard the usual periodization of Eastern Europe's history since 1948 and concentrate on a different classification relevant only to the development of nationalism.26

In the living memory of all those alive at the end of the Second World War, nationalism was one of the strongest, if not the strongest, ideological and emotional force in society. The new regimes, embarked on transforming the people over whom they ruled into "Communist men," preached that nationalism was one of the great falsehoods and evils of modern times, and had to be eliminated if for no other reasons than because it made difficult, if not impossible, cooperation with the fraternal people and governments within the rapidly evolving Soviet zone of influence. Yet at the same time, special care was taken to allow minorities to live their own lives by giving them autonomous regions on the Soviet model. The seeming contradiction was not noted, but the establishment of these regions did as little to eliminate nation-based antagonisms as did the preachings of the ruling parties. While anti-nationalism and internationalism were the ideals, once again promulgated by governments, nationalism made its appearance in a new form in the dispute between Stalin and Tito.

National Communism

Without any doubt Tito's biggest sin, in the eyes of Stalin, was refusing to take dictation from Moscow. Tito differed from the master of the Kremlin in various ways. What was wrong with Tito's approach to the reorganization of Yugoslavia and, it was hoped, the entire Balkan Peninsula into a federal state? After all, the Soviet Union too was made up of several states. The names of the Soviet Republics showed that they had been established along ethnic lines. Why was it a mistake to organize

III

these states too along national lines? Tito could not even be accused of having invented the principle of "Communism in one state." This was, as he reminded Stalin, one of the strongest arguments Stalin used against Trotsky.27 Tito rejected the manner in which Communism was being built in the Soviet Union. His goal -- like Stalin's -- was Communism, and yet he believed that every state had to find its own means to achieve it in accordance with the economic and national realities faced by its party. Tito in fact declared that Communism had to be adjusted to local conditions thus inventing what was first called Titoism and, after he found imitators, National Communism.28 By doing this, he destroyed one of Marxism's original claims to fame, its scientific character. The laws of science do not change from country to country, but, according to Tito, the laws of Marxism do. What this argument meant was extremely significant for Communists all over the world and challenged the Soviet Union's supremacy in the Communist fraternity.

In Yugoslavia, then, National Communism made its appearance when elsewhere nationalism was still considered a sin by Communists. The name given to this new ism is correct. The noun is always more important than the adjective that modifies it. Tito's goal was to introduce Communism into his country, and he made the required tactical concessions without which he could not have operated -- in spite of his wartime successes -- in a multinational country. National Communism retained several characteristics of interwar nationalism. It continued to be propagandistic, self-righteous, state-centered, and officially determined, but also had a most important new feature: nationalism, was subordinated ideologically and ceased to be a goal in its own right.

Old Nationalisms Survive

After 1956 old-fashioned nationalism surfaced in both its late-nineteenth century and interwar forms. At first voiced rather timidly and experimentally, it became more and more vocal as time passed. Disputed lands occasionally became issues again. The Bessarabian question can be discussed in Romania today, and the Macedonian one is very much alive in Bulgaria. I do not include the Transylvanian issue and will discuss it under a different heading. The just-cited territorial questions are reminiscent of the interwar, government-directed version of East European nationalism. The Albanians in Kosovo might have a great variety of goals in mind, including a separate state within Yugoslavia or secession followed by union with Albania. Whatever they have in mind, their activities and aims are the same as were those of the state-builders in the second half of the last century.29 The Slovaks have had clear goals of a similar nature ever since Czechoslovakia was established. By the mid-1980s they appear to have achieved most of them thanks to the reforms introduced during the Prague Spring in 1968-69.30 Some of these old nationalisms survive everywhere in Eastern Europe, color all other versions to some extent at least, and make cooperation of the various "fraternal states" very difficult.

Communist Nationalism

A third version of nationalism in Eastern Europe emerged after the 1956 events in Hungary. It was first expressed in János Kádár's often quoted statement, "all those who are not against us are with us," and blossomed fully in his country. It re-emerged in the ideas of the Prague Spring in 1968 and in the Eurocommunist movement which adopted most of the Czech ideas. Its last clear expression was the Solidarity movement in Poland.31 This third version is communist nationalism, which is still a mixture of two theoretically exclusive ideals, but now the nationalist element is dominant. Once again government- and party-sponsored, this approach includes a state that does anything but wither away, a government that is legitimate because it has popular support, and goals that are purely national and anything but international. It differs from the nation- and state-building varieties of the preceding two periods by being less enemy- and more homefront-centered and by retaining at least the semblance of ideological unity with the other socialist or people's republics.

Communist nationalism can easily coexist with ethno-nationalism or "new ethnicity" which is not simply an East European phenomenon, but is very much visible in this part of the world, too.32 In a sense ethno-nationalism reverses the classic historical development from ethnicity to nation and finally to nationalism. It is a reaction to two developments in history. The first is what we have already discussed repeatedly, how nationalists tried to conquer and subsequently dominate government, which they considered legitimate only if it followed the nation's wishes. Also mentioned has been the fact that this horse (nation) and carriage (government) sequence has been reversed during the last sixty and especially the last forty years, that nationalism is now formulated by governments, and that the population is asked to accept as its goals those proclaimed by the men in power. Thus, in a sense, nationalism no longer legitimizes governments, instead serving as the justification for what the authorities demand from the people. The old horse does not enjoy being the cart, especially because in the modern state centralization has reached extreme proportions. The people feel that they have very little in common with the faraway, extremely impersonal, and powerful government. They might obey its orders, might even agree with the power-holders, but emotionally they do not see eye to eye.

The modern, industrial, urban environment is the second major cause for the emergence of ethno-nationalism. It has created a milieu in which the average person feels lost, depersonalized, and often insecure. Environment and state no longer produce feelings of security and belonging; "the

III

conditions of our time" have transformed nationalism into a governmental doctrine and left the nation behind, forcing its members to search for something else with which they can identify. This something else is "new ethnicity."

The new ethnicity differs sharply from the one that existed roughly two hundred years ago when the modern concepts of nation and nationalism developed. It is neither nation- nor state-building, and can recognize the existence of nation and state into which it wants to fit as perfectly acceptable and legitimate. The new ethnicity is not secessionist, demands only autonomy, and is often satisfied with social, cultural, and economic autonomy without also claiming political self-determination. The great debate in Yugoslavia today is between autonomists and centralizers, and the Slovaks appear to be satisfied with what they achieved some twenty years ago. Excepting some hotheads, the Slovaks, Croats, Slovenes, and so on are realists who know that in our days it is better for them, for reasons of economy and security, to live in a state which is larger and more powerful than would be one whose borders followed ethnic demarcation lines.

The new ethnicity is operative even among minorities whose numbers were diminished by the massive shifts of people after the Second World War. The Hungarians are the single largest group remaining outside their country in Eastern Europe. We never hear of those living in the Vojvodina because the Yugoslav authorities have reacted correctly to the Hungarians' new ethnicity there. In contrast, the problem of Hungarians in Transylvania is constantly discussed and not only in the countries involved.33 The Romanian state is strong enough to keep its minorities quiet, and Hungary is not interested in regaining Transylvania, but it is very interested in the treatment of Hungarians in that province. The Transylvanian Hungarians would probably be happy with the lot of the Vojvodina Hungarians, and this would please Budapest too. Unlike the Yugoslav authorities, the Romanian government apparently does not differentiate between the new ethnicity and old-fashioned revanchist chauvinism. Only this can explain Bucharest's minority policy, which is the continuation of the attitude of the interwar status quo nationalists, and the issue it made of the publication in Budapest of a three-volume History of Transylvania.34 One can hardly find a better example of the survival until today of the presumptively indefeasible, **pugnacious nationalism** of the interwar period than the full-page advertisement attacking this work which the Romanian government placed in <u>The Times</u> of London.35

Modern states and governments can co-exist with the new ethnicity if they understand its nature. Is ethno-nationalism a true form of nationalism? I think so, but admit that this can be debated. If we disregard it, we are still left with several types of nationalism in Eastern Europe today. They are not two variants of the same nationalism that we discussed for the interwar period; they appear to be distinctly different kinds of nationalism. I believe that they are, after all, only different manifestations of a new nationalism which is typical of Eastern Europe <u>only</u>.

East Europeans, irrespective of the kind of nationalism that expresses their feelings, live in a world in which the official truth, some form of Marxism, is accepted by all, at least in theory, and in which numerous supernational institutions, including the Warsaw Pact and CMEA, appear to be permanent features. To these basic indicators of an international order must be added coordinated foreign policies, compulsory teaching of the Russian language in all schools, and repeated declarations of solidarity with states and nations which the average person does not consider even friendly. It is not difficult to see why people believe that an attempt has been made consistently since 1945 by a foreign power, the Soviet Union, to force all of them into a uniform, denationalized mold. This power has proved at least three times -- Hungary 1956, Czechoslovakia 1968, and Poland 1981 -- that it has the means to enforce its dictates, directly or indirectly, if local feelings and ambitions go beyond what it considers acceptable. It is therefore not surprising that people and nations fear being forced into a supernational framework that is not clearly defined, never clearly or comprehensively explained, but is big, frightening, strange, impersonal, and -- most important -- nationally deracinating. It is something they wish to resist because they prefer the clearly defined, comprehensive, clearly expressed, manageable, familiar, and, therefore, comfortable national identity. It is this identity that the remnants of pre-1945 nationalists, national communists, and communist nationalists defend against the real or imaginary dangers they face. This defensive nationalism is the true, specifically East European nationalism of the last forty years into which all other expressions of nationalism fit. It is not necessarily anti-Russian, anti-Soviet or anti-Marxist/Bolshevik in a clearly expressed ideological sense, but it is defensively anti-everything, clear or unclear, that is equated with the assumed although unexpressed aims of the Soviet government. Present-day East European nationalism is <u>defensive nationalism</u>.

III

ENDNOTES

1. Boyd C. Shafer, <u>Nationalism: Myth and Reality</u> (New York: Harcourt, Brace and World, 1955), p. 5.

2. Ernest Gellner, <u>Nations and Nationalism</u> (Ithaca and London: Cornell University Press, 1983), p. 125.

3. Elie Kedouri, <u>Nationalism</u> (London: Hutchinson University Library, 1960), p. 9.

4. Carlton J. H. Hayes, <u>Essays on Nationalism</u> (New York: The Macmillan Co., 1926), p. 5.

5. Hans Kohn, <u>The Idea of Nationalism</u> (New York: The Macmillan Co., 1948), p.16.

6. Louis L. Snyder, <u>The Meaning of Nationalism</u> (Westport, CT: Greenwood Press, 1954), pp. 196-97.

7. A very important study dealing with this issue is John A. Armstrong, <u>Nations Before Nationalism</u> (Chapel Hill, NC: University of North Carolina Press, 1982).

8. Peter F. Sugar, "External and Domestic Roots of Eastern European Nationalism," in Peter F. Sugar and Ivo J. Lederer (eds.), <u>Nationalism in Eastern Europe</u> (Seattle and London: University of Washington Press, 1969), pp. 3-5.

9. Anthony D. Smith, <u>Nationalism in the Twentieth Century</u> (New York: New York University Press, 1979).

10. Gellner, <u>Nations and Nationalism</u>, p. 125.

11. Peter F. Sugar, "Ethnicity in Eastern Europe," in Peter F. Sugar (ed.), <u>Ethnic Diversity and Conflict in Eastern Europe</u> (Santa Barbara and Oxford: ABC-Clio, 1980), pp. 419 ff.

12. Hugh Seton-Watson, <u>Nations and States</u> (Boulder, CO.: Westview Press, 1977), pp. 21-22.

13. V. I. Lenin, "Critical Remarks on the National Question," first published in <u>Prosveshcheniye</u>, Nos. 10-13 (1913) in <u>Collected Works</u> (Moscow: Progress Publishers, Fifth Printing, 180), Vol. 20, p. 25.

14. J. V. Stalin, "Marxism and the National Question," first published as "The National Question and Social-Democracy," in <u>Prosveshcheniye</u>, Nos. 3-5, (1913) in <u>Collected Works</u> (Moscow: Foreign Languages Publishing House, 1953), Vol. 2, p. 317. The

arguments developed in this article were presented in shortened but often identical wording in "The Immediate Task of the Party in the National Question," presented to the 10th Congress of the Russian Communist Party on Feb. 5, 1921. Ibid., Vol. 5, pp. 16-30.

15. Ernest Gellner, "Ethnicity between Culture, Class and Power," in Peter F. Sugar (ed.), Ethnic Diversity. pp. 269-70.

16. Peter F. Sugar, "External and Domestic Roots," pp. 47-54.

17. A summary of all beliefs in early "freedom fighters" and of the materials on which these were based was presented for Bulgaria in a very scholarly fashion by Bistra Cvetkova, Hajdutstvoto v Bulgarskite Semi prez 15/18 Vek (Sofia: Nauka i Izkystvo, 1971). Most East European literatures have similar works.

18. Miklós Toldi is today an example of the Hungarian national hero who reaches high honors coming from a lowly social background. He never existed, but was created by the epic poem Toldi written by János Arany in 1846. Appearing on the scene much later, but playing a similar role by today in the popular mind would be figures like the "good soldier Schweik" or -- in a negative sense -- Pan Tadeusz.

19. Nineteenth-century Romanian historiography, beginning with the publications of the first parts of Nicolae Balcescu's Istoria Rominilor sub Michaiu Voda Viteazul in Revist romina pentru stiinta, litere si arte in 1861-63 depicted Michael the Brave (1593-1601) as a modern Romanian nationalist consciously trying to unify the three Romanian Principalities. Once again, only one of several possible examples.

20. The best known and often quoted examples of historians who wrote good history, but occasionally inserted in their works passages serving nationalist aims, were the Czech Fratisek Palacky, whose famous ten-volume Geschichte der Böhmen first appeared in Prague between 1836 and 1867 and the Hungarian Kalman Thaly whose work was centered on the late 17th and early 19th centuries. Similar, but lesser known figures were active all over Eastern Europe.

21. The relevant literature is too rich to be listed and the citing of a few titles only would not be judicious. Let us note that François Fejtö, who edited a study for the 100th anniversary of the revolutionary year, chose as the English title of his work (originally published in French), The Opening of an Era: 1848 (New York: H. Fertig, 1966) indicating that he saw in the events of this year not the culmination of liberal agitation, but the beginning of a new Europe. It is also significant that even a small people, the Slovaks, not too active in 1848 produced a

III

collection of documents dealing with the event of that year, under the editorship of Daniel Rapant, between 1950 and 1961 under various titles (Dejiny Slovenskeho postavnia R. 1838-49 and Slovenska Povstanie Reku 1848-49) filling eight thick volumes.

22. In spite of its age, the best introduction to Panslavism is still Hans Kohn, Pan-Slavism; Its History and Ideology (Notre Dame, IN: Notre Dame University Press, 1953).

23. For a good, short explanation of the Nacertanije see Michael Boro Petrovich, A History of Modern Serbia, II (New York and London: Harcourt, Brace, Jovanovich, 1976), pp. 231-33. For Kossuth's ideas turn to Zsigmond Pál Pach et al. (eds.), Magyarország Története, X (Budapest: Akadémiai Kiadó, 1976-), Vol. VI, pp. 709-13. The pre-World War I plans of Dmowski can be found in his Myśli nowoczesnego Polaka (Lvov: H. Altenberg, 1907).

24. It is worth remembering that Eastern Europe contained the states that had lost the most and gained the most in World War I. Hungary (not counting the Croatian lands) lost 67 percent of her territory and 58 percent of her population. Romania's territory increased by 112 percent and her population by 113 percent.

25. Besides the works of Smith and Gellner already cited numerous works deal with this transformation, including: American Universities Field Staff (K. H. Silver, ed.), Expectant People, Nationalism and Development (New York: Random House, 1963); Glen St. J. Barclay, 20th Century Nationalism (London: Weidenfeld and Nicolson, 1971); Karl W. Deutsch and William J. Foltz (eds.), Nationbuilding (New York: Atherton Press, 1966); Karl W. Deutsch, Nationalism and Social Communications (Cambridge, MA: M.I.T. Press, 1966); Anthony D. Smith, Theories of Nationalism (London: Duckworth, 1983).

26. The customary division of Eastern Europe's history since the establishment of Communist rule is the following: The Stalinist Period, 1945/8-53; De-Stalinization, 1953-56; The Diversification of Communism, 1956-68; attempts at individual national existence within the limits of the Brezhnev Doctrine, 1968-80; the last seven years have not yet acquired a generally accepted label.

27. For the Stalin-Tito controversy, see: The Soviet-Yugoslav Dispute: Text of the Published Correspondence (London: Royal Institute of International Affairs, 1948).

28. The literature covering the events in Eastern Europe is immense. This and subsequent footnotes cannot even list all of the most important titles and those listed should be considered simply as samples of what is available. On Titoism see: Wayne S. Vucinich (ed.), At the Brink of War and Peace: The Tito-Stalin Split in Historical Perspective (New York: Columbia

University Press, 1982); Josef Kalvoda, Titoism and the Masters of Imposture (New York: Vantage Press, 1958); Charles P. McVickers, Titoism: Pattern for International Communism (New York: St. Martin's Press, 1957). Władysław Gomułka was, for a time, considered the second Tito, but, at least to some extent, he turned out to be an old-fashioned Communist. For details see either Frank Gibney, The Frozen Revolution (New York: Farrar, Straus and Cudahy, 1959), or Nicholas William, baron Bethell, Gomulka, His Poland and His Communism (Harlow: Longmans, c. 1969). Finally, for national communism good introductions are, among others, Howard Machin (ed.), National Communism in Western Europe (London-New York: Methuen, 1983), and Peter Zwich, National Communism (Boulder, CO: Westview Press, 1983).

29. Sinan Hasani, Kosovo, istine i zablude (Zagreb: Center za informacije i publicitet, 1986) is somewhat biased, but contains much valuable material. The best study in a western language is Jens Reuter, Die Albaner in Kosovo (Munich: Oldenburg, 1982). A good short English summary can be found in Pedro Ramet, Nationalism and Federalism in Yugoslavia, 1963-83 (Bloomington, IN: Indiana University Press, 1984), pp. 156-71. The most recent work on Kosovo is Milos Misovic, Koje trazio republike Kosov 1945-85 (Belgrade: Narodna Knjiga, 1987).

30. See the chapter "Federalism and the Slovak Problem," Gordon H. Skilling, Czechoslovakia's Interrupted Revolution (Princeton: Princeton University Press, 1976), pp. 451-89.

31. On the developments in Hungary in the years after 1956, the best book is T. Iván Berend, Gazdasági útkeresés, 1956-1965 (Budapest: Magvető, 1983). On the Prague Spring see the already cited work by Gordon H. Skilling. On Eurocommunism the work of Santiago Carillo, Eurocommunism and the State (Nan Green and A. M. Elliott, trans.), (Westport, CT: Lawrence Hill and Co., 1971) is basic. Other works recommended include: Rudolf Tokes (ed.), Eurocommunism and Detente (New York: New York University Press, 1978) and François Fonvieille-Alquier, L'Eurocommunisme (Paris: Fayard, 1977). The literature on Solidarity by now is massive. Good introductions to the subject include: William F. Robinson (ed.), August 1980: The Strikes in Poland (Munich: Radio Free Europe Research, 1980); Lawrence Weschler, Solidarity (New York: Simon and Schuster, 1982); Neal Ascherson, The Polish August (Harmondsworth: Penguin Books, 1981).

32. To my knowledge it was Walker Conner who first used the term ethno-nationalism in "The Politics of Ethnonationalism," Journal of International Affairs (January, 1973), 27, pp. 1-21. See also his "The Ethnopolitical Change and Governmental Response," in Peter F. Sugar, Ethnic Diversity pp. 147-84; Peter F. Sugar, "From Ethnicity to Nationalism and Back Again," in Michael Palumbo and William P. Shanahan (eds.), Nationalism: Essays in Honor of Louis L. Snyder (Westport, CT - London: Greenwood,

III

1981), pp. 67-84. Anthony D. Smith wrote about this subject too in *The Ethnic Revival* (Cambridge-New York: Cambridge University Press, 1981) as did several sociologists including Hugh Donald Forves, *Nationalism Ethnocentrism and Personality* (Chicago: Chicago University Press, 1985), and John F. Stack, Jr. (3ed.), *The Primordial Challenge; Ethnicity in the Contemporary World* (Westport, CT: Greenwood, 1986).

33. A somewhat biased presentation of the problem of Transylvania can be found in Anne Fay Sanbord and Geza Wass de Czege (eds.), *Transylvania and the Hungarian-Romanian Problem* (Astor, FL: Danubian Press, 1979).

34. Bela Kopeczi et al. (eds.), *Erdely Tortenete*, III (Budapest: Akademiai Kiado, 1986).

35. "A Conscious Forgery of History under the Aegis of the Hungarian Academy of Sciences," *The Times* (London), April 7, 1987, p. 7.

IV

Government and Minorities in Austria-Hungary – Different Policies with the same Result*

I.

The number of studies dealing with nationalism is practically endless. But, nobody has yet succeeded in producing a definition of nationalism that has become universally accepted. Although I have been bold enough to advance a typology of Central and Eastern European nationalisms,[1] I am not ready to suggest an answer to the crucial question: what is nationalism? Fortunately this was not the task assigned to me by the editors of these volumes. Other scholars were asked to present, in other chapters, the histories and developments of the nationalistic movements of the various people living in the numerous lands ruled by the Habsburgs between 1848 and 1918. My task is to present an overview, a comprehensive framework, for the stories my colleagues will relate.

In spite of the elusiveness of the essence of nationalism, I must say a few words about it to show in which sense I am using this concept. My understanding is based mainly on the analysis of Hans Kohn which shaped my ideas about nationalism more than the works of other authors.[2] Nationalism is an expression of old feelings such as love of kin, home, the well known and familiar, the traditional values of one's immediate surroundings and social milieu. It is, in this sense, not dissimilar from patriotism, even localism. Yet, nationalism is a modern, updated, much stronger expression of these attachments. "Nationalism is inconceivable without the ideas of popular sovereignty preceding – without a complete revision of the position of ruler and ruled, of classes and castes."[3] It is an updating of patriotism in accordance with the demands for change which the principle of popular sovereignty imposed on society. It is, therefore, a modern ideology dating roughly from the period of the French Revolution.

The principle of popular sovereignty implies not only a great reliance on the "people", but also an attempt to organize them. "The growth of nationalism is the process of integration of the masses of the people into a common political form. Nationalism therefore presupposes the existence, in fact the ideal, of a centralized form of government over a large and distinct territory."[4]

IV

2 [7-8]　　　Government and Minorities in Austria-Hungary

Nationalism, according to the opinion of most experts presented in a sketchy form following Hans Kohn, is a fairly recent phenomenon in history although with roots stretching back far into the past. It appears as a force in the centralized, modern state in which popular sovereignty is accepted as the basis of all political power. Having established the period of the appearance of nationalism in history and described the circumstances in which it can develop, the question of what it really is still remains unanswered. The one undisputed feature of all definitions of nationalism is the recognition that it is the expression of the will and aspirations of a nation. It is the common consciousness of a group of people identified as a nation, "a group of individuals that feels itself one, is ready within limits to sacrifice the individual for the group advantage, that prospers as a whole, that has groups of emotions experienced as a whole, each of whom rejoices with the advancement and suffers with the losses of the group...Nationality is a mental state or community in behavior."[5] I accept this definition of nationality and nation, and, consequently, regard nationalism as the expression of a nationality-based group psychosis. Nationalism is, therefore, not static but ever changing in accordance with the mood and the circumstances that produce it that a given nation wishes to bring into the open at any given moment in history. "Nationalism is a state of mind. The process of history can be analyzed as a succession of changes in communal psychology..."[6]

This chapter attempts to analyze a very specific historical process, the changes of the "national moods" of the various people in the Habsburg state. There were, of course, as many moods and as many separate developmental processes as there were nations living under the scepter of the Habsburg rulers. These were influenced by numerous local factors which applied only to a single given ethnic group. All these will be discussed in other chapters dealing with the various nationalities individually. What I try to do is to disregard these differences and to find those influences that applied to all of them giving these various national developments a common direction whose final expression induced many scholars to consider nationalism as one of the most important if not the crucial cause for the dissolution of Austria-Hungary.[7]

With the opinion of all these experts I agree only partially. Among the various peoples of the dual monarchy nationalism certainly developed in a direction that was hostile to the unchanged existence of the state and produced, by the last decade of its existence if not somewhat earlier, enough mutual hostility and plans based on these conflicts to endanger Austria-Hungary. But I do not blame "nationalism" for this development, nor do I consider the historical process that produced it as inevitable. I reject, without imputing that the cited experts hold this view, the explanation that a multinational state could not have survived in the "age of nationalism". What happened cannot be changed, and speculation about what might have happened is meaningless. What I propose to do is to present my explanation of why the collective nationalisms of all the nations living in Austria-Hungary became mutually exclusive and a mortal illness for the state.

The one thing all the people in the Habsburg state had in common was the government, and after 1867 governments, of his Imperial and Royal Majesty whose person and historical-legal claims to rule over them was the tie that bound them together. These governments were the overriding reality binding local variants of issues together into common problems whose resolution affected everybody living in Austria and later Austria-Hungary. I see in the interaction of the various people with their only truly "common" and permanent institution, the government (or governments)—closely tied to the crucial figure of the ruler—the overriding cause that produced "the succession of changes in communal psychology", the development of a certain type of nationalism which affected all of them as well as the government (or governments) and, consequently, the stability of the Austro-Hungarian state structure.[8]

This chapter will be devoted to the study of the just mentioned interaction and will attempt to show how it produced not simply Czech, or Croatian, or Romanian nationalism of a certain variety, but a certain kind of overriding macro-nationalism into which all the national feelings of the various people fitted. Different as these feelings were, when they produced macro-nationalism they turned out to be, with very few exceptions, anti-Austria-Hungary in their collectively expressed aspirations.

Before I turn to this task, I would like to make a few additional remarks which, just as those I presented about nationalism, will be sketchy but will attempt to introduce some considerations about Austria-Hungary and its people that will be used in the main body of this chapter.

II.

The rulers and statesmen of the Habsburg realm cannot be accused of misreading the portents of change which they saw all around them. Certainly they tried, beginning with the reign of Maria Theresa, to centralize, and to integrate "the masses of the people into a common political form". Under rulers like Joseph II and Francis I, centralization was pursued with great vigor while, at the same time, serious attempts were made to diminish the differences between the institutions of the various lands and people. They did this at a later time in history than many of their fellow monarchs had done further to the west. In a sense they lacked the necessary time to complete successfully the task of centralization, which took centuries to perform in France and England, because soon they had to face the problem posed by the first demands of the newly emerging ideal of popular sovereignty. While recognizing it, the rulers and statesmen in Vienna did not embrace it as they did centralization, but tried to resist it. To what extent they should be blamed for this action, and the extent to which they had no other alternative given the legal restrictions imposed on them by feudal contracts and by the structure of the society in the various lands over which they ruled, is not important for our purposes, but the fact that this new trend was resisted is. The centralization and politization processes remained incomplete because they were not paralleled by the social and bureaucratic, by the legislative and organizational transformations that would have completed the full "modernization" of the state. Yet Austria never lacked men who realized that the transforming process was incomplete. From the turn of the nineteenth century practically to the last moment of the existence of Austria-Hungary several plans were submitted by people in and out of government which tried to complete the process of transformation hoping, by doing what they proposed, to create a supranational nationalism designed to replace the outdated and ineffective concept of *Kaisertreue* as the common focus for the loyalty of all people.[9]

These attempts at reform never produced determined far reaching action. As a result Austria, and after 1867 Austria-Hungary, remained a curious half-way house presenting many modern ornaments affixed to a basically feudal structure. This was particularly true of the governmental structure which was of paramount importance for the development this chapter attempts to trace. The analysis of governmental action in Austria-Hungary presents, consequently, more difficulties than a similar task would in the case of any other modern state.

After 1867 there was the Common Ministry in Vienna with a vague constitutional position and little ability to govern, and an Austrian and Hungarian government and a sub-government in Croatia. Transylvania had lost its administrative independence, but there were still seventeen provincial governments in the Austrian half of the state (die im Reichsrate vertretenen Königreiche und Länder) and fifty-two county governments in the Hungarian half. To these must be added to the Crown Council which decided such important issues as war and peace, and we wind up with seventy-four "governments" with varying rights and competences, but each capable on its own of making decisions. One only has to remember the turbulent histories of the Bohemian Diet or the Croatian Sabor, or the manner in which the Hungarian county governments prevented the execution of the various laws, especially those of 1868 on nationalities and education passed by the Hungarian parliament, to realize how influential these small ruling units were in shaping popular opinion and consequently the development of nationalism.

The existence of all these authorities points to the major problem which the "central authorities", the ruler, and the governments in Budapest and Vienna faced. We can begin looking at these "central authorities" by asking how centralized they were in the late nineteenth century. Only Bismarck's Germany had a central, imperial government that had to operate through the local governments of the constituent states, but was strong enough, both under the Iron Chancellor and later under William II, to make its views and power prevail. Austria-Hungary operated with three often antagonistic central governments, hardly an ideal solution for a "modern, centralized state". The seventeen Austrian provincial governments and the Croatian Sabor had very distinctive and often far-reaching spheres of jurisdiction, "historic rights", which survived from the Middle Ages as a result of incomplete centralization. Less far reaching legally, but no less traditional and effective were the prerogatives of the Hungarian counties that mirrored the rights of medieval local estates.

This harking back to rights of the past in Hungary had its parallel in Austria too. The February Patent of 1861 established curiae—landlords, chambers of commerce, townspeople and peasants—the "modern estates", as units with a right to send representatives to the various local assemblies which in turn selected the representatives of the various lands in Vienna. For the last two groups the right to vote was tied to the payment of a rather high tax which meant that the landowners, the old nobility, continued to dominate the political scene. When the local assemblies lost, in 1873, the right to select representatives for the Lower House of Parliament, electors to this legislative body were determined by the same old curiae principle which remained in force until general manhood suffrage was introduced at the end of 1906.[10] In a sense, in both halves of the dual monarchy, the ancien regime was maintained at least in politics, while the governments in Budapest and Vienna tried to assert central authority along the same lines which prevailed in the great western states.

This was in itself confusing, but the various people of the state, not only the minorities, had little understanding and use for the medieval features of the state in which they lived. These remnants of the past had nothing to do with their social, economic, or national aspirations, and set a general tone that directed the development of the rising middle class or such movements as liberalism into very peculiar channels, making them in most cases unsuitable for roles which they played in the west. Government was confusing, often contradictory, at best inefficient and at worst exasperating. Labels of political parties were often meaningless. Social mobility tended toward the outdated, supra-national, aristocratic values reserved to the few only.

In a society in which everything was organized along strictly hierarchical lines that appeared immutable, where social classes were almost totally insulated from one another and had within them numerous sub-divisions, it was practically impossible to organize social action. National groups were also ranked hierarchically according to the privileges which they enjoyed, making the cooperation of social groups on the same level even more difficult because of national differences. Under these circumstances it was very hard to challenge the governmental structure.[11] Mutual distrust, going back at least to the events of 1848, made it equally exasperating for any serious reform-bent movement to gain followers in an effectively wide enough geographic region. One has only to think of the failure of the ably led socialist movement to realize that no idea was capable of going beyond the language barrier in the search for followers.

The reverse is also true. If people distrusted each other almost as much they did "government" which was much too complex and bewildering to be understood, those in power had equally little faith in those whose affairs they were running. It is this mutual distrust that supplies the answer to the often raised question why no state-directed nationalism developed in the Habsburg lands. The state that could have made claims on its citizens' loyalty, a strong, single, centralized state that had everybody's welfare in mind, was never established. For this the statesmen in Vienna and later also in Budapest can only partially be blamed. The great mutual distrust of the various classes, ethnic groups, and governments made this impossible, and simply Habsburgstreue was no substitute for nationalism in the 1848-1918 period. With practically all political and social avenues of self-expression closed to them, the various people in the monarchy had to fall back on themselves to assert their hopes and aims. While this tendency was certainly centrifugal producing multiplicities of nationalism, it was by no means by definition the cause of the dissolution of Austria-Hungary.

During the decade of neoabsolutism, the only period after 1848 when a serious attempt was made to create a unitary state out of the lands ruled by Francis-Joseph, most of a nationalities showed a tendency to cooperate. Indecision in Vienna, fiscal difficulties, and a faulty foreign policy brought this period to an unsuccessful end. Another half-century elapsed before the majority of Southern Slavs finally accepted the fundamentally secessionist Yugoslav idea in their Fiume and Zadar resolutions in 1905, and as late as 1914 the Czechs and Poles were not yet certain where their future was rosier, within or outside Austria-Hungary, although they finally opted for the second alternative. The nationalism of the various people in Austria-Hungary was first of all local-historical and would have been satisfied with home rule in a federatively organized state. The ruling elements did not trust them, rejected this alternative, and saw in every manifestation of national self-assertion a tendency towards treason, while the various nations saw in practically every law and regulation a new attempt to suppress them. Both sides reacted first with growing suspicion and then with increasing hostility to the other's every move. Moves and countermoves escalated and transformed home-rule oriented nationalism into a force that finally destroyed even the vague unity of lands which the Habsburgs had fitted together during centuries. In the following pages an attempt will be made to trace these moves and countermoves and to show how each of these represented a step along the road leading towards more and more exclusive nationalism and finally to the situation in which Austria-Hungary had to cease to exist.[12]

Those who made these moves in the process of developing their various nationalisms, the people of the dual monarchy, are usually grouped together according to various criteria. I reject one of these, the distinction between "historic" and "non-historic" nations. It is based solely on political considerations and is, therefore, much too narrow. More importantly, after 1848, in the period under discussion, there was not a single nation in all the Habsburg lands that did not claim to be the heir to an ancient and glorious state (even if this states were as far in the past as the Great Moravian Empire), that did not claim historical continuity for itself in the lands it inhabited, and that did not make a serious effort to prove that the cultural-literary reform movements of the eighteenth and nineteenth centuries rested on the past accomplishments of its sons.

8 [13-14]   Government and Minorities in Austria-Hungary

It would be mistaken to claim that all nations in Austria-Hungary were equal in their economic, cultural, and political developments or that they even claimed that this was the case. Another commonly used distinction is that of majority and minority, also called the ruling and ruled, nations. These nations are divided also into those groups who had co-nations across the border and those who lived entirely within the borders of the Habsburg state. While these are much more satisfactory categories, they are by no means fully adequate for our analysis.

In the strict sense of the word the Germans in the Austrian and the Magyars in the Hungarian half of the dual monarchy were minorities, and in the entire monarchy their percentage in the total population was even lower.[13] Nevertheless if we disregard the fact that in the Transleithan lands the Germans were not the ruling nationality, we can provisionally accept for them and the Magyars the label of "ruling nations". However, this ruling supposed majority often displayed behavioral characteristics usually associated with ruled or minority nations.

In any organized society a minority is a group, irrespective of its numerical size, that for a great variety of objective or subjective reasons is either feared and therefore subjected to discriminatory treatment by the power-wielding segment of society, or feels itself consciously deprived, as a group, of its rightful share in the material wealth, opportunity, political rights, cultural expression or any combination of these. Only the politically dominant group is able to pass legislation which, although it may purport to protect the rights of minorities, in fact legalizes majority fears and limits the scope of minority action. This legislation follows rather than creates the awareness of existing differences in either or both, the majority and the minority.[14]

Given this definition of minority status and attitudes, the behavior of the Bohemian Germans becomes quite understandable. They were steadily losing their role as the power-wielding segment of society, and, as potentially ex-power wielders, were more prone to developing minority fears and attitudes than to adopt a belief in equality and coexistence. Magyarization policies in Hungary can also be viewed as the result of a fear on the part of the Magyars that was not too different from that of the Germans in Bohemia. The case of the Bohemian Germans is a good indication why even the expression of "ruling nation" is not fully satisfactory. In 1848 Germans clearly ruled Bohemia, but by 1918 they had lost their power monopoly. They did not lose during these sixty years their economic, political, social and cultural privileges. It appears more accurate for this reason to speak of nations with and without privileges instead of ruling and ruled nations.[15]

Germans and Magyars are the only nations that can really be considered privileged in Austria-Hungary. The fate of the others was not uniformly the same. For this reason the concept of semi-privileged nations has to be introduced. Among these were the Poles who dominated Galicia in every respect and wielded much power even in Vienna. After 1861 the dominant position of the Poles in Galicia rested on a quasi-constitutional basis. The dominant position of the Croats in Croatia-Slavonia, another of the people who must be considered semi-privileged, had a centuries-old constitutional basis recognized anew by the *Nagodba* in 1868. Certainly by about 1910 the Czechs secured for themselves a position, both in their lands and in Vienna, that would place them in this category too. There can be little doubt that in Dalmatia the Italians enjoyed certain privileges denied to the Slav population of the province.

The nations without privilege were the Serbs, the Croats living outside Croatia-Slavonia, the Italians anywhere except in Dalmatia, the Ukrainians, Romanians, Slovaks, and Slovenes. Their varying attitudes also indicate how difficult it is to speak of any given nation's nationalism or national goals. The importance of these groupings can be suggested by listing them according to these categories.[16]

Nation	Number	Percentage of total population
A Privileged Nations		
Germans	11.987.000	24,27
Magyars	9.945.000	20,34
Total	21.932.000	44,61
B Semi-privileged Nations		
Czechs	6.436.000	13,02
Poles	4.968.000	10,05
Croats (in Croatia-Slavonia)	1.833.000	3,70
Italians (in the Coastal Provinces)	382.000	0,75
Total	13.619.000	27,52

Government and Minorities in Austria-Hungary

C Nations without privileges		
Ukrainians	3.992.000	8,07
Romanians	3.180.000	6,42
Slovaks	1.968.000	3,97
Other Croats and all Serbs	1.874.000	3,78
Slovenes	1.253.000	2,57
Italians (in Tyrol)	386.000	0,80
Total	12.653.000	25,61

These distinctions between the various people of Austria-Hungary are certainly not perfect, but they are better breakdowns than those usually employed by scholars. The other major division which can be found in almost all studies of the people of Austria-Hungary is—as previously indicated—that between nations with co-nationals outside the state and those living entirely within the borders of the Habsburg lands. The importance of this distinction is the absence or presence of alternative national homes that these people might or might not consider as preferable to Austria-Hungary when formulating their plans and goals. Looking at this differentiation we get completely different divisions than those we found when we grouped the various nationalities according to privileges. Using the same 1910 figures employed previously and the political situation in Central and Eastern Europe at the same time we find the following:

Nation	Number	Percentage of total population
A Nations with no co-nationals outside Austria-Hungary:		
Magyars	9.945.000	20,34
Czechs	6.436.000	13,02
Slovaks	1.968.000	3,97
Slovenes	1.253.000	2,57
Total	19.602.000	39,90

Government and Minorities in Austria-Hungary

B	Nations with co-nationals but no state outside Austria-Hungary:		
	Poles	4.968.000	10,05
	Ukrainians	3.992.000	8,07
	Total	8.960.000	18,12
C	Nations with co-nationals and states outside Austria-Hungary:		
	Germans	11.987.000	24,27
	Serbs and Croats	3.707.000	7,48
	Romanians	3.180.000	6,42
	Italians	768.000	1,55
	Total	19.642.000	39,72

For the study of the nationalism of the people under the scepter of the Habsburgs it is not only significant that the correlation between the first and second breakdown of the various nations is minimal, but it is also important to note that over sixty percent of the Emperor-King's subjects had co-nationals outside the territory of the monarchy. These people, who could theoretically shift their allegiance, included the Germans, the largest single ethnic group and one of the two privileged nations. The behavior of the various *Grossdeutsch* parties which, in the twentieth century, paralyzed for all practical purposes the workings of the Reichstag makes the significance of this fact more than clear. If we consider the propensity of numerous Magyars to see in the Ausgleich a less than satisfactory solution, it becomes clear that one of the major contradictions in Austria-Hungary was the fact that the nationalism of the privileged nations was not entirely centered around the state they dominated. Yet, these nations expected all others to be loyal to the dual monarchy. The Germans and Magyars demanded a focus for the nationalism of their fellow citizens which they themselves accepted only with reservations. The resulting contradictions in policy in Vienna and Budapest could only confuse and alienate the other people. Their nationalism, therefore, deviated more and more from the line demanded from them by the privileged nations. As a result even nations like the Czechs and Slovenes, who had no co-nations outside Austria-Hungary began, in the years preceding World War I, to push for solutions that entailed the dissolution of the monarchy. If the Czechs' influence on the Slovaks during these late years of the dual monarchy is also considered, no nation is left—irrespective of where their co-nationals lived—that did not at least envision a solution to its problems that was basically hostile to the continued existence of Austria-Hungary.

Having presented, although in a very rudimentary form only, a few basic ideas concerning nationalism, government in Austria-Hungary, and the manner in which I approach the numerous people living in this state, I can begin to survey the historical process—the interaction of governments and people—that produced not only the nationalisms of the various nationalities but also the macro-nationalism which proved to be fatal to the Habsburg state.

III.

In November 1848 Prince Felix Schwarzenberg became the head of Austria's government. On the 27th of this month he presented himself and his program to the diet which sat at Kroméřiž (Kremsier) and worked for a reconstruction of the Habsburg state along federative lines. His opening declaration made it quite clear that he disagreed with those present and favored a unitary, highly centralized state. It took slightly more than three weeks before he also indicated (on December 12) that the state which he favored would be absolutist and would in its totality (not just the German and Czech lands as previously) be part of a reorganized German Confederation which it would have to dominate. Basically this remained the thesis of Vienna until 1866, and only the means to achieve the goals of Schwarzenberg were open to discussion and experimentation. These statements produced, quite obviously, the dissolution of the Kroméřiž assembly once it reached a federalist solution (March 7, 1849), and served as the foundations for the period of neoabsolutism.

This period was inaugurated with the Sylvester Patent of December 31, 1851. It has been correctly described as the system in which those who were loyal to the House of Habsburg in 1848 received as their reward the same treatment which those who fought it got as a punishment. While some of the measures taken by the authorities, like the school reform introduced by the minister of education, Count Leo Thun-Hohenstein, were progressive, they were all promulgated by fiat with total disregard of the rights of the "historical units", whose existence offered a basis for the agreement which at least the realm's liberals reached at Kroméřiž. The unity of these liberals broke up very soon. Most Germans accepted Schwarzenberg's Great Germany idea, a stand that made their cooperation with the various Slavs of Cisleithania impossible. On the other side of the river the separation of Transylvania, Croatia and the Vojvodina from Hungary proper quickly ended such attempts at liberal cooperation as existed even as late as May 1849 among Serbs, Romanians and Magyars. The fact that these new units received no rights, but were simply administrative entities ruled from Vienna made little difference. The similarity of their and the Magyars' situation did not produce cooperation because the Magyars considered the existence of these additional administrative units simply as further signs of hostility towards them not by Vienna, but by the people who inhabited them.

The situation was not too dissimilar in Galicia. The Polish-Ukrainian unity which existed in 1848 at the Slav Congress of Prague had disappeared by the time the Diet of Kroměříž assembled. The ruling Polish aristocracy, which took a strongly anti-liberal and anti-Ukrainian stand in 1846 and 1848, needed support which it could only get from Vienna. With the appointment of the older Count Agenor Gołuchowski as governor of the province began the mutual interdependence between the central government and the Polish nobility that lasted to the end of the existence of the Habsburg monarch.[17] Vienna gained dependable allies, and Galicia acquired political leadership that was anti-liberal, anti-Ukrainian, and only to some extent nationalistic.

A problem, which created more trouble after 1867 than any other, also appeared in the neoabsolutist period. This was the language problem. Just as in the days of Joseph II, and for the same reason, the use of German was pushed as the official language in army, schools, courts, publications of decrees and laws. After 1854 German became the "official" language of the empire. A centralized state, which, hopefully, was to be inhabited by one "Austrian nation", had to have one language, according to the strong centralist. While this stress on German hurt all non-Germans equally, it produced not unified, but local resistance with each nation emphasizing its own language, and indirectly, its own identity. This insistence on the use of languages became a constant factor in the history of nationalism in the Habsburg domains. While immediate reaction was not possible, once the pressure of the central government was slightly relaxed, after the issuing of the October Diploma (Oct. 20, 1860), two cultural societies, the Romanian *Astra* (1861)[18], and Slovak *Matica Slovenská* (1863)[19] joined the older *Matica Srpska* (1826, the cultural establishment of the Orthodox Metropolitanate of Karlovci), *Matica Česká* (1830), and *Matica Hrvatska* (1842) in their renewed literary and linguistic activities. Their activities were reinforced by numerous newspapers among which the Czech *Národni Listy* (1861), the paper of the Serb liberal Svetozar Miletić, *Zastava* (1863), the Slovak *Pešt' budinska vedemost'* (early 1860's), and the Romanian *Concordia* (1861) are indicative of this new trend. They were soon joined by others. Equally important was the question of schools, but this became crucial only somewhat later, after the *Ausgleich*.

While these, mainly cultural manifestations, were part of a wider reassertion of the demands of 1848 or earlier, they were, with the exception of the demands of the Italians, by no means hostile to the monarchy. The various people did not wish to become germanized, to be transformed into citizens of Greater Germany, or to be absorbed by the larger nationalities. While they rejected the notion of an "Austrian nation", they were quite willing to become good Austrian citizens, or more correctly, loyal subjects of the House of Habsburg. The exception of the Italians is easy to explain. The cause for the new trend in Vienna, the war of 1859, had inflamed Italian feelings much more than those of the other nationalities, and the defeat of the imperial forces meant more to them than to the other people of Austria. The Italians' irredentist plans became much more ambitious as expressed by the pamphlet "Trieste e l'Istria, a loro ragioni nella questione italiana", published in 1861. This new Italian line produced some interesting results. It made the Croats anti-Italian, and led by Eugen Kvaternik and Ante Starčević they expressed their feelings through the Party of the Croatian Right which, among other things, described in its program the borders of Greater Croatia, the Triune Kingdom, which included lands claimed by the Italians. This forced the Italians of the Adriatic coast, those who raised the question in the first place, into a much more pro-Austrian position. Their co-nationals in the Tyrol became the extreme Italian nationalists.

The Croatian state of which Kvaternik and Starčević spoke when they established their party was based on the largest possible extension of land to which the Croats had a "historic right", but they were willing to enjoy these rights under the scepter of the Habsburgs. There was room in it for their fellow Roman Catholics, the Slovenes, but the Serbs were excluded. Here clericalism, so important for the future of not only Slovene and Croat politics, but for much of Austria, becomes clearly discernible for the first time among a non-German people.

The decade that followed the end of fighting in Hungary saw the emergence of conservative-clerical and Great German trends joining the liberal which had expressed itself clearly previously. It polarized political thinking within each nationality making a united stand more difficult. It also produced sharp division between non-German nationalities weakening the arguments based on "historic rights". The decline of the force of these arguments, coupled with the language question that reappeared with great force during the same ten years, strengthened those who took ethnic identity, national self-determination, as the starting point for their plans for the future. In the period of neoabsolutism the issues which became crucial during the next period appeared, but they did not threaten the unity of the realm. More divided than ever, the people living in the Habsburgs' domain looked to Vienna as the supreme judge and arbiter who would solve their disagreements and satisfy their demands.

This Vienna-centered search for solutions on a home rule and cultural liberty basis began with the October Patent, survived the establishment of Austria-Hungary, and went down to final defeat only with the collapse of the negotiations of Prime Minister Count Menyhért Lónyai with the various minorities of Hungary and with the failure of Count Sigmund von Hohenwart's government in Austria to achieve an agreement with the Czechs. These events of 1872 and 1871 respectively, ended another period of only slightly more than a decade during which the various lines hardened considerably, making subsequent negotiations, let alone agreements, extremely difficult.[20]

IV.

The October Patent and the February Diploma of 1861 (Feb. 26), the latter designed to clarify the first and to serve as "the unalterable constitutional law" of the realm, represent an attempt to find a compromise between centralization and the federative solution. The details are not important for the issues under consideration, what matters is that these documents reopened the debate concerning the interrelationship of the Habsburg lands. Diets were called back into session and served as the sounding boards for various views. A few days before the second of these two documents was made public, the Croat Imbro I. Tkalac published in the Viennese *Ost und West*, which he edited from 1861 to 1863, his assessment of Austria's future. He denied that Austria could ever become a nation state, but insisted that it had to become a modern, European state, a state in which the law would reign supreme. This state had to permit its various people not only the "organic development of their personalities", but also "the reconciliation of their national and political differences".[21]

He was looking for a solution within Austria for the ills that affected the various nations.

Finding this solution was a very difficult task. The Magyars were unwilling to begin talks with Vienna until the three regions detached from Hungary had been reunited with her territory, but such a move would have made talks with numerous minorities on both sides of the Leitha practically impossible. The stubbornness with which Francis-Joseph clung to the October-February principles deserves admiration. They were an attempt to find a basis for limited local rights within a unified state in which all nations would have equal duties and privileges. He gave up this stand only after Austria's defeat by Prussia. This event coupled with the bankruptcy of the state demanded a prompt solution of the constitutional impasse. Yet, men like Tkalac foresaw the outcome of the centralist-federalist search long before the ruler accepted it. Shortly after he was forced to leave Vienna in 1863 because he stressed the federalist half of the program too strongly, Tkalac stated, in a memorandum submitted to the Italian minister of the interior, that the centralizing tendencies of Vienna would prevent the finding of a satisfactory solution to the Habsburg lands' problems and would force the Austrian Germans to turn to the Magyars. Hungary

> will be unable to refuse the hand extended to her by Austria. The latter will find in this agreement a strong enough support to fight its recalcitrant nationalities. True enough, the Austrian government is afraid of dualism which will, with one stroke, shift the point of gravity of the state, but faced with the dilemma of either losing Hungary or satisfying her with extreme concessions, it will certainly opt for the latter solution.[22]

Yet, before Tkalac's predictions became reality the efforts of the government to find other solutions produced lasting results which, like those during the period of neoabsolutism, were not foreseen. The Reichsrat, a central parliament after the February Patent, with which Anton von Schmerling had to deal as the emperor's chief minister, was dominated by Germans and by the conservative curiae. The same was true of the local assemblies in the Austrian half. The central parliament never really worked because some people, notably the Magyars, Italians and Croats, always abstained from its sessions. To remedy this situation and

Government and Minorities in Austria-Hungary

make governing possible, the "constitution" included an "Emergency Ordinance Paragraph" (Notverordnungsparagraph) which made it legal for the government to issue ordinances with the binding force of law whenever the Reichsrat was unable to function. This paragraph served as the model for the famous Paragraph 14 of the post 1867 Austrian constitution. Together with the gerrymandering which produced the central local majorities between 1861 and 1867, the two precedents were created that continued to be used after the Ausgleich and were bitterly resented by all, adding to the distrust of central government.

The situation was further confused by the fact that the emperor and his minister considered the Hungarian Diet, which assembled in May 1861 in Budapest, as a legislature whose status did not equal the Reichsrat's. The Hungarians refused this interpretation, had their assembly dissolved, and thus were legally not represented anywhere. Until 1865 the Magyars' absence made them the standard bearers of all who championed local rights and made the negotiations with the minorities in Transleithan lands very difficult.

The authorities banked more on the Poles and Czechs than on the people living in historical Hungary. To get the Czechs to Vienna, Francis-Joseph consented, in 1861, to his coronation as King of Bohemia, a promise he did not keep and broke again ten years later. The Czechs, in a minority in the Reichsrat, were constantly attacked by German centralists. The most virulent of these, Eduard Herbst and Karl Giskra, came from Bohemia. Led by Edward Gregr and František Rieger, the Czechs withdrew from Vienna in 1863 for a period of sixteen years during which they boycotted the central legislature.[23] Their action created an additional precedent, cut them off from cooperation with the Poles, but gave them great support at home. This unified following was shattered by the leaders of the "Old Czechs" in siding with the Russians against the Vienna government. Not only did this move make Polish-Czech cooperation impossible, but it split the Czechs too and signalled the beginning of the "Young Czech" movement.

Schmerling was in a curious position. He leaned on Germans in Austria attempting to create a strong centralized state, but in the Hungarian lands tried to support the nationalities against the Magyars. Pro-Slav in one half of the state, anti-Slav in the other he pursued a policy that confused everybody and made nobody believe him. The developments on the other side of the Leitha show somewhat similar tendencies.

When the Hungarian Diet was called into session, the Slovaks, led by the lawyer Štefan Daxner, met at Turčiansky Sv. Martin where, on June 6, 1861, they drew up a memorandum which they submitted to the Hungarian assembly.[24] This memorandum, while significantly reasserting the old brotherhood between Magyar and Slovak, demanded equality for the two nations, especially equality of language and the use of Slovak as official in the "North Hungarian Slovak District" (Hornouhorské Slovenské Okolie) together with the establishment of a Slovak Law School. Once again we see the primary emphasis placed on language, although the demand of territorial self-rule (the Czech demands served as the model) also made its appearance. That Magyars in Budapest refused to receive the memorandum is less important than is the deep cleavage it produced in Slovak ranks. Some people felt that it was unrealistic, in 1861, to go back to demands voiced in 1848, and preferred to find a common ground with the "liberals" in Budapest and Vienna. While the unyielding attitude of Rieger and company[25] produced the Young Czechs in Bohemia, the opponents of the memorandum formed their group, the Nová škola, in Slovakia. Here too we see then the two trends we observed when looking at Vienna. The difference between two nations, Slovak and Magyar, sharpened, and divisions began to appear in the Slovak camp.

Under completely different circumstances somewhat similar developments occurred in Transylvania. As a separate administrative unit, Transylvania was not forced to deal with the diet that assembled in Budapest in 1861. As long as Vienna tried to keep this province separate from Hungary, it could disregard its traditional ruling minority, the Magyars, who were the most likely to object to the province's separate status. The government also assumed that it could count on the support of the German minority, and concentrated its attention on the Romanian majority which had not rights, had nothing to lose and everything to gain. Here was a potential force which Vienna could court and gain, creating a situation not dissimilar from that prevailing in Galicia.

In 1861 Francis-Joseph received a Romanian delegation in Vienna and subsequently granted permission for the holding of a Romanian national conference in preparation for the session of the Transylvanian Diet. It assembled in 1861, in Sibiu and not in the Magyar stronghold of Kolozsvár (Cluj), its traditional meeting place. During the meeting of the national conference a split, not unlike the one among the Slovaks, occurred among the Romanians. There was no disagreement on demanding complete equality with the other nations in Transylvania, but one segment, led by Bishop Andreiu Şaguna, supported a "realistic policy" and

Government and Minorities in Austria-Hungary

cooperation with the Vienna liberals, somewhat along the line of the Slovak Nová škola. Another faction, led by the newspaper editor Gheorghe Barițiu, insisted on a large number of specific guarantees as the price of collaboration including, once again, the free use of the Romanian language because he felt that "our language is not safeguarded and, therefore, neither is our nationality".[26] Șaguna carried the day and his ideas were incorporated in a memorandum submitted to Francis-Joseph.

With the Magyars boycotting the Sibiu Diet in July 1863, the Romanians achieved equality for their nation, language, and two churches in Transylvania. The laws embodying these changes were considered legally passed by Vienna and totally illegal by the Magyars. To these gains were added the establishment of *Astra* and the separation of the Romanian Orthodox Church from the jurisdiction of the Serb Metropolitanate at Karlovci. Vienna was on its way toward gaining the loyalty of an important people, and had it continued on this course it would have healed the split in the Romanian ranks and secured the backing of Barițiu's faction also. Yet Vienna soon gave up this line, and opted for the Magyars who were, after all, the same people without whom, as Tkalac had predicted, Vienna could not find a way out of its dilemma.[27]

The change came in 1865. Francis-Joseph was gradually moving away from his minister whose anti-clericalism he resented, whose policies were not bringing any result, and whom the Magyars considered totally unacceptable as a negotiating partner. When the leader of the Magyar moderates, Ferenc Deák, published his nation's demands in an Easter Sunday editorial in *Pesti Napló* which the emperor found moderate and acceptable, he changed ministers. The new leader of the government, Count Richard Belcredi, promptly dissolved the Reichsrat which had no working majority anyhow, ruled with the help of the emergency paragraph, and began the search for a new basis for the reorganization of the state.

Before he could produce anything the war with Prussia took place, and he too was replaced. Yet, even before these events occurred, a sharp change took place in Vienna's Transylvanian policy. A new diet was called into session, this time at Kolozsvár, based on the old franchise regulations which were suspended when the Sibiu diet was elected. While Șaguna was willing to make the Romanian views heard even at this diet, the followers of the Barițiu, following the Czech example, declared a boycott widening the split in the Romanian ranks and giving the Magyars an even larger absolute majority than they would have had under ordinary circumstances. The diet of 1865 promptly annulled the laws passed two years earlier and proclaimed the union of Transylvania and Hungary. The Romanian protest was not even answered by Francis-Joseph who opened the Budapest Diet of 1865 in person. In this assembly the Transylvanian Magyars were already fully represented. The Magyar-Romanian split became a chasm and the division among Romanians sharper than ever.[28]

No nation had uttered a single demand prior to the Ausgleich that was not compatible with the unity of the Habsburg lands. Nevertheless, the chances for a solution diminished. The continuous and often totally unexplained changes in governmental policy, and even worse in the ruler's, produced dangerous precedents, a growing lack of confidence, increasing hostility among nations, and splits within the various national groups. Under these circumstances the Ausgleich, which had to be concluded rapidly for fiscal and foreign policy reasons, could be nothing but a minimal solution giving the government the tools for surviving on the domestic and international scene. It could not, at the same time, solve the problems that had grown constantly since 1848. It is significant that the Ausgleich did not even find full acceptance among the Germans and Magyars whom it put in the saddle. Among both the compromise had numerous enemies and within a short time it split these nations into factions. This is extremely significant because among the Czechs, Slovaks, and Romanians the passive resisters and boycotters gained the upper hand for a time, thus leaving the political field mostly to the Germans and Magyars.

The Ausgleich produced another, very significant, and in many ways contradictory change in the political make up of what became Austria-Hungary. In Hungary it led to the disappearance of the Transylvanian and Vojvodina districts and assemblies and, in spite of the Nagodba, fully subordinated Croatia and its sabor to the ruling of the Magyar parliament and government. It strengthened centralization and the central government although the latter still had to cope with the masters of the counties. Furthermore, the Deák-Eőtvős-Andrássy group that negotiated the Ausgleich had such tremendous prestige in Hungary that it was able to establish the authority of the government on very firm basis before it disappeared from the political scene. On the other hand, the situation in Austria was completely different. To make the Ausgleich an agreement between two equal partners, Austria received a constitution, but this document retained the various historical units with their diets and rights, specified them, and thus continued the contradictory policy of centralized diversity. From the very beginning, the governments in Vienna were never able to follow a really forceful line. They had to rely on coalitions which were always multi-national, representing the interests of various "lands" and people. While the Vienna line grew more and more democratic as time passed, the Magyar grew more and more autocratic, producing another contradiction. Yet, at the beginning of the post-Ausgleich period both governments tried to put their halves of the new common house in order.

With the Germans split between conservatives, clericals, Great Germans, and liberals, any Austrian government needed the support of some non-Germans to have a working majority in the new Reichstag. The Poles could be counted on to support the government in most instances as long as their position in Galicia was maintained, but their backing was not enough. The problem became extremely sharp after Prussia's victory over France which polarized German differences even further. This was shown in the 1870 elections and the defeat of the liberals. Count Sigmund von Hohenwart, the leader of the conservatives, took over the government in February 1871. He favored decentralization and tried to come to an agreement with all non-Germans, especially the Czechs. On October 10, 1871, the Bohemian Diet submitted its demands requesting equal status with Germans and Magyars. This demand meant total federalization, and soon the other nationalities joined the Czechs in their demand for home rule. Hohenwart was willing to negotiate on this basis, and offered, for example, autonomous districts to the Italians in the Tyrol. He soon found himself in an impossible position. His proposals, like the ones he offered to the Italians, were rejected by the various people as insufficient, and the Czechs, especially, sure that they would get what they wanted, stood firm. Yet without a compromise any solution appeared impossible. Francis-Joseph, now a firm supporter of the Ausgleich, sided with his new foreign minister, Andrássy, who saw in the federalization of Austria a danger for Hungary and thus a breach in the Ausgleich agreement. Furthermore, the emperor was afraid that federalization would impair the effectiveness of the army. Hohenwart thus found himself rejected by the nationalities, sharply attacked by the German centralists, and in opposition to the ruler and the Magyars.[29] He had no choice but to resign, leaving the nationalities, whose hope had soared very high, totally despondent. The great economic crisis that soon followed temporarily pushed the constitutional question into the background, but it emerged again with full force during Count Eduard Taaffe's "Iron Ring" government.

The Ausgleich did not satisfy the various people in Austria, and from 1867 to the fall of Hohenwart Vienna tried to make the new Austro-Hungarian structure acceptable by attempting to satisfy them with administrative and franchise reforms. This was not enough any more. Their experiences since 1848 made the nationalities dubious of any reform that did not make them masters of their own houses. Policies had changed too often and too drastically during the past two decades and, furthermore, they saw no reason why they should be satisfied with less than what the Magyars had received from the crown. Yet, the years 1867-1871 were a period in which at least the dialogue between the government and the various people was still going on. True enough, a new element had entered the picture. The central government now negotiated simultaneously with the deputies of the nationalities in Vienna and with the various provincial diets. The party alignments as well as the compositions of parliamentary delegations and diet representations were often dissimilar. Representatives of a given nationality naturally spoke differently in Vienna than in the capital of their land. The voices of the nationalities were thus fragmented even further, making it very difficult for the government to figure out who really spoke for the majority of any given nation. This added factor made the work of future governments even harder than it already was up to 1871.

The situation in Hungary started on a promising note. One of the first laws passed by the Hungarian Parliament, the "Law of Equal Rights for the Nationalities" (XLIV/1868),[30] was very liberal. The peace-makers in Paris in 1919-1920 used it as their model when they drafted their version of minority rights without coming near to the generous clauses of the Magyar law. Coupled with this law was the "Primary Education Act" (XXXVIII/1868) giving the nationalities, at least on the elementary school level, practically everything they could have demanded in the use of their languages in the schools. Both laws rested on the assumption that all citizens of Hungary formed one political nation, but recognized the right of other nationalities to total equality limited only by the political unity of the nation. Of course, much depended on how this limitation of rights was interpreted, but there can be no doubt that the framers of these laws, Eőtvős and Deák had the broadest and most liberal interpretation in mind.

The laws were much too liberal for the gentry that ran the county administrations. Although the nationalities law stipulated that the chief county officials, High-sheriff (főispán), and Vice-sheriff (alispán) should be non-Magyars in counties where the majority was non-Magyar, not a single non-Magyar official ever held any of these posts. The county gentry was successful in blocking not only this, but most of the pro-nationalities clauses of the laws, from becoming effective by using their local executive power to interpret the intent of the various laws.

Government and Minorities in Austria-Hungary

The nationalities who by the turn of the century often demanded the strict application of the laws of 1868 as the price for their collaboration with the Budapest government, opposed them in 1868. Minority deputies in Parliament objected to the way in which these laws were passed without they being heard, while in the regions which they represented and where boycotters were in the majority the opposition was even sharper. Once again, as in Austria, distrust of everything coming from the government was one of the major motivating forces. It went hand in hand with a demand for the recognition of "historical rights", something which did not have to be stressed in Austria where the old territorial units had been retained. Typical of this passivist-boycotter reaction was the *Pronunciament de la Blaj* which the Transylvanian Romanians issued on May 15, 1868. It rejected the Ausgleich, asked for the reestablishment of Transylvania's independence, demanded the enforcement of the laws of the Sibiu diet and democratic franchise regulation for Transylvania's diet. The Slovaks also held firm to the demands they had formulated earlier. The reaction of Budapest was sharp, producing the first arrests in a long sequence of such moves.

The story of the Croats and the Nagodba is too well known to warrant repetition, and will be discussed again in the chapter dealing with the Croats. All that has to be noted is that while their special status within the Lands of the Crown of St. Stephen saved them from the treatment other nationalities received, they too lost much, were deeply divided, and their majority was as much opposed to the Nagodba as the other nationalities were to the various laws passed in Budapest.[31]

Among the Magyars themselves there were deep cleavages. The Kossuth or Independent Party was weak in these early years, but a party, representing mainly the county gentry, the Resolution Party, led by Kálmán Tisza, represented a strong challenge to the ruling group and the Ausgleich. Their influence grew after 1871 when Eötvös died, Deák retired from active politics, and Andrássy moved to Vienna as Minister of Foreign Affairs. Tisza's party, recruiting followers among the same social group that supplied most of the backing for Deák and his friends, gained an amazing 116 seats in the election of 1872 signaling the beginning of the dissolution of Deák's party. The Deák party, needing new strength, turned to the nationalities with whom the new Prime Minister, Count Menyhért Lónyai, started negotiations formally in January 1872. He was too weak to carry his party with him, soon got involved in financial scandals, and achieved very little beyond starting talks with the Croats. These produced, under his successor, József Szlávy, a slight readjustment of the Nagodba

IV

which left the Croats as dissatisfied as before. With these talks, just as with those of Hohenwart in Austria, the last exchanges between governments and nationalities under half-way favorable circumstances came to a close. While in Austria attempts were made again and again to form multinational coalitions, in Hungary the trend was just the contrary. With the disintegration of the Deák party and the creation of the Liberal Party, a fusion of Deák's and Tisza's followers, leadership passed to the chauvinistic gentry element that followed the latter, and a new period in Magyar non-Magyar relations began.

V.

So far we have followed certain parallel developments producing fairly similar results in all lands. The various nationalities became more and more confused by the policies of the governments, trusted them less and less, and began to stress those goals which were, to an ever increasing degree, self-centered. They split concerning the means to achieve their goals, but all agreed on a minimum of cultural-linguistic independence and demanded rights to settle their own problems in the territories which they inhabited. Some suggested active participation in the political life of the state, hoping to use the various central and local legislative bodies as sounding boards and, if necessary, battlegrounds. Others hoped to achieve their aims by abstention from all political life expecting to paralyze legislatures and political life forcing the various governments to come to terms with them. Yet, as late as the middle of the 70's voices advocating secession or independence were hardly heard let alone heeded. What the leaders of the various factions forgot was that in both halves of the monarchy the electoral regulations were stacked against them, that the governments could practically always produce a quorum, and that, if nothing worked, there was Paragraph 14 to which at least the Viennese authorities could turn. The governments resented both the activist and passivist tactics of the nationalities. They began to consider them as hostile to them, to the state, and even to the ruling house, and were less and less willing to offer concessions. They began to expect counterproposals if not outright rejection of their suggestions. In spite of this general attitude, serious differences began to emerge between governmental action in Austria and Hungary.

Beginning with the middle 1870's the situation in the two halves of the state became more and more dissimilar. From 1879 to 1893 Austria was governed by the same man, Count Eduard Taaffe who held the position of prime minister for a longer time than anybody else. For practically the same period, Kálmán Tisza was the prime minister of Hungary, holding the reins of power from 1875 to 1890. It is not surprising that the lines that were still somewhat fluid when these two men took power were hardened almost into their final shape by the time they left office. While the two prime ministers followed different approaches in dealing with the nationalities, both men's policies produced the same results. By the time Taaffe and Tisza resigned, the hostility of the nationalities put the survival of Austria-Hungary in serious doubt.

When he took office, Count Taaffe was an experienced bureaucrat without any strong ideological attachment. His task was the same which Hohenwart failed to accomplish, the creation of a strong and stable majority in the Reichsrat. He could rely on some Germans and the Poles and tried to secure the cooperation of as many Slavs as possible, but principally that of the Czechs. The German liberals and other parties that represented mainly the middle class were against him, and his main opposition in the chamber was German. Adding the Czechs to the German clericals and conservatives as well as to the similarly aristocratic Poles produced the "iron ring", with whose help he maintained himself in office as long as he did.[32] He placed a Czech in his cabinet whose key member was a professor from Kraków university, Julian Dunajewski. He secured the cooperation of the Czechs by promising vaguely to satisfy their demands. Ending their long boycott of parliament the Czechs, now dominated by the Young Czech faction,[33] appeared in Vienna only to make clear that their goal was still the same, parity with Germans and Magyars in the state.

As soon as the first Taaffe cabinet faced parliament with the first major bill, military appropriations, it became clear that Taaffe had to pay for the Czech votes. He produced a language ordinance that obliged all administrators and judges in the Czech lands to conduct business in the language demanded by those whose problems they handled. This pleased the Czechs who as a rule could use both Czech and German equally well, but brought a storm of protest from the Germans who only rarely spoke Czech. The result of this ordinance was the rapid increase of Czech functionaries in Bohemia and Moravia. The Czechs pushed their advantage and in 1882 secured the splitting of Prague university into German and Czech institutions.[34] Even lower schools became the issue soon, and Taaffe's policy permitted the setting up of Czech elementary schools wherever forty Czech children lived within a half mile radius from the school's location. The lowering of tax qualifications for voting favored not only the Czechs, but also the other Slavs and the poorer Germans.[35] Among the last mentioned the Socialist Party was now able to become significant, splintering the German forces even further.

Naturally, all these moves were violently opposed by most Germans, and to please his conservative and clerical followers Taaffe placed schools in Austria proper under the supervision of the Catholic church. While in this manner Taaffe maintained a comfortable majority for his government in Vienna, he created serious problems for himself in the provinces, mainly in Bohemia. Here, helped by the 1882 franchise reform, the Czechs gained a majority in the local diet in 1883. This produced the German demand for separate German und Czech administrative districts in the land, something which they had rejected when the Italians demanded it in the Tyrol.[36] This time the Czechs refused the proposal, and for the first time the Germans boycotted a legislature, the Bohemian, from 1886 to 1890. In 1890 Taaffe tried to settle problems in Bohemia by bringing together representatives of the two nations, but, significantly, he did not invite the Young Czechs who were the dominant force in the Bohemian diet.[37] This conference produced the division of Bohemia into Czech and German administrative and judicial districts, which naturally, placed the Young Czechs in a position where they felt obliged to fight to the finish. The scenes in parliament were nothing short of scandalous with deputies fighting with their fists, and Prague was placed under martial law. Taaffe's policy had failed: the Czechs, the mainstays of the "iron ring", were now more hostile than they had been eleven years earlier.

It was almost impossible for Taaffe to fall back on a broader German base for support. The Germans felt threatened by Taaffe's attempt to transform Austria into a "Slav state", and in 1882 some of them established a Pan-German party which proposed, in the well known Linz program of that year, the handing over of the Polish and Southern Slav provinces to Hungary taking the rump of Austria into the closest possible economic relations with Germany in preparation for an Anschluss.[38] Thus it was among the Germans, in reaction to the concessions made primarily to the Czechs, that the first movement that advocated the dissolution of Austria-Hungary emerged. Although not directed against the existence of the state, the new Christian Socialist party, which weakened the clerical backing of Taaffe, was equally anti-Slav, anti-Jewish, and also anti-Hungary, and thus, in the long run, equally inimical to the maintenance of the state structure created by the Ausgleich.

IV

Government and Minorities in Austria-Hungary

The situation was no more favorable in the other Austrian provinces. In Galicia two Ukrainian movements made their appearance. While Vienna's backing of the Poles made these people strong supporters of Taaffe and Austria-Hungary, it made it quite clear to the Ukrainians that they could not gain even minimal concessions under the existing system. Consequently both Ukrainian movements aimed at the dissolution of the dual monarchy. The larger movement worked for independence, the smaller for union with Russia. The actions of the central government and the Galician diet made the Ukrainians even more determined to go their own way, joining, in this curious fashion, the German nationalists with whom they never made a common cause.[39] Thus among two nations, the Germans and the Ukrainians, nationalism produced its first anti-Austro-Hungarian fruits. Taaffe's reliance on Czechs and Poles to maintain his rule created this situation.

In the southern Slav districts Taaffe tried to befriend the Slovenes only to produce sharp clashes which pitted them against their German neighbors. Slovene leadership was in the hands of the Catholic clergy which sympathized with the Croat Party of the Right and was often anti-German, and, where Slovene and Italian lived together, even anti-Italian. In Trieste, the Italian dominated city council outlawed the Slovene language with the backing of the Germans. The same situation prevailed in Dalmatia where the Italians relying on Vienna clashed with the southern Slavs. These same two nations, the Germans and Italians, feuded in the Tyrol. Thus even before 1890, when Taaffe had a majority in parliament, things began to fall to pieces in all provinces. His somewhat pro-nationality policies encouraged the non-Germans, frightened the Germans, and sharpened the confrontation of various people everywhere. Maneuvering all the time without really facing issues, Taaffe created a situation which a quarter century before World War I made Austria the battleground of conflicting nationalisms. Taaffe tried to back out of the corner into which he worked himself by electoral reform. This, so he hoped, would placate the various nationalities who would get even stronger representation while it would also strengthen the nationalistically more moderate German lower classes producing the basis of a new coalition. His bill, practically universal male suffrage, alienated the Poles fearing the Ukrainian vote without bringing renewed Czech support for the government. Equally opposed were most of the established German parties who feared the Christian Socialist and Pan-German vote. Left without a majority Taaffe was forced to resign in 1893.

Taaffe tried to make a multinational state work by creating a multinational governmental block and by permitting the various nationalities more or less free expression. This is certainly to his credit, but the lack of any clear, strictly enforced policy spelled not only his doom, but also that of any future attempt at multinational cooperation.[40] All he achieved was free discussion, but it lacked focus and did not clarify differences for which nobody, least of all the government, offered solutions. Antagonism increased in the provinces while Taaffe's eyes were fixed on Vienna. Finally even the central parliament degenerated into a battleground where police had to separate the combatants. Relative freedom of speech under Taaffe permitted the vocalization of maximum demands, including for the first time a few that had the dissolution of Austria-Hungary in mind. Nationalism reached a dangerously self-centered, uncooperative and uncompromising state in the Austrian half of the monarchy.

Kálmán Tisza was just the opposite of Count Taaffe. He had a policy, knew exactly what he wanted, and tolerated no expression of views opposed to his. Just before he came to power, in 1874, the transition government of István Bittó passed an electoral reform law that was tailor made for Tisza's dictatorial practices. It adopted a version of the Austrian curia system which was even more discriminatory than was that across the Leitha. The nobles had a right to vote, and so had members of certain professions. The third and fourth groups, whose right to vote was based on property and tax qualifications, were further subdivided into urban and rural groups. The requirements were considerably lower in the urban category in which the nationalities were less numerous. All the requirements were very stringent. In Hungary proper 7,5 percent of the population was entitled to the vote, but in Transylvania only 3,2 and in Croatia slightly less than 2 percent. Furthermore, open voting and gerrymandering further assured that elections went in accordance with the government's wishes. Finally, electoral results officially announced often had little in common with the votes cast. This system, which remained unchanged until 1918, produced such disparities as, for example, a total of 5.161 voters in twelve electoral districts of Transylvania which were sparsely populated by Magyars, while a single Romanian district had 5.275 electors.[41] No wonder that with the exception of the forty Croats who had a seat in parliament in accordance with the Nagodba but could vote only on issues concerning Croatia, the Budapest parliament never had more than a handful of representatives from the nationalities even when they did not abstain from participating in the elections.

Government and Minorities in Austria-Hungary

In spite of this "reform", the old party needed help, and Tisza and his friends merged their faction with it creating the party of Free Principles, usually called the Liberal Party. The first of these two names fit Tisza and his rule better. He had to give up all the principles which he advocated until then to become the leader of the new party. He declared at that time that he valued his fatherland more highly than his principles, and his policy continued to be free of any dogmatism except for two, certainly not very liberal, points: he became the staunchest supporter of the Ausgleich (which he had rejected until 1875), and the determined foe of the lower classes, but especially the nationalities.

What Tisza's rule meant for the nationalities became clear soon after he became prime minister. By the end of 1875 all three Slovak high schools and the Matica Slovenská were closed down, starting a trend that, by 1911, reduced Slovak elementary schools to 440 from 1,921 that were operating when the Ausgleich was concluded. The Romanians were able to maintain four and the Serbs one church-supported high school, but these too lost much of their independence. On the lower school level these nationalities suffered just as the Slovaks did, while the Ukrainians never had many schools in Hungary. The Serb deputy Michael Polit was excluded from Parliament in 1875 for defending the Slovak institutions, while the leader of the Serbs, Svetozer Miletić, was jailed, in spite of his parliamentary immunity, when he favored the Serbs in their war with the Ottoman Empire in the same year.

It is very difficult to follow the action-reaction sequence of governmental and nationality action in Hungary in the same way as it was possible in Austria because the make-up of the legislature in Budapest left the nationalities little choice but "passivism". The two largest nationalities, the Romanians and Slovaks, abstained from political activity in Budapest almost totally from 1875 to 1906. The various school laws, for example those of 1879, 1883, and 1891, clearly show that magyarization was the policy of Tisza and his government.[42] Minority languages were not tolerated in the courts, street names could be printed only in Magyar, and all official notices were published in this language only. In Hungary the language question was not simply an attempt to find an administrative language for the realm, it was a clear policy of denationalization.[43] Béla Iványi-Grünwald, a county official in Slovakia, expressed this tendency with great clarity when in his book, *A Felvidék* (The Mountain Region), he wrote:

> The secondary school is like a huge machine, at one end of which the Slovak youths are thrown in by the hundreds, and at the other end of which they come out as Magyars.[44]

The author of these lines was not only a trusted official of the government, but at the same time the president of FEMKE (Felvidéki Magyar Közművelődési Egylet—Hungarian Public Culture Society of the Mountain Region), a supposedly private, but heavily subsidized, association whose aim was to transform Slovaks into Magyars by press, theater, etc. Wherever nationalities lived in greater numbers such societies were established: EMKE for Transylvania, and DMKE for the Vojvodina Serb regions.

The nationalities, who, with the exception of the Serbs, were hardly ever represented in parliament, tried to find effective local countermeasures to the magyarization pressure and also attempted to formulate long range goals. Among them the Slovaks were at the greatest disadvantage. They had no church of their own, unlike the Serbs and Romanians, and their great Roman Catholic masses were under the influence of a clergy which, with few exceptions, backed the Magyar line. The politically conscious segment of the population was extremely small, and the people to whom they tried to appeal were either educated in Magyar schools or too unsophisticated for political action. "The alliance of the thin stratum of the Slovak intelligentsia and the general masses of the people became the basic question of Slovak political life..."[45] The division between Memorandists and the Nová škola made the task of the Slovak leadership even more difficult. The Slovak National Council of the Memorandists became more and more pro-Russian in a Pan-Slav sense and the dominant force as the Nová škola's line of cooperation with the Magyars was totally discredited by Tisza's policy. In 1884 the council reasserted its passivist policy, although it tried to take part in county and municipal politics. Under the leadership of Svetozár Hurban Vajansk the movement turned more and more towards Russia and began to look for solutions in various Pan-Slav ideas, which entailed an existence independent from Hungary. It was not a very effective or fruitful line, but produced a centrifugal tendency which gained strength rapidly after Tisza fell from power.

In Transylvania too the passivists were in the saddle. Under Barițiu's leadership the Romanian National Party was established in 1881.[46] The program of this party contained little that was new: autonomy for Transylvania, equality of languages and creeds, the enforcement of the laws of 1868, and universal suffrage. Tisza's government reacted sharply pointing out that only one nation lived in Hungary and any "national" party that was not Magyar had, therefore, nothing but the dissolution of the state in mind. The party, at this stage, was certainly not yet preaching secession, but in 1887 decided to submit a memorandum to the emperor.[47] General Trajan Doda, who ran for Parliament that year simply to voice in Budapest the points made by the memorandum, was condemned to jail for a speech he made in the house.[48] While Francis-Joseph pardoned him, Ioan Slavici, who published his speech in his newspaper, went to jail. The 1890 meeting of the party reacted by voicing for the first time secessionist ideas, speaking of a single Romanian nation of eleven million people. Thus, once again, measures of the government sharpened the opposition of a nationality to the point where it could be viewed as "disloyal".

In Croatia, where Tisza's relative, Count Károly Khuen-Héderváry, ruled as banus from 1875 to 1903, the strained relationship between Serbs and Croats continued, helped along by the banus's blatant favoritism for the Serbs. But within the Croat camp proper also various views were heard ranging from the pro-Magyar Unionist Party's to the Party of the Pure Right for whom even the Starčević party was not Croat enough. While here Khuen- Héderváry had some success with his divide and rule policy, he was unable to secure a majority favorable to him or to Hungary.

In Hungary too, where the major opposition, the Independent Party, still denied the validity of the Ausgleich, other opposition parties made their appearance also. They united, in 1886, for the first time, over a minor issue, the celebration of the 1848 revolution. It grew into a major problem touching on the unity of the Austro-Hungarian army. The ensuing debate weakened Tisza's position considerably by the time the 1890 army bill came before the house. He won this debate, but when he opposed granting citizenship to the exiled Lajos Kossuth, the scenes in the Budapest parliament paralleled those in the house in Vienna. Without being voted down Tisza resigned, continuing to run his party from behind the scenes.

Tisza's policy, which was just the opposite of Taaffe's, produced the same results. Antagonism between the Magyars and the other nationalities increased to the point where among the Slovaks, Romanians and Croats the first views demanding more than home rule were expressed. By the end of his prime ministership, just as at the end of Taaffe's, the various nationalisms seemed, and in the long run proved to be, irreconcilable. One question must be raised at this juncture. Why could the prime ministers of the halves of Austria-Hungary pursue diametrically opposed policies leading to the same disastrous results when the emperor-king had enough power to force his will and policy on both? Various answers have been offered both complimentary to and critical of Francis-Joseph, but the fact remains that he did not use his powers. The most likely explanation is that he was too removed from reality, too narrowly bound by the views of the circles in which he moved, too fearful of the future of the realm which he saw safe as long as dualism existed, to realize what really occurred in his various lands. Thus, while Austria lacked a determined domestic policy and Hungary pursued a catastrophic line, there was no Austro-Hungarian, imperial, or Habsburg position that the various people of the monarchy could have taken as the supreme expression of state policy. In a country that did not even have common citizenship, in which only Kaisertreue or Habsburgstreue were recognized as binding on everybody with equal force, the absence of an imperial line to which these loyalties could have been directed could only reinforce the centrifugal tendencies which the policies of the two prime ministers brought forth.

VI.

The next period, that saw the seeds of the Taaffe-Tisza period grow into an unpenetrable forest, ends with the introduction of universal male suffrage in Austria at the end of 1906 and with the appointment of Sándor Wekerle as prime minister at the end of the 1905-06 constitutional crisis in Hungary.

Taaffe's immediate successor dropped the controversial electoral reform issue. Just as Taaffe, Prince Alfred Windischgrätz needed the Poles to produce a majority in parliament, but he fell from power when he proposed the introduction of classes in the Slovene high schools that would have established parallel education in German and Slovene. Great German and Christian Socialist forces were by this time so strong that a seemingly minor issue like this was sufficient to produce a crisis. His successor, the Polish count, Kasimir Badeni, began by lifting the state of siege in Prague and securing the return of the Young Czechs to an apparently reconstituted iron ring. He succeeded, with the help of the Czechs, in creating in 1897, a fifth electoral curia, but then he had to face the Czech problem again. Without solving it, Austria could not remain viable. The German parties were too split and too hostile to cooperate with each other, and the Czechs had to be added to the Poles to produce a solid Slav basis for the ruling of a state which was, supposedly, dominated by Germans.

Badeni proposed separately for Bohemia and Moravia two reforms. The first would have made the two languages absolutely equal in all state offices, while the second gave all state employees three years to learn the language which they did not yet speak.[49] Bedlam returned to parliament paralleled by bloody street riots in all major German cities forcing Badeni's resignation. The next government also failed to solve this problem, and in 1898 Prime Minister Count Franz Thus-Hohenstein tried a new approach. Instead of presenting projects to parliament he attempted to negotiate with the various parties. The Germans in Bohemia were once again agitating for separate administrative districts, with the Czechs opposed. Although parliament was not sitting, the government ruled with the help of Paragraph 14, the news of negotiations was enough to bring the demonstrators to the streets again. "National passions had reached such a feverish pitch that even a reasonable and careful politician was prevented from taking the road leading to mutual understanding unless he was willing to accept the odium of being called a traitor."[50]

What made the prime minister's position even more difficult was the fact that any Czech solution was, without any doubt, soon to serve as the model for solving other nationality problems. No uniform basis for a general solution could be found. Germans in Bohemia demanded separate administrative districts along linguistic lines willing to grant them to nobody but the Italians in the Tyrol. In the Tyrol the Italians were satisfied with this solution, but opposed it elsewhere, even in Dalmatia where they were a small minority, and demanded the maintenance of "historic rights." In Silesia the Poles supported rights for minorities, but denied them to Ukrainians in Galicia. While in Silesia and Moravia the possibility of a Czech-German compromise existed, in Bohemia chances for an agreement were minimal. Under the circumstances any attempt to find a general solution had to fail.

Paragraph 14 saved Austria until 1905, when, in connection with events in Russia and Hungary, court circles turned once again to electoral reform as the panacea for all ills that plagued Austria. It was the hope of these circles that universal suffrage would produce supranational mass parties based on religious or professional lines cutting across national lines and thus diminishing national antagonism. At the end of 1906 an electoral law based on universal male suffrage was passed, but it retained certain qualifications, especially taxation, and created unequal electoral districts.[51]

While the electoral reform was debated, prime minister Max von Beck succeeded in making the Badeni regulations palatable to the Moravian diet.[52] This solution served as a model, in 1910, for the language compromise in the Bukovina, and just before World War I broke out, in Galicia. Yet the Bohemian, Italian, and Southern Slav problems remained unsolved. Beck resigned, in 1908, in the midst of an international crisis, for reasons that had nothing to do with nationality problem.

Between Tisza's resignation and 1905 nothing changed in Hungary. His successors continued to follow his various policies. After Tisza's departure from the prime ministership, the Romanians decided to submit their petition, first discussed in 1887, to the emperor. After reworking it, they presented their document in Vienna on June 1, 1892, but the ruler turned it over, unread, to the Hungarian government. The prime minister, Count Gyula Szapáry, labeled the action of the Romanians unconstitutional, but his minister of Justice disagreed with him. After some hesitation the petitioners were tried and received various prison sentences. The Slovak lawyers, the only ones willing to handle the defense, withdrew in the middle of the trial protesting the actions of the judge.[53] After the trial, in 1894, the Romanian National Party was ordered dissolved. One of the reasons given for this action by the ministry of justice was the accusation that the party was acting under the influence of a foreign power. While this was not the case, it was true that after 1891 a Romanian Cultural League operated in Bucharest trying to help those across the border mainly by placing scholarships at the disposal of their students. Thus some connections existed across the Carpathians, just as they existed in the South between the Slavs and Serbia, the Bohemian Germans and Germany, and the Italians with Rome. The nationality question had spilled across the borders of Austria-Hungary and became part of the international problems facing the Habsburg state.[54]

Magyar intransigence was the most clearly expressed by Baron Dezső Bánffy who was prime minister between 1895 and 1899. His goal was a unitary Magyar state in which nobody but Magyars were to live. He declared that "without chauvinism it is impossible to found the unitary Magyar state,"[55] and stated that this end made all means acceptable. His election campaign of 1896, in which troops were used to assure that the nationalities and opposition parties received practically no representation, was the most scandalous in Magyar history. Yet even the attacks by

Government and Minorities in Austria-Hungary

Magyars in parliament did not change Bánffy's policies. When the emperor-king forced him to resign, the change to the "mild and liberal" Kálmán Széll brought no relief for the nationalities. He proclaimed that the only "categorical imperative [was] the Magyar state-idea...which every citizen should acknowledge...and subject himself unconditionally to it... The supremacy and the hegemony of the Magyars is fully justified."[56]

Yes, it was under Bánffy that the nationalities were permitted to hold a congress in Budapest where the Serb, Slovak, and Romanian representatives took the first step away from passivism and abstention. They demanded the recognition of their rights and democratic reforms without the slightest chance of being taken seriously. Yet with this session begins a new phase in their political behavior that became pronounced around 1903, but before we turn to events during that year a few words must be said about the nationalities' action since 1890.

Very important changes occurred in Slovakia. A new generation had grown up and tried new ways to solve the problems which it faced. Here several political movements made their appearance including the clerical Slovak People's Party of Andrej Hlinka. It worked not only for national goals, but also aimed to create a certain autonomy for the Slovak Catholic Church. Much more important, in the long run, was another movement strongly under the influence of Thomas G. Masaryk and closely identified with the journal *Hlas* (1898-1904) that picked up the Czechoslovak idea. By 1901 this movement created the Slovak National Party under the leadership of Vavro Šrobár and Milan Hodža, gave up the old memorandist program and passivism, and worked for both reform in Hungary and for closer cooperation with the Czechs. A cultural renaissance paralleled this political awakening. These were modest but very significant beginnings. The Czechslovak movement deserves special attention because it implied a thorough revision of the structure of Austria-Hungary without advocating the dissolution of the state. It was relatively easy to see, at least in theory, how the Czechs could have achieved home rule within Austria, but a Czech-Slovak union demanded the reconstruction of both halves of the state. While the Slovaks, with the exception of a few leading figures, never became very active in politics, the existence of the Slovak National Party was considered a grave danger by the ruling Magyar circles who intensified their pressure, trying to kill this movement by speedy magyarization of the Slovaks.

In Croatia the Unionists and National parties continued to operate, and after 1896 they were joined by the Croatian Party of the Pure Right that split the Croatian Party of Right, and soon thereafter by the Croatian Peasant Party. The Pure Right, led by Josip Frank, was not only violently Croatian in its nationalism, a strict upholder of the Triune Kingdom idea, and thus immune to Yugoslav propaganda, but also strongly clerical.[57] This allowed it to establish good relations with the clericals in Vienna, with the circle of Archduke Francis Ferdinand, and with the clericals in Slovenia. Once again, just as in Slovakia, we see the development of a movement which, while remaining loyal to the Habsburg state, broke the line dividing Austria from Hungary by searching for solutions in Vienna and not in Budapest.

Yet Frank was not the only one who had contacts in Austria. When banus Khuen-Hedervary finally left Croatia to become prime minister of Hungary, the Serbs and Croats began to work together. They collaborated during the large protests of 1903 and suffered equally under the martial law that was imposed. Their case was taken to Vienna by a Croat delegation from Dalmatia and Istria, but they were not received by Francis-Joseph. Out of this common move came the crucial events of 1905.

As is well known, the constitutional crisis in Hungary erupted over the army bill which the emperor-king wanted passed in 1904. István Tisza, the son of Kálmán, who was prime minister since 1903, could not push the bill through parliament and called for new elections. A coalition made up of the Independent Party led by Ferenc Kossuth, the Constitutional Party led by Count Gyula Andrássy Jr., and the People's Party under Count Aladár Zichy won the election of January 1905. Tisza not only resigned but dissolved his party. The dual monarchy faced a serious crisis when this coalition became the majority in parliament. Two thirds of the seats won by the coalition were in the hands of the Independent Party that had always denied the validity f the Ausgleich and now tried to restructure the relationship between the two halves of Austria-Hungary.

Francis-Joseph was not willing to yield, refused to entrust the coalition with forming the government and appointed a caretaker cabinet under Baron Géza Fejérváry. A constitutional struggle had begun and was of great significance to the nationalities. They had always been rejected by the liberals who had just disappeared and their petitions were not even read in Vienna. Now a new force appeared on the scene that challenged the policies of both Hungary's masters for the past fifty years and Vienna. They ended their passivism, reorganized and returned to the political scene.

In Croatian lands far reaching changes took place. Led by the Croatians from Dalmatia, Franjo Supilo, the Croats and Serbs, coming from all parts of Austria-Hungary, first met in Rijeka (Fiume) on October 4 and then twice in Zadar on October 16 and November 18, 1905.[58] The two nations declared that they were members of a single nation and agreed that they would act as one irrespective of the artificial borders of Austrian and Hungarian provinces separating them. Their program was still based on the Triune Kingdom concept, on a renegotiation of the Nagodba satisfying them, but it included really democratic demands as far as the franchise, freedom of speech and press, etc. were concerned. This coalition had numerous possibilities. It could follow the vague promises coming from the circle of Francis Ferdinand, it could opt for a Yugoslav solution and union with Serbia, or it could collaborate with the opposition in Budapest. It represented an important political force because, with the exception of Frank and his followers, it included all Croat and Serb parties of both halves of the monarchy. Under the circumstances prevailing in Hungary the coalition followed Supilo's line. As a Dalmatian, he was more afraid of Vienna than of Budapest, and both in Zagreb and Budapest the forces of the coalition cooperated with the Hungarian opposition. The other minorities, first of all the Romanians, who chose this moment to give up passivism, had a similar choice.

Not only the nationalities had a choice. Following the line pursued at the same time in Vienna, Francis-Joseph saw in universal suffrage, that would have weakened all established Magyar parties, the solution of the crisis. József Kristóffy, from the circle of Francis Ferdinand, served as minister of the interior in the Fejérváry cabinet, pushed the universal suffrage measure and sought an agreement with the nationalities. The Magyar coalition in opposition did the same. Both sides had a great opportunity because these suddenly vocal people presented amazingly modest and reasonable demands.

Unfortunately neither side took the nationalities seriously. The Magyar coalition was too deeply imbued with the idea of Magyar supremacy to consider earnestly cooperation with the nationalities that universal suffrage would have entailed. Yet the nationalities were siding with them, and with their help the Magyars could have pressured their ruler for serious concessions. Francis-Joseph, on the other hand, gave up the franchise idea and with it all possible claim on the nationalities' loyalty when on, April 9, 1906, he came to a secret agreement with the Magyar coalition which was basically nothing but the capitulation of the Magyar leaders. The elections of that month gave the Magyar coalition

380 out of the total of 413 seats, but also brought more nationality deputies than ever before, twenty-five, to parliament.

These deputies were soon in trouble. They were received with open hostility and within weeks several of them were again standing before judges in spite of their parliamentary immunity. The ex-opposition now in power proved just as chauvinistic as the defunct liberals had been. The well-known Apponyi School Laws that would have magyarized all non-Magyar, even the confessional schools, if in the years to come it would not have encountered too much clerical opposition, were submitted to the house in 1907. The nationalities' deputies fought against this bill in vain just as the filibustering of the forty Croats could not prevent the passage of a new Railroad Service Act prescribing the Magyar language on the Croatian lines. These two laws, the latter introduced by executive order, finally convinced the nationalities that they would never get anything in Hungary.

This can be seen most clearly in Croatia where the local legislature, the sabor, gave the people their own forum. In spite of severe repression and large scale bribery, the Croato-Serb coalition held together and won large majorities in each election. The new banus, Baron Paul Rauch, governed without the sabor for years, and the famous Zagreb and Friedjung trials only added to the discontent of the Southern Slavs. The annexation of Bosnia-Hercegovina and the new mood in Serbia, were the added external influences that pushed the Croato-Serb coalition more and more into a secessionist Yugoslav direction. By 1910 only the Slovenes were still vacillating, but the great majority of Croats and Serb had decided in favor of the Yugoslav solution.

By different roads the Austrian and Hungarian governments reached, once again, the same destination. In the period that had passed since Taaffe and the older Tisza left power, they produced a sharp division in their German and Magyar camps, several major crises, street riots, martial law, and government by decree. In many cases the disturbances were the result of controversies centered around the nationalities. These people never received anything, became more and more hostile to the existing order and began to formulate plans that would have, as a minimum, destroyed the state structure created by the Ausgleich introducing Czech-Slovak and Yugoslav autonomous units. By the end of the crisis years in Hungary even these tendencies had been surpassed. Great Germans, Italians, most Southern Slavs, and increasingly the Romanians followed the direction previously taken by the Ukrainians and were formulating plans that involved the dissolution of Austria-Hungary.

Government and Minorities in Austria-Hungary

The Czech-Slovak idea could be realized as well outside as inside the Habsburg domain although no clear separatist tendency had yet emerged. The Magyars, once the opposition surrendered to the ruler, were still the firm upholders of the Ausgleich and the state it created, and the Slovenes had not yet succumbed to the Yugoslav idea. This is very little to show for almost fifty years of work aimed at making Austria-Hungary function as a viable state. The remaining years, those during which universal suffrage produced new combinations in the Viennese parliament and which saw the old Magyar liberals reassume power under another name as well as those of the First World War brought little change and not much has to be said about them.

VII.

The first elections that were held after universal suffrage had been introduced (June 17, 1907) brought to Vienna representatives of 28 different political parties. The 243 Germans represented seven factions. The Czechs had 82 deputies, who came from six parties but worked together in the Czech Club, and another 23 Social Democrats, while the Polish Club's 72 members represented five parties with another 7 Poles following the social democratic line. The Ukrainians' 13 deputies came from three parties, the 19 Italians from the same number of factions, and the 24 Slovenes from two. There were also 5 Croats, 5 Zionists, 4 Romanians from the Bukovina and 2 Serbs in the Reichsrat.[59] All these people were, although for different reasons, united in their opposition to the demands of the Magyars, but agreed on nothing else. The speech from the throne, opening parliament, stressed that all nationality differences had to be subordinated to the unalterable goal of the crown to maintain Austria-Hungary's great power position, but it made no impression on those in the house. National differences became paramount again when the events in the Balkans inflamed feelings and Prague was once again placed under martial law. Professor Hantsch analyzed the problems facing this assembly correctly when he pointed out that as a result of the suffrage reform

> Austria had a democratic parliament, but still did not have a democratic government because the ministers continued to receive their mandate from the ruler to whom, and not to parliament, they were

> responsible. Thus parliament and government represented two different political philosophies that were contradictory.⁶⁰

Given this lack of unity in principle and the numerous contradictory party and nationality affiliations, the best that could be achieved were, once again, unstable working coalitions that could solve nothing and fell apart rapidly. The various ministries that followed each other had nothing to offer as far as new programs or ideas were concerned and, after 1908, got more and more involved in concentrating their attention on foreign affairs. The unresolved questions continued to fester, and the tendencies which began to manifest themselves during the previous periods among the nationalities grew stronger under the influence of both domestic and international developments. It was much too late in 1906 to point to missed opportunities, yet one must note that the new Czech leaders, such as Masaryk and Karel Kramař, still clung to a federative solution within the Habsburg domain when they formulated their plans. The more extreme of the two, Kramař, declared as late as 1908

> that nobody can deny the clear and obvious fact well known to everybody that our nation can work relatively the best for its cultural, political and economic advancement within the framework of Austria.⁶¹

Naturally, he and his friends saw other alternatives too and turned to them when the government refused to cooperate with them. Vienna soon ceased to function in a manner that would have made negotiations with it possible. Looking more and more to events outside the state, following the line of the Hofburg, unable to master the complicated factional-national situation in the Reichsrat, governments began to operate almost exclusively with the help of Paragraph 14 without even referring to parliament. Under these circumstances the nationalities began to follow even more determinedly their own road turning more and more sharply away from Austria-Hungary.

If in Austria relatively little changed after 1907, in Hungary an even sharper line emerged. Professor May was correct when they entitled his chapter dealing with the years that followed the replacement of the Fejérváry government "Hungary Militant." Knowing well what happened in Austria, all Hungarians knew that sooner or later electoral reform would come to Hungary too, but all Magyars, irrespective of their party affiliation, were opposed to it. This stand against reform produced an even more frantic magyarization designed to create a Magyar majority by the time the inevitable came to pass.

Among the Slovaks a serious attempt to decapitate the leadership, that began with the jailing of Hlinka and Šrobár for "incitement" in 1906, expanded and concentrated mainly on the Catholic and Lutheran churches whose clergy supplied much of the political leadership. In Croatia and Transylvania the agitation continued, but the crucial events occurred in Hungary. By the end of 1909 the relationship between the ruler and the coalition had deteriorated, and early in 1910 Francis-Joseph turned to another caretaker government recalling Count Khuen-Hédervary to the prime ministership. The younger Tisza saw in this move an invitation to reconstitute his party and established the National Work Party. Khuen-Hédervary outdid even the Bánffy elections using 194 battalions of infantry and 114 cavalry squadrons in the 1910 elections producing an overwhelming victory for the new party. The number of nationality representatives was reduced to five Romanians and three Slovaks. While the prime minister continued in office, the real master of Hungary from this moment until his resignation in 1917 was István Tisza. His views are, therefore, of great importance.

By 1910 Tisza was thoroughly frightened by the rising nationalism of the various nationalities, but especially the Slavs. He became, therefore, the strongest partisan of the existing Austro-Hungarian state that could survive only, according to him if in it the Magyars acquired leadership. Vienna had to accept this view that excluded any federalization, because, said Tisza, Hungary "cannot allow itself to be placed in a position to be outvoted by the others."[62] With government in Austria practically paralyzed, the continued ascendency and finally leadership of the Magyars in common affairs was certainly a distinct possibility. To achieve this goal, the Magyars had to make certain that they remained masters in their own house (including Croatia) and had to increase the number of "Magyars" to the detriment of the other inhabitants of the land.

In the first speech which Tisza gave in the newly elected parliament, he addressed himself to the nationality problem. He told his "non-Magyar fellow-citizens", that they "must first of all reconcile themselves to the fact that they belong to a national state, which is not a conglomerate of different races, but which one nation had conquered and founded, upon which one nation has stamped the ineradicable impress of its individuality." He promised fair treatment to all, but declared war on "agitators" making clear that he would not tolerate "national parties." He addressed himself specifically to the Romanians "because of all races in the country national consciousness beats most strongly in their breast," and invited them to work with him, but, in the same breath, warned them that they could not form parties because when they do "they are already denying the political unity of the Magyar nation." "With this shade of opinion," he ended, "there can be no negotiations; it must be fought, and if we conquer, we must destroy it."[63]

Thus Tisza came out for the continued and unchanged existence of Austria-Hungary to be dominated more and more by a fully magyarized Hungary. This policy resulted in the suspension of constitutional rule in Croatia. Placed under imperial commissioners the Croats made three attempts on the lives of these functionaries. Of the new attempts of magyarization the detachment of seventy-five parishes from the Uniate (Romanian) church and their attachment to the Catholic (Magyar) church is a typical example. These moves were paralleled by further trials of minority journalists and politicians and by the growing separatist tendencies of the various nationalities.

Tisza, who became prime minister again in June 1913, was somewhat of a realist and read the signs correctly. The Balkan wars induced him to reestablish constitutional government in Croatia and to attempt a compromise with the Romanians. The Romanian demands were by no means excessive. They asked for the use of their language in schools, courts and in public announcements and ordinances, freedom of press and assembly, help for economic development in regions which they inhabited, and certain electoral reforms. When Tisza, admitting that these requests were justified, rejected them nevertheless as incompatible with his goal of a Magyar Hungary, the Romanians reverted to their 1881 program and any further talks proved useless.

Here we have, once again, a parallel case to what we have observed in Austria. Austrian leadership was unable to take advantage of the relative moderation of the new Czech spokesman. Tisza, just as his Austrian colleague, faced new leaders, Iuliu Maniu and Alexander Vaida-Voevod, both future prime ministers of Romania, but in 1912-14 they were primarily interested in bettering the position of their people and, therefore, amazingly moderate. In January 1913 Vaida-Voevod, in an article published in *Österreichische Rundschau*, still wrote that a Greater Romania reaching to the Tisza river born with Russian help was a pipe-dream. Tisza could not agree with even men of this stamp. Unlike his

Austrian counterparts, he had an ideology and a goal for the sake of which he rejected demands which even he had to admit were reasonable. The lack of principles in Austria produced the same result that rigid principles brought about in Hungary. While the lack of principles only permitted the gradual drifting away of nationalities in Austria, their presence in Hungary accelerated this trend making the position of nationalities practically untenable within the exiting state structure.

It was under these circumstances that Austria-Hungary entered World War I. Little if anything must be said, in the context of this chapter, of the war years. The war, especially after it turned definitely against the Central Powers, only opened new vistas for the nationalities who could now count on the backing of those who fought their masters. Just as understandable are the moves of the various governments who took measures, as soon as the war began, against leaders whom they did not trust unavoidably reinforcing centrifugal tendencies. The attempts at reconciliation that were made, especially after Francis-Joseph's death, came too late and under circumstances unfavorable to Austria-Hungary. Tisza held out against concessions until he finally had to resign in the summer of 1917, and the futility of his successors' attempts to come to an agreement with the nationalities of Hungary who were, by that time, committed to the Yugoslav, Czechoslovak, and Greater Romanian ideologies, have been described well too often to require repetition. It is my contention that by the summer of 1914 the problems raised by nationalism were indeed insurmountable and that the war only accelerated the process. While nationalism was not by definition incompatible with the existence of Austria-Hungary it finally spelled the dual monarchy's doom as a result of the developmental sequence described in this chapter.

VIII.

At the very outset, I quoted Hans Kohn to the effect that nationalism "presupposes" the existence of a centralized form of government. This statement is equally valid for societies (mainly those of Western Europe) who acquired a strong, centralized state before they developed their nationalistic feelings, and for those (mainly in the Americas and the "third world") who became nationalists before their "modern" nation states were established. Austria-Hungary and its numerous people do not fit either alternative. The realization that centralization had become a necessity and the ideal of nationalism penetrated the realm of the Habsburgs simultaneously. It, therefore, proved equally impossible to develop a nationalism fitting a preexisting state or to create one to satisfy the demands of nationalism.

If one looks back far enough, one hundred years before 1848, it is easy to see that the rulers, from Maria Theresa to Francis-Joseph, worked diligently at centralization, but the Habsburgs never really understood the force of nationalism. This new ideal gradually gained influence among the various people. Yet centuries of coexistence produced a strong enough bond to make them search originally for a solution, even for the problems raised by nationalism, within the framework of the curious state structure that the Habsburgs had pieced together over the centuries. This willingness to cooperate both with each other and the rulers changed during the period 1848-1918 into hostility of each nation for all others. Even Habsburgstreue was at best Franz-Josephstreue by 1914.

This chapter tried to show how the readiness of nationally conscious people to cooperate in a large centralized empire evaporated and was replaced not only by a great variety of mutually antagonistic nationalism, but a macronationalism encompassing them all and demanding the dissolution of Austria-Hungary. The argument has been advanced that this drastic change occurred as the result of the inability of the governments to deal with their people, to understand their responses to legislation, and to gain their trust. In a sense, this chapter described, although it did not define, nationalism by presenting it in action.

Those responsible for the government, the ruler and his chief advisers and ministers, must bear the major share of the responsibility for this development, but the circumstances under which they performed their duties were certainly not making their task an easy one.

Austria, and later Austria-Hungary, was not truly a centralized state and did never have a strongly and consistently expressed overall policy. Francis Joseph resembles more a romantic medieval knight than a modern statesman in his scrupulous avoidance of everything that could have been interpreted as a violation of the Ausgleich or the rights of the Königreiche and Länder. It is impossible to be loyal to a non-existing state, to agree or disagree with reasons of state that are never expressed, or to develop any form of nationalism under these circumstances. Kaisertreue was supposed to replace nationalism as the cement holding the various people together within what was considered to be a state. In the "age of nationalism" this was simply not a satisfactory substitute.

If Austria-Hungary was not a state and had no policy, Hungary was certainly a state and, taking the term considerably more loosely, so was

Government and Minorities in Austria-Hungary

Austria. In the absence of a central policy, the governments of these two states had practically unlimited powers to act on their own within the framework of dualism. Conceivably an over-all policy could have emerged as a result of close cooperation between the two governments and careful coordination of their actions. Some concurrence was made mandatory by the Ausgleich (affairs to be regulated in common and common affairs), but it did not extend to the internal affairs of the two states and these were crucial in the development of nationalism. On the contrary, the two governments produced diametrically opposite internal and nationality policies. Not only did this fact confuse the nationalities, but often produced intervention—not foreseen by the Ausgleich—of one government in the affairs of the other whenever it believed that the internal policies of its partner endangered its own approach to similar problems.

The nationalities policy of the Magyars was not, as it would appear at first sight, based on strength, but on weakness and fear. The strong can be generous and conciliatory; the weak are afraid to make concessions. Magyar nationalities policy after 1867 is the best example of what happens if a minority (as defined in this chapter) acquires most privileges in a state and builds a policy on the assumption that these are endangered by others who would like to share them. Hungary was not only ruled by an ethnic minority with maximum privileges, but all people in that state, including most Magyars, were suffering from the manifestations of micro-minority, a minority within the minority, mentality. Magyar policy can only be explained by this "microminoriterianism." When Tisza the younger, after assuming the prime ministership for the second time, became the greatest champion of the maintenance of Austria-Hungary albeit under increased Magyar influence, he expressed this feeling perfectly. Only within the state structure created by the Ausgleich could a minority maintain its privileges guaranteed to it by this agreement; only in Austria-Hungary could the gentry count on the help of other aristocracies in trying to keep its social position within the Magyar nation; yet it had to extend its influence even into Austria to make certain that no challenge to its position developed "across the border." Of course, neither Tisza nor the other Magyar leaders thought of themselves and what they did in these terms—they were Magyar patriots defending a millenary state—but their behavior can be ascribed either to their micro-minoriterianism or simply to stupidity. They were often extremely intelligent and capable men leaving only one possible explanation of their behavior.

IV

The privileged minority on Cisleithania was strong. Its strength was based on confidence gained from a habit of leadership on the European scene, economic achievements and quasi monopoly, and belief in its ability to manage under all circumstances. Consequently this minority, and within it the leading element, was much more generous than the Magyars were, and concessions were readily offered to the nationalities. The great difficulty Austria's privileged minority faced in communicating with other nationalities was that while it acted for Austria, not a well defined state, it was not Austrian, but German. Pan-Germans and Great-Germans were a small segment of the German population of Austria, but every member of this nationality was consciously German. They acknowledged that they lived in Austria, were citizens of Austria, and subjects of the Emperor of Austria, but their language and culture were German and deeply rooted in German history. It was very difficult for Germans who were proud of being Germans to convince the other nationalities to cease to be Czechs, Poles, Slovenes (living in Austria, citizens of Austria, etc.) and to become Austrians. It was this impossible task that those Germans who believed in the Austrian state tried to accomplish.

These were the circumstances under which the governments' actions produced the development of nationalism described. In my opinion, the governments remain chiefly responsible for this development in spite of these difficulties because I reject the only other alternative which this sketchy description of circumstances might suggest, namely that Austria and after 1867 Austria-Hungary were ungovernable because they lacked *all* attributes of a modern state. They lacked *some* characteristics of the centralized nation state. They could not be governed in accordance with the ideas of the Magyar gentry, the Austrian aristocrats, and some people in court circles, but they could have been ruled following other principles constantly suggested by would be reformers. Those who were the political masters of Austria-Hungary were the creators of the nationalisms of the various people living in that state. These, including the macronationalism whose main feature was hostility to the dual monarchy, finally destroyed the realm of the Habsburgs not because nationalism could not be accommodated within a multinational state, but because those who shaped nationalism in Austria-Hungary did not try to understand it and work with it.

Notes

* - In this essay I refer repeatedly to the subsequent chapters of a volume of which my contribution was to be the first. It was written in the early 1970's. After waiting several years, I inquired about the date of publication and was told that a change in plans made the inclusion of my contribution questionable. I withdrew it and subsequently offered it to another publisher.

1 - Peter F. Sugar, "External and Domestic Roots of Eastern European Nationalism," Peter F. Sugar and Ivo J. Lederer (eds.), *Nationalism in Eastern Europe* (Seattle-London; University of Washington Press, 1969), pp. 3-54.

2 - Hans Kohn, *The Idea of Nationalism* (New York; Macmillan, paperback edition, 1961).

3 - Kohn, *Nationalism*, p. 3.

4 - *Ibid.*, p. 4.

5 - Walter B. Pillsbury, *The Psychology of Nationality and Internationalism* (New York-London; Appleton & Co., 1928), p. 5 quoted by Kohn, *Nationalism*, p. 12.

6 - Kohn, *Nationalism*, p. 18.

7 - See, for example, Hugo Hantsch, *Die Nationalitätenfrage im alten Österreich* (Wien; Herold, 1953), p. 64; Oscar Jászi, *The Dissolution of the Habsburg Monarchy* (Chicago; Chicago University Press, 1929), p. 7; Robert A. Kann, *The Multinational Empire*, 2 vols. (New York; Columbia University Press, 1950), II/p. 293; Arthur J. May, *The Habsburg Monarchy, 1867-1914* (Cambridge: Harvard University Press, 3rd printing, 1965), p. vii; Hugh Seton-Watson, "Übernationale Monarchie und Nationalstaat," Richard G. Plaschka und Karlheinz Mack (eds.), *Die Auflösung des Habsburgerreiches; Zusammenbruch und Neuordnung im Donauraum* (München; Oldenbourg, 1970), p. 368; Erich Zöllner, *Geschichte Österreichs von den Anfängen bis zur Gegenwart* (Wien; Österreichischer Bundesverlag, 1961), p. 431.

8 - The only other truly "common" institution that influenced the life of citizens directly, the army, never touched the lives of women. Men, with the exception of professional soldiers, had only limited contact with the armed forces.

9 - For a good summary of the numerous reform plans see Kann, *Multinational Empire*, II/pp. 3-219.

10 - A good example of the working of the curia system is the Bohemian Diet of 1873. The first curia elected 75, the second 15, the

third 72 and the fourth 79 deputies. In the urban districts an average of 11,666 electors chose one representative, in the rural district 49,081. Electors in the urban districts also differed from one region to another. In Prague, with its mixed German-Czech population, 14,500 inhabitants were entitled to a deputy, but in the purely German Reichenberg (Liberec) slightly more than 8,000 had the same right. Hugo Hantsch, *Die Geschichte Österreichs*, 2 vols., (Wien; Styria, 2nd ed., 1953), II/p. 380.

11 - For the isolation of social classes along national lines see Peter F. Sugar, "The Nature of non-Germanic Societies under Habsburg Rule," *Slavic Review*, XXII/1 (1963), pp. 1-46 and Fran Zwitter, *Les Problèmes nationaux dans la Monarchie des Habsburgs* (Beograd; Comité national yougoslave des sciences historiques, 1960), pp. 19-23.

12 - The chronological breakdown of the following sections is based, with some slight modifications, on the one introduced by Zwitter in *Les Problèmes*.

13 - According to the 1910 Austro-Hungarian census Germans made up 34.79 percent of Austria's population, and the Magyars 47.66 percent of Greater Hungary's (including Croatia-Slavonia). If all Habsburg lands, including Bosnia-Hercegovina, are considered, the total German population amounted to 23.32 and the Magyars to 19.35 percent of the state's inhabitants.

14 - This definition of "minority" was worked out in a seminar at the University of Washington by the doctoral candidates Mrs. Victoria F. Brown, Mr. David Goldfrank, Mr. David Lester and Mrs. Nancy Weil.

15 - To my knowledge, Oscar Jászi was the first scholar to group the nationalities of Austria-Hungary according to the privileges they enjoyed. The grouping presented in the following pages is mine.

16 - Figures rounded out to the nearest thousand, percentages to the nearest hundredth of a percent. Minor groups totalling 1,254,000 people (2.31 percent) in a total population of 49,458,000 (excluding Bosnia-Hercegovina) according to the 1910 census were disregarded.

17 - For this cooperation see Konstanty Grzybowski, *Galicja 1848-1914. Historija ustroju politycznego na tle historii ustroju Austrii* (History of Galician Political Institutions) (Wroclaw; Zaklad Narodowy im Ossolinskich, 1959).

18 - Vasile Curticapeanu, "Intemeierea societătii "Astra" si rolul in cultura poporulul romăn," (The Establishment of the "Astra" Society and its role in the Culture of the Romanian People), *Studii* XIV/6 (1961), pp. 1439-63. A French version of it is "La formation de la société "Astra" et son rôle dans la culture du peuple roumain," *Revue Roumaine d'Histoire*

(1962), pp. 529-46. For more details see: *Die Rumänische Kulturbewegung in der Österreich-Ungarischen Monarchie* (Bucureşti; Ed. Acad., 1966) by the same author.

19- Julius Mésároš, *Matica Slovenská v našich dejinách* (The Matica Slovenska in our History) (Bratislava; Vydavatel'stvo SAV, 1963).

20- Erich Fischer, "The Negotiations for the national Ausgleich in Austria in 1871," *Journal of Central European Affairs*, II/2 (1942), pp. 134-45.

21- *Ost und West* (February 20, 1861) quoted by Angelo Tamborra, "Le compromis Austro-Hongrois de 1867 et l'Italie." Paper presented to the International Congress on the Ausgleich on 29 August, 1967 in Bratislava.

22- Tamborra, quoting from Tkalac, "Coup d'oeil sur la situation intérieure de l'Autriche" paper submitted to Ubaldo Peruzzi.

23- Stanley Z. Pech, "Passive Resistance of the Czechs, 1863-1879," *Slavonic and East European Review*, XXXVI/3 (1958), pp. 434-52.

24- František Bokes, "Mad'arske projevy protimremorandovér, 1861," (Anti-memorandist Magyar statements in 1861) *Historica Slovaka* I/II (1940/41), 278-86; L'udevit Holotik, "Memorandum slovenského národa z roku 1861," (The 1861 Memorandum of the Slovak Nation) *Historicki Časopis*, XI (1963), pp. 3-30; Daniel Rapant, "Viedenské memorandum slovenskéz roku 1861," (The Slovak Memorandum of 1861 in Vienna) (Turčiansky Svätý Martin; Matica Slovenská, 1943).

25- Stanley Z. Pech, "F.L. Rieger; The Road from Liberalism to Conservatism," *Journal of Central European Affairs*, VII/1 (1957), pp. 3-23.

26- Victor Cherestesiu et al, *Din Istoria Transylvaniei*, 2 vols. (Bucureşti; Ed. Acad., 1963, 2nd edition), II. p. 193.

27- For the crucial period of 1860-65 in Transylvania see; Keith Hitchins, "The Romanians of Transylvania and Constitutional Experiments in the Habsburg Monarchy, 1869-1865," *Balkan Studies*, V/1 (1964), pp. 89-109.

28- On the Romanian reaction to the policy change in Vienna see Keith Hitchins, Românii din Transylvania şi compromisul dualist (1865-1869)," *Studdi*, XXI/2 (1968), pp. 289-316 and its English version, "The Romanians of Transylvania and the Ausgleich, 1865-1869," *Revue Roumaine d'Histoire*, VII/2 (1968), pp. 197-232, and Cornelia Bodea and Josif Kovács, "Les Roumaines de la Monarchie des Habsbourg et le compromis de 1867," *Revue Roumaine d'Histoire*, VII/3 (1968), pp. 359-370.

29 - Zöllner, *Geschichte*, p. 419.

30 - The Romanian text was first published on August 27, 1868 in No. 26 of *Federatiunea*. A Hungarian translation is available in Gábor G. Kemény, *Iratok a nemzetiséqi kérdés történetéhez Magyarországon a dualizmus korában* (Documents relating to the nationality question in Hungary in the dualist period), 2 vols., (Budapest; Tankönyvkiadó, 1952-56), I/pp. 83-4. The problem is discussed by Stefan Pascu and Carl Göllner, "Lutte des Roumaines de la Monarchie des Habsbourg contre le Dualisme," *Revue Roumaine d'Histoire*, VII/1 (1968), pp. 39-56.

31 - A comparison of the attitudes of Hungary's minorities can be found in Peter F. Sugar, "The Reaction of the Croats, Romanians and Slovaks to the Ausgleich, 1867-1875," presented at the International Congress on the Ausgleich on August 30, 1867 in Bratislava.

32 - The "Iron Ring" consisted of 78 German, 57 Polish and 54 Czech deputies when Taaffe first organized this coalition. For the story of the "Iron Ring" see William A. Jenks, *Austria under the Iron Ring* (Charlottesville: University of Virginia Press, 1965).

33 - H. Gordon Skilling, "The Politics of the Czech Eighties," Peter Brock and H. Gordon Skilling (eds.), *The Czech Renaissance of the Nineteenth Century* (Toronto; University of Toronto Press, 1970), pp. 254-81.

34 - H. Gordon Skilling, "The Partition of the University of Prague," *Slavonic and East European Review*, XXVII/69 (1949), pp. 430-49.

35 - The tax to be paid to qualify was halved, giving the vote to those paying five Florins in direct taxes.

36 - A good short summary is Helmuth Stradal, "Die Lage der Italiener in der österreichischen Reichshälfte nach dem Ausgleich 1867," presented to the International Congress on the Ausgleich on Sept. 1, 1867 in Bratislava. For more details see Hans Kramer, *Die Italiener unter der österreichisch-ungarischen Monarchie* (Wien; Herold, 1954) and Theodore Veiter, *Die Italiener in der österreichisch-ungarischen Monarchie* (Wien; Verlag für Geschichte und Politik, 1965).

37 - Karel V Kazbunda, "Krise české politiki a videnská o t. zv. punktace roku 1890," (The Czech Political Crisis during the so-called negotiations in Vienna in 1890) *Česki Časopis Historicki*, XL (1934), pp. 80-103, 310-14, 491-528 and XLI (1935), pp. 41-82, 294-320, 514-54.

38 - Jiří Kořalka, "La montée du pangermanisme et l'Autriche-Hongrie," *Historica*, X (1965), pp. 213-53.

39 - Ivan L. Rudnytsky, "The Ukrainians in Galicia under Austrian Rule," *Austrian History Yearbook*, III/2 (1967), pp. 394-429 and Ivan Zeguc, *Die Nationalpolitischen Bestrebungen der Karpatho-Ruthenen, 1849-1918* (Wiesbaden; Harrassowitz, 1965).

40 - Professor Hugo Hantsch, a leading expert on Austrian history, disagrees with this evaluation of Taaffe's achievements. His argument that Taaffe did not create the problems, but was simply unable to master them does not take into account the mistakes which he made. Hantsch, *Geschichte*, II, p. 453.

41 - May. *The Habsburg Monarchy*, 85-6 and R.W. Seton-Watson, *The History of the Roumanians* (Hamden; Archon Books reissue, 1963), p. 403.

42 - Prior to the passing of the Apponyi school laws greatly reducing their numbers, the nationalities had, in 1904, the following elementary schools: Romanians, 2,339; Slovaks, 477; Germans, 305; Serbo-Croats, 154; Ukrainians, 64. *Ungarisches Statistisches Jahr buch*, XII (1904), p. 357. The effectiveness of the school policy introduced by Tisza becomes clear when it is realized that the nationalities, 52.34 percent of the population, controlled less than 21 percent of the elementary schools even before their large scale magyarization.

43 - A good example of what magyarization meant is supplied by Daniel Rapant, *K pociatkom mad'arizacie*, II, (About the Beginnings of Magyarization) (Bratislava; Univerzitat-Filozofická fakulteta, 1927).

44 - Quoted by Seton-Watson, *Roumanians*, p. 400.

45 - L'udevit Holotik, "Slovak Politics in the 19th Century," *Studia Historica Slovaca*, V (1967), pp. 35-55. Quotation from p. 38.

46 - Constantin Nuțu, "Partidul National Român din Transylvania și problema unirii," (The Romanian National Party of Transylvania and the Problem of Unification) *Studii*, XXI/6 (1968), pp. 1009-38.

47 - Matei Ionescu, "Monumente din lupta iredentei romăne transilvane in anii 1884-1887," (Memorial from the irredentist Struggle of the Transylvanian Romanians in the year 1884-1887), *Studii*, XX/3 (1967), pp. 511-22.

48 - Th. Tripcea, "Din memoriile și corespondenta lui Traian Doda," (About the Memoirs and Correspondence of Traian Doda), *Studii*, XV/4 (1962), p. 927-9.

49 - Berthold Sutter, *Die Badenische Sprachenverordnungen von 1897* (Graz; Böhlau, 1960).

50 - Zöllner, *Geschichte*, p. 431.

IV

51 - Germans, 34,78 percent of Austria's population, received 43 percent of the seats in parliament. Roughly the same advantages were given to the Italians in Dalmatia, the Poles in Galicia and the Romanians in Bukovina. Zöllner, *Geschichte*, p. 434. For a complete survey of the electoral reform see William A. Jenks, *The Austrian Electoral Reform of 1907* (New York; Columbia University Press, 1950).

52 - Hans Glassl. *Der Mährische Ausgleich* (München; Fides, 1950).

53 - On this incident and the growing Romanian-Slovak cooperation see Stefan Pascu, "Relations roumano-slovaque à la dernière due XIXe siècle," *Revue Roumaine d'Histoire*, (1968), pp. 385-96.

54 - Salamon Wank, "Foreign Policy and the Nationality Problem in Austria-Hungary, 1867-1914," *Austrian History Yearbook*, III/3 (1967), pp. 37-56.

55 - R.W. Seton-Watson, *A History of the Czechs and Slovaks* (Hamden; Archon Books reissue, 1965), p. 272.

56 - Jászi, *The Dissolution*, p. 321.

57 - Mirjana Gross, "Geneza Frankova stranke," (The Beginnings of the Frank Faction), *Historijski Zbornik*, XVII (1964), pp. 1-83.

58 - Mirjana Gross, *Vladavina Hrvatsko-srpske koalicije, 1906-7* (The Rule of the Croato-Serb Coalition, 1906-7) (Beograd; Kultura, 1960).

59 - Hantsch, *Geschichte*, II, p. 488.

60 - *Ibid.*, p. 489.

61 - *Ibid.*, p. 522.

62 - May, *The Habsburg Monarchy*, p. 483.

63 - Excerpts from Tisza's speech of July 12, 1910 are given in R.W. Seton-Watson, *Roumanians*, p. 428.

V

AUSTRIA–HUNGARY AND THE BALKAN CRISIS: AN INGENIOUS IMPROVISATION

Although the recurrent crises in the Balkans during the nineteenth century evoked great concern in the foreign ministries of the European powers, historians, except those of the Balkan states, have paid surprisingly little attention to them. The crisis of 1875–78, ending with the Congress of Berlin, June 13–July 13, 1878, is the exception. The literature dealing with it is voluminous,[1] and even textbooks discuss it.[2] It is, therefore, superfluous to recount the series of events that began at the end of 1874 with disturbances in Hercegovina and ended with the signing of the Berlin Protocol.[3] During these years the position of Austria–Hungary changed repeatedly in response to the constantly changing situations in the Balkans and on the international diplomatic scene. If the Ballhausplatz emerged from the Congress of Berlin as one of the victors (Great Britain being the other), it owed its success to the clever improvisation of the imperial and royal minister of foreign affairs, Count Gyula Andrássy.[4] This paper will explore the reasons for the various shifts in Austro–Hungarian attitudes in searching for a solution for the Balkan crisis of 1875–78.

Writing about another Balkan crisis, Roger V. Paxton has remarked,

> Diplomatic histories of "Great Powers" often reveal that... [they] fail to design foreign policies which can easily adjust to substantive changes: ...Instead of devising several contingency strategies... these governments frequently vacillate. ...This decision-making process becomes complicated when the problem under consideration is entangled in a web of revolutions, wars and diplomatic intrigues.[5]

The crisis of 1875–78 had all these elements — revolutions, wars, and diplomatic intrigues — and the Great Power to which these pages are devoted, Austria–Hungary, certainly vacillated. While the lack of a clear foreign-policy line and the absence of contingency plans are in most cases signs of poor diplomacy, in the case of Austria–Hungary they simply reflected the com-

V
THE BALKAN CRISIS

plicated and confusing domestic situation, which made a clear-cut foreign policy practically impossible. This situation must be understood by anyone who attempts to analyze the various diplomatic positions taken by Austria—Hungary during the years under consideration.

After the *Ausgleich* of 1867 that created Austria—Hungary, this new empire had three ministries: an Austrian ministry responsible to the Austrian parliament, a Hungarian ministry responsible to the Hungarian parliament, and a common ministry with three portfolios responsible to the emperor-king. The common ministries of foreign affairs, national defense, and finance could not function without the budgets annually allotted to them by the two parliaments, to which they owed only the nominal duty of reporting through the peculiar institution of the delegations.[6] That the two parliaments wanted the common ministers to act in conformity with their wishes goes without saying. The Hungarian position was stronger in this respect than the Austrian because the Hungarian prime minister had the right to be consulted on foreign affairs while the Austrian did not. Furthermore, the position of the Hungarian prime minister, who always dealt with a parliament in which he had a large majority backing him and practically no minority representation, was much stronger than that of his Austrian colleague, who more often than not was the leader of a coalition government facing a lower house in which minorities, especially Czechs and Poles, held numerous seats.

While it is hard to identify a clearly defined Austrian approach to foreign affairs in the second half of the 1870s, the Austrian government had to pay close attention to public opinion, at least as it was expressed by minority deputies, all of whom were pro-Slav and, with the exception of the Poles, often pro-Russian. Hungarian views were much clearer although by no means without contradiction. Andrássy and his colleagues were liberal nationalists and therefore sympathized with the national liberation movements in the Balkans. This attitude contradicted two other considerations. The more important was fear of Russia, which the Hungarians considered the greatest danger to their country's future because of its expansionism and its Pan-Slavism. They tended to see Russia's sinister maneuvering behind most manifestations of Slavic nationalism. Russia was the enemy and had to be thwarted, while other Slavs were to be handled accordingly. The second consideration was limited to the Balkans, where the Hungarians were interested in maintaining the status quo. They did not see any danger to themselves in the weak Ottoman Empire, which, if it disappeared, would, in their view, be replaced by the Russians or Russian-dominated states. On the contrary, they regarded it as extremely useful. Andrássy summarized this attitude concisely at the Crown Council of January 29, 1875: "Turkey is of almost providential usefulness for Austria. Her existence is in our best-understood interest. She maintains the status quo of the small states and denies, to our advantage, their aspirations. If Turkey did not exist this troublesome task would become ours."[7] The resulting Hungarian approach to the Balkans was, therefore, one which relied on improvisation depending on Balkan developments and the role Russia played in them. The continued existence of the Ottoman Empire, the bulwark against Russian expansion, had to be supported as long as possible. If the Ottoman Empire were to dissolve, Austria—Hungary would have to gain the loyalty of the Balkan people, detaching them from Russia and attaching them to herself.[8] This was not only in her own but in Europe's interest.[9] Only if the disintegration of the Ottoman Empire and the expansion of the Balkan states created the threat of Russian domination of the Balkans would Austria—Hungary have to act to secure for herself the territories on which her safety depended. In 1875 this alternative appeared to be developing: Andrássy expressed his fears at the already mentioned Crown Council when he argued for a strong policy: "Should Serbia and Montenegro acquire Bosnia and Hercegovina, creating a new state complex that we do not or cannot oppose, then we would be relinquishing our own existence and assuming the role of 'the sick man.' "[10]

Whatever Andrássy's views, and however much they were in accord with Hungarian wishes, he had to fit them into a foreign policy that took into account the opinions of the emperor-king and the military. These differed sharply from his own. Court circles were conservative, looked at foreign affairs as a prerogative of the crown, and even after 1870 were expansionist, although they recognized the altered European situation and were ready to change tactics. In contradiction to Andrássy's views, the court preferred agreement with Russia, possibly even an alliance, and considered partitioning the Balkans with the great Eastern power.[11] The military circles, dominated by Archduke Albert, the ruler's uncle, and Feldmarshalleutenant Beck, were also conservative, pro-Russian forces influencing foreign policy.[12] The military's influence was in part the result of the realization that *Realpolitik* was the only method possible in an age dominated by Bismarck. Francis Joseph himself made this clear when he informed those present at the Crown Council of February 17, 1872, that when "Andrássy accepted his portfolio he agreed to the principle that the conduct of foreign affairs must be in harmony with military interests."[13] The foreign minister made this even clearer on the same occasion by explaining that "the result of the last war is that might comes before right; consequently, no state can be certain today to maintain its rightful position unless it makes it a basic principle in all its calculations that it has to be capable of securing with arms the goals it strives to achieve by peaceful means."[14]

While *Realpolitik* gave the army a say in foreign affairs, the military had its own interests that it wanted pursued, especially in the Balkans. After the

V
69 THE BALKAN CRISIS

Napoleonic wars the Habsburgs had acquired Dalmatia, a thin strip of land on the eastern shore of the Adriatic. In spite of its great strategic value, this new province was militarily indefensible because of its location and shape. From the military's point of view, Dalmatia had to be not only retained but also secured by acquiring a supporting landmass. Two years before his death, Field Marshal Joseph Radetzky had proposed the occupation of Bosnia—Hercegovina. Ten years later, Admiral Baron Wilhelm Tegetthoff had made the same request, and Beck reiterated it repeatedly between 1869 and 1875.[15] After 1867 this demand was further complicated by a basic constitutional question: if and when Bosnia—Hercegovina was annexed, who would conduct the annexation? The Dual Monarchy consisted of two equal states each of which could gain territory and population by annexing a new region, thus upsetting the balance between them. Neither half was willing to let the other grow without compensation, while at the same time both were loath to accept additional Slavs. Before 1875 this problem was not acute. Yet, whatever the situation, the army was never in a position to pursue its own goals or give the diplomats the backing that Andrássy considered necessary.

Whereas the armed forces had been fully reorganized by 1875, they were still extremely weak in comparison with other forces. Austria—Hungary, the second largest state in Europe, was economically a second-rate power. Her agricultural production was excellent, but only 15 percent of her population worked in industry, and consequently her iron and steel production, so crucial for the military, was even lower than that of Belgium. Road and railroad networks were inadequate.[16] Furthermore,

> the parliamentary bodies... controlled the military expenditure of the Monarchy. The eternal parsimony of the Austrian and Hungarian governments and their parliaments was an important cause of the weakness of the military forces. ...From 1890 until 1912 the Monarchy fell steadily behind the other Great Powers in military potential. By 1913 Franz Joseph's subjects were spending more than three times as much money on beer, wine and tobacco than on the entire armed forces of the Dual Monarchy.[17]

The stinginess of the legislatures predated the period of this statement. Dominated by antimilitaristic liberals in the years under consideration, they never gave the military the financial means it needed. After the beginning of the economic recession in 1873 the armed forces fared very badly. Some figures illustrate this weakness (table 1).

The cumulative effect of this budgetary policy emerges clearly from figures that compare total military expenditures between 1867 and 1892 as calculated by the Austro—Hungarian chief of staff's office. The expenditures are given in French francs (no figures for Great Britain are given):[18] France,

23,154,480,000; Russia, 22,426,371,000; Germany, 14,208,000,000; Italy, 6,822,411,000; Austria–Hungary, 7,004,511,000. No wonder, then, that by 1875 "some observers doubted that Austria–Hungary could sustain a major war without foreign subsidy" and that in 1877 the monarchy negotiated for such help with Britain.[19] Military men not only were conscious of the disparity in power between their country and Russia but also realized that the various political orientations of the different ethnic groups living in Austria–Hungary deprived them of issues behind which the population could be united enough to support a war. Even Archduke Albert admitted that public opinion was against war and that the army could consider only defensive action.[20]

Finally, all those involved in framing Austria–Hungary's foreign policy were bound, at least to some extent, by the provisions of the Three Emperors' League in force since the spring of 1873, which stipulated that the rulers of Germany, Russia, and Austria–Hungary must consult one another on issues of common interest. Vague as this agreement was, it was taken seriously and produced, between 1875 and 1878, a voluminous correspondence between Francis Joseph and Tsar Alexander II. The problem was that in the Balkans the interests of these two rulers were not common but contradictory.

When in 1875 a series of events began to unfold in the Balkans involving "revolutions, wars, and diplomatic intrigues," those involved in directing Austro–Hungarian foreign policy had to reconcile their wish for maintenance of the status quo in the Balkans and the continued existence of the Ottoman Empire with the desirability for internal politics of a benevolent attitude toward the Balkan Christians and their cause. In deference to the sympathies of the large Slavic population of their own state, they had to reconcile their determination not to permit the creation of a major Slavic state south of the Danube–Sava line that might act as a magnet for conationals living north of it with a friendly attitude toward the cause of the revolutionaries. They had to cooperate with Russia because the weakness of the military did not permit opposing her, yet they had to make certain that the tsarist empire did not achieve its goals in southeastern Europe. In spite of constitutional difficulties and their abhorrence of including more Slavs in Austria–Hungary, they had to make plans for intervention and even territorial acquisitions should this be the only alternative to Russian domination of the Balkans. Practically any course of action open to the Ballhausplatz was certain to alienate important segments of public opinion and require funds that the parliaments, reacting to public opinion, were unlikely to make available. Under these circumstances it was impossible to formulate a clear policy line. It is not surprising that the first decision taken was simply to wait and see how events unfolded. After all, uprisings against Ottoman rule were nothing new in the

V
THE BALKAN CRISIS

Balkans, had not involved the Great Powers directly since the end of the revolution in Bucharest in 1848, and usually ended with the Ottomans reestablishing order. The last uprising in Hercegovina, in 1858–62, had been put down by fifty thousand Ottoman soldiers. Yet this time the situation was different. Serbia and Montenegro were deeply interested, and the Ottoman government appeared to be neglecting its duty as pacifier of a region that bordered on Dalmatia.[21] Therefore, Austria–Hungary had to attempt to produce by diplomatic means some solution that would calm the insurgents, be acceptable to the Ottomans, Serbs, and Montenegrins, and make the Dual Monarchy appear a friend of the Slavs. Any diplomatic campaign with these goals in mind could succeed only if it involved Russia.

The interests and prestige of both states were involved. Both realized that if a peaceful solution were not found they would face greater difficulties. Therefore, they agreed to put pressure on the Ottomans and force them to institute reforms that would satisfy the insurgents and end the revolt. They approached the Porte jointly with this suggestion, but what they proposed, in rather vague terms, was rejected by the revolutionaries as not going far enough and by the Ottoman government as excessive.[22] Andrássy's hopes of maintaining the political status quo in the Balkans while gaining the gratitude of its Christian inhabitants had been disappointed. In August of 1875, Prince Aleksandr Gorchakov submitted a proposal to Vienna suggesting that the two powers demand that the Ottoman Empire give Bosnia and Hercegovina autonomous regimes similar to that enjoyed by Romania.[23] Prior to Serbia's and Montenegro's declaration of war and the Bulgarian uprising this proposal made some sense, but in Andrássy's opinion it showed clearly that Russia was pursuing her own goals and totally disregarding the interests of the Dual Monarchy. He described Gorchakov's plan as "purest nonsense," pointing out that "autonomy might be practicable for an entirely Christian region, such as Bulgaria; but such a weak system of government would never be able to maintain order in Bosnia, with its warring Moslem, Catholic, and Orthodox populations."[24] The result could only be annexation by Serbia and/or Montenegro, something that was totally unacceptable to Austria–Hungary. Anything was better than this solution, even the incorporation of these provinces into his own country. Only the Ottomans or the Austro–Hungarians could be masters of these provinces. In 1875 Andrássy wrote in an aide-mémoire: "It is not permissible to push Turkey out of the two provinces. On the contrary, she must be supported as long as possible with advice and by urging reforms on her. Nevertheless, at a given moment we must step into her place whenever she proves incapable of protecting the provinces."[25]

Since Gorchakov's proposal excluded both the Ottoman Empire and the Habsburg Monarchy from Bosnia–Hercegovina, Andrássy was forced to make counterproposals. His first move was unrealistic. He still clung to the illusion that the status quo in the Balkans could be maintained, thus sparing Austria–Hungary the need to give preference to some of her contradictory aims over the others. He hoped that if Russo–Austro–Hungarian pressure on the Porte could be increased by associating the other Great Powers with it, the Ottomans would yield. This is what he proposed to the various governments of Europe in the so-called Andrássy Note of December 30, 1875. This approach had no chance of success. No action was taken either by the two states most closely interested in Balkan development or by the other powers.

Intervention became much more likely after the Bulgarian uprising of April 1876, which finally produced Ottoman intervention and the "Bulgarian Horrors" that shocked European public opinion. On May 12, 1876, Andrássy, Gorchakov, and Bismarck met in Berlin. The Russian chancellor submitted a plan that basically consisted of military intervention in Bosnia–Hercegovina and a demand for a congress of the Great Powers to resolve the Eastern Question. To the Austro–Hungarian minister this solution was totally unacceptable. Military intervention on the part of his country without lengthy preparation of various kinds was impossible, whereas Russian intervention was anathema. A conference of the Great Powers, also calling for careful and lengthy preparation, might possibly bring results favorable to the Balkan Christians, but in this case they would owe gratitude to all those who attended it, thus diminishing the influence of Austria–Hungary in southeastern Europe.

What exactly happened in Berlin on that day is not clear. Obviously very tense negotiations took place that ended in the total retreat of the Russians.[26] Late in the evening the Berlin Memorandum was issued. A victory for Andrássy, the document called for a return to his policy of pressure on the Ottoman Empire, which was now requested to grant the various insurgents a two-month armistice and to use this time period for reforms and pacification. To show that the powers meant business, Andrássy agreed to Gorchakov's demand to send warships to the straits, but in exchange Gorchakov agreed to drop the plan for a Great Power conference. This was the last time that Andrássy was able to avoid painful decisions. Once the Bulgarians had joined the Hercegovinians and Bosnians in revolt and the Ottoman army had intervened, the chances of a peaceful settlement were practically nonexistent and public opinion in Serbia and Montenegro made intervention by these two states a foregone conclusion.

Six weeks after the Berlin meeting, Serbia declared war on the Ottoman Empire, and Montenegro followed two weeks later. The war created a new situation, and the two powers most closely involved had to ask themselves a simple question: What position do we take if the war is won by the Ottomans, and how do we deal with the small states should they emerge

V

THE BALKAN CRISIS

victorious? It was obvious that should they be unable to find an answer to this question satisfying to both of them a very serious crisis would emerge. This was the situation for which the Three Emperors' League had been created.

Russia and Austria–Hungary acted promptly. Within a week of Montenegro's declaration of war, Francis Joseph, Alexander II, and their major policy makers got together at Reichstadt (today Zákupy) in Bohemia. The result of these talks, known as the Reichstadt Agreement, was simply a gentlemen's agreement between rulers in keeping with the provisions of the Three Emperors' League. The document to which historians refer emerged as the *Résumé des pourparlers secrets de Reichstadt du 8 juillet 1876*, dictated by Andrássy on that day to the Russian ambassador in Vienna.[27] It was, as its title indicates, a secret agreement.[28]

In the event of an Ottoman victory, according to the *Résumé,* the two powers were to make certain that Christians under Ottoman rule were not harmed. Serbia and Montenegro were to retain their present borders, and no Ottoman troops were to be reintroduced into Serbia. Serbia was not to be allowed to declare her full independence, although Montenegro was to be recognized as a sovereign state. The Porte was to be asked to introduce the reforms in Bosnia–Hercegovina that her inhabitants had demanded when they revolted.

At first sight this solution appears to be in line with the policy pursued up to then by the Ballhausplatz: no military intervention and the reestablishment of the status quo ante. It is intriguing to speculate what prompted the Russians to retreat from their position as rapidly as they did in Berlin in May and to accept Andrássy's line in July, but this question would lead too far away from the topic of this paper. Actually, the Russians gained quite a lot by this agreement. Montenegro, then their favorite, was to gain full independence in spite of her defeat, Serbia was to owe her continuing existence at least in part to Russia, and in the arrangements that were to protect the Balkan Christians (Bulgaria, Rumelia, and Bosnia–Hercegovina) Russia was to play a decisive role. These developments certainly did not please those in Vienna, Andrássy included, whose primary goal was to keep the Russians away from the Balkans. Concessions were made by both sides in order to retain the chance of cooperation and to exclude the other powers from a region they considered in their sphere of influence.

It was much more difficult to reach an agreement on what to do in the event of an Ottoman defeat. At Reichstadt certain basic lines of action were outlined, but the need for further consultations was recognized. The two states agreed that for the security of Dalmatia the region between Dalmatia and Croatia (basically Bosnia) must be kept out of Serbian hands. Yet, the victors could not be expected to be satisfied with nothing, and should they be forced to return home empty-handed they would blame Russia and Austria—Hungary. This was something both powers wanted to avoid. In the case of the Dual Monarchy the reaction of its Slavic population would also have created serious internal problems. Therefore, Serbia was to receive some territory in Bosnia and the Sanjak of Novi Pazar, while Montenegro was to get some Hercegovinian territory and a port on the Adriatic. "The remaining territory of Bosnia and Hercegovina can be annexed by Austria—Hungary," stated the *Résumé*. The borders dividing the two provinces were not defined. Russia was to regain Bessarabia (lost in 1856) and enough territory in Asia — once again without defined borders — to equal her partner's territorial gains. Greece was to receive Thessaly and Crete, while Albania, Bulgaria, and Rumelia were to gain autonomy. The borders of these states also remained unclear. No major state was to be created in the Balkans. Should the Ottoman Empire collapse completely, Constantinople and some territory around it were to be declared a free city.29

Andrássy clearly would have had to abandon, in the event of an Ottoman defeat, his favorite solution, but the outcome would still have been acceptable. Montenegro and Serbia would still have owed some of their gains in part to Austria—Hungary's intervention; while the Dual Monarchy would have been forced to face the constitutional problem of annexation and the unwanted increase of her Slavic population, this action could have been sold to the governments and parliaments as the lesser of two evils, since the creation of a major Slavic state on the empire's southern borders was ruled out; Russia would have been excluded at least from the western Balkans; the breakup of the Three Emperors' League and military intervention by Russia would have been avoided; and Andrássy could have hoped to be able to match Russian influence in the newly autonomous states. This was a new policy, dictated by events over which Austria—Hungary had no control, and it was the first of many improvisations.

The Ottoman armies rather easily defeated the Serbs and Montenegrins, who were forced on October 31, 1876, to ask for an armistice. The victors refused to settle the war on the conditions stipulated by the Reichstadt Agreement and granted the armistice only after they had received an ultimatum from Russia. The possibility of an Ottoman—Russian war alarmed Britain. On her initiative, the ambassadors of the Great Powers prepared new peace proposals at the Constantinople Conference. These demanded even more from the Ottomans than had Russia and Austria—Hungary at Reichstadt. The Ottomans responded with a surprise: they transformed the empire into a constitutional monarchy, submitted the powers' proposals to an ad hoc conference of Muslim and Christian notables, and on their recommendation rejected the European demands.

It was obvious that Russia, having delivered an ultimatum to the Ottomans, would have to act. Austria–Hungary was not unprepared. Already during the summer of 1875, as soon as Serbia had declared war, Francis Joseph had instructed the general commanding in Croatia, Baron Anton Mollinary, to prepare plans for intervention in Bosnia–Hercegovina.[30] The army was, therefore, ready for at least limited action. Even before the Constantinople Conference broke up, Andrássy, predicting Russian military intervention, sent an aide-mémoire to his ambassador in St. Petersburg explaining that Austria–Hungary could not permit Russian troops to enter Serbia or any region in the western Balkans because

> when Russia begins to fight Turkey and to lead the forces of these countries [Serbia and Montenegro] the struggle acquires a completely different complexion. Cooperation with Serbia and Montenegro will transform a European action into a Slavic movement, the Christian-humanitarian approach will change into a one-sided Orthodox one, and the war will take on the features of a revolution. ...If Russian action brings under one roof all the, until now, isolated Slavic aspirations and thus turns into a propaganda campaign addressed to all Orthodox Slavs, then public opinion among our most important people, the Germans and Hungarians, will judge the existence of the Monarchy endangered by Russian action and will not permit the governments to remain passive observers.[31]

It would appear from this statement that Andrássy, seeing in Russia the greatest danger to his country, was ready to move against her under certain circumstances. While the general staff prepared contingency plans for a campaign against Russia in 1876, Archduke Albert and Beck made it clear that such a war would be too expensive for Austria–Hungary, would drag on forever, and could not be won; it was simply out of the question.[32] Andrássy's choices were limited by the position taken by the military leaders. Fortunately, the Russians were also eager to avoid a confrontation, leaving the door open for further negotiations and improvisations.

The Russians first approached Vienna with a plan that amounted to the virtual partition of the Balkans between the two states. "This proposal conformed with certain traditions of Austrian and Russian foreign policy. There were several individuals in the imperial capital who would have accepted it gladly, but Andrássy rejected it."[33] After receiving the Ballhausplatz's answer the Russians tried without success to get assurances from Germany that in the event of a war between two emperors in the Balkans, the third would remain neutral.[34] Andrássy too turned to Bismarck, who told him that balance-of-power considerations and the Polish situation would leave Germany no choice but to come to the aid of the apparent loser.[35] Under these circumstances Vienna and St. Petersburg had to get together and hold the additional consultations indicated by the Reichstadt Agreement.

Negotiations conducted by Andrássy and Novikov produced the Budapest Convention.³⁶ When the first, military part of the convention was signed the Constantinople Conference was still sitting, but the Russians were already thinking of war and wanted to secure Austria–Hungary's neutrality. Andrássy was convinced that Russia would take military action, and he knew that neither the military nor public opinion would permit the use of Austro–Hungarian military forces; events in the eastern Balkans, where the hostilities would occur, were too far from the monarchy's borders to permit calling military intervention there a "defensive war." He had to retreat to the minimal position of keeping Russia away from Serbia and Montenegro. He was, in fact, in a very weak bargaining position. Should St. Petersburg have gone to war, even without an agreement with Vienna, he could not have done anything to prevent it. Fortunately for him, the Russians were eager to secure their flanks before starting hostilities. The military part of the convention was the result of these mutual desiderata. It stipulated that in case of a Russo–Ottoman war, Serbia, Montenegro, and the Sanjak of Novi Pazar would be considered neutral territory by the Russians, who would not send troops into them. In exchange, Austria–Hungary promised to remain neutral and to prevent diplomatic intervention by the concert of the Great Powers. In the event of a Russian victory, Bulgaria was to receive practically full autonomy. Bosnia–Hercegovina might either receive limited autonomy or fall to Austria–Hungary in accordance with the Reichstadt Agreement; this question was left open for further negotiations.³⁷ Tsar Alexander II was at first outraged, saying "all these conditions are unacceptable, and I cannot understand how Novikov could have agreed to them," but finally even he accepted them.³⁸

The additional convention is of greater interest not only because it is much more specific but also because it was open to contradictory interpretations that soon became a bone of contention. While Gorchakov excluded from this document any consideration of possible territorial gains by Russia in Asia, his country's right to annex Bessarabia in accordance with the Reichstadt Agreement was reiterated. Austria–Hungary received the right to annex Bosnia–Hercegovina, and Serbia and Montenegro were to gain additional territory in the Lim region and the Sanjak of Novi Pazar, with Montenegro also receiving the port of Bar (Antivari) on the Adriatic. Andrássy clearly made the agreement concerning Serbia and Montenegro reluctantly. By dividing the territories in question the two states would acquire a common border, and merger at a later date could create a "major Slavic state" on Austria–Hungary's southern border. To prevent this from happening, Austria–Hungary reserved to herself the right to take special measures in the Sanjak to safeguard her commercial interests in the Balkans. Crucial for Andrássy, and the source of future disagreements, was the third paragraph of the additional convention, which stated "that in case of either a territorial reorganization or the dissolution of the Ottoman Empire the establishment of a large, compact Slavic state is forbidden; in exchange Bulgaria, Albania, and what is left of Rumelia [basically present-day Macedonia] could become independent states."[39] Having the creation of a major Slavic state excluded from the possibilities and instead establishing three relatively small ones were critical for Andrássy. The problem this paragraph created stemmed from the possible dissolution of the Ottoman Empire and was eventually to become important in Austro–Hungarian–Russian relations, as will be shown below.

The Budapest Convention, concluded under the shadow of an approaching war, represented a serious retreat by Andrássy on several fronts and the abandonment of considerations previously presumed to be important. The idea of securing Serbia's friendship had been given up, and, consequently, the danger of creating serious opposition among the monarchy's Slavs had increased. The annexation of Bosnia–Hercegovina raised military and financial questions that required answers from the army and the two parliaments and presented the first serious constitutional complications since 1867. The liberal approach to nationalism was forgotten. Andrássy had fallen back on the cornerstone of his foreign policy, anti-Russianism, and even in this respect he had had to make concessions that only two or three years earlier he would have rejected out of hand. What he secured was a Russian-free western Balkans and a southeastern Europe in which no large state took the place of the Ottoman Empire, whose support he also had to jettison. Under these circumstances, it is hard to speak of a foreign policy; it makes more sense to see in Austria–Hungary's position a defensive stand dictated by circumstances. Diószegi points out, correctly, that Austria–Hungary took a grave risk in signing the Budapest Convention. If the Dual Monarchy could not prevent Russian military action prior to the outbreak of the war, what measures could she take against a victorious Russian army stationed in the Balkans should St. Petersburg, under the influence of victory, decide to disregard this agreement and reorganize the peninsula in accordance with its own wishes?[40] It was only about a year before Andrássy had to find an answer to this question.

On April 24, 1877, Russia declared war on the Ottoman Empire, and her armies began to move south through Romania, with which she had concluded an agreement making this possible. On May 11 Bucharest also declared war on the Ottoman Empire.[41] At first the hostilities went as expected. On June 26–27 the Russian–Romanian forces crossed the Danube, and by July 19 they had managed to cross the Shipka Pass, reaching the valley of the Tundzha River. One more mountain range had to be crossed before the advancing forces reached the Maritsa River basin, an easy highway to Edirne (Adrianople) and Constantinople. The fortifications around Plevna proved to be a serious obstacle, and the advance was halted there later in July. This somewhat calmed Europe's fears,[42] and it also cooled Russian enthusiasm. "On 26 July the tsar assured Franz Joseph that he had no intention of permanently occupying Bulgaria, or of introducing any 'democratic' elements there; that the Powers could assert their interests in the final peace settlement, and that Russia, for her part, would hold scrupulously to the Reichstadt agreement."[43] This was reassuring, and Andrássy played a very cautious game. When Great Britain suggested a military alliance, the Ballhausplatz refused it and confined itself to agreeing with the Foreign Office only on the limits of Russian territorial gains.[44]

The situation changed drastically when, on December 10, 1877, Plevna fell. This victory decided the war, and the Russian forces advanced rapidly to the outskirts of Constantinople, halting only at San Stefano (Yesilköy). Beginning in the middle of December, several notes were exchanged between Francis Joseph and Tsar Alexander II and their leading ministers. What emerged clearly from this exchange of ideas was that the positions of the two powers now diverged drastically. According to the Russians, the Ottoman Empire was in dissolution, creating an altogether new situation that made previous agreements obsolete. This was St. Petersburg's interpretation of the third paragraph of the additional convention. Andrássy's view was completely different. He did not recognize a lost war as a cause for dissolution and had for years opposed accelerating the process of dissolution of the Ottoman Empire by outside intervention.[45] Dissolution, according to him, had to be the result of a long process in which "internal gestation" brought about a gradual disintegration.[46] He once expressed himself on this subject humorously but clearly when he stated that "the situation with it [dissolution] is the same as it is with becoming bald. When does the process begin and when does it end?"[47] The new Russian position, which, among other provisions, ceded parts of Bosnia–Hercegovina to Serbia and Montenegro, created the major Slavic state of Bulgaria, in which Russian troops were to remain for two years, and gave Russia practically a free hand in Asia, was totally unacceptable to the Austro–Hungarian minister. Andrássy did not object to the creation of a Bulgarian state, because "Russia, once she has accomplished her mission, can easily leave Bulgaria again without endangering her interests. This country possesses all the prerequisites for an independent existence. After her reorganization she will remain Bulgaria."[48] What Andrássy had in mind was that while Russia had a legitimate interest in Bulgaria and was the power that could help her, Bulgaria was strong enough to be truly independent. What he objected to was only Bulgaria's proposed borders and the length of the Russian occupation. Russia was clearly violating the Reichstadt and Budapest agreements. Gorchakov admitted this but explained that *force majeure* made it inevitable.[49] In spite of numerous

V

THE BALKAN CRISIS

Austro–Hungarian protests, Russia did not change her position; her single-handed reorganization of the Balkans was the basis of the preliminary Peace of Edirne of January 31, 1878, mainly the work of Count Nikolay Ignatyev.[50]

From the Austro–Hungarian point of view, the worst of all possibilities had to be considered. Cooperation with Russia had become impossible; Turkey might, indeed, withdraw from Europe; Serbia and Montenegro would owe all their gratitude to Russia, whose influence in the western Balkans would become supreme; and a major Slavic state, occupied by Russian troops, was emerging in the eastern and central Balkans.

Yet, Andrássy's position was not hopeless. Russia's behavior had seriously alarmed Britain and violated the Paris Treaty of 1856. He could now return to Gorchakov's idea, which he had rejected only a little time earlier, of a conference of the Great Powers. Bismarck was cool, in February 1878 still recommending direct Austro–Hungarian–Russian negotiations. Great Britain, on the other hand, now became very active. Russia held back, waiting to see how the European situation developed. It was encouraged by Bismarck's position but leery of Britain. Andrássy obtained assurances from London that in the event of common action by the two states Austria–Hungary would receive a subsidy making mobilization possible. He was no longer bound by the Three Emperors' League and hoped that under the circumstances the various forces influencing foreign policy would unite behind a clear plan of action.

The British not only offered military subsidies to the Dual Monarchy, but, on February 15, 1878, ordered their fleet to cross the Dardanelles and anchor at Constantinople. London was ready to go to war if Austria–Hungary joined her. The crucial decision was made in Vienna on February 24, 1878. Under the emperor's presidency, the ministers of both governments and the military leaders discussed the monarchy's next move. At this meeting Andrássy recommended war with Russia in alliance with Britain and demanded first 600, then 200 million gulden in credit for this purpose. He pointed out that this was possibly the last chance for Austria–Hungary to settle her Slavic problem with the help of Europe. His position was somewhat weakened by Bismarck's "honest broker" speech (made on February 19 in the hope of calming the British), which opened the door to a possible last effort to find a peaceful solution. If Andrássy really wanted war, he was disappointed. Only the Hungarian prime minister, Kálmán Tisza, backed his proposal.[51] The Austrian representatives made it clear that among the Slavs only the Poles would welcome a war with Russia and that the Germans of Austria were anything but enthusiastic. Finally, the army-court circles led by Archduke Albert continued to cling to their conservative and pro-Russian views. Thus "the absence of a unified foreign policy paralyzed the multinational Monarchy in spite of the favorable turns in the international situation. Although English financial backing was available, no Austro—Hungarian mobilization occurred. Because of Austro—Hungarian passivity the guns of the British ships also remained silent."[52] All that Andrássy salvaged from this meeting was the permission to ask the two parliaments for a credit of 60 million gulden to strengthen the forces on the southern border. When this issue was debated in the legislatures, he made it clear that the money would not be used to enter Bosnia—Hercegovina. That Bosnia—Hercegovina was later occupied became one of the reasons for Andrássy's fall.[53]

While the Russians did not know what had happened in Vienna on February 24, they saw clearly that Austria—Hungary was not mobilizing and that the British fleet remained inactive. Encouraged, they dictated the Peace of San Stefano to the Ottomans on March 3, 1878. Kars and Batum, in Asia, became Russian, as did Bessarabia; Romania, Montenegro, and Serbia became fully independent states; and a Greater Bulgaria, including Rumelia, with nearly 5 million inhabitants came into being. This state cut off Bosnia—Hercegovina and Albania from what remained of European Turkey. Fortunately for the Ottomans, not only Austria—Hungary but Britain found this solution unacceptable. From March to June the various European governments prepared themselves for the Congress of Berlin. The story of this congress is, as I have said, too well known to demand repetition. Austria—Hungary emerged from this meeting very well. Greater Bulgaria was dismantled and the major Slavic Orthodox state in the Balkans disappeared; Serbia and Montenegro were denied a common border; Russian prestige in the Balkans and in Romania diminished considerably; the right of Russia to station troops in the new Bulgaria was limited to nine months and in the new Ottoman province of Eastern Rumelia to three months;[54] the Ottoman Empire did not cease to exist in Europe and still stretched to the shores of the Adriatic in Albania; and Bosnia—Hercegovina was occupied, not yet annexed, by Austria—Hungary on the request of the powers assembled in Berlin.

It would appear that Andrássy, after twisting and turning for three years, achieved his goals. His country gained the territory for which its military leaders had clamored for many years, the western Balkans were under Austro—Hungarian influence, the Russian danger was, once again, averted, and the Ottomans were still the neighbors of Austria—Hungary. All he had to give up of his numerous original desiderata was the friendship of the Balkan Slavs. Yet he and his country did not gain all these advantages as a result of a clear-cut, consciously and determinedly followed foreign policy. No such policy existed. All the decisions the Ballhausplatz made during these crucial years were retreats forced upon it by events. Only during the February—July 1878 period, when Vienna was certain of Britain's full support and, increasingly, of Bismarck's diplomatic help, did Austria–Hungary follow a clear line in her demands and actions in preparing for and during the sitting of the Berlin Congress. Diószegi is right in saying that the successes of the Dual Monarchy at Berlin were the result "primarily of favorable turns in international relations"[55] and to a much lesser extent of her own ability to act. Austria–Hungary was a "great power" with vital interests in the Balkans, but given the complications created by the *Ausgleich,* her economic and military weaknesses, the multinationality of her population, and the diversity of views of her policy makers, she was unable to formulate and pursue a consistent foreign policy even when major events occurred on her border that could affect her very existence.

TABLE 1

DEFENSE ESTIMATES AND EXPENDITURES BY COUNTRY, 1870 AND 1880

	Estimates (in million Pounds Sterling)		*Per capita Expenditures*	
	1870	1880	1870	1880
Germany	10.8	20.4	5s. 4d.	9s.
Austria–Hungary	8.2	13.2	4s. 6d.	7s. 1d.
France	22.0	31.4	12s. 2d.	16s. 9d.
Great Britain	23.4	25.2	14s. 9d.	14s. 5d.
Italy	7.8	10.0	5s. 9d.	7s. 3d.
Russia	22.0	29.6	5s. 4d.	6s. 3d.

Source: A. J. P. Taylor, *The Struggle for Mastery in Europe, 1848–1918* (Oxford, 1954), p. xxviii.

NOTES

1. Among the numerous monographs dealing with the 1875–78 crisis are the following: Karl O. Frhr. von Aretin, ed., *Bismarcks Aussenpolitik und der Berliner Kongress* (Wiesbaden, 1978); Bertrand Bareilles, ed., *Le rapport secret sur le Congrès de Berlin adressé à la S. Porte par Karathéodory Pasha* (Paris, 1919); Vasco Čubrilović, *Bosanski Ustanak 1875–1878* (Belgrade, 1930); Milorad Ekmečić, *Ustanak u Bosni*

1875–1878 (Sarajevo, 1950), also available in German translation, *Der Aufstand in Bosnien, 1875–1878* (Graz, 1974); P. K. Fortunatov, *Vojna 1877–1878 gg. i osvoboždenie Bolgarii* (Moscow, 1950); Sergei M. Gorianov, *Le question d'Orient à la veille du traité de Berlin (1870–1876) d'après les archives russes* (Paris, 1948); Imanuel Geiss, *Der Berliner Kongress, 1878: Protokolle und Materialien* (Boppard am Rhein, 1978); David Harris, *A Diplomatic History of the Balkan Crisis of 1875–1878: The First Year* (Stanford, 1936); Gisela Hünigen, *Nikolaj Pavlovic Ignat'ev und die russische Balkanpolitik, 1875–1878* (Göttingen–Zürich–Frankfurt, 1968); Barbara Jelavich, *The Habsburg Empire in European Affairs, 1814–1918* (Chicago 1969); David MacKenzie, *The Serbs and Russian Panslavism, 1875–1878* (Ithaca, 1967); William N. Medlicott, *The Congress of Berlin and After*, 2d ed. (Hamden, Conn., 1963); Ralph Melville and Hans-Jürgen Schröder, eds., *Der Berliner Kongress von 1878* (Wiesbaden, 1982); Alexander Novotny, *Quellen und Studien zur Geschichte des Berliner Kongresses, 1878*, 2 vols. (Graz, 1957); Alfred F. Pribram, *The Secret Treaties of Austria–Hungary*, 2 vols. (Cambridge, Mass., 1920–21); Franz Ronneberger, *Bismarck und Südosteuropa* (Berlin, 1941); Georg H. Rupp, *A Wavering Friendship: Russia and Austria, 1876–1878* (Cambridge, Mass., 1941); Theodor von Sosnosky, *Die Balkanpolitik Österreich–Ungarns seit 1866*, 2 vols. (Stuttgart, 1913–14); Mihailo D. Stojanović, *The Great Powers and the Balkans, 1875–1878* (Cambridge, 1939); Benedict H. Sumner, *Russia and the Balkans, 1870–1880* (Oxford, 1937); Bruce Waller, *Bismarck at the Crossroads: The Reorientation of German Foreign Policy after the Congress of Berlin, 1878–80* (London, 1974); Walter G. Wirthwein, *Britain and the Balkan Crisis, 1875–1878* (New York, 1935).

2. See, for example, Gordon A. Craig, *Europe since 1815* (New York–Chicago–San Francisco–Toronto–London, 1961), pp. 276–81; Carlton J. H. Hayes, *A Generation of Materialism* (New York–London, 1941), pp. 25–34; H. Hearder, *Europe in the Nineteenth Century* (New York, 1966), pp. 160–63; Charles and Barbara Jelavich, *The Establishment of the Balkan National States, 1804–1920* (Seattle–London, 1977), pp. 141–57; Alan Palmer, *The Lands Between* (New York, 1970), pp. 83–87; Robert R. Palmer and Joel Cotton, *A History of the Modern World*, 4th ed. (New York, 1978), pp. 615–19; Norman Rich, *The Age of Nationalism and Reform, 1850–1890*, 2d ed. (New York, 1977), pp. 230–33; Leften S. Stavrianos, *The Balkans since 1453* (New York–Chicago–San Francisco–Toronto–London, 1958), pp. 393–412; Ferdinand Schevill, *The History of the Balkan Peninsula* (New York, 1922), pp. 393–406; F. Roy Willis, *World Civilizations*, vol. 2 (Lexington, Mass.–Toronto, 1982), pp. 1228–29; Robert Lee Wolff, *The Balkans in Our Time*, rev. ed. (New York, 1974), pp. 69–71, 82–85.

3. The major turning points of the crisis prior to the Berlin Congress were as follows: Disturbances began in Hercegovina at the end of 1874. By the summer of 1875, this province was in full revolt, and in July the Bosnians joined the uprising. April 1876 brought insurrection in Bulgaria. On June 23 Serbia, on July 2 Montenegro declared war on the Ottoman Empire. Both requested an armistice on October 31. The Constantinople Conference was held December 12, 1876, to January 18, 1877. On April 24, 1877, Russia declared war on the Ottoman Empire. December 10, 1877, saw the fall of Plevna. On December 14 Serbia reentered the war. The Armistice of Edirne was declared on January 31, 1878. The San Stefano Treaty was signed on March 3, 1878.

4. Count Gyula Andrássy von *Csík-Szentkirály* and Kraszna Horka (1823–90) was Hungarian prime minister 1867–71 and imperial and royal minister of foreign affairs 1871–79.

5. Roger V. Paxton, "Russian Foreign Policy and the First Serbian Uprising; Alliances, Apprehensions, and Autonomy, 1804–1807," in Wayne Vucinich, ed., *The First Serbian Uprising, 1804–1813* (Boulder, 1982), p. 41.

6. The Austrian and Hungarian delegations consisted of twenty members of the upper and forty of the lower houses of the two parliaments, elected by their colleagues. They met at least once a year. The common ministers' reports to them in practice

consisted of accounts of the events of the previous year, demands for funds, and vague statements about the future.

7. Horst Haselsteiner, "Zur Haltung der Donaumonarchie in der Orientalischen Frage," in Melville and Schröder, *Der Berliner Kongress*, p. 237, n. 33.

8. István Diószegi, "Die Anfänge der Orientalpolitik Andrássys," in Melville and Schröder, *Der Berliner Kongress*, p. 252. Diószegi also indicates that in 1868, while Andrássy was Hungarian prime minister, he even suggested to the then imperial and royal foreign minister, Baron Friedrich Ferdinand Beust (1809–86), that the monarchy should persuade the Ottomans to hand over Bosnia–Hercegovina to the Serbs because they constituted the cornerstone of its Balkan policy.

9. Ibid.

10. Haselsteiner, "Zur Haltung der Donaumonarchie," p. 230, n. 7.

11. See Gunther E. Rothenberg, *The Army of Francis Joseph* (West Lafayette, 1976), p. 91, and István Diószegi, "Az Osztrák–Magyar Monarchia külpolitikája a kiegyezés után" (hereafter "Foreign Policy"), in *Magyarország Története tíz kötetben*, vol. 6, ed. Endre Kovács and László Katus (Budapest, 1976–), pt. 2, p. 903.

12. Archduke Albert (1817–95), grandson of the emperor Leopold II, became inspector general of the imperial and royal army in 1869 and held this post until his death. Friedrich von (after 1906 Count) Beck–Rzilkowski (1830–1920) was head of the emperor's military chancellery (1867–81) and then chief of staff (1881–1906).

13. Haselsteiner, "Zur Haltung der Donaumonarchie," p. 228, n. 4.

14. Ibid., p. 229, n. 6.

15. F. R. Bridge, *From Sadowa to Sarajevo: The Foreign Policy of Austria–Hungary, 1866–1914* (London–Boston, 1972), pp. 71–72. Radetzky (1766–1858) was Austria's military hero in 1848–49 and from 1849 to 1857 governor of Lombardy. Tegetthoff (1827–71) commanded the Austrian navy in 1866 and subsequently became its commander in chief.

16. Diószegi, "Foreign Policy," p. 898.

17. Bridge, *From Sadowa to Sarajevo*, p. 23.

18. The figures for total military spending are in Rothenberg, *The Army of Francis Joseph*, p. 106. The conversion rates of major currencies in the 1870s, according to the 9th edition (1878) of the *Encyclopaedia Britannica*, were as follows: 1 Austro–Hungarian gulden = 2.27 French francs, 2.00 German marks, 0.62 rubles, and 11 ½ d sterling.

19. Rothenberg, *The Army of Francis Joseph*, p. 78.

20. Haselsteiner, "Zur Haltung der Donaumonarchie," pp. 230–31.

21. The Ottomans did not send their army into the Balkans prior to the April Uprising in Bulgaria in 1876.

22. István Diószegi, "A keleti kérdés és az osztrák–magyar külpolitika" (hereafter "Eastern Question"), in Kovács and Katus, *Magyarország Története*, pp. 1181–82.

23. I was not able to find the exact date of the Gorchakov note. Prince Aleksandr Mikhailovich Gorchakov (1798–1883) held various important positions in Russia. Between 1856 and 1882 he was the tsar's chancellor. The content of the note is described in Bridge, *From Sadowa to Sarajevo*, p. 74.

24. Ibid.

25. Ede Wertheimer von Monor, *Gróf Andrássy Gyula élete és kora*, 3 vols. (Budapest, 1910), 2: 329. A German version, *Graf Julius Andrássy, sein Leben und seine Zeit*, 3 vols. (Stuttgart, 1913), also exists. Wertheimer considered this statement so crucial that he italicized it in his work.

26. Bridge publishes as his Documents 6 and 7 two telegrams, both dated May 12, 1876, sent from Berlin to Francis Joseph by Andrássy. The first was sent at 2:36 P. M. and the second at 10:35 P. M. In the afternoon the minister reported to his ruler on Gorchakov's unacceptable proposal, but by evening he was able to communicate the satisfactory conclusion of the day's work (Bridge, *From Sadowa to Sarajevo*, pp. 394–96).

27. Wertheimer, *Gróf Andrássy Gyula*, vol. 1, p. 406.

28. Besides the two emperors, Gorchakov, and Andrássy, the only persons promptly informed of the *Résumé's* contents were Eugene Petrovich Novikov (1826–1903), Russian ambassador in Vienna, 1870–80; Count Alois Károlyi von Nagy-Károly (1825–89), Austro–Hungarian ambassador in Berlin, 1871–78; and Baron Ferdinand von Langenau (1818–81), Austro–Hungarian ambassador in St. Petersburg, 1871–80. Even Bismarck was not told about the agreement until later (Wertheimer, *Gróf Andrássy Gyula*, vol. 2, pp. 409–10).

29. For details of the Reichstadt Agreement, see the relevant sections of the works cited in n. 1 and Bridge, *From Sadowa to Sarajevo*, pp. 77–78; Diószegi, "Eastern Question," pp. 1183–84; Wertheimer, *Gróf Andrássy Gyula*, vol. 2, pp. 408–10.

30. The order was given on June 30, 1875, to Lieutenant Field Marshal Baron Anton Mollinary von Monte Pastello (1820–1904) (Rothenberg, *The Army of Francis Joseph*, p. 93).

31. Wertheimer, *Gróf Andrássy Gyula*, vol. 2, pp. 487–88. The note was dated December 16, 1876.

32. Rothenberg, *The Army of Francis Joseph*, p. 94.

33. Ibid., p. 101.

34. Diószegi, "Eastern Question," p. 1183.

35. Ibid., p. 1184.

36. The Budapest Convention consisted, in fact, of two conventions. The first, a military agreement, was concluded on January 15, 1877, and the additional convention, predated to the same date, on March 18, 1877. They were considered interrelated, and unless both were observed neither was valid.

37. For details, see Bridge, *From Sadowa to Sarajevo*, pp. 81 ff., and Wertheimer, *Gróf Andrássy Gyula*, vol. 2, pp. 492 ff.

38. Wertheimer, *Gróf Andrássy Gyula*, vol. 2, p. 492.

39. Reprinted in the original French in Wertheimer, *Gróf Andrássy Gyula*, vol. 3, p. 112, n. 1.

40. Diószegi, "Eastern Question," p. 1184.

41. For details on Russo–Romanian negotiations and Romania's entry into the war, see the first half of Dan Berindei, "The Romanian War of Independence (1877–1878)," in Ştefan Pascu and Ştefan Ştefanescu, eds., *Pages from the History of the Romanian Army* (Bucharest, 1975), pp. 133–43.

42. On July 1877, the British cabinet decided to declare war on Russia should its forces occupy Constantinople and not evacuate the city promptly.

43. Bridge, *From Sadowa to Sarajevo*, p. 83.

44. Diószegi, "Eastern Question," p. 1185, and Bridge, *From Sadowa to Sarajevo*, p. 84.

45. For his views as early as 1871, see Diószegi, "Foreign Policy," p. 909.

46. For this interpretation of dissolution, see the statement made by Andrássy on January 29, 1875, in Haselsteiner, "Zur Haltung der Donaumonarchie," p. 232.

47. Wertheimer, *Gróf Andrássy Gyula*, vol. 2, p. 494.

48. Ibid.

49. The *force majeure* explanation was used by Gorchakov on February 12, 1878 (Bridge, *From Sadowa to Sarajevo*, p. 85).

50. Count Nikolay Pavlovich Ignatyev (1832–1908), a leading Russian Pan-Slavist, was his country's ambassador in Constantinople 1864–77. During the war he was the foreign policy adviser and, therefore, the leading diplomat on the spot of the commander in chief of the Russian armies, the brother of the tsar, Grand Duke Nikolay Nikolayevich (1856–1929). To what extent Ignatyev was following his own inclinations or orders from St. Petersburg at Edirne and later at San Stefano is not clear. Bridge believes that he was never informed of the Budapest Convention (*From Sadowa to Sarajevo*, p. 85).

51. Kálmán Tisza von Borosjenő and Szeged (1830–1902), like Andrássy a revolu-

tionary in 1848—49, was the leader of the Hungarian Liberal party and prime minister from 1875 to 1890.

52. Diószegi, "Eastern Question," p. 1187.

53. Peter F. Sugár, *Industrialization of Bosnia—Hercegovina, 1878—1918* (Seattle, 1963), p. 24. Wertheimer and other admirers of Andrássy claim that he resigned for reasons of health. The fact remains that the process of his resignation began when the delegations drew up a list of accusations against him in December 1878, including the charge that he had misused the 60 million gulden.

54. After Berlin, Bulgarian territory was limited to the region between the Balkans in the south and the Danube in the north. Eastern Rumelia lay between the Balkan and Rhodope ranges. The territory south of the Rhodope remained Ottoman.

55. Diószegi, "Eastern Question," p. 1190.

INTERACTION WITH POLITICS AND RELIGION

In spite of containing more essays than do the previous two sections, this one needs only the shortest introduction. Nationalism, like other ideologies, beliefs, customs, habits and all other manifestations of a given society's existence, is influenced by and influences all of them. Five of the studies are devoted to various aspects of group existence in Eastern Europe and show that all of them depended, to a larger or smaller extent, on the contemporary manifestations of nationalism. Of the interactions of nationalism with other social forces, the one with the political establishments is the most obvious, but not the most interesting. The role religion played and plays in the formulation of national identity and nationalism is the most interesting phenomenon in Eastern Europe. Catholicism is a mark of 'Polishness', but not a prerequisite of 'Hungariannes'. Orthodoxy does not define a Bulgarian, Romanian or Serb. What was more important in the dissolution of Yugoslavia: the country's multi-ethnic or multi-religious composition? To answer these questions scholars invented expressions like religioethnicism and *Konfessions-Nationalität* and others. Whatever expressions are used and whatever the answers are that are given to the religion/nationalism question, the issue is still unsolved and will demand further study. These two interrelationships – politics and nationalism, and religion and nationalism – are the central themes of items VI–X.

The last piece is my evaluation of an entire century's developments, or, rather, the lack of them. It is the last essay I wrote, and fairly recent. I may change some of my views in the future, but right now item XI contains the summary of forty-five years' involvement with Eastern European nationalism. This is a good reason for not commenting on it and letting each reader do this for him/herself.

VI

CONTINUITY AND CHANGE
IN EASTERN EUROPEAN AUTHORITARIANISM:
AUTOCRACY, FASCISM AND COMMUNISM[1]

The purpose of this paper was the presentation of a historical overview of the various forms of authoritarianism in modern Eastern Europe. This simple statement already requires the introduction of three definitions: what is authoritarianism; what regions of Europe are to be considered Eastern Europe; and what period of the history of this region is to be considered "modern"?

The second and third of these questions are easy to answer in light of the consensus achieved by those who worked with Eastern European problems since World War I. Eastern Europe, somewhat arbitrarily, is that part of Europe that lies between the German and Italian speaking part of the continent to the west of it and the Soviet Union and Turkey to the east. The modern period in the history of the people living in this area begins at the end of the 18th century within a relatively short span of a few years. The relevant bench-marks are the third partition of Poland (1795), the death of Joseph II, the Emperor-King of the Habsburg realm (1790), and the beginning of Sultan Selim III's rule (1798). These events completely changed the political climate in the affected regions and set in motion developments that, in the long run, produced the present day situation in Eastern Europe. It should be remembered that these selected starting years for the modern period in Eastern Europe coincide with the French Revolution, an event which produced significant results in this part of Europe too.[2] It was one of those important and steady "foreign" events without which development in this region cannot be understood properly.

It is much more difficult to define authoritarianism. Many scholars have written about it, but I found no acceptable definition. According to Huntington and Moore "authoritarian systems are nondemocratic ones,"[3] while, according to Kirscht and Dillehay, "the most useful way to define authoritarianism appears to be in terms of cognitive style—close minded cognitive functioning."[4] While somewhat clearer, even the definition of Webster's

Dictionary is not very helpful: "Authoritarianism," says Webster, is a "concentration of power in a leader or an elite not constitutionally responsible to the people."[5]

The definition offered by the dictionary only slightly masks the assumption clearly stated by that of Huntington and Moore: authoritarianism can only be understood as a deviation from democracy. Furthermore, it should also be noted that authoritarian regimes in modern times operate, in spite of the dictionary's statement, in countries with very elaborate constitutions making it impossible for their critics to attack them for their unconstitutional behavior. The best and most recent example of such a confrontation was the "Charter 77" which appeared in Prague in January 1977.

Most importantly, these definitions assume that democracy is by definition the accepted goal of all people, the inevitable end result of modern political development, the ideal that serves as the norm for measuring the value of other political systems. This approach is not unlike that of the Marxists who see an inevitable progression of mankind from slavery through feudalism and capitalism to socialism. Donald Treadgold has recently expressed this American tendency to see historical development as a predestined process when he said:

> Lacking any structured analysis of differing human societies, the tendency of Americans has been to assume a unilinear view of events. That is, the assumption has been that all societies are traveling approximately the same economic and social road towards 'modernization' ... or economic development which at a certain point reaches 'take-off' ... or something else. ... Once it was assumed that all nations were destined for democracy for which the world must be made safe. ...[6]

In judging authoritarianism, we must get away from this unilinear, involuntarily Marxist American approach. This point was made clearly by Vernon Aspaturian in the instructions he sent to those invited to the conference on authoritarianism:

> Authoritarianism, like its polar counterpart democracy, has developed and changed over the years in response to diverse forces, and continues to exhibit a durability and vitality as an autonomous and separate system, with its own capacity to evolve, adapt, change and develop. The tenacity and vigor demonstrated by authoritarianism suggests strongly that we can no longer, with calm assurance, assume that 'authoritarianism' somehow represents a primitive stage of development of which democracy is a higher stage towards which it evolves. Rather, authoritarianism is a parallel and alternative system, capable of evolving into democracy or simply into 'higher' and more sophisticated versions of authoritarianism, just as democracy can evolve into higher forms of democracy or evolve (not

necessarily 'devolve' or degenerate) into authoritarianism. Authoritarianism can be viewed as a distinctive family of political systems and can stand by itself and serve precisely the same societal functions and purposes as democratic systems, but within a different value framework.[7]

In his instructions Vernon Aspaturian also stressed that today more than 75 per cent of the globe's more than 150 governments are authoritarian, but added that "many of these... bear little resemblance to earlier authoritarian systems because the cultural, technological, philosophical and geographic mix of these societies are substantially different."[8]

I accept these statements of Treadgold and Aspaturian and must, consequently, give a definition of authoritarianism that will serve as the basis for an analysis of its various manifestations in Eastern Europe. In arriving at this definition I was influenced by a recent article of Mihály Vajda.[9] My definition is the following:

Authoritarianism is a political system in which separation of civil society and the political state has not been realized, in which the pluralism of economic, political and ideological power has not been achieved, and in which—consequently—all civil and political power and decision making is reserved to an individual or group claiming—for a variety of reasons—to possess the authority to act for the entire polity.

As all definitions, this is certainly not a perfect one, but it will allow differentiation between earlier forms of authoritarianism such as autocracy, in which power was lodged, at least theoretically, in a single individual, the ruler, who acted by the grace of God or other divine authority and between more contemporary forms of dictatorship, including fascism and communism, whose authority is based on an often mythical ideology and which require group participation in power inspite of the required leader figures. The offered definition will also serve to differentiate between the various subvarieties of autocracy, fascism and communism, and will permit the discussion of their specifically Eastern European variants.

II

Before turning to Eastern Europe proper, another set of problems needs elaboration. It centers around the fact that some states developed into democracies and others, the majority, into authoritarian entities. The long quotation from Aspaturian ends with the assertion that democracy and authoritarianism serve the same goals, "but within a different value framework." The simplest approach to this problem of "value framework" is the well known one: each group of people—the inhabitants of a political unit, the state, are such a group—is basically interested in two things: freedom and security. Freedom and security are value frameworks. A facile, but nevertheless basically correct assumption would be that those polities whose value framework was built around freedom developed into democracies and those who valued security more became authoritarian states. Hidden behind this assumption is another one that accepts that different people at various times in history had a chance to make a choice and that they made it consciously. Every historian knows that this seldom if ever occurred. Time, place, developmental level, foreign pressures, strength and weakness of whoever represented authority are among the numerous, and for Eastern Europe crucial, variables that determined this, in most cases unconscious, choice. There are no universal rules or patterns that help us understand why and how any given group of people made a certain decision. Even Marx realized that his neatly structured developmental pattern was not valid for lands in which the Asiatic mode of production insured the supremacy of a basically unchanging bureaucracy. Yet, today even these states have changed and are ruled by various forms of authoritarian governments. In their cases foreign influence was the decisive factor. On the other extreme we have the Eastern European countries that have known—in one form or another—feudalism and do not fit into either the Marxist or non-Marxist evaluation based on this fact. Capitalism and socialism have not followed feudalism organically in the Marxist sense in Eastern Europe, nor do they conform to the "mountainous evidence ... that democracy requires centuries of social, political, and legal experience in pluralistic handling of problems; that so far only post-feudal countries [including Japan] have successfully instituted democracy; that premature attempts at democracy may produce lasting failure...."[10] Eastern Europe had centuries of pluralistic handling of problems, although in a more limited form than Western Europe, but it developed bureaucratic machineries and not democracy. There was no Asiatic mode of production in Eastern Europe, but

> very early in the process of political development the administrative bureaucracy, or in some cases (such as Yugoslavia and Poland) the military, had emerged as autonomous forces in the political arena. Contrary to popular belief this administrative-military complex, for our purposes 'bureaucracy' was not the handmaiden of established social classes or the national community as a whole, but eventually became an interest group in its own right.[11]

While Andrew Janos made this statement about inter-war Eastern Europe, it is equally true of earlier centuries. As my old high-school history professor pointed out, "Holy Bureaucratius" became the patron saint of Eastern Europe at the latest with the accession of Maria Theresia in 1740. Once again an easy assumption presents itself. Eastern Europe, a region that had known different forms of feudalism and even pluralism, tended towards authoritarianism because this suited the self-interest of the dominant political force, the bureaucracy. Yet, one only has to look at France in the same period, in the eighteenth century after the death of Louis XIV, to see an equally powerful bureaucracy in action, but a completely different development.

Moving away from a Marxist or quasi-Marxist analysis and remembering that feudalism is not simply a mode of production, but also a social and political order, another interpretation presents itself. In the feudal society the main reason for the system's existence was the need for individual and collective security. The military-bureaucratic masters were responsible for it irrespective of the size of their domain. Yet, it would be mistaken to call their regime autocratic although it was certainly authoritarian. The separation of civil and political society and the absence of pluralism which, according to the definition just presented, mark a society as authoritarian were not issues that interested society. These became important considerations only when the modern state and society developed. It is my belief that in the timing of this development, in the sequence of events that brought it about, in the presence or absence of foreign pressures during the process, and in the level of mass participation in the transformation lies the real explanation for the unconscious opting for freedom or security, for democracy or authoritarianism in post-feudal Europe. In this respect practically all non-European lands—with the exception of North America and Japan and possibly India—followed the Eastern and not the Western European model.

Kenneth Jowitt, thinking about similar problems, although in a different context, came to very similar conclusions. He expressed them so well that I will use his definition for my purpose.[12] Jowitt sees the end of the feudal period in the appearance of

> 'the factually absolutist state' (in contrast to the theoretical absolutism of the Middle Ages). The defining characteristic of this ruling organization was a hierarchy of officials whose status and loyalty were in significant respects defined without reference to their social-familial position and commitments. The emergence of the 'officials' as a politically and administratively defined group ... provided the substantive dimension for the process of structural differentiation that was occurring in the relationship between central and regional elites and between the elite and non-elite sectors of society.[13]

This explanation sees absolutism following feudalism a long time before capitalism made its appearance. This absolutism, upheld by an independent professional, highly structured bureaucracy created the modern, centralized state in which the "relationship between state and society was strictly hierarchical, largely extractive and coercive, and defined in terms of mutually exclusive statuses (official and subject) rather than complementary roles (citizen and official).[14] The exclusive and hierarchical structure of the centralized state resulted finally in the emergence of the autocratic ruler as the head of the bureaucratic hierarchy whose members derived the legitimacy of their position from the sanction of the autocrat and not—as in feudal society—from a right by birth. The relationship between ruler and official was mutual; the ruler could not rule without the bureaucrats whose power depended on that of the ruler.

This development occurred in Eastern Europe too but two or three centuries after it took place in England and France. The most drastic changes occurred in the years following the dates given above for the beginning of the modern period in this region. With the partitions of Poland the power of the old ruling classes was ended and the administration was placed into the hands of officials who owed their positions entirely to the appointments given to them by the rulers. In the Habsburg lands a similar, professional bureaucracy was created by Maria Theresia (and her actions were reinforced by those of her son, Joseph II) who realized the need to transform her realm into a modern, centralized state. With the rule of Selim III began the displacement of Ottoman officials who held positions because they were members of the "professional Ottoman" class by bureaucrats who held office simply as a result of imperial appointment.[15]

At this point the parallel development between Western and Eastern Europe ends. Feudal states were transformed into centralized ones in both regions, but the differences—to be discussed in the next section of this study—are more important than the similarities when the development of authoritarianism is traced. In the newly centralized states anywhere in Europe civil society and the political state were still not distinctive entities. Their separation needed an additional development, the transformation of the subject into the citizen.

The importance of civil society as an independent entity within the political structure of the state emerged when the centralized state became the nation state. Obviously, this transformation had to wait until the concept of modern nationalism emerged and until this new focus of loyalty became of primary importance to the majority of the inhabitants of any given political unit. Furthermore, the ruling elements (ruler and bureaucracy) too had to accept this new idea and give it scope for action. It does not matter why the leaders of the centralized state fell into line—necessity, conviction, or opportunism—they did so gradually or suddenly mainly under the influence of the Enlightenment, the French Revolution, and the emergence of the capitalist economic system. According to Jowitt, the three main features of the nation state that permitted the differentiation between civil society and the political state transforming the subjects into citizens were the following: First, the nation state "was the only political organization with societal scope to be based on the individual . . . Second, the individual as a political actor was strengthened and legitimated by both capitalism and liberalism . . . Third, the national polity was more *inclusive* in its membership than the state polity."[16] Only when the individual became a citizen did he acquire the right of choice that produced pluralism in society.

Nationalism and the nation-state emerged in Eastern Europe too. Superficially the developmental sequence there resembles that in the west whose unfolding Jowitt traces. Yet, once again, the differences are more important than the similarities. Of this problem I have already written repeatedly, but will return to it again, in the different context, shortly.[17] The differences between the Western and Eastern European developments are crucial when the question is asked: why did a seemingly similar post-feudal development produce democracy in Western and authoritarianism in Eastern Europe as the dominant political system? The answer to this question explains the reasons for the unconscious choice the citizens of the various nation states made in modern times when they had a chance to influence the type of government under which they lived.

III

Modernity, in the sense outlined in the first part of this paper, hit Eastern Europe suddenly. When Poland disappeared, the lands of this chaotic state at the end of what her historians call the critical century, became parts of three other political units. In two of these, Russia and Prussia, the transformation creating the centralized state with its massive bureaucracy was in the last stages, while in the third, the Habsburg realm, it was well advanced.[18] While the three partitioning powers were certainly behind the western states in "modernity," they were way ahead of Poland in which the feudal order had not changed at all. In the numerous lands of the Habsburgs the situation was practically the same. Maria Theresia and her son faced not only a rigidly feudal order in their various domains, but also an almost unbelievable variety of laws, habits and customs when they decided that drastic change was overdue and set out to create a single, centralized state. The Ottoman Empire, practically in full dissolution in 1789, was typical of the state of which Kenneth Jowitt wrote when he referred to theoretical absolutism. What Selim III attempted was to create a factually absolutist state in which central administration and uniform laws were to replace a variety of local polities compared to which even the Habsburg domain was ordered and uniform.[19] In each of these cases the change came suddenly as a result of a ruler's decision and without the cooperation of a bureaucracy that developed gradually from the midst of the affected population. In Poland the subjects of the partitioning powers took over; in the Habsburg lands the ruler's coworkers were recruited mainly from the lower nobility of the hereditary, German speaking provinces; in the Ottoman Empire they represented a new element educated along novel lines that made them equally alien to Muslim and non-Muslim, Turk and non-Turk. Centralization, successful everywhere but in the Balkans, was uniformly resisted, but the resistance was not uniform.

While all "modernizing" rulers mentioned so far were "westerners" in the sense that they followed the models presented by western European states whose power they envied and wanted to acquire, their opponents were both "westernizers" and traditionalists. At first the traditionalists were in the majority. Their aim was to frustrate change and retain their power and significance based on the old feudal order. By the time of the Congress of Vienna, the "westernizers" were the rulers' most dangerous antagonists in East-Central Europe and their importance in the Balkans was increasing. The difference between these "westernizers" and the rulers stems from the various features of the model states which they wished to introduce. The rulers were interested in centralization and an up-to-date political state structure, while their opponents were interested in those aspects of the western model that gave significance to civil society. The partisans of the centralized and of the nation state faced each other.

Several crucial differences between the developments in Western and Eastern Europe emerge from these few facts. In the west the rulers and their bureaucracies were native sons of the states which they gradually transformed; in the east they were "foreigners." In the west the transformation was gradual; in the east it was sudden. In the west several centuries elapsed before the centralized state was transformed into the nation state; in the east the two concepts appeared practically simultaneously and were espoused by antagonistic forces. In the west both, the centralized and the nation state, evolved parallel with societal, economic, and ideological changes in accordance with the overall development of the various countries in the east these concepts were borrowed, often did not fit local situations, and were, therefore, misunderstood and often adapted to solve local problems to which they were not applicable.

To these, rather obvious, differences several others must be added. It is very important to remember that in the west the centralized state predated the great economic transformation that produced capitalism. By the time this new state was again changed and became the nation state, the size, education and power of the middle class had grown to such an extent that it was able to confront ruler and the bureaucracy and demand rights first for itself, then for other segments of the population to counter-balance those held by the masters of the centralized state. The nation state was based solidly on the mental and financial power of the middle class. In the east both the centralized state and the nation state concepts appeared and were advocated prior to the economic transformation of these lands in which the middle class was still insignificant. Here the "modernizer" was, at the same time, the "industrializer" because he saw in the modern economy the power base on which the type of state he advocated could be built. The west had time to think about the changes that occurred over the centuries and produced men able to justify them. The autocratic, centralized state was ably defended by Machiavelli, Bodin, Hobbes, and even by Hegel and Treitschke, while the democratic nation state found its advocates in Locke, Rousseau, Bentham, and John Stuart Mill, to mention only a few. One looks in vain for thinkers of this magnitude in Eastern Europe. In this part of the continent the crucial issue was not ideological; the state needed no explanation or justification. In contrast to the west, the importance of foreign elements in the transformational process is striking.

Another feature of the Eastern European building of the "modern" state—totally absent in the west—is its defensive character. Both rulers and their "westernizing" opponents advocated change because they realized their relative weakness. The rulers felt weak when they compared themselves to those who sat on the thrones of the west, and their antagonists felt weak when confronting their "foreign" rulers. They both sought power. The rulers did this by accepting a western model and by creating a tool, the bureaucracy, that they could use in building a state that was to give them power equal to those whose superiority they acknowledged tacitly or overtly. Those who opposed them tried to infiltrate and, if possible, capture the bureaucracy in which they saw the instrument of power within the state. Consequently the bureaucracy became indispensable to both parties in the dispute and developed into the independent interest group mentioned by Andrew Janos. The aim was to gain power; the state, its form and control were the tools that allowed one to capture and subsequently to wield it. According to Erich Fromm, the authoritarian personality is sadistic-masochistic.[20] I believe that it is the result of the power hunger of those who suffer from inferiority complexes.

What emerged in Eastern Europe between the end of the 18th century and roughly the middle of the next was the autocratic, centralized state run by a more-or-less despotic ruler with the help of a steadily growing bureaucracy. The aim of this ruling element was to add economic strength to its political mastery to acquire power that equaled that of the western states. Their weaknesses—including those who ruled in the emerging new "nation" states in the Balkans—were their separation from the masses of the subjects; the lack of capital, a middle class, and technology; the rapidity with which the west was transforming itself further increasing the power gap between it and the east; and, with the transformation of the western centralized state into the nation state, the multinationality of their subjects. Yet, they saw no solution to their problems except increasing their power hoping to acquire enough of it to permit them to catch up with the west and silence their internal enemies. These regimes were those to which Vernon Aspaturian referred when he wrote about "earlier systems of authoritarianism."

The next fifty years, roughly the second half of the 19th century, saw the gradual weakening of the power of the autocrat, but not the diminishing of authoritarian rule in Eastern Europe. The form but not the essence of rule changed. Interestingly, in the 1830's and 40's Eastern Europeans began to move towards true liberalism and nationalism of the kind Mazzini was preaching. These two trends were cut short by the defeats of the revolutions in mid-century. Ideas were defeated by power. Before ideals could be realized power had to be wrested from those who opposed them. By the time the ex-revolutionaries occupied positions of power they had forgotten their ideals. Liberalism survived only in the label of parties, and nationalism was transformed into more and more exclusive chauvinism. The weak beginnings of movements that might have favored democratic developments died on the barricades and battle fields of 1848-49. The autocrats regained full control of their domains. Yet, their success was more ephemeral than real. Slowly the goals for which the centralized state had been created by them began to be realized. Communications improved, literacy levels rose, industries made their appearance and in the growing cities the middle and working classes became important.

While the working classes—once they became conscious of their identity and interests—pursued goals similar to similar classes elsewhere, they were either too weak to become a serious political force, or had to compromise with trends that were considerably stronger than the ideals they advocated. Socialism became the only true ideological basis for politics, but, as the example of Austrian Social Democracy proves, had to make concession to other forces, primarily nationalism, that made it ineffective.

The middle classes had many of the characteristics of those of the west, but differed from them even more sharply. Their basic values were not those of the industrial and financial groups in the west, but those of the local gentry. The son of an upper middle class father in Eastern Europe preferred legal studies to any other education because a law degree coupled, if possible, with good connections and mild corruption could secure him a position in the bureaucracy and transform him into a "gentleman." The bureaucracy grew rapidly, needed new recruits and followers, and in addition needed additional sources of income to keep up with the rising living standards and costs. This cooperation between the bourgeoisie and the bureaucracy produced political parties which represented (judging by the number of eligible voters) mainly themselves. The real struggle was not that between ideologically motivated groups or those representing various social or economic interests, but between members of the same narrow social circle whose aim was to capture the government in order to gain control over the bureaucracy, its power and prestige. In most cases even this struggle was illusory because the bureaucracy controlled it by managing the elections in favor of a given party or coalition which it favored at any given moment. The rulers had no choice but to share power with this new combination of bureaucrats and politically active newcomers. The state became too complicated for them, but they retained control over foreign and military affairs which they considered to be the most important and the right to dismiss from office personalities that offended them. Autocracy was over, but authoritarian government continued because those in power not only made certain that it was limited to a narrowly defined political oligarchy, but also that its position remained inviolate. What Fritz Fellner wrote about Austria is true of all of Eastern Europe.

> ... it is quite significant that the political language ... is made up of words taken from war and fighting, using terms of strategy, tactics, and military planning. Political parties quite often were called 'fronts' ... the political opponent was never seen as a partner with whom one might exchange the command post for a certain time ... the political opponent was always the enemy to be destroyed. Political victory was a victory only when the opponent was annihilated—not only as a political force, but physically.[21]

The truth of this statement is borne out by the long tenures in power of "ruling parties." The number of politicians who, although not annihilated physically, experienced jail or exile before "seeing the light" and gaining admission into the circle of power wielders was large including such men as Andrássy, Brătianu, Pašić, Stambulov, and many others. Rule, although shared more widely than before, continued to be exclusivist, authoritarian, hierarchical and basically determined by the bureaucracy. Power still remained the aim of rule, but to this was added, in the second half of the 19th century, the militaristic approach to politics discussed by Fellner.

Unchanged also were foreign considerations. Austria, later Austria-Hungary, and Russia were still weak great powers when compared to Great

VI

Britain, France, and later Germany. The acquisition of power equal to that of the strong great powers was still the primary purpose of government and required the continued unfailing obedience of the citizens. That the inhabitants were considered citizens, that parties were permitted, that parliaments functioned, that rulers became "constitutional monarchs" are also clear indications of the influence of the western model. Yet, all these changes were at best skin deep; under this thin layer of western veneer the reality remained unchanged.

That this pseudo-transformation could be introduced and maintained without serious opposition and criticism by the masses can be explained by three factors. The first of these has already been discussed: the suddenness of change from feudal to centralized state that caught the inhabitants of the various lands unprepared and the fairly advanced tools of power (military, police, communications, machinery, etc.) that those who brought about the change were able to use to enforce their will. The second factor is the historically determined attitude of the masses towards their masters.

In the feudal period both of the great power centers with which every individual came into contact, the state and the church, were organized as monolithic hierarchies and demanded total obedience in the name of power and absolute truth respectively. Those who were not members of the "political nation" or the various churches were not only not supposed to think and reason for themselves but were also deterred from doing so by cruel punishment or the promise of same in the afterlife. To make certain that these deterrents were effective the masses were given as little information beyond the minimal they needed to know. The result was not indifference or blind obedience, but a kind of stoicism whose major features were the belief that life is inevitably hard, but that those who make it unbearable will sooner or later disappear if left alone and not moved to act by disobedience. This feeling was especially strong when either the temporal or spiritual masters were foreigners. This attitude made the masses cautious, unused to thinking for themselves, inclined to ignore everything not relevant to everyday living, and accustomed to hierarchical structures. In the west the situation was similar during the early Middle Ages, but centuries of slow change transformed this world view before the centralized state made its appearance. In Eastern Europe this way of looking at life remained unchanged into the early nineteenth century. The bureaucratic-hierarchical centralism of the new state structure was, consequently, easily enforceable.

Ironically, it was the bureaucracy of the centralized state that had to move the masses out of their stoic acceptance of life and make them active participants in society because the modern state could not be built without them. The masses had to be educated, but in this lay the only serious danger

EASTERN EUROPEAN AUTHORITARIANISM

to the power monopoly of the autocrats and the bureaucracy. The solution produced the third factor; an educational system that combined the acquisition of needed skills with the continued willingness to let others think. Not only was the newly emerging educational system strictly controlled by the ministries of education—nowhere was this control stricter than in France—but it was structured in a manner that made "the recognition of pluralist values" impossible. "People were not readied for compromise, but rather were taught to obey and believe, not to challenge or show initiative. ... Worship of heroes, worship of war, worship of sacrifice were the main themes of teaching in history and literature."[22] The heroes extolled always included those who wielded power at any given moment; the wars in which one had to be ready to fight alwys included the political ones of the day; and the sacrifices were to be made for the good of the state. Having gone through an Eastern European education for twelve years I can attest to its effectiveness. Propaganda in the days of modern communications is a very effective weapon, but never more so than when it is directed at the young in the guise of education. In Eastern Europe it succeeded admirably in "modernizing" the masses' knowledge without significantly changing their basic attitude towards the authorities.

The features and actions of the powerful in the second half of the 19th century are not only characteristic of the Polish and Habsburg lands, but also of the small states that gained their independence in the Balkans. In these states too the acquisition of power in the country and the extension of the state's power at the expense of neighbors were the main aims of authoritarian governments. While they were less independent from foreign influences, especially in their foreign affairs, than were their larger neighbors, the enforcement of authoritarian rule at home was considerably easier south of the Danube-Sava line than north of it. The introduction of the modern state was even more sudden in the south than it was in the north; the number of those who had the financial independence and minimal education to get involved in politics was much more limited in the Balkans than it was in East-Central Europe, and the population was even more ignorant, backward and, due to long Ottoman rule, even more conditioned to blind obedience. Given the more primitive structure of society, the political wars in the Balkans were more cruel and bloody than in the lands of the three emperors, but the power of the autocratic bureaucracy was less limited and more absolute.

The "independent, nation states" of Eastern Europe that entered the first World War were, when viewed with their factual political systems in mind, centralized autocracies dominated by narrowly recruited bureaucracies. The state structure, modeled on that of the west, made it inevitable that some differentiation between civil society and the political state had that went way beyond what they wanted to achieve. Some of these interim leaders accepted the more extreme trends (Stojadinović and Imrédy) while the others disappeared from the political scene.

The next period is usually and incorrectly considered the period of fascism or of fascistic regimes.[26] Let us not forget that the only government that took power in Eastern Europe with a fascist program was that of Octovian Goga in Romania that lasted for 44 days between December 1937 and February 1938. When Ferencz Szálasi became Prime Minister of Hungary, in October 1944, he had no power and simply served his German masters whose troops had occupied the country.

The various royal, military, and one-party dictatorships in power in Eastern Europe in the late 1930's and during World War II had adopted many features of German National Socialism not so much to satisfy the local movements of the extreme right, but to please Hitler on whose good will their countries' very existence depended. Once again, we see a good example of foreign influence dictating the nature of the East European authoritarian regimes. Nevertheless, the local fascistic movements are significant. Not only did they represent a force that favored the growing concentration of all power in fewer and fewer hands, but they also present, for the first time, examples of true mass moblization of the political activity of the lower strata of society, and the importance of ideological commitment. Two features of this extremist movement are of significance for this study. First, the fact that the leadership was socially and nationally marginal and appealed mainly to those segments of society which were the farthest removed from any possibility of sharing power. Codreanu was of Ukrainian origin and his family name was Zelenski. Szálasi's family was Armenian with Greek relatives. These men became the most outspoken advocates of racism and racial purity. Codreanu's strength was in the villages, and Szálasi had to turn to that part of the country too once he became the puppet master of Hungary. It was exactly this, the most revolutionary element, the marginal people and the peasantry, that the Communists failed to mobilize when they achieved power after the Second World War. What is important when Eastern Europe is analysed as the home of authoritarian regimes is the realization that all dictatorships or right wing extremist movements demanded this type of government, that the mass movements that occasionally backed them did the same, and that all dictatorships operated through the existing bureaucracies whose membership hardly changed. The members of this professional class were not interested in ideology or the nature of the regime they served, they were only interested in keeping power in their own hands even if they had to accept the existence of a self-appointed "leader." The so-called fascist period in Eastern Europe changed the trappings, but not the essence of government and hardly touched those who exercised effective power. The bureaucrats had no convictions beyond their belief in their own importance, power, and their right to function as they saw fit. They had served emperors, kings, presidents, prime ministers with various party labels, had survived one world war and were confident that they would outlive the second. They would have served the masters of the post-1945 regime equally well provided that these granted them the power and immunities they had enjoyed for nearly two centuries. Unfortunately for them, the new regimes had other plans.

V

No period in Eastern European history had produced a scholarly and popular literature comparable to that dealing with the last 35 years. It is, therefore, not necessary to review in detail the manner in which the Communists gained power in the various countries, the Tito-Stalin dispute, the events of 1956 or 1968, to mention only a few of those historical events that are familiar to all of us. Historians and political scientists, who hardly ever agree on anything, have even accepted an identical periodization for the various sub-periods marking changes in the overall picture of communist domination. One of these, the years 1948-53 are probably the only ones that can be justifiably labelled as totalitarian.

Yet, looking at all these well known developments with the single aim of judging the type of authoritarian rule prevalent in Eastern Europe at any given moment some interesting and fairly new generalizations can be made. It is not difficult to see in the first main period, 1948-56, the perfectly autocratic power of men like Tito, Rákosi, Dimitrov, Gottwald and others. These were the years of the so-called personality cult. The fact that these masters were satraps once removed from the true power source in Moscow made relatively little difference as far as their conationals were concerned and reintroduces a feature familiar from previous years, the importance of foreign influence. What differentiates these red masters from those who preceded them was the absence of a ready made governmental machine on which they could rely. The members of the old bureaucracies were shunted aside as "fascist," and given the weakness of the local communist parties they were almost impossible to replace. Communist parties are structured hierarchies ever since Lenin's days, and in Eastern Europe the similarly organized bureaucracies became more and more identified with membership in the single-party or front organizations in the inter-war period. Unless one wanted to be called a capitalist or imperialist it was impossible to propose any other than the hierarchical-party-bureaucracy structure. The color, the ideological mythology, changed, but the nature of rule remained the same. In a sense, there was little difference between the governments of 1939 and those of 1953. The old bureaucracies were proud of their positions and knew how the various tasks had to be accomplished. The first years of communist rule saw functionaries in office who occupied their positions either because they were true believers, pre-1945 party members, or clever opportunists. The first group was in almost all cases unqualified to perform the duties assigned to it, while the second was either too clever or too timid to stick its neck out and developed a mastery in idle paper shuffling. Never in its collective history has Eastern Europe known such inefficent rule! Looking at the 1948-56 period one could call it the years of autocratic totalitarian inefficiency. This is the reason why the various parties were unable to react effectively to Stalin's death, to "collective leadership" in the Soviet Union and to Krushchev's "Secret Speech" of February 25, 1956. These events totally bewildered the true believers and made the cautious even more careful to the point of total inactivity. The party and governmental machineries, which were anyhow identical, ground to a standstill. This circumstance alone explains the events of 1956.

The various leaders of the Eastern European communist parties had learned their lessons in 1956, and Krushchev was willing to listen and to experiment. As a result the last fourteen years were the most significant as far as Eastern Europe's role in the history of authoritarianism is concerned. It produced national communism and communism with a human face.

National communism differs from communism in one state whose first variant was advanced by Stalin in his struggle with Trotsky and whose more up-to-date version was articulated by Tito in his debate with Stalin. Communism in one country does not compromise the basic beliefs of a Marxist-Leninist nor does it call into question the role of the party in society; it simply advocates either tactical, temporary measures with a return to the "straight line" predicted for the foreseeable future (Stalin), or demands the freedom to use previously untried means to achieve the quickest possible transformation of a given country into a communist state (Tito). National communism is willing to compromise with ideology to a certain degree and is ready to weaken the influence of the party in society. This willingness to make real concessions to public opinion and demand was the result of 1956. Several reasons account for this development. No leader could be considered "infallible" any more; the lessons of 1948 were relearned—ideology by itself does not solve problems; to avoid inefficency the base from which people in responsible positions were recruited had to be broadened; the political state had to establish a working relationship

VI

EASTERN EUROPEAN AUTHORITARIANISM

with civil society. The major directions in which the party leaderships moved to achieve these goals involved "the search for domestic legitimacy ... the search for an economic management formula ... and the assertion of national raison d'état in domestic and foreign policies."[27]

While the emphasis on one or more of these three major goals differed from state to state, the over-all direction was the same everywhere. Because the stress differed from place to place the resulting regimes and *communisms* also began to take on various forms, but allowed the emergence of civil society—even if in a limited form—in each state. This meant that if and when the party apparatchik saw "strains arise between ideology and reality he [was] able to adjust the former without causing irreparable damage to himself and to the group."[28] With the emergence of the beginning of civil society the transformation of the centralized into the nation state began ironically under the auspices of communism. With the emergence of *communisms* and the party members' willingness to bend ideology to suit reality, the history of Marxism took a new turn.

The search for efficiency and the willingness to recruit qualified people for the various tasks strongly affected the governments' operations too. Numerous old bureaucrats, or if not they then their children, found their way into offices again. They performed reasonably well right from the beginning and the party leaders were pleased with them. Several of them joined the party to buttress their newly regained or acquired positions and merged with younger, better trained party members. The result was the emergence of what Milovan Djilas called the New Class. It was in fact the old class, the bureaucratic class, in the new garb of aparatchiki. By the next important turning point, 1968, this old-new class was firmly established, acting in the authoritarian manner of previous bureaucracies not serving but dispensing favors. Most importantly, its attitude toward the rest of the population and its view of itself reverted to that of previous office holders. The national communist regimes procalimed a new ideology, but the authoritarian government reverted to its previous Eastern European pattern: it had a powerful leader, was dominated by a clearly defined "class," the bureaucracy, was under the influence of a foreign power, tried to maximize the concentration of power in its hands, was still interested in catching up with economically more advanced states, and in the name of the "national" good demanded obedience and conformity from the population at large. Although more powerful than any previous regime it was anything but totalitarian having recognized the need for "legitimacy" and having allowed some room for the activities of civil society. These regimes represent, referring back to the statement of Vernon Aspaturian, a "more sophisticated version of authoritarianism."

VI

In the years 1956-68 the question was often asked: how long will the Soviet Union tolerate the deviationist behavior of her Eastern European client states? The answer came with the invasion of Czechoslovakia during the night of August 20, 1968. This intervention made it clear that the Soviet Union was willing to tolerate national communism but not communism with a human face.

The events in Czechoslovakia leading up to the events in the summer of 1968 are well known. What the Czechs and Slovaks tried to do can be described also in terms of the definition of authoritarianism I offered at the beginning of this study. First they attempted to enlarge the scope in which civil society was free to operate and, then, went even further and demanded the pluralism of economic, political and ideological power. It is very important to realize that they did not have the liquidation of the communist party or its leading role in the state in mind. The party was supposed to retain its dominant and even domineering role in a true nation state in which limits were set on pluralism to prevent the erosion of authoritarian control. The vaguely expressed aim of the Prague Spring was a Marxist democratic authoritarianism or authoritarian-democracy. The Soviets believed, probably correctly, that this new, curious form of Marxism was unworkable, but was, nevertheless, dangerous for the world Communist movement and especially for the continued mastery of Eastern Europe by the Soviet Union. The Prague Spring was not intended to abolish Communism, to change authoritarian into democratic government, to alter the basic structure or ideology of party or state. It simply moved several steps further, too many according to Soviet judgment, on the road leading from totalitarian to national communism. It represents another evolution within the framework of authoritarianism.

While the Prague Spring failed, its spirit lives on. Jiří Valenta argues that Eurocommunism is the result of the events in Czechoslovakia and that its aims are modelled on those expressed by the Prague reformers. He states that "the term [eurocommunism] as they [Enrico Berlinger, Santiago Carillo, and Georges Marchais] use it, is not meant to define a concept or a coherent doctrine, but rather to describe the trend toward independence and the adaptation of communist tenets to conditions of their own countries, which would be free of the lack of democracy noted in the USSR and the East European countries."[29] This quotation repeats in condensed form several of the arguments previously presented. The aim is to introduce democracy into communism or, in other words, to retain a centralized authoritarian regime in which civil society's scope is enlarged to the extent that a certain degree of pluralism can be incorporated into everyday life. This trend was first expressed in Czechoslovakia in 1968. It does not represent a break or change, but simply a new, tentative evolutionary direction in the development of one form of authoritarianism. It is a notion that could never have been voiced without the development of national communism and is one that Eastern Europe contributed to the history of communism and authoritarianism. It is the result of the defensive nature of all Eastern European authoritarian regimes mentioned earlier in this paper. Communism was introduced into the region by force by a foreign power. This power is so overwhelming that it cannot be opposed openly and that its continued presence must be taken for granted. Therefore, the East European communist bureaucracies, the "new classes," had to develop a new variant of the imposed, foreign theme—communism—to justify their position, power, and reason for existence in the eyes of those whose support they sought. This new variant was national communism whose outgrowth was communism with a human face and its Western European version, Eurocommunism.

The Soviet Union could invade Prague, but the existence of Eurocommunism is not ground enough for an invasion of Western Europe. Yet, the Soviet Union needs not only the Eastern, but also the Western European Communist parties' support in its struggle with the Chinese Communist Party. It, therefore, fears Eurocommunism, fears any new development in Eastern Europe, and since the 1975 Helsinki agreement fears the possible infiltration of democratic ideas into its Eastern European domain. As a result, the Soviet authoritarian regime has become even more defensive than it was already all through its existence. As a result in the later 1970's emerged "a Soviet policy to consolidate the 'world socialist system,' namely to integrate Eastern Europe with the Soviet Union... beyond the point of return.... The dynamics of interaction between national forces for change and the new Soviet thrust for integration will shape conditions in Eastern Europe in the eighties...."[30] As this quotation indicates the Soviet Union and her version of Communism are attempting to counter the challenges of China and Eurocommunism by establishing nearly total control over Eastern Europe. If Moscow succeeds the history of Eastern European authoritarianism will end, but if the masters of the Kremlin fail Eastern European authoritarianism might continue to evolve further from the point where it was halted by the Soviet forces entering Prague. Which of these alternatives will become reality and what the next form of Eastern European authoritarianism will be should it be allowed to evolve further cannot be predicted at the moment of writing. I am only fairly certain that given the history of authoritarianism in Eastern Europe the political regimes of this region will not be transformed into democracies for many decades to come.

NOTES

1. This paper was written for a conference devoted to Authoritarianism in the Fall of 1979. It is based on materials available at that time. Important works dealing with my subject, including Andrew Janos, *The Policy of Backwardness in Hungary, 1825-1945* (Princeton: Princeton University Press, 1982), have appeared since then. I decided to submit my original paper to the *East European Quarterly*, but wish to direct the readers' attention to works, like the one just cited, which shed further light on the topic.

2. For a good overview of the influence of the French Revolution in Eastern Europe see: R. R. Palmer, *The Age of the Democratic Revolution, A Political History of Europe, 1760-1800*. II (New York: Alfred A. Knopf, 1959, 1964), esp. pp. I, 103-8, 373-97, 422-9; II, 86-96, 135-174.

3. Samuel P. Huntington and Clement H. Moore, "Conclusion: Authoritarianism, Democracy and One-Party Politics," in Huntington and Moore (eds.), *Authoritarian Politics in Modern Society. The Dynamics of Established One-Party Systems* (New York-London; Basic Books, Inc., 1970), p. 509.

4. John P. Kirscht and Ronald C. Dillehay, *Dimensions of Authoritarianism: A Review of Research and Theory* (Lexington: University of Kentucky Press, 1967), pp. 132-3.

5. *Webster's Seventh New Collegiate Dictionary* (Springfield, Mass.: G. & C. Merriam Co., 1967), p. 59.

6. Donald W. Treadgold, *The U. S. and East Asia: A Theme with Variations*. Presidential Address delivered on August 11, 1979 at the Honolulu meeting of the Pacific Coast Branch of the American Historical Association, p. 22.

7. Vernon V. Aspaturian, *Conference on Authoritarianism in Eastern Europe*, p. 1.

8. Ibid.

9. Mihály Vajda, "Is Kádárism an Alternative?" *Telos*, 39 (Spring, 1979), pp. 172-9.

10. Treadgold, *The U.S. and East Asia*, p. 23.

11. Andrew Janos, "The One-Party State and Social Mobilization: East Europe between the Wars," in Huntington and Moore, *Authoritarian Politics*, p. 205.

12. Kenneth Jowitt, *State, National, and Civic Developments in Contemporary Eastern Europe*. Professor Jowitt kindly gave me a multigraphed copy of this paper. I have not yet seen it in print. Subsequent page references are to the multigraphed version of this paper.

13. Ibid., pp. 1-2.

14. Ibid., p. 2.

15. For an explanation of "professional Ottoman" see Peter F. Sugar, *Southeastern Europe under Ottoman Rule, 1354-1804*. Volume V. of Peter F. Sugar and Donald W. Treadgold, (eds.), *A History of East Central Europe*. (Seattle and London: University of Washington Press, 1977), pp. 34-43, 272-3.

16. Jowitt, *State, National and Civic Developments*, pp. 4-5.

17. For example see: Peter F. Sugar, "External and Domestic Roots of Eastern European Nationalism," Peter F. Sugar and Ivo J. Lederer (eds.), *Nationalism in Eastern Europe* (Seattle and London: University of Washington Press, 1969), pp. 3-54 and "From Ethnicity to Nationalism and back again," in Joseph Palumbo and William O. Shanahan (eds), *Nationalism. Essays in Honor of Louis L. Snyder* (Westport, CT.: Greenwood Press, 1981), pp. 67-84.

18. In the case of Russia, I refer to the changes begun by Peter the Great and brought to an end, for a relatively short period, by Catherine the Great. In the case of Prussia the corresponding figures are Frederick William I (the Great Elector) and Frederick II (the Great). The Habsburg transformation had made great progress by the time of the first partition and was practically completed when Poland disappeared.

19. The Russian and Prussian developments are generally well known. For Selim III's reforms see: Stanford J. Shaw, *Between Old and New. The Ottoman Empire under Sultan Selim III, 1789-1807* (Cambridge, Mass.: Harvard University Press, 1971).

20. Erich Fromm, *Escape from Freedom* (New York-Toronto: Rinehart & Co., 1941), pp. 141-79.

21. Fritz Fellner, "The Background of Austrian Fascism," Peter F. Sugar (ed.), *Native Fascism in the Successor States, 1918-1945* (Santa Barbara: A.B.C.-Clio, 1971), pp. 18-9.

22. Fellner, ibid., p. 18.

23. Janos, "The One-Party State," p. 209.

24. Ibid., p. 218.

25. Peter F. Sugar, "Conclusion," Peter F. Sugar (ed.), *Native Fascism*, p. 150.

26. Fascism is used here to denote any "right wing" totalitarian movement that aims to establish a government possessing the six features enumerated by Carl J. Friedrich and Zbigniew K. Brzezinski, *Totalitarian Dictatorship and Autocracy* (Cambridge, Mass.: Harvard University Press, 1956), pp. 9-10.

27. Teresa Rakowska-Harmstone, "Nationalism and Integration in Eastern Europe; The Dynamics of Change," in Teresa Rakowska-Harmstone and Andrew Gyorgy (eds), *Communism in Eastern Europe* (Bloomington and London: Indiana University Press, 1979), p. 209.

28. Janos, "The One-Party System," p. 232.

29. Jiři Valenta, "Eurocommunism in Eastern Europe; Promise or Threat?" in Rakowska-Harmstone and Gyorgy (eds.), *Communism in Eastern Europe*, p. 291.

30. Rakowska-Harmstone, "Nationalism and Integration," pp. 309-10.

VII

**FASCISM IN INTERWAR EASTERN EUROPE:
THE DICHOTOMY OF POWER AND INFLUENCE**

The interwar decades, the years 1919-39, have often been called the period of the "long armistice." It makes good sense to look at the period covered by this paper in this light not only because World War I raised more questions that it solved, not only because several states—notably Germany, Hungary, and Bulgaria—were consciously looking ahead to the "next round" practically from the moment the shooting stopped, but mainly because, for well-known reasons, a feeling of dissatisfaction, uncertainty, and even fear pervaded the thinking of victors and losers alike. The Italians and even some French believed that their governments sold them short and did not secure for them the advantages to which the great sacrifices made during the war entitled them. The losers blamed their governments either for the defeat or for signing peace settlements that were unacceptable. In spite of the creation of the League of Nations, no effective international organization or mechanism was established that could have alleviated frustration and fear and served as the broad framework for the solution of the numerous social and economic problems that proved too big for the individual states to tackle successfully.

Besides the above-mentioned international difficulties and the growing dissatisfaction of their populations, governments also had to face such problems as the conversion of economies from war to peacetime production; the integration of demobilized soldiers into the economy; inflation; the need for social, educational and land reforms; the social and communication problems created by new borders; and,

Eastern Europe in the 1970s, eds S. Sinanian, I. Deak and P.C. Ludz. Copyright © 1972 by Praeger Publishers. Reproduced with permission of Greenwood Publishing Group, Inc, Westport, CT.

VII

finally, the less tangible but extremely important need to understand and adjust to a profoundly changed self-image of workers and peasants.

If these conditions convinced more and more people all over Europe that the known political systems were bankrupt, turning them away from the traditional political parties, one cannot be too surprised. Nor should it be cause for amazement to discover that when the people looked for ways to solve the many problems they faced, the new means that they devised to achieve their goals placed unprecedented powers in the hands of the authorities. The war had reinforced two trends already extant: the long-term historical one toward centralization and reliance on the all-powerful state, and the shorter but equally well-established trend of judgment on the basis of integral nationalism. Even the Marxists of various shades who ostensibly rejected nationalism followed, in a sense, these same tendencies. The state was replaced by the party or by the dictatorship of the proletariat, and the class took the place of the nation. Nationally or internationally oriented, this "politics of despair" produced the totalitarian movements of which Bolshevism and Fascism are the best known examples.

The best short definition of totalitarianism in my opinion was given in 1956 by Zbigniew Brzezinski:

> a system where technologically advanced instruments of political power are wielded without restraint by the centralized leadership of an elite movement for the purpose of effecting a total social revolution, including the condition of man, on the basis of certain arbitrary ideological assumptions proclaimed by the leadership in an atmosphere of coerced unanimity of the entire population.[1]

Together with Carl J. Friedrich, Brzezinski also enumerated six features that every regime must possess simultaneously to qualify as totalitarian.[2] Fascism qualifies as a totalitarian regime both under the definition just presented and in accordance with the six Friedrich-Brzezinski criteria.

Before we turn from totalitarianism in general to Fascism in particular, a few words must be said about Eastern Europe. This region—from Poland in the north to Greece in the south—is that part of Europe that lies between Germany, Switzerland and Italy in the west and the U.S.S.R. and Turkey in the east. It includes the Austro-Germans and those Bielorussians and Ukrainians who lived in interwar Poland. I know of no perfect definition of Eastern Europe. The one just presented delimits the area surveyed in this paper.

Everything that was said of the situation in Europe at the end of World War I existed in still sharper form in Eastern Europe.

FASCISM IN INTERWAR EASTERN EUROPE

The political, economic, and social dislocations produced by the war in Eastern Europe were much more fundamental and thorough than they were in the West. National antagonisms were sharp, affecting numerous people with disparate ethnic origins whose habitats overlapped and whose identity was not always easy to establish. Among the Eastern European workers and peasants the war produced an even deeper break with their prewar self-image than it did in the West, and the need for basic reforms was much greater here than in any other part of Europe, with the exception of Russia. Democratic political traditions were weak if they existed at all, and societies in general lacked the strong middle class that in the West was a political force in its own right while also serving as a bridge between the so-called upper and lower classes. Eastern Europeans in power understood even less well than those in power in the West the profound changes wrought by the war, and were unable to deal with them. They mastered the first wave of revolutionary fervor that was socialist or communist inspired, outlawed its leaders, parties, and ideologies, leaving only one direction open to those who wanted change at any price. For reasons that will be discussed later, they were unable to deal with these people, making Eastern Europe the ideal region for fascist agitation.

Brzezinski gave us a good short definition of totalitarianism, and he is not the only one who was able to do this. It is much more difficult to find an equally satisfactory short definition of Fascism. Francis L. Carsten takes more than seven pages at the end of his excellent book to define this movement;[3] Ernst Nolte gives various definitions on different levels in his well-known Three Faces of Fascism, winding up with a complicated, three paragraphs-long definition;[4] and numerous other authors are equally unsuccessful in defining succinctly this form of totalitarianism. The difficulty they faced is well summed up by S. J. Woolf, who begins the Introduction to the volume European Fascism that he edited with the following sentences:

> Perhaps the word fascism should be banned, at least temporarily, from our political vocabulary. For like other large words—democracy, reactionary, radical, anarchy—it has been so misused that it has lost its original meaning; or, at least, it has been so overlaid with newer and broader connotations that the narrower, historical sense almost seems to require apologetic inverted commas.[5]

Later on the same page he adds, "the word, unfortunately, has certain commode-like tendencies—the more you stuff into it, the more it takes."[6]

VII

This commode stuffing began almost as soon as Mussolini gained power in Italy and certainly became a popular pastime among would-be Führers after Hitler's <u>Machtergreifung</u>. The definition became hopelessly blurred during World War II when so-called antifascist liberation movements or antifascist fronts were established everywhere, mainly by the communist resistance movements, to bring all those they fought under a common label. Finally scholars have added to the confusion by inventing such additional expressions as clerico-Fascism and monarcho-Fascism.

Fortunately it is not my task to succeed where others much better qualified than I have failed. While I do not have to define Fascism, I must indicate which Eastern European movements are considered fascist when the contrast between their power and importance is investigated in these pages. The movements considered were all "totalitarian" in the sense previously given. They were revolutionary in their desire to change the socioeconomic structure of the countries in which they flourished. Yet, primarily nationalistic, their planned revolutions were considered more of a return to the old national values than a new departure. This apparently contradictory goal of conservative revolution is somewhat clarified when one thinks of other men who in earlier days tried to do the same thing. For example, the nineteenth-century Ottoman reformers, whose goal was a thoroughgoing change in their state, called their movement <u>Tanzimat</u> (purification) to indicate their loyalty to the national past and traditions. Another approach to this curious contradiction is to call fascists the representatives of the "new" Right in the sense in which Eugen Weber used this term.[7] In this chapter the label Fascism will be applied to those political movements that were aiming at the establishment of totalitarian regimes (as defined by Brzezinski) with a chauvinistic, anti-internationalist, conservative-revolutionary program in mind. Although Eastern European movements fitting this working definition followed either the "German" or the "Italian" model, that difference must be disregarded in this chapter that, by its very nature, must concentrate on common features and attempts to generalize.

Limiting Fascism in this manner, men like Dollfuss, Pilsudski, Horthy, Carol II, Alexander, or Plastiras cannot be considered fascists while Seyss-Inquart, Piasecki, Szalasi, Codreanu, Pavelic, and Metaxas—to give only a few examples—qualify as representatives of Eastern European Fascism. With a very few honorable exceptions there has been nothing written since 1945 by those who have access to the documentation, the Eastern European scholars, about the movements led by these and other men.[8] Western scholars, on the other hand, have published enough to allow specialized investigations of several aspects of Eastern European Fascism on the basis of the

FACISM IN INTERWAR EASTERN EUROPE

material that they have presented.[9] One of these aspects—the contrast between the power and the great importance of the Eastern European fascist movements—is of great importance for the understanding of political developments in this region during the "long armistice."

The fascists of Eastern Europe proudly stressed that modern political anti-Semitism was born in their lands, that the Nazi movement had its origins in Georg von Schönerer's prewar movement, and that their post-1918 movements were "homegrown," not needing Italian or German examples. While there can be no doubt that native Fascism existed in Eastern European lands, it is also true that these movements were politically insignificant prior to the second half of the 1930s, when "foreign" developments helped their growth,[10] and that, with the exception of the short-lived government headed by Octavian Goga in Romania from December 28, 1937, to February 10 of the next year, no fascist party achieved power in Eastern Europe prior to the years of World War II when Hitler placed several fascist leaders at the head of satellite governments.*

This lack of success does not mean that the fascists of Eastern Europe represented only the "lunatic fringe" that nobody but themselves took seriously, nor, more importantly, that they were not extremely influential in shaping the policies of those in power to whom they were officially opposed and by whom they were often imprisoned. The influence of these native, politically unsuccessful, often suppressed movements becomes even more amazing in view of their lack of unity. In each country several fascist parties competed for the allegiance of a relatively small segment of the population. They were led by "Führers" whose activities were often exhausted by ridiculous posturing and who presented disjointed and badly formulated programs.

In his excellent short comparative study presented at Moscow in the summer of 1970, Lacko pointed out that in our region there was no strong middle class, no strong and politically conscious

---

*This government included among its members Professor Alexander C. Cuza and the future master of Romania, General Ion Antonescu. While I consider General John Metaxas, the archigos (Führer) of Greece from 1936 to 1941, a fascist, I see him as a fascist without a movement (he tried to organize one after he came to power) and for this reason look at his regime as authoritarian only, although dressed up in a fascist garb. This leaves Goga's regime as the only fascist regime in Eastern Europe prior to World War II.

VII

working class—with the exceptions of Czechoslovakia and Austria, no democratic tradition, and no true political pluralism to limit the appeal and expansion of Fascism in the way they limited it in "highly developed" Western societies with the exception of Germany. Nor was Eastern Europe, with the exception of Albania, a truly "backward" region where traditional, basically patriarchal peasant societies presented a similar barrier to Fascism. In Eastern Europe "conditions conducive to fascism and its manifestations made their appearance soon and with great force to the point where both on the ideological level and in the domain of political methodology it exercised a considerable influence on the reactionary tendencies of Central and Eastern Europe."[11] According to Lacko, three main reasons accounted for the ease with which Fascism functioned here. The social structure and the general historical evolution was the first, nationalism the second, and the third was the traditions concerning power, institutions, and the views concerning the proper functions of the state.[12]

Society as a whole, although it had some classes (workers, tradesmen, professional people) that depended on trade and industry, was still dominated by a landholding upper class in close alliance with the impoverished gentry and civil servants and supported vaguely by a group of small shopkeepers and artisans. These people, in Weber's terms the "old Right," held power, were deathly afraid of losing it, together with their wealth and social position, and, while incapable of adjusting to the demands of the other social strata, were far from being homogeneous themselves.

Historically speaking, our states were all "new" states in 1919-20, despite their long histories and traditions. They faced within their new borders new social and economic problems and tried to solve them either by political integration of previously disparate lands (Regat and Transylvania, Czech lands and Slovakia, the three parts of partitioned Poland, the various provinces of the Kingdom of Serbs, Croats, and Slovenes) or by revisionism (Hungary, Bulgaria, and to some extent Greece). When it became obvious that social and economic problems could not be solved by political expedients, the leaders of the Eastern European states faced a choice: they could turn to social and economic reform or they could adopt even more repressive political measures. Unwilling to consider the former solution, which would have undermined their power base, they turned to the latter alternative during the late 1920s and early 1930s. But by this time the fascists had already made their claims to represent the tendencies to which the "old Right" was now willing to turn.

The problem of nationalism and its virulence in multinational Eastern Europe is too well known to demand discussion. Let me only remind you of a few very relevant facts. Most of the states of post-World War I Eastern Europe were only slightly less

multinational than was the Austro-Hungarian monarchy. In the interwar period these multinational states were either trying to integrate their newly acquired territories and citizens or were attempting to upset the new political order. Both activities enhanced even further the already virulent nationalistic feelings and tendencies of the people involved. The attempts of those in power to find political solutions for all ills aggravated the situation by raising the question of who was really "reliable," and by manufacturing criteria of "reliability."
This search for standards of national dependability led—not unnaturally, given the traditions of Eastern Europe—to equating nation with race. External enemies presented little problem, but the "internal enemy," the group responsible for the failure of the leaders to solve their countries' problems in the 1920s had to be found. When the leadership "discovered" this enemy, the people who were different from them and, therefore, by their definition, not truly part of the nation as they themselves were, it not only turned out that these people belonged to those professions or social strata to which the leaders did not belong, but it also became obvious to those who studied nations with the help of a racist microscope that they were of different ethnic origin. It was at this juncture that the large scale "politization" of anti-Semitism, a long standing prejudice of many Eastern Europeans, occurred. The role of this new political anti-Semitism in Eastern European Fascism is relatively well known. For this reason, although it would deserve detailed discussion, it will not be discussed at length in this chapter. Suffice it to direct the reader's attention to the significance it had in helping the fascists in recruiting followers. By the time the leaders, who might have felt this way for a long time, were ready to make statements of this sort, they found, once again, that they were entering a form of nationalism that the fascists had already defined and claimed as their own.

    The people of Eastern Europe had lived for centuries in absolutist empires (Habsburg, Romanov, and Ottoman). Even when these states changed and became constitutional monarchies or when newly formed, independent, constitutional states took their place in the nineteenth century, power remained in the hands of the old ruling elements that operated under the new circumstances only slightly differently from the manner in which they had run affairs previously. On the lower levels of administration the change was even less marked. The little bureaucrat, usually the younger son of a great family or an impoverished member of the elite, was a gentleman dispensing favors in a more or less arbitrary manner and would have resented being considered a public "servant."

    The military establishments were even more authoritarian than the civil services and were run by the same social element. The churches also fell neatly into this authoritarian picture. Not only did they preach "the only saving and true dogma," a set of beliefs that could not be questioned, but they were also strictly structured along lines of authority with the pinnacle of power once again in the hands of men who came from the same social milieu that furnished the military officers and bureaucrats. Finally, the church was often "national," if not necessarily in its structure then in its symbolism. It was hardly possible to be a Serb and a Roman Catholic at the same time. Not being a Catholic and trying to be accepted as a Pole was equally difficult. Schools, highly centralized and strictly controlled, reinforced this tendency created by state, army, and church, and preached reliance on the state and the authorities as a public virtue.

While it was difficult, given the newly found self-consciousness of large segments of society, to maintain this demand for unquestioning acceptance of everything handed down to a chain of authority, it was by no means impossible. Centuries of training had drilled a certain discipline and, more importantly, a certain attitude into the majority of the population. Most people were used to being led, felt comfortable with dogmas handed to them, and lacked the habit, practice, and, in most cases, the education to think and act on their own. While the old beliefs and dogmas were dated and had lost their appeal, the habit of relying on them remained and all that had to be done was to present new ones.

Marxism in its various forms tried to do this, but failed. Some of the early manifestations of what later became the "new Right" also understood the need for dogma. But these, like the Szeged idea in Hungary, were voiced too soon before the new lines of power emerged clearly. The reason for the failure of the "old Right," the rulers of interwar Eastern Europe, was that they tried to operate with the help of old ideas and never formulated ideologies that could have been disseminated with the help of the state apparatus which they controlled.

The "new Right" did exactly what the "old" failed to do. It tied the traditional and the revolutionary together, attempting to infuse new meaning into the familiar structures of state, army, school, and, when possible, church. The Ustasa stressed Roman Catholicism, Croat nationalism, and, when they achieved power, returned to such old trappings as the uniforms of the old Austro-Hungarian army to stress continuity while presenting a new program. The apostolic double cross was the symbol of the Slovak Peoples' Party, and in Romania Codreanu went even further by calling his movement the Legion of the Archangel Michael, using religious symbolism as often as possible and making Orthodoxy the first precondition of real Romanianism. The fascists understood the need for leadership and dogma and used old bottles for their new wine.

FACISM IN INTERWAR EASTERN EUROPE

The remaining pages of this chapter will attempt to spell out in some detail the generalizations presented so far and to show how and why these produced the curious contrast between the very slight political power the fascists enjoyed and the great influence that they exerted. It is my conviction that the picture I will paint has validity for the entire region in spite of the fact that it does not and cannot cover all the variations that occurred and that most samples cited will refer either to Hungary or Romania, the two states that had the largest fascist movements and for which more material is available than for the others.

After the failure of communists and socialists as well as some peasant-based movements to alter the established political patterns of Eastern Europe, the old leadership element was firmly in the saddle again everywhere. No challenge seriously disputed their supremacy after the failure of the communist coup in Bulgaria in 1923. Even those politicians who were not outright conservatives— the major figures in Czechoslovakia or Poland for example—had reached political maturity before 1914 and were set in their ways. All of them were leaders, and, although not the main spokesmen of their parties, they demanded loyalty and obedience from their followers, and looked at politics as a form of war, in that the object is the elimination of the enemy. Their values were usually the same as they had been before the war, and in more ways than one they tried to reestablish the old order under new circumstances.

In their first task, the elimination of the leftist opposition, they were fairly successful. They had the wholehearted cooperation of the future fascists who, in these early years, usually were members of the ruling parties. These parties aimed at gaining a political and power monopoly, to put the organs of the government and state—at least at election time—in the service of the party, to erect barriers against any possible challenge from the left, to equate themselves and their often narrowly selfish interests with those of the state and nation and with true patriotism. They were, naturally, declared enemies of the Soviet Union and everything it represented; they favored economic change to the degree that it was required to get as near to autarky as possible without, however, weakening the mainly agrarian interests of their own followers; they favored the parliamentary form of government, not in its true democratic form, but only as a fashionable mechanism that allowed them to give their rule the veneer of popular approval and legality.

All these parties and leaders were more or less conservative, politically well schooled but ignorant of economic and social problems, highly nationalistic, and firm believers in the state as the embodiment of national sovereignty, power, and as an instrument for ruling.

They certainly had dictatorial tendencies, but these were not totalitarian. They had something paternalistic in them that told them that any method that would keep the ignorant from making mistakes—and the gravest would have been the removal of the truly knowledgeable from power—was not only acceptable but for the public good, and their dictatorial tendencies and methods were in direct correlation to the real or imaginary dangers they saw around them. Unfortunately, as already indicated, their sense was purely political; consequently, political moves, including a gradual but steady move toward dictatorship, were their answers to challenges that were not political in nature. Coupled with the serious crisis produced by the Great Depression, their misreading of the problems of society finally bankrupted their policy and forced them to look, if not for a new approach, then for modifications in this approach and for new allies.

This was the moment when the influence of the fascists began to become serious. Anti-Marxism, nationalism, the belief in political warfare that would end with the victory of the only true approach to the nation's future greatness, an elitist outlook on society, an egotistical self-centered approach to public life, a disdain for all who either were unwilling or unable—because they were congenitally, racially, not of the nation—to see the "truth" were some of the features the "old guard" leaders and fascists had in common. The major difference between the two was one of degree. This difference is well illustrated by the case of the Arrow Cross ideologist, Ödön Malnasi who, in 1937, was indicted on the basis of Law III/1921 originally passed in Hungary to justify the outlawing of the Communist Party. Malnasi published a fascist work, Sincere History of the Hungarian Nation, in which, among other things, he advocated land reform. This, according to the court, represented "an indictment of the system of large estates which sustained the Hungarian state over the centuries." He was condemned because, in the words of the Supreme Court of Hungary, "the crime of insulting the nation can be committed not only by a Bolshevik but also by a well-known anti-Bolshevik and patriotic scholar."[13]

This example brings to light one of the main differences between the "old" and the "new" Right, between outright conservatism and conservative revolutionism. Malnasi and other fascists were just as elitist as the orthodox conservatives were and their interest in the peasants was neither altruistic nor based on a true recognition of economic realities. While some of them were vaguely Populists, their main goal was to take over the leadership of their respective countries from the "old guard." This required something of a social revolution, a certain egalitarian leveling, the raising up of the lower bureaucracy to the level of the upper or, in other terms, the opening of the upper reaches of power to the gentry, the gentry-imitating segment of the middle class, and the lower bourgeoisie. This demand for change also represented the desire of a younger generation to replace its elders on the political stage. Attacks like Malnasi's were well designed to enlist broad support, but their goal was the undermining of the economic bases of the groups that the fascists proposed to replace.

The "old Right" knew which social and political order was to be maintained or, in the case of the Polish National Democrats, to be introduced to its own advantage, while the "new Right" simply wanted power to impose a new order—about which, in Eastern Europe, it was usually very vague—by totalitarian means often modeled on those of Stalin. The fascists were social déclassés, people whose pretensions were not matched by their social or economic positions and who faced the danger of sinking even lower. They could have turned to any form of extreme or totalitarian solutions, but under circumstances in which "the radical left is crushed or otherwise eliminated . . . , where nationalism appears to be a necessary political stance, as in the new nations struggling to free themselves from economic and political bonds that independence has not removed," it was the rightist form of totalitarianism that became almost the natural, logical solution for those who wanted drastic change.[14]

The Eastern European fascist would probably have turned to the right even had his choice been broader than it was. As a true déclassé, he wanted to climb socially, not to lose his identity completely as he would in the full-scale leveling suggested by Marxist theory. He wanted and felt entitled by birth, education, ability, and determination to have what those in power already had. He stood for that for which the ruling group stood, but in an extreme form that included broadening the criteria for those who enjoyed power and privileges just enough to include him. His great advantage over those who ran the various Eastern European states was that he was not in power. This allowed him a somewhat freer hand in analyzing and assessing the situation, permitted him to put his finger on some real problems like the need for land reform, made it possible for him to criticize and to advocate change, and, when the relatively moderate methods used by the "old guard" rulers failed to solve the problems, to attack them for their "softness," demanding drastic, violent, totalitarian change.

I hope it has become clear from what has been said that a close connection existed between the "old" and the "new" Right in Eastern Europe. This connection was based on social origin (nobility in the broadest sense of the word—a relatively small segment of the middle class that was truly "national" and contained the déclassés of the nobility), on occupation (land holding, free professions, civil and military services), on belonging to the "true nation" in the most

VII

limited ethnic-racial sense of the word, and on numerous common fears and goals. This group could also be described as the composite of a small upper and a broader lower layer of the socioeconomic "in" group within every state in Eastern Europe. This close connection explains both the strength and weakness of Fascism in Eastern Europe, and, in the final analysis, its influence out of all proportion with its true political strength.

In Western and Central Europe many of the fascist leaders were not déclassés but parvenus, while in Eastern Europe the situation was just the contrary. President Hindenburg's background could not have been more different from Hitler's than it was, and the same holds true of Mussolini and the leaders of Italy. Counts Istvan Bethlen and Fidel Pallfy or Sandor Festetics in Hungary came from the same class. Gajda, Stribrny and Benes among the Czechs, Rydz-Smigly and Piasecki in Poland, and most of the political opponents in the other countries fall into similar pairs. The Nazi Hohenzollern, Prince August Wilhelm, was considered by most of his class an aberrant, but the role of Albrecht von Habsburg in Hungary was regarded as a power play within "proper" circles. The number of military officers going beyond playing roles in veterans' and other "patriotic" organizations into outright fascist leadership was much higher in Eastern than it was in Western and Central Europe. The same was true proportionally of civil servants and professional people.

Consequently, in Western and Central Europe the fascists had to start their movements "out in the cold," had to oppose those in power, and work for a Machtergreifung. They represented an alternative in truly pluralistic societies and reached down into the large masses trying to find support. On the other hand, the Eastern European fascists began their political careers, in almost all cases, within well-established parties or movements whose leaders were not alien to them, and they never thought of reaching too far down the social ladder for support even if in some cases it came from the "lowest" classes. They could hardly have acted in a different manner. They had to work, at least to some extent, with people with whom they identified but who were better situated politically and financially than they were. Otherwise they would not have had any financial or social basis for their activity unless, and this they refused to do, they cooperated with people they regarded as their inferiors.

But the rulers' choice was also limited. The further they moved away from true democracy, the closer they got to dictatorship and, because they needed some additional support, the more they needed the backing of the fascists, those people in their own camp whom they considered too extreme and socially not quite equal or too young. The clearer it became that those in power needed help, the more obvious it became that the policies of the governments were doomed to failure, and the less important it became for the fascists to revolt openly against the existing order. Time was running in their favor, and in the not-too-distant future they saw the moment when those running the show would have to turn to them, accepting the personalities and methods they advocated as the least of many possible evils.

This relatively close relationship between the wielders of power and the fascists had numerous advantages and disadvantages for the latter. Let us begin with the disadvantages. First of all, the connections between the two groups were too close both on the ideological-programmatic and on the personal level. The fascists in Eastern Europe were never able to condemn the policies of the governments they wanted to replace with the vehemence and sharpness of their Central and Western European counterparts. Only those who went beyond mere fascism into outright treasonable activities aiming at the dissolution of the state—the followers of Henlein, Tuka, and Pavelic—could equal their Western fellow fascists in this respect. Furthermore, with the exception of Czechoslovakia, no Eastern European government ever could be accused of "Bolshevist leanings" because socialists were never allowed a share of power even in a coalition. The programs of the governments usually pointed in the right direction from the fascists' point of view, and the most the fascists could do was to accuse the ruling groups of going too slowly, too cautiously, maybe only half-heartedly in the right direction.

Secondly, the personal relationships were often too close. Polish fascist movements could and were systematically absorbed by government-sponsored political movements in 1937-38; men like Ljotic and Szalasi treated the heads of their states with amazing respect, sometimes even deference, making it difficult for them to attack governments supported by an Alexander or a Horthy as unacceptable. Furthermore, these relatively friendly personal relations protected the fascists to a considerable extent from prosecution, making it politic not to break them. As a result only the very extremist fringe of the fascist movements, once again with the exception of those who were also antistate, men like Piasecki, Gajda, Baky, Sima—to mention only a few examples—operated in Eastern Europe exactly as the fascists did in the rest of Europe. These men were relatively minor figures in their respective fascist movements but, together with those who were aiming at the dissolution of the states in which they operated, the Ustasa, the Sudeten parties under various names, and a segment of the Slovak Peoples' Party, had a limited although sometimes very important appeal to certain segments of the population.

The close connection between the "old" and the "new" Rights also worked to the latter's disadvantage when, especially in the

1930s, connections with Italy and Germany became essential for their states. Even the years of World War II began with this tendency unfavorable to the hard-core fascists. It was much more advantageous for Mussolini and Hitler to work with men with fascistic sympathies, with people like Imredy, Gömbös, Stojadinovic, Antonescu, or Tiso who were well-established politicians with well-functioning party machines, than to champion a Böszörmenyi, Szalasi, Pavelic, Sima, or Tuka. Only certain well-known events toward the middle and end of World War II forced Hitler finally to turn to the latter group of men, and, when he finally did, his own satraps became the real masters and not the fascists who were then nominally in power.

Finally, this close relationship also prevented the fascists from gaining power without foreign intervention either in the interwar years or during World War II. While the general trend favored them more and more, and while they were able to capture positions in the governments (Austria, Hungary, Romania), sometimes placing one of their men even in the top position, they never came to power in their own right, with the already-mentioned Romanian exception. Following the deepening crisis at home, following their own personal, if not always political, inclinations, and reacting to changes in Germany, the "old" Right gradually was able to take on more and more features of the "new" without adopting the "new's" most extreme demands or tactics and in this manner keep the fascists from power.

This listing of circumstances that worked against the fascists explains not only why their parties remained politically relatively insignificant, but it also indicates some of the reasons for their steadily growing influence. Operating in countries whose policies they more or less approved—leaving aside for the moment the antistate movements—the fascist parties of Eastern Europe grew within a framework that was favorable to them. It is much easier for authorities to move against people whom they do not need and who attack them than against people who belong to the social stratum whose support they require and whose only "crime" is to demand that the governments go faster and farther on the road that they were already following. In the middle 1920s and especially in the early 1930s even the antistate fascist parties began to influence the policies of governments who attempted to save the integrity of their states. Prague had to make concessions to Tiso to keep Tuka in the background and was, in the last moment, ready even to compromise with the extreme demands of the Sudeten. The Sporazum in Yugoslavia can also be considered in this light. It was a compromise concluded by the central authorities with the moderate Macek faction of the Croatian Peasant Party in an attempt to take away the nationalist plank from the Ustasa-dominated extremist wing of the party.

FASCISM IN INTERWAR EASTERN EUROPE 27

The circumstantial advantages also include the fact that the fascists were a more determined and active group than were their friends in government circles. Permit me to illustrate this point with a personal experience. When I was 19 years old and worried about the trends around me, I sat with a group of other young people discussing politics. One of them was an impoverished member of the aristocracy. When his turn to speak came he said something like the following: "I neither think nor worry much about politics. I have a fairly well paying governmental job that involves almost no work and gives me lots of free time. If nothing changes, I will get promoted to jobs with even more pay and less work. Should the monarchy be reestablished, I will get a position within the royal household to which I am entitled by birth and will make even more money doing absolutely nothing. If the fascists take over, my cousin, the well-known fascist leader, will take good care of me. In the unlikely case that the reds should come to power, I will go to England and sponge off our English relatives. So why should I worry about political trends."

While this young man's situation was certainly not typical, his attitude was. Those who had jobs often thought as he did, and those for whom the government could not find positions that they considered suitable became déclassés and joined the ranks of the fascists. Educational restrictions placed on Jews and certain social classes, or simply operating through financially erected barriers, produced more and more young men who came from the "correct" circles, who obtained degrees and felt that these, coupled with their social and national-racial background, entitled them to sinecures. But even the most swollen bureaucracies had their limits of absorption, leaving more and more "proper" young men dissatisfied and ready to join the fascists.

The last two disadvantages mentioned, the choice that Hitler and Mussolini could exercise in handling out patronage in Eastern Europe and the ability of some key politicians to move further to the right with ease, are indications of the first of two major reasons why the fascists, usually leaders of relatively small parties never in power, were as influential as they were. They did represent an alternative when the masters of Germany and Italy looked at Eastern Europe. This was important, especially after the Great Depression, when practically every country in the region would have faced total economic collapse without its trade with Germany. Under these conditions Hitler had a choice, but the leading Eastern European politicians really did not. The theoretical choice they had was no choice at all. They could and did turn increasingly toward the extreme represented by the fascists. The alternatives either were displeasing the master of Germany, thus courting economic disaster and, therefore, finally failure and political oblivion, or—provided they had a

VII

conscience—abdication, leaving the onus of cooperation with Hitler to the fascists themselves. Giving up power is hard for any politician, even for one with a conscience. Those who had it usually retained power and, consequently, moved closer to fascist policy, either believing or fooling themselves by stating that their action spared their countries the rule of local fascists. Just by being around, by representing an alternative for the foreign masters of Eastern Europe, the fascists of the region were able to influence and in some cases dictate policy.

Many politicians in Eastern Europe did not have a conscience, or if they had one it did not exclude the following of a fascist-type policy. These men always sympathized with and often advocated in one form or another the policies preached by the fascists, but were simply better tacticians then the avowed fascists and waited until it was to their advantage to make a switch. Here the social, educational, and other backgrounds that the "old" and "new" Rights shared created the framework within which each could operate with relative ease. For all these reasons the established politicians were able to and did steal the thunder of the fascists, but it would be a mistake to attribute the need they felt to outroar the fascists simply to economic conditions and German-Italian influence. Home conditions demanded it too.

As has been indicated repeatedly, all the Eastern European countries faced serious problems after World War I, and, once the old guard reestablished its political supremacy in these states by eliminating their opponents, development could move only in one direction. Yet even before the Great Depression and Hitler's Machtergreifung it became fairly obvious that the policies of the numerous governments had failed to solve the ills of the region. Change became more and more unavoidable, and unless those in power changed their approach drastically, introducing the real social and economic reforms that would have undermined their own position, they had to turn further to the right, toward the policies already advocated by fascists of the various countries. The groundwork for this turn had already been laid not so much by the vague and confusing platforms of the Eastern European fascist parties, but by the relatively few individuals placed in crucial positions in society.

These men were army officers, clergymen, and, much more importantly, newspapermen and teachers. They not only represented "authority" for people who were used to being led, but were in fact in posts of authority. Furthermore, among people who were to a large extent either uneducated or undereducated, they were a privileged elite because of their knowledge. Finally, in these scarcely pluralistic societies where their number in the total population was much smaller than in Central and Western Europe, they carried a

FASCISM IN INTERWAR EASTERN EUROPE

disproportionate weight.* These people represented a small but crucial element in society whose cooperation was vital for those holding power, notwithstanding the fact that most of them were state employees. It was this group of people also that had the specialized training and the detachment from involvement in day-to-day petty politics to view the national scene "objectively," to see some of its basic problems, and to advocate changes that the governments were unwilling to introduce. Because the really important and influential members of this group came from the same social stratum that furnished the members of both the "old" and "new" Rights, the changes they advocated were seldom democratic, let alone socialistic. The advocates of reforms of a truly popular nature quickly lost positions and influence. It was among these men that the fascists found their most important sympathizers. These, not the party theoreticians, were the individuals who produced the thunder the politicians in power could steal from the fascists.

A well-placed newspaperman could influence thousands of readers; in the army barracks the peasant recruit got not only military training but indoctrination; an anti-Semitic or patriotic sermon in a village church carried much weight; and most of the déclassés were not only the products of the schools, but also carried with them the Weltanschauung that their teachers, mainly the history and philosophy professors, imparted to them. Newspapers were not too numerous and universities even less so. It was easy to mold the readership and even easier to shape the future members of the elite, the university and even the high school graduates, in the image of a few men. Those whom the press and the schools did not reach, the army did. While these armies had no political commissars, everybody familiar with the armies of interwar Eastern Europe knows that the run-of-the-mill officer performed a commissar's duty with great effectiveness. Public opinion, and consequently whatever pressure it could exercise, was shaped by a few men.

It was among this group of crucially placed people that the fascists found—if not party members or even sympathizers—then at least people who shared many of their ideas and were also able to formulate and propagate them with great and far-reaching effectiveness. At least two of the four groups, the newspapermen and the teachers, were also among those who, like the other professionals, had to compete for positions with those, first of all the Jews, whose origins could easily be labeled not quite acceptable from the national

---

*This was true even in the Slovak and Ruthenian parts of Czechoslovakia.

point of view. This made their cooperation with the fascists even easier. They not only were the formulators of ideas that later, in the hands of the politicians moving to the right, became policy, but they also shaped the public climate that, together with the apparent bankruptcy of official policy and later with Italo-German influence, put tremendous pressure on the governments by the late 1920s and early 1930s. This was pressure not only to introduce change but to change in the direction demanded by both a faction of the intellectual elite and of the fascists.

In this identity of views among these two groups we find the second major reason explaining the influence wielded by the Eastern European fascists. While the governments had the power either directly (army and school), or indirectly (church and press) to influence if not to determine the membership of this influential segment of the intelligentsia, it was the fascists who politicized their ideas and turned them into instruments of pressure for the type of change that they favored.

These, then, are the circumstances and reasons that made me write previously that our "states would have produced something that without Mussolini's choice of a label for his party we would possibly not have called fascist, but which, in its essence and numerous manifestations, would have amounted to nearly the same thing."[15] These are also the circumstances and reasons that, while keeping the fascist parties relatively small and away from power, gave them a disproportionate influence in determining the social, economic, and, especially, political policies of most Eastern European governments in the years that both fascists and most other influential politicians considered to be the period of the "long armistice."

NOTES

1. Zbigniew K. Brzezinski, "Totalitarianism and Rationality," The American Political Science Revue, I, 3 (September 1956), 754.

2. Carl J. Friedrich and Zbigniew K. Brzezinski, Totalitarian Dictatorship and Autocracy (Cambridge, Mass.: Harvard University Press, 1965), 2d rev. ed., pp. 9-10. In summary these criteria are: 1. an official ideology; 2. a single mass party led by one man and including in its membership a relatively small percentage of the population; 3. a terroristic police apparatus including a political police; 4. a technologically conditioned monopoly of all means of mass communications; 5. a similar monopoly of all armed forces; 6. a centrally controlled and directed economy.

3. Francis L. Carsten, The Rise of Fascism (Berkeley and Los Angeles: University of California Press, 1967), pp. 230-37.

FASCISM IN INTERWAR EASTERN EUROPE 31

    4. Ernst Nolte, Three Faces of Fascism (New York, Chicago, San Francisco: Holt, Rinehart and Winston, 1965), p. 429.
    5. S. J. Woolf, ed., European Fascism (New York: Random House, Vintage Book, 1969), p. 1.
    6. Ibid.
    7. Hans Rogger and Eugen Weber, eds., The European Right: A Historical Profile (Berkeley and Los Angeles: University of California Press, 1965), pp. 1-28.
    8. If one disregards Austria and the publications of emigrés, only Hungarian books deserve mention: Kalman Szakacs, Kaszaskeresztesek [The Scythe-Cross Movement] (Budapest: Kossuth Könyvkiado, 1963); Miklos Lacko, Nyilasok, Nemzetiszocialistak, 1935-1944 [The Arrow Cross, National Socialists, 1935-1944] (Budapest: Kossuth Könyvkiado, 1966); Peter Sipos, Imredy Bela es a Magyar Megujulas Partja [Bela Imredy and the Party of the Hungarian Rebirth] (Budapest: Akademiai Kiado, 1970). Lacko also presented a short comparison of Eastern European Fascisms at the XIII International Congress of the Historical Sciences in Moscow in August 1970, Le Fascisme—Les Fascismes en Europe Centrale-Orientale (Moscow: Editions "Naouka," 1970).
    9. Practically all studies dealing with Eastern Europe or individual countries in this region during the interwar period discuss Fascism. Their number is too great to permit listing them. Of the specific works dealing with Fascism already cited, the following sections deal specifically with Eastern Europe: Carsten's fifth chapter; in Woolf's volume, Chapter 5, written by K. R. Stadler, is devoted to Austria, Chapter 6 (J. Erös) to Hungary, Chapter 7 (Z. Barbu) to Romania, and Chapter 8 (S. Andreski) to Poland; the volume by Rogger and Weber has chapters on Austria (Andrew Whiteside), Hungary (Istvan Deak), and Romania (Eugen Weber). These same three countries are also discussed by Eugen Weber, Varieties of Fascism (Princeton-New York-Toronto-London: D. Van Nostrand, Anvil Pocketbook, 1964). A detailed study of Hungarian and Romanian Fascism can be found in Nicholas M. Nagy-Talavera, The Green Shirts and the Others (Standford: The Hoover Institute Press, 1971). Peter F. Sugar ed., Native Fascism in the Successor States, 1918-1945 (Santa Barbara, Calif.: A.B.C.-Clio Press, 1971) contains two essays each on the following countries; Austria (Fritz Fellner and R. John Rath), Czechoslovakia (Jan Havranek and Joseph F. Zacek), Hungary (György Ranki and George Barany), Poland (Henryk Wereszycki and Piotr S. Wandycz), Romania (Emanuel Turczynski and Stephen Fischer-Galati), Yugoslavia (Dimitrije Djordjevic and Ivan Avakumovic).
    10. The explanation for this early lack of success given for Hungary by Lacko, Nyilasok, p. 17 is more or less valid for the region as a whole.

11. Lacko, Le Fascisme, p. 9.
12. Ibid., pp. 10-15.
13. George Barany, "The Dragon's Teeth: The Roots of Hungarian Fascism," in Sugar, ed., Native Fascism, p. 76.
14. Rogger and Weber, The European Right, p. 11.
15. Sugar, "Conclusions," in Sugar, ed., Native Fascism, p. 156.

VIII

The Historical Role of Religious Institutions
in Eastern Europe and Their Place in
the Communist Party-State

According to Karl Marx, religion "is the 'opium of the people,' because it holds out hopes of an illusory happiness and thereby diverts them from the struggle for their real happiness."[1] Happiness in this life is achievable and superior to the "illusory" happiness in the afterlife. I doubt very much that this issue of real happiness bothers any communist, let alone the leaders of the various ruling communist parties in Eastern Europe today. Bothered by the "materialism" and "hooliganism" in their societies, especially among the younger generations, they would certainly have no objections if these people lived in accordance with principles like those stipulated by the Ten Commandments. Christ's command, love thy neighbor as thyself, was repeated although in different words by the communists' principle, from each according to his ability, to each according to his needs. There is no reason why a follower of any of the monotheistic creeds could not live in accordance with its commands, hoping to save his or her soul and, at the same time, be a model member of a communist society.

Feuerbach and all those who followed him, including Marx, Engels, and their disciples, were atheists on philosophical grounds in a world which, until 1917, did not force them to test their principles in the "real world." By that time they had a tradition and a vast literature which they could quote or misquote, interpret or misinterpret, in their efforts to make themselves masters of states in which they achieved supremacy irrespective of the manner in which they came to power. It was, therefore, the easiest to base action on this material and, among other things, turn atheism into something like the religion of the communist state.

VIII

Historical Role of Religious Institutions

Atheism, a denial of the existence of God, is not what interests communist regimes. They are not even antireligion or anticlerical when practical considerations supplant theoretical ones, as they do when the parties become governing parties; what they are under these circumstances is antichurch. This statement requires some clarification.

Religion has several explanations in our dictionaries. The one I have in mind, "one of the systems of faith and worship,"[2] demands more from a religious person than simply a belief in God or gods; it demands an intelligent and deep understanding of the basic tenets, the dogmas, on which faith rests and, equally important, the proper interpretation of the services. A true Christian must not only accept on faith but understand the dogmas of Virgin Birth, the nature of the Trinity, etc., and the meaning of transubstantiation and other aspects of the services. To be truly religious, in this sense, demands not only faith but a certain insight of which relatively few people are capable and which religious instruction and catechism classes alone cannot provide. Without this understanding, religion becomes folk religion, a combination of half-understood or misunderstood tenets and practices, local traditions, and even superstitions, and—at least in some cases—the survival of premonotheistic traditions survive. Folk religion is based on the fear of God's anger and on the hope of eternal life in paradise; it has little to do with the true understanding of the essence of any given religion to which its practioners theoretically belong. The great peasant masses of Eastern Europe lived out their spiritual lives on this level. It presented no real danger to anybody or to communism, because by its very nature it is adaptable to local circumstances and demands. An intelligent communist would not and could not be afraid of it.

Anticlericalism is much older than Voltaire's famous battle cry, *Écrasez l'infâme!* The infamous thing which Voltaire attacked was in part folk religion, "bigotry, intolerance and superstition," but it was mainly what he saw as upholding these horrible things: "the power of the organized clergy."[3] The power of the organized clergy that challenged the state, forcing the emperor Henry IV to go to Canossa in 1077, that dominated education and publishing in Voltaire's day, and that, in the nineteenth and twentieth centuries, brought the emergence of Christian Socialism and numerous other political parties was always resented by the laity. Bismarck based his entire Kulturkampf on the assumption that the Center party would obey the orders of the pope and not those of the emperor.

Where were the limits of the clergy's legitimate concern? Did they use their influence over the faithful, people whose understanding seldom went beyond the described folk religious level, and the strength which their organization gave them to become dominant in fields which had nothing to do with their legitimate concern, the saving of the souls? What was, for that matter, the limit of anybody's legitimate activity? The ancient Romans already gave their answer: *ne sutor supra crepidam*.[4] Clearly the clergy went too far for the liking of modern political man, who invented the principle of the separation of church and state. This is the answer to successful anticlericalism; it defines the role of the priest, minister, rabbi, etc., as the old Romans defined the shoemaker's. In this sense the communists are anticlerical too, but not more so than numerous other political parties were and are.

Any religion claims to have "the truth" and, therefore, to be able to tell those who are willing to listen how to live on this earth to earn or hopefully be predestined to eternal happiness in the thereafter. This "truth" is absolute and demands the undivided loyalty of those who accept it. What Bismarck asked from members of the Center party was not undivided loyalty to emperor and state; he asked that they give to Caesar what belonged to him, and he was quite willing to allow them to give to God what was his. The Second Reich was not totalitarian in the sense that it demanded the undivided, total devotion of its citizens. The communist party and any state in which it gains power is totalitarian in this sense. The party's "truth" demands undivided loyalty. This is the reason for its antichurch stand irrespective of which church is involved. Party, state (dominated by the party), and church are *institutions* claiming total loyalty and, therefore, they are inevitably in conflict. The church does not ask, Are you truly religious or do you follow a version of folk religion? It simply says, You are officially a member of this church, you must give it your undivided loyalty unless you want to end up in hell, purgatory, limbo, or some other similarly pleasant place. The party does not ask, Do you understand and believe in what is today the officially sanctioned version of Marxism (Marxism-Leninism, communism, bolshevism, etc.)? It simply says, Unless you cooperate with us you are an outlaw and must suffer the consequences. The problem is that nobody can owe undivided loyalty simultaneously to two institutions. Probably most people would like to owe such loyalty to nobody, but this is an alternative unacceptable to those who make claims on their devotion.

As far as successful communist parties are concerned, they can tolerate no organization or institution that might possibly offer an alternative focus of loyalty—even if it were not the primary one—in the countries in which they govern. Other institutions must either be eliminated altogether, as were the Boy Scouts, or they must be transformed and absorbed by the party apparatus in a manner for which the German National Socialists invented a perfect term: *Gleichschaltung.* Only the Albanians claim to have abolished religion, meaning that they have abolished all religious organizations, institutions, and manifestations, and even their claim must be questioned when taken literally. True believers in Albania are still true believers. The other East European communist regimes recognize that the various churches could neither be eliminated by fiat nor be *gleichgeschaltet* and must, therefore, be constantly watched and disciplined.[5]

In Eastern Europe at present the party is the institution that has enough power to enforce its will, threatening the very existence of all other institutions, and the church is the one resisting *Gleichschaltung,* asking this modern political shoemaker to stick to his last. The church —irrespective of which one it is—has to strive, before anything else, to safeguard its existence, dogmatic base and unity, contact with the believers, and the freedom of those functions that make this contact possible and meaningful. Only if it is able to achieve this primary function can the church get interested in protecting other principles and rights in which its members and the population at large might be interested. When it tries to do this, any church acts in a manner which the communist party will consider an intervention into affairs which are none of the church's business. The churches are not the only institutions or organizations capable of challenging the party-state in this manner —Solidarity played this role in Poland for sixteen months in 1980–81—but they have been the most important ones in Eastern Europe since World War II. Their roles and effectiveness vary greatly. Historical development is one of the factors which account for this difference, and the following pages of this chapter will be devoted to a summary overview of the churches' place in East European society.

ORTHODOXY

Nationalism is the tradition or ideology which created the greatest difficulties for the novel and internationalist creed which the communists tried to introduce into Eastern Europe. It would be a logical expectation to see the various Eastern Orthodox churches in the forefront of nation-centered resistance to communism, with Roman Catholicism and the various Protestant churches playing a less important role. While the final break between the Eastern and Western church occurred in 1054, the developments which separated the two were much older and, besides theological differences, rested on church-state relations which were very different. At the famous and important Council of Nicaea, in 325, Emperor Constantine I (305–37) played an important role and laid the basis for his successors' dominance of the Eastern church. He was a strong and effective ruler who deserved being called the Great by historians. At the same time the rulers of the West were weak. When, in 452, the Huns of Attila neared Rome, the defense was not organized by Emperor Valentinian III (425–54), but by Pope Leo I (the Great) (440–61). In the East the emperor protected the church, in the West the pope protected the emperor. The Attila episode can be placed in the broader context of the centuries-long Great Migration of People (*Völkerwanderung*). It sapped the strength of the Western Roman Empire, which gradually lost its provinces and then even Italy to the newcomers before the Herulian king, Odoacer, deposed the last emperor in 476, leaving only the church as a universal institution in Europe outside the borders of the Byzantine (Eastern Roman) Empire. The Western (Roman Catholic) church did not give up its claim to supremacy and universality even after Pope Leo III (795–816) crowned the king of the Franks, Charles the Great (771–814), emperor in 800. Because of this universalist claim that never recognized national differences or boundaries, it is rather surprising that the Catholic church became the "most nationalistic" of churches in states under communist rule; the Protestants and Orthodox were—in theory—better suited to play this role.

The Byzantine emperors not only increased the influence which Constantine the Great established over the church, but they were much more successful in dealing with the various new elements streaming into Europe from Asia. They either defended their borders successfully or allowed the wandering people—in their case mainly the future southern Slavs—to settle in their domain as their subjects or vassals. The first major influence that changed the life of the new arrivals was Christianity. By the end of the tenth century most Serbs had become Eastern Christians, while the Bulgarians date their conversion from even earlier, the end of the ninth century. The Croats lived outside Byzantium and, therefore, became Western Christians.[6] What these people saw was a powerful ruler who was also master of his church. Thus, when they attempted to break away from Byzantium, they not only called their rulers emperor (tsar), but to prove their might and independence established national churches. The first Bulgarian tsar, Simeon (893–927), assumed this title in 924 and to justify it changed the title of the head of the Bulgarian church from archbishop to patriarch (Preslav patriarchate). At the same time Ohrid (in Yugoslavia today) became an important center of Bulgarian culture. This city became the site of the second Bulgarian patriarchate in 1232 during the reign of Ivan Assen II (1218–41).[7] These two patriarchates are the prime indicators that under Simeon and Ivan Assen the Bulgarians had important, independent states of their own. The story of the Serb Orthodox church is also closely connected with Serbia's most glorious moments in the late Middle Ages. Stefan Nemanja I (1168–96) established a strong, united state, and his son, Stefan Nemanja II (1196–1223), completed his work. The brother of the latter, Saint Sava, became the head of the Serbian church with a traditional center at Peć (Ipek).[8] The somewhat similar relationship between Muscovite (later Russian) rulers and the church is well known.

The Byzantine (Greek), Bulgarian, and Serbian lands were gradually absorbed into the Ottoman Empire between 1354 and 1453. The religious institutions of these people also had to adjust to the dictates of the new political masters. After several steps taken by earlier sultans, the full-fledged "Ottoman system" emerged after 1453 when Mehmed II (the Conqueror) (1444–46; 1451–81) gave it its final form.[9] He followed, in many ways, the Byzantine model, considering himself the new emperor whose capital city he had just conquered. Not bound by Christian tenets, dogmas, customs, and traditions, it was even easier for him than it had been for the rulers of Eastern Rome to consider clergymen who were inferior to himself to be members of a branch of government. His Muslim worldview forced him, in a sense at least, to pay attention to the clergy, religious "functionaries" whom he had to recognize and respect following the Prophet's dictum, while he not only could disregard but also strove to eliminate lay officeholders and hereditary masters, who could lead the various conquered people against him.[10] The resulting *millet* system recognized no nationality, only differences between the sultan's subjects along religious lines. One of these *millets* was the Orthodox whose head, the patriarch of Constantinople (Istanbul), whom the sultans considered to be an administrative functionary, was responsible to them for the good behavior of all Orthodox.[11]

This well-known development in the life of the Balkan Christians reinforced the already established rank order—emperor (sultan) followed by the patriarch. The *millet* system did not differentiate between ethnic groups; it recognized only Orthodox people who had to obey one religious leader, whose powers went way beyond the traditional and the purely religious. A stronger institution emerged that was clearly acting in the name of the state.

Unity of dogma, organizations, and even ceremony are basic considerations for ecclesiastic leaders at the best of times and even more so when the lay authority to which they owe allegiance is of a different faith. The patriarchs of Constantinople always resented the establishment of other patriarchates by the Balkan peoples and in the name of safeguarding church and faith used the power given to them by the *millet* system to recentralize the Orthodox church, eliminating even the usage of Church Slavonic in the services.[12] The church became "Greek" to the point that modern Serb, as well as Bulgarian, historians speak of the double "Ottoman-Greek yoke." The reemergence of the independent Balkan states was either followed by the establishment of their own "national" churches (Serbia) or followed the reestablishment of independent ecclesiastical institutions (Bulgaria).[13] Clearly, this Greek-dominated establishment did not lend itself to "nationalistic" movements by Slavs. That some of the early nationalists were clergymen is understandable because one had to be literate to become familiar with new ideas.[14] The Greeks also established their own national church as soon as they gained their independence because Constantinople remained subject to a foreign ruler. These new Balkan Orthodox churches became what they had been prior to the arrival of the Ottomans—state institutions.

The Romanian story reflects this "eastern tradition," although the

Romanians were neither Slavs nor subjects of Byzantium. They retained their internal independence as vassals of the Ottomans. The formation of the Wallachian state is usually dated from the reign of Basarab (ca. 1330–52) and that of Moldavia from roughly the same time, when King Lajos I (the Great) of Hungary (1342–82) liberated the territory of the future state from the Mongols' rule and established a march district there.[15] Following the by then well-established practice of Orthodox rulers, the princes of these states organized their own churches. More interesting is the story of Transylvania. In this multinational region, under Hungarian rule since the early tenth century, Hungarians, Germans known as Saxons, and Székelys were "political nations" with full and equal rights. The Orthodox faith was not "recognized" but only tolerated, and its followers had no freedoms. In Transylvania, the Uniate church was formally established by the Act of Union of 1698.[16] Orthodox clergymen who joined the new church became the most privileged and best educated Romanians of Transylvania and, by the eighteenth century, the main spokesmen demanding equal treatment for their conationals. The Orthodox, still the majority of Transylvania's Romanians, had to do something to produce a "national church" of their own, independent from the Serb-dominated archbishopric of S. Karlovci. This they achieved in 1865. There were now "two Romanian national churches" working for the equality of Romanians in the Habsburg Empire and after 1867 in Hungary.

Just as the Constantinople patriarchate was considered the "Greek church," so all other Orthodox establishments were "national churches." Ironically, this very fact made them relatively ineffective as centers of national (or any other) opposition to communism. They were considered to be institutions of the "ruling establishment" of which they were a part. This view was not simply something "taken for granted," but—with few notable exceptions prior to and since the communist takeover—corresponded to reality. While the Bolsheviks in Russia were much too weak and preoccupied with other affairs when the Russian patriarchate, in abeyance since 1700, was reestablished on October 30, 1917, they did not abolish it subsequently but tried to make it, once again, a governmental institution. After World War II the successful East European communists did the same in Orthodox lands.

The only seeming contradiction, the popularity of the Orthodox church in Macedonia, does not negate but rather confirms the evaluation presented. Macedonia, a republic in the Yugoslav Federation, the first Macedonian state in modern times, had to ward off both Bulgarian and Serb claims and propaganda after Tito established it at the end of World War II. In the roughly twenty years that followed, something like a true Macedonian self-identity developed in this republic whose citizens must have looked at the establishment of the Macedonian Orthodox church in 1967 as a confirmation and legitimation of their existence as a separate nation. Now they too had their national church, although this should not have been important to them, as true communists.

The populations of countries with Orthodox majorities have become accustomed to equating the "national church" with the "church of the establishment." When the establishment fell into communist and thus theoretically antireligious hands, the Orthodox clergy, with few notable exceptions, did not know how to act as members of a nonestablishment institution and did not take the stance that would have made them the leaders of national resistance to either communist internationalism or Soviet domination.

ROMAN CATHOLICISM

The Roman Catholic prelates were even more a part of the establishment than were their Orthodox colleagues. Anybody even vaguely familiar with the role the clergy played during the Middle Ages and the early modern period anywhere in Catholic and later Catholic/Protestant Europe knows this too well to require any argument. The archbishop of Esztergom was not only the primate of the church in Hungary, but also was entitled to the rank of prince and the position of first baron (zászlósúr) of the realm. The position of the primate in Poland, the archbishop of Gniezno (later Gniezno/Warsaw) was comparable. Both states considered themselves the *regnum marianum* and the savior of western Christendom, facing the Orthodox and the Muslims threatening from the East. While the position of the church was seriously challenged during the Reformation, the Counter-Reformation was successful in both states and reestablished the eminent position of the Catholic church. The clergy's role in administration and politics was always of primary importance.[17] Therefore, the most important bishoprics, if not all of them, were usually entrusted to those segments of the

VIII

aristocracy that those in power favored whenever a given see became vacant. When the role and importance of the church in the history of these two countries is considered, the conclusion cannot be avoided that they were an integral part of the establishment; but at the same time it should be remembered that the church always stressed its supranationality and universality and strongly resisted any attempt aiming to create national Catholic churches.

The situation in Croatia comes closest to that in Poland and Hungary. This is the case not only because of the long period during which Croatia was a land of St. Stephen's Crown—although not an integral part of Hungary—worn for some four hundred years by the members of the House of Habsburg, but also because most of those heading its most important dioceses (Split, Zagreb, and later also Djakovo) were aristocrats and very active in politics. It is, therefore, of some interest to compare the position of these three churches in their respective lands in their communist period.

Without any doubt, the Polish Catholic church offered the most formidable opposition to a communist government anywhere since 1945. This has several reasons, but the historical is the one that is discussed in this chapter. It was after the partitions that the Polish church became the symbol of Polishness in the eyes of practically all Poles. Massive Russification following the uprising in 1832 practically eliminated all Polish institutions and made Russian dominance of public life in the Russian areas practically universal. What was left was the Catholic church. It became the symbol of Polishness and Polish resistance, with every move taken by St. Petersburg to weaken it interpreted as a further attempt to eradicate the Polish nation from the face of the earth. After the insurrection of 1863 the situation became even worse. The establishment of an Orthodox archbishopric in Warsaw and the transfer of the Roman Catholic seminary to St. Petersburg were deeply resented by everybody, not only the clergy. Under these circumstances, being a Catholic was not only a religious but also a nationalistic "duty."

The Catholic church became the symbol of Polishness in Prussian held lands also. Here the "enemy" was not Orthodox but Lutheran. This was made obvious to the Poles by Bismarck's Kulturkampf. This "struggle" was political not religious in essence, and while it could be considered anti-Catholic it was certainly not anti-Polish. Yet, having watched the events in Russian Poland, by the 1870s the Poles saw in every anti-Catholic move an anti-Polish one. The church was, here too, the persecuted victim of anti-Polish sentiments and thus the living symbol of Polishness.

In the Austrian part of Poland, Catholicism was not persecuted. The growing liberalism of the Austrians, especially after 1867, made possible the growth of Jewish emancipation and the emergence of Ukrainian nationalism (often associated with the Uniate church), two manifestations which threatened the Polishness of the Galician lands. Again, the Roman Catholic church emerged as the bulwark of pure Polishness. To these local developments must be added another, very important fact. After the Third Partition, the only Polish institution that remained intact and could unite all Poles was the church, despite its universalist claim. If for no other reason than this, it had to develop into the national symbol which it had become by 1918 when Poland was reborn as a united state.[18] After the Fourth Partition, in 1939, the Catholic church was, once again, the only surviving "Polish" institution and quickly reverted to the role which it ceased to play only some twenty years earlier. It continued to see itself in this light once the hostilities ended in 1945, and many Poles agreed with this assumption. Thus the Polish Catholic church had a strong historical base on which it could base its struggle and the Poles a long-established symbol of resistance.

The Croatian Catholic church has to be ranked in second place should anybody try to rank Catholic churches in terms of effectiveness as national symbols. Here the long-term historical factors are less important than they were in the Polish case, but the shorter-range events play a more important role. In Croatia Catholicism became important after the modern ideology of nationalism made its entry into the Balkans and, especially, after the Illyrian movement set in motion the Yugoslav movement.[19] In a united southern Slav political unit (irrespective of its location in or outside the Habsburg domain) Catholics were in the minority. Catholicism, as both a religion and a cultural orientation, differentiated Croat and Slovene from the Orthodox, mainly Serb, brethren. Croatianism became equated with Catholicism. True enough, the Slovenes were Catholics too, but they did not have the long history of independence and political activity which the Croats had, and when they entered politics, in the second half of the nineteenth century, their parties were clerical and, thus, usually pro-Habsburg. This left the Croats to carry the national/religious banner both before and after the creation of the Kingdom of Serbs, Croats, and Slovenes, later renamed Yugoslavia. A Serbo-Croat-speaking Catholic is still automatically considered to be a Croat, and the Croats have still not settled their differences with the Serbs. Yet the Catholic church plays a less important role as a symbol and institution of resistance here than in Poland. I believe that two major factors account for this. First, the great nineteenth-century leaders of the church, including bishops Josip Stadler (1843–1918) and especially Josip Juraj Strossmayer (1815–1905), were not followed by similarly outstanding people with true leadership quality in the interwar period. Second, the role of the Catholic church, or at least some of its priests, during World War II made the position of this institution as a Croat—and not *Ustaše*—symbol somewhat questionable. Consequently, the church was forced on the defensive for too long to be able to play a leadership role.

The fact that the Hungarian Catholic church is the least prominent today of the three churches being compared has its historical reason too. Three important events took place almost simultaneously in Hungarian history. The great defeat of Mohács and the beginning of uninterrupted Habsburg rule both occurred in 1526, and the beginning of the Reformation in the country came soon thereafter. It should also be remembered that from 1526—when a Habsburg and a non-Habsburg were both elected as king—until 1699, the Hungarian nobility, the politically important segment of the population, had a choice: they could support the ruler in Vienna or the one in Cluj (Kolozsvár, Klausenburg)—the successor of the second king elected in 1526, the prince of Transylvania. The nobility, therefore, had a choice, something which nobles elsewhere did not have.

Two of the major goals of the Habsburgs were the creation of a centralized empire and the support of the Counter-Reformation. Therefore, in the mind of the Hungarian nobility, Catholicism and the elimination of Hungary's special status within the Habsburg domain became two undistinguishable entities associated with Habsburg, that is, "foreign" rule. When they adopted and fought for the principle of religious equality and freedom, they fought the Habsburg-supported Roman Catholic church and, most importantly, they fought for the rights and privileges of their country, that is, their estates. This is why both before and after 1699, princes of Transylvania, even those who were Catholics themselves, fought for the rights of Protestants as an important part of the national liberties which they wanted to safeguard.[20] In this manner protonationalism became identified with anti-Habsburg sentiments and a distrust of the Habsburg-protected and, therefore, Habsburg-loyal Catholic church. This opposition centered east of the Tisza river, where the largest city, Debrecen, became known as the Calvinist Rome. The Reformed church became the symbol of opposition and of national independence because the nobility of eastern Hungary, and to some extent Transylvania, followed it.

Today there are far too few members of the Reformed church in Hungary to make it the institution that can challenge the supremacy of the Communist party. The Catholic church was always the establishment church, even after the Habsburgs had to relinquish the throne of Hungary after World War I, and the role played by Jozsef Cardinal Mindszenty (1892–1975), especially after 1956, certainly did nothing to change the population's image of its role in society.

Czechoslovakia is the one remaining country in which the overwhelming majority of the population is, at least nominally, Roman Catholic. The masters of Prague certainly do their best to make the activities of the Catholic church as difficult as possible, and Josef Cardinal Beran (1889–1969) more than earned his reputation as the defender of his church and human rights. Yet, the Czech nation does not look at the Catholic church as the institution that symbolizes its historical or present identity. The most glorious days in Czech history are connected with the Hussite-Táborite period.[21] This fifteenth-century movement was not only a forerunner of the Reformation but also a true social revolution at the same time. It was defeated after a long struggle, as was the Reformation a century later, at the Battle of the White Mountain in 1620. The Counter-Reformation made the Czech lands practically solidly Roman Catholic but failed to eradicate what many experts have called the "Hussite spirit" of the people. Even if this spirit, which supposedly dominates even the Czech Catholic church, has become nothing more than a myth by now, it is hardly possible for a people which sees the moments of its most glorious national greatness in a reformist movement to transfer this feeling to an institution that rests on the defeat of this historical event.

While the Táborite forces of Jan Žižka (d. 1424) operated in Slovak territory too, the religious development and, consequently, the position

VIII

of the Catholic church to the present was very different. As has been mentioned, the Croats had important bishoprics usually occupied by Croat bishops. When the Uniates in Transylvania became the spokesmen of the Romanians in this principality, the Orthodox, the majority, successfully fought for an independent church of their own and, once they got it, joined the Uniates in fighting for their people. The real importance for a people in having its "own church" is not so much this very fact, but the ability of this institution to maintain schools, hospitals, and other social institutions through which it can influence its flocks' every weekday also. The Slovaks never had a Catholic church—or any other church—of their own during the roughly one thousand years they spent under Hungarian rule. After Žižka's troops disappeared, the mastery of the Catholic church was only slightly challenged by Lutheranism, which was adopted by the German-speaking minority in Slovak lands and also by a small proportion of the Slovaks. The Lutherans had their church and, therefore, their schools. In these, Lutheran Slovaks also studied, with the result that most of the early Slovak "modernizers" and "nationalists" from Jan Kollár (1793–1852) to L'udevit Štúr (1815–56) and Pavel Jozef Šafařík (1795–1861) were Lutherans. The mainly illiterate masses, religious in the folk-religious sense, distrusted if not these "heretics" then at least their church, which could not become the symbol of Slovak revival. There were Roman Catholic reformers too, beginning with Anton Bernolák (1762–1856) and ending with the first truly popular political leader Andrej Hlinka (1864–1938). They too had to struggle against the uneducated, superstitious attitude of their people, and while these clergymen became very well known and liked, their church could not profit from their eminence because the hierarchy remained Hungarian and, therefore, anti-Slovak until the end of World War I. Thus, prior to 1918 the Catholic church, while popular in the folk-religious sense, did not emerge as a "national" institution. The symbol and major culprit (to some extent, at least, unjustifiably) of the World War II period was another clergyman, Jozef Tiso (1887–1947), placing the Slovak Roman Catholic church in the same defensive position which the Croatian faced after 1945. It was another Catholic church which could not function successfully as an alternate institution facing the Communist party.

VIII

THE MUSLIMS OF BOSNIA

So far, the "major churches" of the "major nations" have been covered. This does not mean that the other religious or ethnic groups are less important, interesting, or—at least to some extent—historically influenced by their attitude toward their leading religious institutions. The Roman Catholics of Bosnia and Slovenia easily come to mind, if for no other reason than because they are members of a faith that has been covered. I will not deal with these people because their ecclesiastical leadership since 1945 has been relatively weak and because their position within Yugoslavia makes any stand they might take secondary to the resolution of conflicts emerging from the Croato-Serb controversy, the country's major "national" problem. Jewish and Protestant communities are too small in Eastern Europe today to offer any challenge to the communist-dominated state. More numerous than these are the Muslims in the Balkans. A few words should be said about these, although chapter 16 will discuss them in detail.

Muslims can offer a position of their own anywhere, but not as a "church," although members of the *ulema* might be prominent among the leaders. It should be remembered that while Islam is a very important religion, it has no clergy, only learned men (*ulema*), and no official "church." Islam came to the Balkans with the conquering Ottomans. With the exception of some of the Muslims living in southeastern Bulgaria, the Balkan Muslims, although often called Turks, were not and are not Turks but converted members of the local population.[22] They had no reason for seeking an independent identity until the end of Ottoman rule at various times in the nineteenth century. Even then they did little because their leaders, including the important members of the *ulema*, withdrew together with the Ottoman army and administration. Thus, no Muslim community emerged capable of political action as a distinct group. The followers of this religion became involved, often prominently, in Albanian and Macedonian movements as members of these nations, not as Muslims. If they oppose the ruling establishment today as religious minorities—Albania, Bulgaria—then they do so because the regimes' decision to move against them for whatever reasons prompted their actions. The one exception is that of the Bosnian Muslims.

The Muslims of Bosnia were numerous and powerful enough even under Ottoman rule to govern their own province, although nominally as appointees of the sultan. When Bosnia-Herzegovina was first occupied (1878) and then annexed (1908) by Austria-Hungary, the position of the Muslims was not altered because Vienna understood that it needed their cooperation to rule the province without difficulty. Benjámin Kállay (1839–1903), who as Austro-Hungarian common minister of finance administered Bosnia-Herzegovina from 1882 to 1903, was especially favorable to them because he was aware of the Yugoslav problem and favored a group that called itself Muslim and not Serb or Croat. It was he who foreshadowed, in a sense, what occurred in Tito's Yugoslavia when the Muslims were recognized as a separate "nation." Kállay wanted to create a Bosnian nation separate from Serbs and Croats and for this needed the Muslims. When Serb and Croat national movements and parties surfaced in Bosnia-Herzegovina, the Muslims moved also, but their leadership was not clerical but laic. They moved as a separate ethnic, not as a religious, group to safeguard their position in Bosnia-Herzegovina.[23] In acting in this manner, they stressed the socioeconomic separation more than the religious one, justifying Kállay's policy to some extent and foreshadowing the developments under Tito. Thus, for something like one hundred years the Bosnian Muslims acted as a separate group identified by its religion, but not for religious reasons and not through an organized religious institution.

CONCLUSION

The number of factors and circumstances that have determined the interaction since 1945 of two major institutions, church (irrespective of the denomination) and party-state, are numerous. Timing is important, as are personalities, the policy of the Soviet Union, the international situation, correct or faulty assessment and tactics on either the party's or the church's part, economic conditions, and reaction to unforeseen occurrences. Thus, history and historically determined circumstances are not crucial and decisive by themselves. Yet without taking them into consideration some of the differences we observe in church–party-state relations cannot be explained fully. Stefan Cardinal Wyszyński (1901–81), a personality of heroic proportions, could not have played in Hungary or Croatia the part that he played in Poland because in these countries the populations' assessment of the importance of their church, for them and for their nations, was and is drastically different from that of the Poles. It was not and is not simply the contemporary party and ecclesiastic leadership that determines the relationship between the institutions which they supervise; they cannot operate without a certain popular acceptance, the "legitimation" which communist leaders tried hard to gain and prove at least since 1956. The churches too need a certain national "legitimation" to act effectively as spokesmen of a great variety of ideals contradicting those of the party. In striving for this popular recognition the historical tradition plays a very significant role, and it was this role which was presented in outline form in this chapter.

IX

Nationalism and Religion in the Balkans
Since the 19th Century

The demise of communist rule in the various states of the Balkans was followed by steadily increasing tensions leading to a bloody civil war. Some of the events which have attracted world-wide interest began even before the critical years of 1989-90. Clever and unscrupulous leaders using the tools which modern media technology put at their disposal can channel and have directed popular sentiment and feelings in directions which suited their purpose. They did this during the long years of communist supremacy, and even more blatantly during the last few years. Shaping public opinion and action is easier when the direction in which the leadership wants events to move coincides with and/or is based on the feelings and wishes of the majority of those whom the leaders wish to mobilize. Each group of humans, from the smallest (the nuclear family) to the largest (nation) is held together by shared self-identifiers. In the Balkans (except Albania) the most pronounced differentiation separating the masses from those who ruled them for about a half millennium was religion, the main if not only criterion accepted and enforced by the masters of the Ottoman Empire. Has this enforced self-identifier survived into the present, or was it changed and if so why and how? This study attempts to answer this basic question.

The historic 19th Century in the Balkans begins with 1789. This region was affected, as were the other lands of Europe, by the French Revolution, but it was also in this year that Sultan Selim III (ruled 1789-1807) ascended the throne in Istanbul, drastically changing the basic philosophy of rule in all the lands of the Ottoman Empire over which he ruled. This long nineteenth century, the primary subject of this essay, ended in 1914 with the outbreak of World War I.

By 1789 the conditions under which the various inhabitants of the peninsula lived varied greatly. The Romanian principalities, never under direct Ottoman rule, were ruled by phanariot hospodars whose tenures in office were short and often rapacious. Montenegro's prince-bishops enjoyed life tenure and

IX

considerable independence in their actions. Some districts of mainland Greece, mainly in the Morea, and most Aegean Islands were administered by members of hereditary local masters who acknowledged Ottoman rule and were not displaced when the Ottomans conquered the Balkans. In Albania and Bosnia-Hercegovina, local Muslim families held sway nominally as Ottoman functionaries, but in fact on the basis of their local prestige and wealth. The Serbs and Bulgarians saw their lands administered either by Ottoman functionaries or by various *âyans* who established themselves in certain regions and ruled as petty local potentates. Everywhere, the overwhelming majority of the people inhabited the countryside and lived the life of cultivators or husbandmen. In the Greek and Romanian lands well established rural demographic patterns were still in place, but in the Slav-inhabited lands the *çiftlik* system had replaced the *timar* by this time making village elders and chiefs important individuals.

In spite of these significant differences all regions were identical in one very important respect besides the already mentioned heavy rural concentration of the population: Orthodoxy was the dominant religion everywhere. In terms of the number of followers, Islam followed Orthodoxy in Rumeli with Judaism in the third place. With Jews residing almost entirely in cities, the countryside was Orthodox and Muslim. If we are to analyze the shifting of the primary self-identifying criteria of the people of Southeastern Europe,[1] the rural-orthodox majority of those living in Ottoman-held lands and their attitudes deserve major attention although we know less about this group than we know of other segments of the population.

Istanbul looked at its subjects in Rumeli as members of various *millets*, making religious identification crucial and the Orthodox Patriarch in Istanbul a person of great importance for the people of the Balkans.[2] Although by the end of the 18th century the intellectual frontier between the Ottoman Empire and Europe had broken down and western ideas and ideals had penetrated into this state, the great majority of the population, being cut off by its illiteracy and immobility, knew nothing of these revolutionary thoughts.[3]

The gradual disintegration of law and order in the Ottoman Empire reached its apogee in the 18th century. The establishment of the *çiftlik*-based life and the emergence of the *âyans* were not the only results of the Porte's inability to rule its provinces. It also gave birth to the klephts, martalose, morlaks, hajduks, uskoks, etc., the various locally constituted armed bands who had their bases in the villages of given neighborhoods and made life very unpleasant to all foreigners, but especially to the representatives of the authorities. Future generations looked back at these bands as the early fighters for their nations' freedom. "Though in real life these guerrillas were pirates and brigands, the epic poetry extols them as champions of the oppressed against the Turks. Thus the Serbian people acquired a whole gallery of Robin Hoods who could be admired and emulated in the struggle for freedom."[4] The same can be said about Greeks and Bulgarians who practiced the same trades and became national heroes one or two generations later. It is also important to note that "the antagonism between the *asker* and *raya* increasingly came to be identified with . . . antagonism between Muslim and Christian."[5]

While the Ottomans looked at the Orthodox *millet* as one group, the Balkan Christians were anything but a united group. Orthodox Churches were historically national churches and symbols of a nation's sovereignty. Their memories of these states and Churches were still alive at the end of the 18th century. The Ohrid archbishopric was abolished in 1767 and the patriarchate of Peć in 1766. The latter's place was taken by the patriarchate of Sremski Karlovci which had been established by Patriarch Arsenije III Crnojević who moved there from Peć in 1690. To these memories and the longing for their Church, the Slav people added their discontent with the manner in which the Patriarch in Istanbul governed his *millet*. Trying to maintain the doctrinal and organizational unity of their Church under very adverse circumstances, the patriarchs of this all-important see forbade the use of Church Slavonic and gave preferential treatment to those who had the proper theological training when appointing bishops. This training was given in Greek in the various seminaries and schools and, consequently, all bishops were Greeks. This fact was deeply resented by the village priests, often poorly trained sons of important local families. They learned the texts required, mainly in Church Slavonic, from their predecessors and recited them from memory without understanding the words they used. The situation was somewhat better in the Romanian Principalities, especially after the beginning of the phanariot period. Local boyars intermarried with and joined the phanariots. "The Greek yoke," mentioned often by Balkan historians and very much resented both then and now, is based on the actions of the Greek hierarch and phanariots.

To the chaotic situation[6] and uncertainty surrounding the people of the Balkans a new element was added by the onset of the 19th century: the ideas and events of the Enlightenment and the French Revolution. Obviously, these were only accessible to those who could travel outside the confines of the Empire or to those who not only could read and write, but could do this also in a foreign language. Those who had these abilities were first of all merchants but included also members of the clergy. The most important people in this group were the phanariots, who had the means to hire tutors or study abroad and who produced some remarkable scholars, innovators and reformers. Several members of the Mavrocordatos family, Rhigas Pheraios, Adamantios Koraës, Agostino Capodistrias and Alexandros Ypsilantis, among others, come easily to mind. Even these few names indicate scientific, literary and political activities of a very significant nature.

The Greeks were not the only ones who profited from the activities of the phanariots. As hospodars of the Romanian Principalities they brought their culture and attitude to Bucharest and Iaşi where they intermarried with the local boyars creating an upper class with innovative tendencies. New ideas were brought to these lands not only from Istanbul, but also from Russia and Transylvania. It was in Transylvania that a Uniate bishop, Ioan Inochentie Micu (later Baron Klein) first proclaimed the Daco-Roman theory explaining the origin of his people and establishing the basis of modern Romanian nationalism.

The Romanians were not the only ones who profited from the activities of conationals living outside the Ottoman borders. Around the patriarchate at Sremski Karlovci numerous Serb institutions developed including a seminary and a school system producing the first learned Serb elite. As is well known, these *Prečani* Serbs, together with those who went to schools north of the border, became the diplomats of the Serbian Revolution and supplied most of the administrators and scholars who helped to establish the modern Serb state.

It is less well known that in 1790 a Serb *sabor* (assembly) met for three months at Temesvár. It was called by the patriarch Mojsije Putnik who died before the *sabor* met on 21 August. In preparation for this meeting the various Serb-inhabited communities in Hungary and the Military Frontier regions not only prepared instructions for their representatives, but also sent *cahiers* on the French model directly to the *sabor*. Several points of view were voiced during the discussions, but the final resolutions reflected the victory of a Serb national trend. The Emperor-King was not only asked to confirm the religious and national privileges granted by his predecessors, but it was also requested that a special vojvodate be created for the Serbs in which they could be self-governing as Croats were in Croatia.[7] Vienna promised everything but, in the end, granted nothing except the continuation of the earlier privileges. What is important to note is that at this congress the Serbs of the future Vojvodina demanded national and not only religious recognition. It is also significant that the important work of Jovan Rajić, *Istorija raznyh slavenskih narodov najpače Bolgar, Horvatov i Serbov* . . . was published in the mid 1790s.

The Transylvanian Romanians were encouraged by "the examples set by the Serbs of Hungary." They too demanded permission to organize their own *mare sober* (great assembly).[8] Several Romanian clergymen, including bishop Gherasim Adamovici, attended the Temesvár meeting. This frightened Count George Bánffy, governor of Transylvania, enough to propose "that the Rumanian and Serbian hierarchies be separated."[9] The government did not grant any of the Romanians' demands. What is important to note is that in the crucial years following the death of Emperor Joseph II (ruled 1780-1790) Uniate and Orthodox cooperated as Romanians.

Thus, at the beginning of the 19th century, Greeks, Romanians, and Serbs could rely on conationals living under better circumstances than they did under Ottoman rule to help them acquire new ideas about themselves and the world at large. The Bulgarians and Albanians had to rely on themselves and, as a result, lagged behind the three other nations in broadening their self-image and basic loyalties beyond their Churches and the immediate surroundings with which they were familiar.

The two nations of the Balkans which were not subjects of the sultan, the Croats and the Slovenes, were Roman Catholics as were most of the other people living in Habsburg-ruled lands. Therefore, the religious differentiation and conflict along confessional lines so important for Ottoman subjects played no role in their self-identification. In 1102, the Croats had elected Kálmán

IX

(ruled 1095-1116), the King of Hungary, as their ruler. From that time on Hungary and Croatia were always ruled by the same sovereign whose representative, banus, was the highest ranking official in the Croatian administration. When the 19th century began the exact constitutional position of the two nations was subject to different interpretations. The Croats "claimed that in constitutional terms a common Hungarian-Croat state, a real union, had been established . . . while the Hungarians claimed they [Croatian lands] were subject provinces."[10]

The Croatian position, clearly expressed in 1790 by the Vice-comes of Zagreb county, Nikola Škrlec, demanded equality for the Croat and Hungarian nations. In this case, nation meant only the "political nations," i.e. the two nobilities. To this demand of equality the request was added, after the Habsburg acquisition of Dalmatia in 1797, that this new province be united with Croatia-Slavonia. These two issues, the constitutional position of Croatia and the demand for the establishment of the "Triune Kingdom," dominated Croatian politics up to the dissolution of Austria-Hungary. What changed, mainly in the 19th century, was the definition of the nation in whose name the demands were made.

The Slovene lands lie geographically outside the Balkans, but are inhabited by a Slavic people who joined Yugoslavia after the First World War. Not only are the Slovenes inhabiting a non-Balkan territory, but their history also differs sharply from that of the other people surveyed in these pages. Their lands were conquered by Charlemagne (ruled 768-814) during his anti-Avar wars lasting from 796 to 803. From this time to 1918 Slovenes lived first in the Holy Roman, then the Habsburg Empire. Their history is a part of that of Central Europe and not of the Balkans. On the one hand, they were never masters of their own house, which was divided into estates of German nobles; but on the other, they profited from being part of the Western World and sharing with its other inhabitants all the major developments from the Renaissance and Reformation to the Enlightenment. They retained their own language and thanks to this, their identity. This linguistic identity was transformed into a national one, to a considerable extent, during the few years between 1809 and 1814 when, together with Dalmatia and certain segments of Croatia proper, the Slovene lands became a part of Napoleon's Illyrian Provinces. Interestingly, religion became part of Slovene self-identification only at a later date.

The first major and successful revolt against Ottoman rule in the Balkans broke out in the Paşalik of Belgrade in 1804. This event and the long struggle it set in motion is well known. A few facts have to be listed, however, because they are of importance for the nationalism-religion focus of these pages. In 1791, Sultan Selim III forbade the janissaries, by this time not much more than a privileged and well armed band of outlaws, to operate in the paşalik. Osman Pasvanoğlu *âyan* of Vidin, became their protector, and when the sultan was forced to make peace with this character, the janissaries were permitted to return to the paşalik. The Ottoman authorities, headed by the paşa of Belgrade, Haci-Mustafa Sinikoğlu were as unhappy with the renewed presence and depredation of the janissaries who obeyed only their leaders, known as *dahis*, as were the Serbs. Thus a community of interests and actions tied the Porte's legal representatives to the inhabitants of the area under their jurisdiction. In 1801, the janissaries killed Sinikoğlu and began to terrorize everybody. Most history books tell us that the Serbs, provoked by their depredations, revolted against the rule of the *dahis* "trying to help the sultan." Preparations for resistance were certainly organized by the *knezes*, but "the spark that kindled the Serbian Revolution was set off not by Serbs, but by the Turkish Janissary leaders, the *dahis*."[11] These men decided that all *knezes* and other popular leaders must be killed, and only after their murderous expeditions began did the Serbs take action in self-defense. Clearly neither their religion nor their national identification prompted the Serbs to revolt although they were conscious of both. As the long struggle dragged on, it took on a more and more "national" character in the eyes of the rest of Europe and in the numerous declarations and diplomatic notes prepared by the Serb leadership. Some of these men might, indeed, have had a clear national concept in mind, but what about the population at large and the fighting men? They fought in self-defense, they fought because they were loyal to their leaders, they fought to revenge wrongs, but did they fight as Serbs for Serbia? I doubt it. Nor did they fight a modern crusade against infidels to save their souls; they fought for something more earthly and practical. Religion alone was no longer a motivating force, but religion was still an important element of their self-image. To describe this half-religious, half-lay identification the expression of *Konfessions-Nationalität* proposed by Emanuel Truczynski is applicable and very helpful.[12] It is an unconsciously formulated self-awareness that melds the religious and ethnic into a new concept with which the majority of a given group could identify. It is no longer purely religious and not yet national; it is neither while it is both. For the history of the people of the Balkans this is a useful concept. Although none of the authors who contributed to the excellent volume edited by Wayne S. Vucinich[13] used Turczynski's concept, several chapters tackle this problem and come to similar conclusions. While some of the *Prečani* Serbs might have thought in nationalistic terms, the motivating ideology of most of those who revolted against the misdeeds of the *dahis* and later fought the Ottomans was something that can easily be identified as the confessional nationality presented by Turczynski.

The forces that motivated the Greeks were more complex and are more difficult to analyze than were those discussed in the case of the Serbs. First of all, Greeks could be found in practically all Ottoman provinces and in numerous foreign lands and were influenced by their immediate surroundings. A second important factor was the composition of the Greek "upper classes." These included, besides the phanariots, the higher clergy, numerous merchants who did not work within the phanariot system, leaders of the various mainland and island communities that were practically self-governing, and the *hocabaşis*, a group of Greek landowners, who often occupied minor administrative positions and worked as hereditary *mültezims* (tax collectors and tax farmers). Maintaining the Ottoman system was clearly in the interest of some of these people. The self-centered behavior and attitude of some of the local chieftains became obvious when they fought each other during the years of the Greek War of Independence. Others were either motivated by honest conviction or were forced to act by the circumstances in which they found themselves. Good examples of this last mentioned group are Alexander Mavrocordatos and the Patriarchs Grigorios and Evgenios. Mavrocordatos wrote that as good Christians the Greeks should "Render unto Caesar the things which are Caesar's" and should not "confuse what is temporary and corruptible with what is divine and eternal."[14] Both patriarchs and 22 other bishops excommunicated, for very obvious reasons, all those who participated in the Greek Revolution.[15] While in the case of the Greeks we have much richer and diverse samplings of attitudes and convictions than we had in the case of the Serbs, the question of what motivated the revolutionaries of 1821 can still not be answered unequivocally.

There can be little doubt that the *Philiki Etairia* became a revolutionary organization after Alexandros Ypsilantis became its leader. It is also clear that he discussed his plans with Tsar Alexander I's (ruled 1801-1825) Greek minister of foreign affairs, Count Ioannis Kapodistrias, although it is not clear which of his numerous plans he shared with this important statesman.[16] Finally, it is also certain that Ypsilantis counted on Russian help, but this was denied him, if it was ever a possibility, because, unknown to him, the Tsar adopted the conservative views of Prince Clemens von Metternich at the Congress of Laibach (Ljubljana).[17] There can be little doubt that Ypsilantis, a highly educated man of the world, familiar with the political trends and philosophies of his time, was a Greek nationalist. The question that can be posed, but cannot be answered is: which of his various plans was nearest to what he truly hoped to achieve? Did he only wish to liberate Greece and if so what borders did he have in mind? Did he contemplate something of a crusade or did he hope that a Balkan-wide revolt would produce something akin to the Byzantine Empire, making him an early advocate of the *Megale* (great) idea? Whatever he had in mind came to naught when his expedition bogged down in the Romanian Principalities.

The second revolutionary movement that began in the Morea at practically the same time succeeded mainly because of the activities and influence of the European (and to lesser extent American) philhellenes, in spite of the fractional in-fighting of the Greeks. That by 1832 the Greeks were nationalists cannot be doubted. That the borders of their new state did not satisfy them is understandable and that, for this reason, the irredentist *Megale* idea dominated Greek thinking for something like the next 84 years is comprehensible. What made their nationalism unique for nearly a century was that it encompassed not only the Hellenic *demos* (people), but the entire Hellenic *genos* (race) making it rather difficult for the neighbors of Greece to understand the limits of Greek aspirations.

When Ypsilantis crossed into the Romanian Principalities he found a local revolutionary movement led by Tudor Vladimirescu in progress. Romanian historians writing since 1945 date the beginning of "modern" Romanian history from this uprising.[18] It is not easy to find a convenient label for this revolt. It was certainly not motivated by religious considerations because the principalities were religiously homogeneous. It was not nationalistic either because it was not directed against the Ottomans. This becomes clear from the often quoted statement Vladimirescu made when meeting Ypsilantis:

> You do not belong here. Go, cross the Danube and fight the Turks. As for me, I do not intend to fight them. I wish to fight only the abuses that tear up my country.[19]

The movement was not a spontaneous rebellion by the abused people to whom Vladimirescu referred; these he had to recruit once he decided that revolt was the only way to remedy some of the social and economic conditions he considered intolerable. His Padeş Manifesto calling his countrymen to revolt made it clear that the enemy was the ecclesiastical and political upper hierarchy which was almost exclusively phanariot. Yet some of the people who were members of this group of enemies not only knew what Vladimirescu was planning, but even financed his movement. I am not the only one who has difficulties in pigeonholing this movement which had national, social and political elements, but no truly dominating ideology. Romanian Marxist historians found an interesting label for Vladimirescu's movement, calling it a "Prolog al revolutiei burgheze" [A Prologue to bourgeois revolutions].[20] Given the absence of a middle class in the Principalities in those years, this explanation makes no sense.

In Transylvania, the Romanians were the "tolerated" nation and the religion of most of them, Orthodoxy, was also only a "tolerated" confession. The Uniate faith, followed by those Romanians who were not Orthodox, enjoyed an "accepted" position as part of the Catholic Church. The well known *Supplex libellus Valachorum*, the petition submitted to the Emperor-King in 1792, demanded not only equality for the Romanian nation with the three "accepted" ones (Magyar, Székely and Saxon) and for the Orthodox Church with the four "accepted" ones (Catholic, Lutheran, Reformed and Unitarian), but also proposed some constitutional changes reflecting the influence of western ideas. This famous document was prepared by clergymen of both religions, i.e. Orthodox and Uniate, to which the Romanians belonged, and showed a remarkable degree of national unity. This unity became even stronger when the so-called second Romanian reformist generation, consisting not only of clergymen, but more and more of well educated laymen, became vocal in Transylvania. These people were Romanians first of all; following a given creed was only a secondary consideration for them. They continued to demand equality for their people and church, but placed emphasis on uplifting their poor and illiterate conationals by establishing schools and publishing books and newspapers. These men, who were active mainly in the 1830s and 1840s, were Transylvanian and Romanian nationalists, although they did not yet think in broader nationalistic terms about possible unity with the Principalities. This makes good sense. Their "oppressors" were fellow Christians, not Muslims and, in spite of the misery of the peasant majority, even this social group lived better than its equivalent in Wallachia and Moldavia.[21]

The second Greek generation after the French Revolution was mostly involved in its struggle with the Othonian system. Party politics dominated public life and became more and more partisan as years went by. The most notable achievements were the "nationalization" of the Church in 1833 and the transformation of Otho's arbitrary regime (1832-1862) into a constitutional monarchy. The first of these two changes was inevitable. The patriarch residing in Istanbul was subject to pressure by the Ottoman government even in religious matters and national churches were the norm for centuries in lands with an Orthodox majority. Otho's regime was not only arbitrary, but also "foreign" in the eyes of most Greeks not only because he was a German, but mainly because his regime was run almost exclusively by Bavarians. Given the nature of Greek politics in those days, one can wonder to what extent the constitutional movement was anti-foreigner, anti-absolutist or simply a move to open the highest offices in the land to ambitious Greek politicians. After all, the corrupt "System" operated on the national level similarly to what is known to Americans as the political machines on the city level of William Tweed in New York or on the state level of Huey Long. While everybody in public life proclaimed his dedication to the aims of the *Megale* idea, the same politicians completely neglected their own countrymen. Nationalism was the official doctrine and those in public life always showed great concern for their unredeemed brothers without doing much if anything for those whose redemption had already taken place.

Among the Slavs, irrespective of where they lived, the

only important developments during these years occurred in the Slovene and Croatian lands. This fact is well illustrated by the title of Wolf Dietrich Behschnitt's excellent work, *Nationalismus bei Serben and Kroaten, 1830-1914*.[22] I refer to the well known Illyrianist Movement and the careers of men like Ljudevit Gaj. The importance of this movement for South Slavic history needs no repetition here. An excellent study dealing with it is easily available.[23] Gaj and his collaborators attempted to show "that [the] Croat and Slavonian tribe is not so insignificant . . . and that the Croats and Slavonians are only a part of the greater Illyrian people, just as in turn the Illyrian people are a part of the great Slav People." This is why they selected the Illyrian appellation for their basically Croat Revival movement.[24] It was this attempt to define Croat/Illyrian as broadly as possible that made the Illyrianists select the štokavian version of Croatian as the basis for their linguistic reforms although this was not the dialect they spoke.[25]

Behschnitt begins his examination of Serb nationalism with a detailed analysis of Ilija Garašanin's *Program of Serbia's Foreign and National Policy at the End of 1844*, better known as the *Načertanije*. This document is well known and has been studied in detail by many scholars. What is interesting is that Behschnitt considers it the first expression of both a vague Yugoslavism and also of Great Serbianism.[26] Ivo Banac sees this document, in contrast to Behschnitt, only as a clear approach to Great Serbianism.[27] This document was certainly a pre-1848 expression of Serb nationalism. The next important document of Serb nationalism discussed at length by Behschnitt, Vuk Karadžić's *Srbi svi i svuda*, (All Serbs and Serbs everywhere) is well described by Banac in a few words: "Karadžić, in short, brought forth a modern Serb national ideology, the purpose of which was to assimilate the vast majority of Catholic Croats and all Bosnian Muslims. . . ."[28] These two authors reach the same conclusion shared by others also. By the crucial revolutionary period Serb identity had moved beyond Orthodoxy and became aggressively national.

The Illyrianists dominated the Slovene scene during the first half of the 19th century, and the Slovenes were, consequently, not narrowly nationalist or Catholic. No major movements existed in Croatia although Croats became gradually more and more aware of their position in the Habsburg domain in response to the growing Hungarian nationalism and, especially, to the actions of the Diet of 1843-44 which replaced Latin with Hungarian as the official language in all lands of the Crown of St. Stephen. The Croats "in turn replaced Latin with their own vernacular as the official language in the autonomous 'associate country' of Croatia-Slavonia."[29] Thus began a growing hostility between two Catholic nations first as an expression of cultural and soon thereafter of political nationalism.

The revolutionary year of 1848-49 was of great importance for the development of nationalism in the Balkans. The revolutionaries were defeated and liberal ideas had to wait for several decades before they were adopted by various governments. Even before the ultimate triumph of liberalism the image which the great masses had of themselves and other nations was altered drastically and permanently. This change was the result of the civil war that raged in Hungary parallel to the struggle between the Magyars and the Habsburg forces. Not only did the banus of Croatia, Baron Josip Jelačić, lead his forces against the Magyars, but the Serbs of the Vojvodina and the Romanians of Transylvania also revolted due to the chauvinistic nearsighted nationalities policy of Lajos Kossuth's Hungarian government. For the first time, peasant masses fought each other as members of nations. The revolts of Serbs and Romanians received help from co-nationals living in Serbia and the Principalities. It became clear to those fighting that their brothers were not fellow (Hungarian) peasants, but those who came to help them from across the borders. The memories of this struggle and the lines of division drawn along national lines never faded from the minds of those who fought in 1848 and were transmitted by them to later generations. After 1848 nationalism became the most important element determining the self-image and loyalty of Serbs, Croats and Romanians, as it was already for the Greeks.

The aim of the neo-absolutist regime known as the Bach Period that followed the Habsburg victory in 1849 was the creation of a highly centralized unitary state. It was as ruthless in dealing with those nations that had fought the Magyars as it was in dealing with the Magyars. Anybody who opposed the centralizing tendencies of Vienna was automatically placed under police surveillance, including the Illyranists Ljudevit Gaj and Ivan Kukuljević among others. Their colleagues Mirko Bobović and Ivan Filipović wound up in jail, and Bishop Josip Juraj Strossmayer, who had opposed the introduction of German as the official language, escaped this fate only because of his position. He was accused of withholding taxes, and military units were sent to confiscate some of his property. The Serbs, who had claimed the right of local self-government since at least the 1790s, had to be satisfied with an additional title given to the ruler, who became Grand Vojvod of the Vojvodina which was not yet a separate administrative region.[30]

In Transylvania the situation was similar. General Ludwig Wohlgemut was given full powers to transform this land into an imperial province as quickly as possible. The Romanians--considered simply an inconsequential *Bauernvolk*--were not consulted or given any new rights or privileges.[31] The Magyars said, quite rightly: the nationalities received as reward what we received as punishment.

After the *Ausgleich*, the position of the non-Magyars in Hungary did not improve and even became worse after Kálmán Tisza became Prime Minister in 1875. The story of Hungary's minorities is too well known to require repetition here and easily accessible in several well known works.[32] All I want to do is stress a few aspects of the story leading to the end of the 19th century.

Reaction to the growing arbitrariness of their Hungarian "partners" provoked two reactions among the Croats. One, tied to the names of Eugen Kvaternik and Ante Starčević, fought for the recognition of the right of Croatia to manage its own affairs in the lands laying between the Danube and Albania and stretching from the Drina to the Adriatic. Later Josip Frank advocated the same rights for Croatia. This super-nationalistic approach paid scant attention to the Serbs of Slavonia, making it easy for Count Károly Khuen-Hérdeváry, banus of Croatia from 1883 to 1903, to organize a majority in the Croatian *sabor* made up of some Magyarone Croats and the Serbs. I see in this clash between a party based on Serbs and the nationalistic Croats the first serious division of the two people, a beginning of hostilities based entirely on nationalistic considerations.

The other trend, less political, more cultural but nevertheless very influential was the Yugoslav movement, a newer form of Illyrianism advocated with growing success by Bishop Strossmayer and Franjo Rački. This movement was at first *Kaisertreu*, aiming at the unity of Croats and Serbs in the Habsburg Monarchy in which they were to be granted equality with the Germans and Hungarians. As all pan-movements, this one too was based on the recognition that Serbs and Croats alone, and especially when disunited, were too weak to fight the two dominant nations of the Habsburg lands. Politically, the union of the two Slavic nations was achieved by the Croato-Serb coalition, the *Hrvatsko-srpska koalicija* of 1905. It aimed at South Slavic unity in the Dual Monarchy, including the Slovenes, and was anti-Frankist and opposed to the plans of the Franz Ferdinand circle. When Franjo Supilo, its most influential founder, retired from politics and when Hungarian politics became less and less tolerant, the HSK lost its popularity. Another, later very important party, the *Hrvatska pučka seljačka stranka* (Croat People's Peasant Party) was established in 1904 by Stjepan Radić. This party too advocated an Austroslav solution until the end of World War I. During the last years before the war, the form of Yugoslavism ready to leave the Dual Monarchy and unite with Serbia, was represented in Croatia by the *Nacionalistička Omladina* (Nationalist Youth) movement. All these parties and movements testified to the existence of a strong nationalist sentiment in Croatia without regard to religious considerations. This was true even of clergymen of the Strossmayer-Rački stamp.

The Catholicism of the Slovenes, their relatively high living standards, and the fact that Austrian rule was much more tolerant than Hungarian rule, produced a less militant nationalism than among the Croats and Serbs. Furthermore, most of the political leaders of this nation were clergymen who sympathized with the equally strongly Catholic circle of Franz Ferdinand. They learned to play a clever game of wait and see, which they continued to play after the First World War with great success in Yugoslavia.

The Serbs of Serbia had their hands full trying to build up their state, resist outside pressures coming from Austria and later Austria-Hungary, digest national humiliations like the defeat in 1885, and take sides or try to keep away from the dynastic struggles that ended only in 1903 with the murder of Alexander Obrenović. Those who killed their king and queen, military and civilian conspirators, were mostly members of the *Ujedinjenje ili Smrt* (Unification or death) society whose aim, as this name indicates, was the unification of all Southern Slavs--Bulgarians excepted--in a Greater Serbia. These grandsons of the Garašanin idea were impatient and ready to use force to gain their ends.

IX

The Great Serbia idea had a more patient, and in the end more successful, champion in the leader of the Radical Party, Nikola Pašić who worked to achieve the same ends by diplomatic means. All partisans of Great Serbia preached South Slavic unity, but wanted to make certain that it would be achieved in a state in which the Serbs will occupy the position of *primus inter pares*.[33]

After the *Ausgleich*, the Transylvanian Romanians found themselves in a worse position than that in which they had been in before 1867. While in Transylvania they had no rights, they were at least the majority of the principality's inhabitants whose rights had to be recognized sooner or later. When their land became an integral part of Greater Hungary they became an important minority, but a minority nevertheless. This fact made collaboration between Uniates and Orthodox an absolute necessity. The collaboration of the two Churches became easier when, in 1868, the Andrássy government's truly liberal minister of cultural affairs, Baron József Eötvös, satisfied a long standing demand of the Romanians and gave them their own metropolitanate which was independent of Sremski Karlovci. This was a very important concession because it made possible the establishment of parochial schools for the majority of the Romanians living in Hungary. This apparently religious move, for which the Romanians had fought since 1848, was also a significant political move.[34]

To return to the Croats and oversimplify a complicated issue: the political thought of the Croats split into Austro-slav (or at least *Kaisertreu*) and secessionist movements. The same was true of the Romanians living in Great Hungary. While cultural life and political action became more and more difficult as the position of Budapest became more and more intransigent, Romanians made significant progress in all respects. Most of their leading political figures, including the future Prime Ministers of post-1918 Romania, Iuliu Maniu and Alexandru Vaida-Voievod, represented their conationals in the Hungarian parliament. Those who despaired and did not believe that life in a Magyar-dominated state had a future for Romanians moved to the Principalities.

The Principalities, united into a Romanian state in 1859, made rapid progress economically and politically. After full independence was achieved in 1878, the two leading political parties, the Liberal and the Conservative, agreed on their next common goal, the creation of a Great Romania which was to include not only Transylvania, but also the Banat, Bessarabia, and the Bukovina. The yearning for this great state was so general on all levels of society that the country's adherence to the Triple Alliance in 1883 had to be kept secret. Irredentism was the basic element of the country's foreign policy from at least 1878 if not already in earlier periods. The only feature of Romanian policy that could be labelled religious was its anti-Semitism, but this had a large economic aspect also.[35]

One additional region of the Balkans had its Habsburg connection--Bosnia-Hercegovina. Here the religious factor of the religion-nationalism equation played a significant role. Together with the Albanian lands, Bosnia-Hercegovina was the westernmost province of the Ottoman Empire until 1878. "At the end of four centuries of Ottoman occupation approximately 38 per cent of the population followed Islam, 42 per cent were Orthodox, and 18 per cent were Catholics."[36] Irrespective of their religious affiliation all inhabitants of the *sancak* were ethnically Southern Slavs and spoke one or the other of the Serbo-Croatian variants. While the population increased by an amazing 68 per cent under Habsburg rule, the religious division hardly changed.[37] Under Ottoman rule, the local Muslim notables were strong enough to run the *sancak* and even forced their nominal superior, the governor, to live in Travnik while they sat in Sarajevo. Not all Muslims were notables. Most of them were simple peasants and lived much as did other peasants belonging to other religions.[38] Christianity survived the long centuries of Ottoman rule mainly thanks to the work of the Bosnian Franciscans.[39]

When, after 1878, Bosnia-Hercegovina was administered and in 1908 annexed by the Dual Monarchy, the Common Minister of Finance was assigned the task of governing this newly acquired province. It was taken for granted that the Catholics would be delighted with living under a Catholic master, but their number was too small to supply the administration with a pro-Austro-Hungarian population base.[40] It was also assumed that the Orthodox would be hostile. For this reason the social and economic positions of the Muslims was not changed; on the contrary, they were courted by Vienna. The antagonism of the various elements of the population, in this case clearly based on religious divisions, was obvious and remained unchanged. This prompted the most talented and able of the Common Finance Ministers, Benjámin Kállay, to invent a Bosnian nationality which

IX

he tried to propagate with all means at his disposal. The murder of the Archduke Franz Ferdinand by young Bosnian Serb nationalists is the best proof of the total failure of this attempt.

Greece was one of the few countries that had no revolution in 1848. Her existence still depended to a considerable extent on the good will of the Great Powers who helped her gain her independence. The British Ambassador in Athens declared that "a really independent Greece is an absurdity. Greece is either Russian or English and since she must not be Russian she must be English."[41] The well known Don Pacifico affair of 1850 and the occupation of Piraeus from 1854 to 1857 by a joint British-French fleet proves that the Great Powers meant what they said.

The Greek revolt of 1862 ousted Othon and brought the Danish George I (Georgios - ruled 1863-1913) to the throne. A new constitution of 1864 signaled a change in Greek politics. The *Megale* idea continued to dominate Greek thinking, but the two leading politicians disagreed on the means to achieve the national goal. Charilaos Trikupis wanted to build up the country economically first and hoped to make foreign policy gains through diplomacy. His approach was opposed by Theodore Deligiannes, a jingoistic firebrand who mobilized the Greek army in 1886 to get "compensation" for the territorial gains made by Bulgaria the year before. He was unsuccessful, but tried again in 1897 when he went further and attacked the Ottoman Empire with catastrophic results. The only territorial gain on the mainland was awarded to Greece by the Great Powers who, at the Congress of Berlin, instructed Istanbul to negotiate border revisions with Athens. When negotiations dragged on for three years, the Conference of Istanbul, to which the Greeks were not invited, awarded Greece most of Thessaly in 1881. The Great Powers, in this case Great Britain, were also responsible for another Greek gain of territory, the acquisition of the Ionian islands, which London handed over as a sort of accession gift when George I became King of Greece. The other focus of Greek irredentism was Crete where successive revolts in 1841, 1858, 1866-68, 1875-76, 1896, and 1909 brought more and more concessions from the Ottomans. From 1897 to 1909 the island was occupied by troops of the Great Powers who came to prevent the expansion of the Greek-Ottoman war to the island. By 1909 Crete was, for practical purposes, ruled by the Greeks, but *enosis*, unification with Greece, had to wait until the Balkan wars. Greece fought these under the leadership of one of her truly great statesman, Eleutherios Venizelos, Crete's gift to Greece. This summary of Greek activities outside the country's borders indicates an expansionist drive pursued with the help of both religious and nationalistic slogans. As far as the Greek population was concerned, the two really were one and the same thing.

The Balkan wars represented an important phase in what is known as the Macedonian question. This question is closely connected with the emergence of modern Bulgaria and Macedonia.

The Bulgarians lived geographically closer to Istanbul than did the other Balkan subjects of the Ottoman Empire. Military and economic considerations also made their lands of primary importance to Istanbul, which, therefore, kept a tight control over the Bulgarians. Nor were the Ottomans the only ones interested in keeping the Bulgarian *sancaks* in the Empire. Similar to the Greek *hocabaşis*, a group of Bulgarians, the *çorbacis* fit well into the existing system from which they profited as also did members of the large Bulgarian merchant community in Istanbul. The first Bulgarian nationalists were members of other merchant colonies living in Belgrade, Bucharest, Odessa, and several other cities. "The first organised armed group of Bulgarians was the small Bulgarian legion formed in Belgrade in 1862 by George Rakovski."[42] It was disbanded almost immediately by the Serbian government at the request of the Ottoman government. Four years later a Bulgarian Central Committee was established in Bucharest by Liuben Karavelov and Vasil Levski. Levski led several filibustering expeditions into Bulgarian lands and was captured and executed in 1873. Other important figures working outside the Ottoman Empire included Georgi Benkovski and Hristo Botev, all of whom have a secure place in the Bulgarian pantheon. They organized revolutionary committees all over the territory of the future Bulgaria, the core of which was clearly delineated by the edict of the Sultan Abdülaziz (ruled 1861-1876) on 11 March 1870. This *firman*, the result of long and persistent pressure by the Russians, created a Bulgarian Exarchate, an autocephalous Church, in spite of the objections of the patriarch.[43] This dignitary quite correctly predicted as early as 1867 that a Bulgarian Church could easily serve as "a bridge to the political independence of the Bulgarians."[44] The traditional sequence of appearance was reversed in this case. In the past, Orthodox rulers who succeeded in establishing states created national Churches. In this case the Church predated the establishment of a state. The dioceses assigned to the Exarchate were situated mainly between the Danube and the Balkan range. That the patriarch excommunicated the clergy and laity of the new ecclesiastical unit had no historical significance. The area assigned to the exarchate did, indeed, become the core of a new Bulgarian state. It was established as a result of the Russo-Turkish war of 1875-1878. The Treaty of San Stefano dictated by the victorious Russians assigned to Bulgaria all those lands which, according to the Article X of the sultan's original *firman*, could possibly be considered Bulgarian. This article allowed any diocese that voted by a two-thirds majority to join the exarchate to do so. The Greek and Serb churches understood this article to mean that if any diocese voted by a two-thirds majority to join them they too could do so. As is well known, the Congress of Berlin changed the borders drawn at San Stefano and limited Bulgaria practically to the same territory that had been assigned eight years earlier to the exarchate. The area between the Balkan and Rhodope range was set up as the Christian-governed Ottoman province of Eastern Rumelia with the remaining lands, Macedonia, returned to the Ottomans. In their small state the Bulgarians showed amazing political maturity and sophistication in setting up their new state.[45] When Eastern Rumelia voted to join Bulgaria seven years later and Serbia tried to prevent this, an equally amazing Bulgarian military victory assured this union. The Bulgarians now had their own *Megale* idea, the aim of which was to regain their country's San Stefano borders.[46]

The tenth article of the sultan's *firman* and the decision of the statesmen assembled at Berlin created the Macedonian problem which is still with us to the present day. The Macedonian question has been studied in great detail for the last hundred years and is too complicated to summarize in a few sentences.[47] What is important for this paper dealing with religion and nationalism is that in this area of the Balkans the nationalisms of three Orthodox states clashed and that one of the weapons all three states used in their struggle was religious. Priests became some of the fighters in this struggle and much too often also its victims. The attempts of the Great Powers to settle the Macedonian question before World War I were unsuccessful. The three Orthodox states of the Balkans fought the two Balkan wars primarily over Macedonia. The activities of IMRO continued in the interwar period. In World War II Bulgaria gained temporary possession over some of Macedonia. It was Tito who tried to solve this question by creating a Macedonian state in the Yugoslav Federation after World War II and who secured the agreement of Georgi Dimitrov for this move. This did not mean that the majority of Bulgarians ever believed that this was a just and final solution of the Macedonian question and that their dreams of regaining the San Stefano borders had ended. They were not the only ones with a "Macedonian question." When Macedonia declared its independence in October 1991, Greek nationalists found a new focus for their feelings. Claiming that only a Greek-ruled area had the right to be called Macedonia and prompted by their paranoiac fear of "Slav imperialism," they not only refused to recognize this state, but also prevented--using their NATO membership--its recognition by the West. The Bulgarians' acceptance of the existence of Macedonia was less the result of praiseworthy restraint than it was a clever political move. The area ceased to be part of Yugoslavia, was obviously anything but Greek, feared Serbia and, therefore, had only Bulgaria as a possible friend. It is noteworthy that Sofia recognized a Macedonian state, but made clear that it does not recognize the existence of a Macedonian nation--I am afraid that we have not seen the last fights in and over Macedonia. Today only the clergy are interested in the religious aspects of the problem in spite of the fact that the secessionist Macedonian state has its own national Church which would certainly be abolished should the state lose its independence. The present situation is far from settled. The future might still hold some new conflicts linked to the territorial problem created in 1878.

    There is not much to be said about the Albanians prior to 1914. They lived in the most neglected region of the Ottoman Empire, divided by the two dialects, Gheg and Tosk, which they spoke, by their tribal social organization, and their religious divisions. Most of the 70% which was Muslim followed Sunni practices; a minority observed rites established by the Bektashi dervishes, who were tolerant of other creeds. Of the rest of the population 20 per cent, mainly in the south were Orthodox Christians and the remaining 10 per cent, mainly in the north, belonged to the Catholic church. The first Albanian movement that gained European attention was the League of Prizren. It was es-

IX

tablished in 1878 to lobby at the Congress of Berlin preventing Serbia, Montenegro and Greece from claiming and receiving Albanian territory. The League continued to exist until it was dissolved by Ottoman armed forces two years later. It was replaced by the similarly short lived Albanian League, 1899-1902. Even after the victory of the Young Turks, relations between Istanbul and its Albanian provinces remained tense. Finally, in 1910, an Albanian revolt broke out in Priština and spread rapidly. It was suppressed and all Albanian institutions and schools were closed. Albania was created by the Great Powers in 1913, on the request of Austria-Hungary. The Dual Monarchy's aim was to keep the victorious Serbs from gaining an outlet to the sea after the Second Balkan war.

The Albanians gained some national heroes from all these activities. They include the Frashëri brothers, Sami and Naim, Haxhi Mulla Zeka and Ismail Kemal Vlora. These individuals and their collaborators were early Albanian nationalists, but the great majority of their countrymen continued in their old established ways. It was the Albanian emigration in the United States that became the germ of the Albanian national life that began after World War I. In 1906, the first Albanian weekly *Kombi* (Nation) began publication in Boston, followed two years later by the establishment of the Albanian Autocephalous Orthodox Church by Fan S. Noli and in 1912 by *Vatra* (the Heart), a Pan-Albanian Federation. During the First World War the newly established Albanian state disappeared and was fully occupied by Austro-Hungarian forces. It had to be reconstituted after the war.[48]

****

I have spent a great deal of time dealing with the historical nineteenth century because it was during those years that nationalism joined religion in the Balkans as a self-identifying criterion demanding the loyalty of the various people. Furthermore, in the present century I have to deal only with three topics that touch on possible conflicts involving both religion and nationalism: the problem of Yugoslavia since its creation; the Turkish problem in Bulgaria, Greece and Cyprus; and the Muslim problem artificially created after the great changes that began in 1988. Of these three topics, the Yugoslav problem has the longest history.

Pseudo-experts and self-appointed pundits discussing

Yugoslav problems like to stress "the centuries-old hostility" infecting the various ethnic groups that became the citizens of the Kingdom of Serbs, Croats and Slovenes after the First World War. Knowledgeable scholars disagree with this interpretation. It is true that Orthodox, Catholics, and Muslims disliked each other and developed unflattering stereotypes describing the customs, habits and characteristics of those belonging to national and religious groups other than their own. There were occasional clashes, but all in all, Serbs, Croats, and Muslim Slavs not only learned to live peacefully side by side, but also began to intermarry in steadily growing numbers. The Slovenes had always lived by themselves and had little to do with the problems of the other three groups.

In my opinion, serious, although still non-violent, disagreements began to separate Serbs and Croats during World War I when discussions concerning a future Southern Slav state began. Émile Haumant, author of one of the earliest histories of Yugoslavia, wrote that Pašić "wanted to achieve Yugoslavia by stages. First came the establishment of Greater Serbia, a Serbo-Croat state next, and Yugoslavia last." He even reports that according to Marko Jakovljević, member of the Yugoslav Committee established at Niš, Nikola Pašić confused Slovenes and Slovaks.[49] All experts agree that Pašić was an advocate of Greater Serbia and that he had this in mind when he announced that Serbia's war aim was the liberation of all Slavs living in Austria-Hungary.[50] He made quite clear what he had in mind when, in 1918, he declared:

> Serbia wants to liberate and unite the Yugoslavs
> and does not want to drown in the sea of some
> kind of Yugoslavia . . . but to have Yugoslavia
> drown in Serbia.[51]

The man who had negotiated the Corfu agreement, Ante Trumbić, had something quite different in mind. While attending the Peace Conference he explained "that although he was for state unity, he was not for a united state. 'This is not a fine point,' he stressed . . . 'but a conception.'"[52]

That Ante Trumbić, Frano Supilo, and the other founders of the Yugoslav Committee had something else in mind is also well known. When the discussions began that led to the Corfu Declaration of 20 July 1917, Pašić argued for the establishment of a unitary, and Trumbić of a federated, state. In spite of this,

IX

Trumbić agreed that the new state had to be a monarchy ruled by the Karadjordjević family. Trumbić, who would have preferred an independent Croatian state, came to the conclusion that a united Southern Slav state was the optimal solution for his people because he "was convinced that, in the event Croatia achieved independence, Serbia would get the lion's share of any contested territory in Bosnia-Hercegovina and elsewhere, as well as Dubrovnik and other coastal areas."[53] The events of 1991-92 justify his premonitions. The Slovenes had no representatives at Corfu. As a matter of fact, the future leader of the Slovene People's Party, Anton Korošec, had proposed two months earlier, on 30 May 1917, in the Austrian Parliament the creation of a Croatian-Slovene state with a position and rights equal to those of Austria and Hungary.[54]

While the Slovenes still pursued their own aims, the Montenegrin Committee in Paris endorsed the Corfu Declaration. In spite of what some Croatian politicians would claim later, this declaration did not stipulate either a centralized or a federal form of government for the future state.[55] Subsequent meetings and declarations did not help either. The final outcome, the centralized state enshrined in the Vidovdan Constitution of 28 June 1921, was simply the result of the fact that the only force available in the lands of the future Kingdom of Serbs, Croats, and Slovenes was the Serb army. If important documents like constitutions can be accepted by a simple majority, this constitution was legal and binding because, in spite of numerous abstentions, thirteen more votes were cast for it than was required for a simple majority. This fact did not impress or satisfy those, primarily the Croats, who were unhappy with the result of the work of the Constituent Assembly. Trumbić voiced his and his fellow Croats' displeasure and declared,

> A centralist system is pushed through under the guise of unity. . . . This system represents a danger to peace and harmony. . . . This constitution will sharpen the tribal conflicts all the more . . . they are today acerbated more than under Austria-Hungary.[56]

The situation did not improve during the inter-war years. Croats continued to look at Serbs as oppressors, and the Serbs saw in the Croats nothing but troublemakers. This confrontation was made worse by the shooting in 1928 of Stjepan Radić and others in Parliament by a fellow deputy, Puniša Račić, and by the growing influence in the ranks of the *Hrvatska seljačka stranka* (Croatian Peasant Party) of the Ante Pavelić-led, fascist, right-wing *Ustaša* movement.[57] The royal dictatorship which began on 6 January 1929, suspended the constitution and established *banovinas* in place of the historic entities making up the country. On 3 October 1929, King Alexander renamed the country Yugoslavia. King Alexander was assassinated in Marseille in October 1934, but his successor, Regent Prince Paul, was not an effective sovereign. In spite of the need for unity, it took five years before, on 26 August 1939, Prime Minister Dragiša Cvetković and Vladko Maček, leader of the HSS, signed the *Sporazum* (Agreement) which was supposed to replace Serb-Croat hostility with collaboration. As the date indicates, it was too late to make a difference.[58] The Slovenes and Bosnian Muslims stayed out of the dispute of Serbs and Croats, and by playing clever politics gained several advantages by siding sometimes with one and then with the other of the two groups. Their behavior was dictated entirely by political considerations, and was intended to gain the most possible for their nations. Even the Bosnian Muslims played a purely nationalistic game. Religious differences had almost nothing to do with their actions. It is my contention that this was true of the Serbs and Croats also. In spite of this contention, it has to be admitted that religion was not unimportant. If a Serb moved to Croatia, adapted his speech to the local usage and fitted perfectly into his environment, he was still considered a Serb if on Sundays he attended an Orthodox service. The same was true of a Croat living in a Serb-dominated region. The views of the members of each nation toward the other were made steadily more and more hostile by the constant accusations, often based on actual practices, which their politicians and the daily press dished out day after day after day. In 1939, Croats and Serbs were less inclined to cooperate with each other than they had been when their common state was born at the end of World War I. Nationalistic politics must carry the major share of the blame for this development.

  The tragic civil war that was fought while the country was occupied by Germans and Italians is too well known to require detailed description. The *ustaša*, *četniks* and partisans were the major actors. The partisans proclaimed their religious and nationalistic neutrality in the name of liberation and the Communist ideology. The *četniks* were Serb nationalists and royalists with clearly defined non-religious motivations for their stand, but they did not refrain from committing violent acts against non-Orthodox people when it suited their purpose. The *ustaša*, Croat super-nationalists and racists, were the most guilty and responsible for the country's massive losses in people and livestock, housing, etc. The Croatian national-socialist state was racist and aimed at the establishment of a purely Croat state. As is well known, the number of people who were driven from their homes was large enough to bring a German intervention halting the process. The Germans were not sorry for the Serbs, Jews, and others who were the victims of this drive. They simply understood that the economy, in which they were very much interested, could not afford the huge loss of workers being caused by the Croatian policy. Unfortunately, the Croatian Fascists also used religion as a criterion in determining nationality. The 1946 trial of Zagreb's Archbishop Alojzije Stepinac did not prove that he was in favor of the mass conversions forced on something like 200,000 Orthodox to turn them into Croats or for the extermination of the Jews, but segments of the Catholic clergy were certainly involved. I doubt that the *ustaša* were religious people. Nazis anywhere generally were not religious, but some of them clearly equated religion not only with nationality, but even with race.[59] These actions of the *ustaša* indicate that nationalism had become the dominant consideration, and that religion had been relegated to be no more than one of the characteristics of national (racial) belonging. This is why the conversion issue became important. It signified the change in national self-identification. *Konfessionsnationalität* had been a vague concept, but clearly *Konfession* was its crucial element. Now it had lost its centrality. What took its place was nationalism. *Nationale Konfession* (national religion) took the place of the concept identified by Turczynski. It had become as difficult to be a Catholic Serb or an Orthodox Croat as it was to be an Orthodox or Protestant Pole.

From 1945 to 1980, Josip Broz Tito was the undisputed master of Yugoslavia. In retrospect, the Croats accuse him of being pro-Serb, while the Serbs maintain that just the opposite was true. Tito was hostile to all forms of nationalism and tried to balance economic, political and party preferences between regions. He tried to make them as independent from each other and the central government as possible. Yet, whenever he attempted meaningful decentralization, hostilities became obvious again and he had to recentralize the state. What he faced was the nationalism of each of the nations living in Yugoslavia. Their nationalism differed and still differs sharply from that of Western Europe and North America. One of these differences, in my opinion, is that in the case of Balkan nationalisms the hatred of others is the dominant feature, while elsewhere the love of one's own nation is the primary element. The second basic difference was mentioned earlier in this paper. In the "west," nationalism developed gradually as the concept of nation broadened, and it became an integral part of representative, parliamentary democracy. In the Balkans this form of democracy is unknown in spite of the parliamentary institutions that were introduced in every state. This is why Tito's decentralization had to fail. This is the reason why Yugoslavia's 1974 constitution also had to fail when, after Tito's death, it was supposed to maintain the viability of Yugoslavia. For a while, the Communist Party was able to keep a semblance of order amid steadily growing difficulties. When Communism began to lose its hold everywhere beginning in 1988 and the old "Balkan type nationalism" took its place, the party leaders also became "nationalists." Using name familiarity and what was left of the party machinery under new names, they had themselves elected presidents of the various republics. Only in Bosnia-Hercegovina was a president, Alija Izetbegović, elected who had not been a Communist.

In the now "democratic" states of Yugoslavia opposition parties made their appearance forcing the various presidents to take gradually more and more extremist positions to show how well they served their people. Slobodan Milošević, still chairman of his renamed party besides being president of Serbia, prevented, in 1991, the assumption of the Federation's rotating presidency by a Croat. It was also in 1990 that Milošević proclaimed that every Serb had the right to live in a Serbian state. He and his followers interpreted this statement to mean that all those areas and regions with a mixed population had to become part of Serbia with the members of the other nations who could or would object forced to leave. This statement by Milošević led to a series of additional statements, actions and confrontations ending in the Declaration of Independence first of Slovenia and Croatia followed by Bosnia-Hercegovina and finally Macedonia. *Četniks*

IX

made their appearance again mostly in the form of Serb officered Yugoslav Army units and the civil war in Croatia and subsequently in Bosnia-Hercegovina broke out. What the Serbs tried to achieve was the "ethnic cleansing" of those regions in the other states which they wanted to attach to Serbia. Naturally, they called the resisting Croats *ustaša* thus reviving the memories of the bloody civil war years of 1941-1945. The Serbs and Milošević are not the only villains in Yugoslavia's tragedy. Franjo Tudjman, the ex-partisan general and now President of Croatia, has long been a rabid Croatian nationalist. This is proven not only by the intermittent troubles he faced while Tito was still alive, but also by his writings.[60] He was the only communist who tried to white wash - at least to some extent - the *ustaša* and was ready to falsify the history of World War II to achieve this goal. From the beginning of hostilities, Tudjman voiced his "nation's" claims to large parts of Bosnia-Hercegovina and discussed the possible partition of this region/state with the Serbs even while fighting them in eastern Slavonia and the Krajina.[61] Given the characteristic features of "Balkan nationalism," the savagery which we are witnessing is really no surprise. Nor should we forget the role of secondary actors. A good example of these is the ex-convict, ex-protégé of Milošević, Vojislav Šešelj. He is an out-and-out fascist, controls one third of the seats in the Serb legislature, and his "tigers" are the most inhumane "fighters" in Bosnia-Hercegovina. I doubt that he obeys anybody or that he and his men would honor any agreement even if Milošević would accept it.

What deserves special attention is the newly coined term, "ethnic cleansing." The Serbs finally found a term to describe what the *SS Einsatztruppen* had done in Poland, Belorussia and Ukraine during World War II and what the *ustaša* had done until they were stopped. The behavior of the Serbs during the last four years deserves being listed as equal in its inhumanity with those for whose actions they invented the appropriate label. Over a million people had become refugees by mid-summer of 1992; the number of the dead and wounded cannot yet be established, but it is growing steadily. In one respect the actions of the Serbs differ from those of the Germans in World War II; the Serbs and even the Croats use confessional criteria in determining who has to be cleansed. Serbs, Croats, Slovenes, and all other inhabitants of Yugoslavia have lived in the same country since 1918. Disregarding dialectic variants, they speak the same language or similar languages (with the exception of the Slovenes). Is what is taking place in what used to be Yugoslavia a new form of the Crusades? Do the Serbs of Bosnia fight heretics (Catholics, 17 per cent of the population), or infidels (the 44 per cent Muslims)? Certainly not. Most of the young fighters grew up under communism and few of them became religious zealots.

What we witness is, first of all, Serb nationalism-imperialism aiming to establish Great Serbia with an outlet/coastline of her own on the Adriatic. This required conquests in northern and western Bosnia and in the Krajina region of Croatia. To create secure western borders for this state, especially for Belgrade, Eastern Slavonia and the west bank of the Drina river had to be attached to Serbia. This Great Serbia was planned as a national state "cleansed" of non-Serb elements. How could these be identified when they speak the same language, lived with "Serbs" in these regions for centuries and were fellow "Yugoslaves"? *Nationale Konfession* supplied the answer to this question because it is an easy, obvious, convenient and historical criterion separating Serbs from Croats. Religion becomes simply an identifying ethnic name tag. Let us not forget that the expression used by the Serbs to define their actions was ethnic--not religious--cleansing.

The Croats had been one of the victims of Serb aggression. Yet, as already indicated, they are no better than are those who attacked them when it comes to chauvinism and the application of *Nationale Konfession* which they were first to use in nationalistic excesses during the second World War. When the Serbs shifted their attention to Bosnia-Hercegovina, having achieved their preliminary goals in Croatia, the Croats backed the Muslims hoping to regain what they had lost in their own country in this neighboring state. After it became obvious that this would not be the case and that the Serbs' *Drang nach der Adria* could not be stopped in the Bosnian mountains, the Croats began to cooperate with the Serbs in preparation for Bosnia-Hercegovina's defeat and dismemberment acting in accordance with the same purely nationalist considerations expressed some seventy years earlier by Ante Trumbić.[62] To counteract the Serb push to the sea, the Croats concentrated their conquests and "ethnic" cleansing on regions east of the Dalmatian border with Bosnia-Hercegovina. In this case too, religion served as a criterion of ethnic belonging.

If religion in itself is of no primary value, but is used as a

IX

nationalistic label, a viable claim to territory and a state requires a national identity. The Serbs and Croats have it. The Muslims lacked it. This is why they, who had been glad when their ethnic identity was recognized albeit with a religious label, now began to call themselves Bosnians giving themselves the double self-identifier enjoyed and utilized by their enemies. Why should this be important? When the world media, following local usage, write or speak of the struggle in Bosnia-Hercegovina, they do not refer to the combatants as Catholics, Orthodox, and Muslims, but as Croats, Serbs, and Muslims. For many readers this could and did mean that two nations are fighting a religious group in their middle, creating a picture which too often brings terrorists to mind.

It is also of interest to note that the newly independent ex-Yugoslav states differentiate between nationality and religion. The Croatian Constitution does not recognize minority rights, but guarantees the free practice of religion. This could protect the few Muslims living in Croatia. On the other hand, it means that it is all right to be Orthodox as long as this does not lead to Serb demands for national rights. The Slovene Constitution grants minority rights to Italians and Magyars, minuscule in number and Catholics like the Slovenes, but the more numerous, equally Catholic, Croats and Germans are not given the same rights. In each case, it is clearly the national identity and not the religious one that the framers of the constitutions had in mind.

Returning to the civil war of 1992-95 in Bosnia-Hercegovina, I doubt, having watched the futile peace process and the continuing atrocities, that anybody is truly in charge of the forces operating in Bosnia-Hercegovina. This does not exculpate those who are mainly responsible for what is occurring. This is true as much for Milošević as for the leader of the Bosnian Serbs, Radovan Karadžić, or the leader of the "Bosnian Serb Army," General Ratko Mladić, Vojislav Šešelj, or the Croatian "soldiers." As Gale Stokes of Rice University remarked correctly, the present leaders of the various nations fighting in what was Yugoslavia have taught a new generation old hatreds and nobody can rein in the murderous feelings which they set free.[63]

What these men offer most of the time is propaganda often of the most ridiculous kind. For example, Karadžić stated on 14 August 1992 on American television that Serbs were not laying siege to Sarajevo, but simply defending their positions under attack by 50,000 Muslims in that city. The well known Bosnian Serb historian, Milorad Ekmečić, wrote recently that the campaign of Prince Eugen of Savoy that liberated those Hungarian and Slavonian territories still under Ottoman rule and led to the Peace of Passarowitz in 1718 was the result of a conspiracy between the Habsburgs and the Papacy with the aim of preventing the absorption of the Croats by the Serbs.[64] That the present problems would not exist had this and other anti-Serb actions not taken place in the past was an obvious conclusion.

While religion is used only as a convenient label to mask the nationalism of the combatants in Yugoslavia, there is a danger that a truly religious war might be in the offing in the Balkans. On the same day on which Karadžić made his statement, another American network interviewed a wounded Serb. This young man stated that he had no choice, but had to fight to prevent a fundamentalist Muslim takeover of the Balkans. This danger does not exist, but not only the Serbs, but Greeks also mention it repeatedly. Almost all Muslims living in Albania, Kosovo, Bosnia, Macedonia, and European Turkey are either Hanafi or Hanbali Sunnis and have nothing to do with any fundamentalism. Yet the fear of Muslim fundamentalism is spreading. I do not know who is responsible for the rumors making the round in Yugoslavia, Greece, and even Bulgaria. The danger is that constant repetition of this "danger" might convince a growing number of people that it really exists.

Not only religious war, but also new instances of "ethnic cleansing" are distinct possibilities in what was once Yugoslavia. Some violence and destruction of property have already occurred in the Vojvodina.[65] If fighting is renewed in Croatia, new displacements of people will occur. What and who will or can prevent the Serb army or Seselj's "tigers" from cleansing Kosovo should they be freed, even if only temporarily, from involvement in Bosnia-Hercegovina? In this province too the victims would be Muslims giving the action not only an ethnic, but also a religious coloring. Would the Albanians of Albania and Macedonia simply watch while their coreligionists/conationals are destroyed? I doubt it. If they should move, could Greece remain neutral? If she gets involved could Bulgaria refrain from acting? This is, of course, the worst possible scenario and it is not likely to become reality. A third Balkan War is something Europe cannot afford. Yet, the possibility of this happening cannot be de-

IX

nied.

    I will not discuss Bulgaria at length. I only wish to point out that she offers an interesting example of how the weakening of Communism increased the nationalist factor in the equations which were supposed to result in policies designed to keep the people loyal to the regimes. The Zhivkov regime gradually built up its anti-Turkish campaign which finally resulted, in 1984, in the expulsion of some 300,000 Turks. Sofia's action was not the result of a religious policy; rather, it was nationalistic. It would be very difficult for a communist regime to be opposed to only one religion. Furthermore, not all Muslims were attacked. Change of names was, seemingly, more important in escaping persecution than was a change of religion. While the Communist regime disappeared and some Turks returned to Bulgaria, the main target of post-Communist Bulgarian nationalism remains the same. Given the history of Bulgaria and the presence in the country of a large and fairly well-to-do minority, anti-Turkism is an easy and obvious means showing the patriotism of those in power. It is not likely to produce a more serious confrontation with Turkey than was the one of 1984. The major interest of Turkey right now is Central Asia and she will not move in the Balkans unless forced by either anti-Muslim or anti-Turkish moves much stronger than were those up to the end of 1995.

    The Turkish issue has a longer and much more complicated history and presence in Greece. While the long Ottoman occupation is always mentioned when the Turkish issue is discussed by Greeks, the present dispute between two NATO members is of more recent origin. At the earliest, it began when, in the Spring of 1921, a Greek force, poorly equipped and badly led, crossed the Aegean Sea hoping to add Ionia to the country's impressive gains in the Balkan Wars. By the fall, the Greeks were in full retreat, and a year later, on 9 September, 1922, the last remnants of their army and much of the population of Izmir (Smyrna) were mercilessly destroyed by Mustafa Kemal's forces. The *Megale* idea was dead and the events that occurred in Izmir rankled. The Turkish-Greek population exchange between 1923 and 1930 involved some 400,000 Turks who were easily absorbed, but in exchange Greece received more than three times that many people who resented being moved, whose life-style was entirely different, who could not be absorbed easily and whose presence was a constant reminder of a humiliating defeat.[66]

IX

The end of World War II and of the colonial regimes all over the world created the issue of Cyprus.[67] Ottoman rule, lasting from 1570 to 1878, saw the migration of Turks to this strategically priceless island. By 1945 Turks made up about 30 per cent of the population. Given the island's importance, this was one colony Great Britain, which had ruled the island since 1878, did not wish to give up. The island is the ideal "aircraft carrier" for any power interested in the Near East and also serves as the best "listening post" for broadcasts and rumors coming from the Arab world and Israel. The Greek majority living on the island was in favor of *enosis*, (unification with Greece) which the Turkish minority feared. It was not until 19 February 1959 that the Zürich-London agreement, signed by Great Britain, Greece, and Turkey, established the Republic of Cyprus. The Greeks were not happy with this solution and neither were the Greek Cypriots. *Enosis* had not been achieved. Archbishop Makarios III, previously a strong advocate of *enosis*, became president of Cyprus and together with his first vice-president, Fazil Küçük, honestly tried to implement the new state's constitution. This became more difficult after Rauf Denktaş took the place of Küçük. During the long years leading to the pact that set up the new republic, a third force, EOKA (The National Organization of Cypriote Fighters) was an active, mainly anti-British, terrorist organization on the island under the leadership of the right leaning Col. Georgios-Digenis Grivas. He temporarily disappeared from the scene after Cyprus became a republic.[68]

This is not the place to go into details on the history of Cyprus from 1960 to 1974. It is enough to note that during these years relations between Greeks and Turks on the island, and consequently also between Greece and Turkey, continued to worsen. The United States and even the Soviet Union got involved in these disputes. On the island three armed forces came into existence: a National Guard of roughly 20,000 men, commanded mainly by officers from Greece; a Turkish Guard of about 15,000 men led by officers who came from Turkey; and EOKA-B established by Grivas before he died in 1973.[69] It did not help that the regime of the colonels, that came to power in Athens on 21 April 1967, formulated its own policies seeking a closer military alliance with Turkey within NATO. Yet the Junta-backed EOKA-B infiltrated the National Guard and, contrary to the Junta's policy, turned this unit into a pro-*enosis* force unacceptable to Turks on

IX

the island and in Turkey. A pro-Makarios, pro-independence, but strongly leftist force was organized by Dr. Vassos Lyssarides. Public law and order disappeared from the island. In an attempt to end this disorder, but even more to save the weakening position of the Junta by acquiring Cyprus, the Junta's last leader, Brig. Gen. Demetrios Ioannides, acted impulsively and unwisely. He was provoked into action by a letter Makarios sent to the puppet President of Greece accusing the Junta of interfering in Cypriot affairs, trying to kill him, committing numerous other crimes, and demanding the withdrawal of all officers of the National Guard. On 8 July Ioannides and the rest of the Junta decided to replace Makarios with a man of their own choice. The rest of the story is well known. The coup set in motion by Ioannides took place on 14-15 July 1974 followed by the landing of Turkish troops six days later.[70] The existence of the Cypriot Turkish Republic established by the victorious Turkish forces has plagued Greek-Turkish relations for nearly 20 years.

Why was it not possible either for NATO or the United States, the supplier of arms to both of her allies, to bring the two countries together and force them into solving their dispute over Cyprus? Why has Greece repeatedly indicated that she fears a Turkish attack, while military observers could not find the slightest indication that an attack was planned? Is Cyprus that important? I may be cynical, but my answer is "no." What makes the Greek-Turkish dispute even more complicated--and a possible rapprochement of Greece and Bulgaria likely--is the discovery of oil in the Aegean Sea during the year of the Cypriot crisis. What definition of territorial waters applies in the Aegean area is not easy to say given the numerous differing answers offered to this question by several states all over the world. None of the possible answers would or could solve this Greek-Turkish problem because of the close proximity of Greek and Turkish territories in the Aegean. The oil deposits and possibly other riches remain unexplored although both, rather poor countries badly need them, and the Balkan's Turkish problem also remains unsolved. The problem is neither religious nor national although past conflicts of both kind are cited by politicians and the media of both countries. It is quite possible that the memories of past controversies help to create the distrust which the two contending parties feel for each other making their negotiations futile to the present, but neither religious zealots nor extreme chauvinists run the affairs of Greece and Turkey. What, then, has prevented meaningful progress in the relations of the two countries? I am afraid it is something much less prosaic than historically rooted religious and national feelings, it is the fear of loss of face and prestige by those who sit at the negotiating tables. This, of course, is true not only of Greeks and Turks; it is a curse from which the entire world suffers.

I find it almost impossible to evaluate the events that have occurred in Albania since the end of Communist rule. The situation is confused to say the least and the major problems are clearly economic. It is ironic, but it appears to be the fact that Communism succeeded in lessening religious, tribal and linguistic differences in Albania and that, as a result, most inhabitants of this country are--for the first time in their history--Albanians first before they are anything else. To what extent this fact, if indeed it is one, will complicate the solution of the Kosovo problem remains to be seen.[71]

Romanian nationalism is, once again, complicating Romania's relations with Hungary in spite of the fact that after the fall of Ceauşescu the chance of solving the nationalistic antagonisms in Transylvania was greater than it had ever been before. Judging by the scanty information I was able to gather, it is my impression that during the winter of 1990-1991 Transylvanian Romanians and Hungarians were ready to cooperate, but that this chance was lost as a result of the Iliescu-Roman government's actions and directions which aimed to prove their national loyalties. Hungarian propaganda which contrasted the handling of Romanian refugees in Hungary with the manner in which Hungarians were treated in Transylvania only added fuel to the fires. The Transylvanian problem will be with us for some time to come even after the Moldavian/Bessarabian question will be settled one way or another.

All these considerations--the Aegean, Cyprus, Transylvania and Bessarabia--although geographically not in the Balkans only add to the problems of the peninsula itself and keep nationalistic clashes going. Some of these controversies might use religious labels as short hand to identify the various camps facing each-other, but the true conflicts are national everywhere today. There is an additional danger. The continued use of religious labels, supposed religious conspiracies, and religious criteria for "ethnic cleansing" might easily reawaken feelings and hostilities that "disappeared" with the Ottomans and their *millet* system. If this occurs and further envenoms "Balkan nationalism," the Third Balkan War will become inevitable. Due to the Bosnian "Peace" agreement signed in Paris on 14 December 1995, NATO troops are now stationed in Bosnia. Their presence there gives the inhabitants of this state at least a temporary respite, but by itself it does not solve the problems of Bosnia, of the other ex-Yugoslav states, or of the Balkans in general. The future remains fraught with serious dangers.

NOTES

[1] Two studies deal with the topic of this essay. Emanuel Turczynski, *Konfession und Nation. Zur Frühgeschichte der serbischen und rumänischen Nationsbildung* (Düsseldorf: Schwann, 1976) and Pedro Ramet (ed.), *Religion and Nationalism in Soviet and East European Politics* (Durham, N.C.: Duke University Press, revised edition, 1989).

[2] Scholars date the establishment of the *millet* system to the year of the conquest of Constantinople when Mehmed II, the Conqueror (b.1432 - ruled 1444-1446 and 1451-1481) appointed Gennadius Scholarius patriarch of all Orthodox. A Jewish *haham başi* was appointed by him soon thereafter. Some scholars give 1461 others 1516 as the year when the first Armenian patriarch was named with jurisdiction over all monophysites. These appointments created de facto *millet* systems. It was only during the rule of Selim III (b.1761 - ruled 1789-1807) that the Ottomans began to use this term and to treat their minorities accordingly. For further reading see, among others: Steven Runciman, *The Great Church in Captivity* (Cambridge: Cambridge University Press, 1968); Timothy Ware, *The Orthodox Church* (Baltimore: Penguin Books, 1963); Theodoros Papadapoullos, *Studies and Documents relating to the History of the Greek Church and People under Turkish Domination* (n.p., 1952); and László Hadrovics, *Le peuple serbe et son église sous la domination Turque* (Paris: Presse Universitaire, 1947).

[3] While military roads were always kept in good repair, most other Balkan roads were passable only during the summer

months. Merchants and tax collectors regularly visited villages and were, more often than not, the peasantry's only contact with the outside world. Rivers, especially the Danube, carried much freight, but even the inhabitants of riverine villages hardly used them for anything besides fishing. Illiteracy was the norm in rural Rumeli with literate individuals the exception to the rule.

[4] Michael Boro Petrovich, *A History of Modern Serbia, 1804-1918*, 2 vols. (New York: Harcourt, Brace, Jovanovich, 1976), Vol. 1, p. 15.

[5] Vladimir Dedijer, Ivan Božić, Sima Ćirković, Milorad Ekmečić, *History of Yugoslavia* (New York: McGraw Hill, 1977), p. 193.

[6] On the chaos in the European provinces of the Ottoman Empire see: Peter F. Sugar, *Southeastern Europe under Ottoman Rule, 1354-1804*, Vol. 5 of Peter F. Sugar and Donald W. Treadgold (eds.), *A History of East Central Europe* (Seattle: University of Washington Press, 1977), pp. 233-247.

[7] On the Serb Congress of 1790 see Gyula Mérei and Károly Vörös, *Magyarország Története, 1790-1848* Vol. 5 in two volumes of Zsigmond Pál Pach (ed.), *Magyarország Története tiz kötetben* [The History of Hungary in ten volumes] (Budapest: Akadémiai Kiadó, 1980),Vol. 5, Part 1, pp. 123-129.

[8] Keith Hitchins, *The Rumanian National Movement in Transylvania 1780-1849* (Cambridge, Mass.: Harvard University Press, 1969), p. 117.

[9] *Ibid.*, p. 118.

[10] Emil Niederhauser, *The Rise of Nationality in Eastern Europe* (Budapest: Corvina, 1981), p. 209.

[11] Petrovich, *Modern Serbia*, p. 27.

[12] Turczynski, *Konfession und Nation*, pp. 188-193.

[13] Wayne S. Vucinich, *The First Serbian Uprising, 1804-1813*. Vol. 8 of the *War and Society in East Central Europe* series (New York:

IX

Columbia University Press, 1982).

[14] Cyril Mango, "The Phanariots and the Byzantine Tradition", in Richard Clogg (ed.), *The Struggle for Greek Independence* (London: The Macmillan Press, 1973), p. 51.

[15] Philip Sherrard, "Church, State and the Greek War of Independence," in Clogg (ed.), *The Struggle*, p. 183.

[16] Douglas Dakin, *The Greek Struggle for Independence 1821-1833* (Berkeley: University of California Press, 1973), pp. 48-49.

[17] E.D. Tappe, "The 1821 Revolution in the Rumanian Principalities" in Clogg (ed.) *The Struggle,* p. 142 quotes from one of Metternich's letters dated 23 February [1821]: "No one believes that the Emperor Alexander and I understand one another thoroughly, and yet it is so..."

[18] Among the works that date the beginning of "modern" Romanian history are: Miron Constantinescu, Constantine Daicoviciu, Ştefan Pascu et al.. *Istoria României* (Bucharest: Editura Didactică şi Pedagogică, 1969); Andrei Oteţea (chief ed.), *Istoria României,* Vol. 3 (Bucharest: Editura Academiei Romîne, 1964); Andrei Oteţea, *The History of the Romanian People,* trans. from Romanian by Eugenia Farca, (New York: Twayne Publishers, 1970); Dinu G. Giurescu, *Illustrated History of the Romanian People* (Bucharest: Editura Sport-Turism, 1981). The best monograph, Dan Berindei, *Revoluţia Romăna din 1821* (Bucharest: Editura Academiei Romîne, 1991) has a good French summary at the end of the volume.

[19] Giurescu, *Illustrated History,* p. 337.

[20] Constantinescu et al., *Istoria,* p. 271.

[21] The section dealing with Transylvania is based on Keith Hitchins, *Rumanian National Movement.*

[22] Wolf Dietrich Behschnitt, *Nationalismus bei den Serben und Kroaten, 1830-1914* (München: R. Oldenbourg, 1980).

[23] See Elinor Murray Despalatovic, *Ljudevit Gaj and the Illyrian*

Movement, (Boulder, Colo.: East European Monographs, 1975).

[24] Ivo Banac, *The National Question in Yugoslavia: Origins, History, Politics* (Ithaca: Cornell University Press, 1984), p. 76, quoting Bogoslav Sulek.

[25] *Ibid.,* pp. 77-78.

[26] Bechschnitt, *Nationalismus,* p. 54.

[27] Banac, *National Question,* p. 80.

[28] *Ibid.,* p. 80.

[29] George Barany, "The Age of Royal Absolutism, 1790-1848," in Peter F. Sugar, Peter Hanak, and Tibor Frank (eds.), *A History of Hungary* (Bloomington: Indiana University Press, 1990), p. 201.

[30] Endre Kovács and László Katus, *Mágyarorszag Története, 1848-1890* vol. 6 in two parts of Zsigmond Pál Pach (ed.), *Magyarország Története tiz kötetben* [The History of Hungary in ten volumes] (Budapest: Akademiai Kiadó, 1979), Vol. 6, Part 1, pp. 479-480.

[31] Keith Hitchins, *Orthodoxy and Nationality: Andreiu Şaguna and the Rumanians of Transylvania, 1846-1873* (Cambridge, Mass.: Harvard University Press, 1977), p. 79.

[32] E.g., Éva Somogyi, "The Age of Neoabsolutism, 1849-1867," in Sugar, Hanák, Frank, *History of Hungary.*

[33] The paragraphs dealing with the Southern Slavs are based on the already mentioned works of Bechschmitt and Banac.

[34] Keith Hitchins' *Orthodoxy and Nationality* is devoted primarily to the Transylvanian Orthodox Romanian's struggle to gain an independent church of their own. He also deals with other issues of importance to the Romanians. It is the best work available for the years which it covers.

[35] We still lack a History of Romania in English which is not ideologically biased. Giurescu's is better in this respect than is

IX

Oteţea's. I have, therefore, relied on the dated work of R.W. Seton-Watson, *History of the Roumanians*, chapters 10 and 13 (Cambridge: Cambridge University Press, 1934) and on Leften S. Stavrianos, *The Balkans since 1453* (New York: Holt, Rinehart, Winston, 1958) chapters 18 and 26, but also checked the works cited in n. 18.

[36] Peter F. Sugar, *Industrialization of Bosnia-Hercegovina 1878-1918* (Seattle: University of Washington Press, 1963), p. 6.

[37] Dimitrije Djordjevic, "Die Serben," in Adam Wandruszka and Peter Urbanitsch (eds.) *Die Habsburger Monarchie, 1848-1918* vol. 3 in two parts (Vienna: Österreichische Akademie der Wissenschaften, 1980), Vol. 3, Part 1, p. 764.

[38] See Robert J. Donia, *Islam under the Double Eagle: The Muslims of Bosnia and Hercegovina, 1878-1914*, (Boulder, Colo: East European Monographs, 1981).

[39] Ivo Andrić, *The Development of Spiritual Life in Bosnia under the Influence of Turkish Rule*. Zelimir B. Juričić and John F. Loud (eds. & trans.), (Durham, N.C.: Duke University Press, 1990), pp. 39-57.

[40] This assumption was incorrect. When Dr. Josef Stadler was appointed Archbishop of Sarajevo in 1882, he found the Bosnian Franciscans badly trained in theology and replaced them in the parishes with priests of his choice. This move alienated most of the Bosnian Catholics. See Sugar, *Industrialization*, p. 38.

[41] L. Bowers and G. Bolitho, *Otho I King of Greece: a biography* (London, 1939), 106 quoted by Stavrianos, *The Balkans*, p. 292.

[42] R.J. Crampton, *A Short History of Modern Bulgaria* (Cambridge: Cambridge University Press, 1987), p. 18. We still need a good, detailed English language history of Bulgaria. Besides Crampton's short history the following are useful: Thomas Butler (ed.), *Bulgaria Past and Present, Studies in History, Literature, Economics, Music, Sociology, Folklore & Linguistics* (Columbus: AAASS, 1976); and Nikolai Todorov, Liubomir Dinev, and Liuben Malnishki, *Bulgaria. Historical and Geographic Outline* (Sofia: Sofia Press, 1968).

[43] Thomas A. Meininger, *Ignatiev and the Establishment of the Bulgarian Exarchate, 1864-1872* (New York: Laymark Editions, 1970).

[44] Stavrianos, *The Balkans*, p. 375.

[45] Cyril E. Black, *The Establishment of Constitutional Government in Bulgaria* (Princeton, N.J.: Princeton University Press, 1943).

[46] For the history of Bulgaria up to the end of World War I see: Richard J. Crampton, *Bulgaria 1878-1918. A History.* (Boulder, Colo.: East European Monographs, 1983).

[47] The literature dealing with Macedonia is voluminous. It includes numerous "official" publication as, for example: Mihailo Apostolski, Bogo Grafenauer, Ljuben Lape, Aleksandar Stojanovski, Jorjo Tadić, *La Macédonie et les macédoniens dans le passé* (Skopje: Institute de l'Histoire Nationale, 1970), a bilingual collection of essays presenting the Yugoslav-Macedonian side of the argument. Voin Bozhinov and I. Panaiotov (eds.), *Macedonia: Documents and Materials* (Sofia: Institute of History, 1978) presented the Bulgarian argument in a very sophisticated form. Of the numerous monographs published, I prefer Fikret Adanir, *Die Makedonische Frage: Ihre Entstehung und Entwicklung bis 1908.* Vol. 20 of *Frankfurter Historische Abhandlungen* (Wiesbaden: Steiner, 1979). A good fairly recent publication is Duncan M. Perry, *The Politics of Terror: the Macedonian Revolutionary Movement, 1893-1903* (Durham, N.C.: Duke University Press, 1988). Douglas Dakin, *The Greek Struggle in Macedonia, 1897-1913* (Thessaloniki: Institute for Balkan Studies, 1966) has become a highly regarded work on the subject. The most recent work is Hugh Poulton, *Who are the Macedonians?* (Bloomington: Indiana University Press, 1995).

[48] In writing this short summary of Albanian activities I relied on Stavrianos, *The Balkans*, pp. 502-506 and on Barbara Jelavich, *History of the Balkans*, Vol. 2: *Twentieth Century* (Cambridge: Cambridge University Press, 1983), pp. 84-89.

[49] Emile Haumant, *La Formation de la Yougoslavie* (Paris: Bossard, 1930), pp. 682-683.

[50] See among others: Michael Boro Petrovich, "Russia's Role in the Creation of the Yugoslav State, 1914-1918," in Dimitrije Djordjevic, *The Creation of Yugoslavia, 1914-1918* (Santa Barbara: ABC-Clio, 1980), p. 74; Dedijer et al., *History*, p. 482; and Ivo J. Lederer, *Yugoslavia at the Paris Peace Conference. A Study in Frontiermaking* (New Haven, Conn.: Yale University Press, 1963), p. 4.

[51] Banac, *National Question*, p. 132.

[52] Petrovich, *Modern Serbia*, p. 647.

[53] Alex N. Dragnich, *Serbia, Nikola Pašić and Yugoslavia* (New Brunswick: Rutgers University Press, 1974), p. 120.

[54] Janko Pleterski, "Die Slowenen" in Wandruszaka and Urbanitsch, *Monarchie*, Vol. 3, Part 2, p. 836; and Banac, *National Question*, p. 125.

[55] I know of no English version of the Korfu Agreement. For the Serbo-Croatian text see: Ferdo Šišić, *Dokumenti o Postanku Kraljevine Srba, Hrvata i Slovenaca* (Zagreb: Matica Hrvatska, 1920), pp. 96-100.

[56] Banac, *National Question*, p. 402.

[57] Dimitrije Djordjević, "Fascism in Yugoslavia, 1918-1941," and Ivan Avakumović, "Yugoslavia's Fascist Movements," in Peter F. Sugar (ed.), *Native Fascism in the Successor States, 1918-1945* (Santa Barbara: ABC-Clio, 1971), pp. 125-134 and 135-143.

[58] Barbara Jelavich, *Twentieth Century*, p. 203.

[59] For a good short summary of Yugoslavia in World War II see: Jozo Tomasevich, "Yugoslavia during the Second World War," in Wayne S. Vucinich (ed.), *Contemporary Yugoslavia: Twenty Years of Socialist Experiment* (Berkeley: University of California Press, 1969), pp. 59-118.

[60] For Tudjman's ideas see: *Bespuća povijesne zbiljnosti* (Zagreb: Matica Hrvatska, 1989) (Deadlocks in Historical Reality) and *Nationalism in Contemporary Europe* (Boulder, Colo.: East European

Monographs, 1981).

[61] *Financial Times* (London), 10 August 1991, p. 22, and 16 January 1992, p. 2.

[62] See p. 40 above.

[63] Under old hatred Stokes understood the feelings generated during the inter-war years by Belgrade's high-handed dealing with the non-Serb people and those resulting from the horrors of World War II. Stokes' comments were made during a roundtable discussion on 15 December 1993, entitled "The Former Yugoslav Republics," at the Woodrow Wilson International Center for Scholars, Washington, D.C.

[64] Milorad Ekmečić, "Budućnost Jugoslavije," (The Future of Yugoslavia), *NIN*, November 16, 1990, pp. 55-59. I am grateful to Professor Ivo Banac for bringing this article to my attention.

[65] See the article and photographs on the "Vojvodina" in *Hungarian Observer*, Vol. 6, No. 5 (May 1993), pp. 2-5.

[66] On the population exchange see: V.M. Boulter, "The Exchange of Population between Greece and Turkey," in C.A. Macartney (ed.), *Survey of International Affairs, 1925*, Vol. 2 (London: Royal Institute of International Affairs, 1925) Vol. 2, pp. 257-266; Idem, "The Settlement of Refugees in Greece, 1923-6," *Ibid.* Vol. 2, pp. 272-279 and Dimitri Pentzopoulos, *The Balkan Exchange of Minorities and its Impact upon Greece* (Paris: Mouton, 1962).

[67] The two histories of Cyprus which I prefer are: Costas P. Kyrris, *History of Cyprus with an Introduction to the Geography of Cyprus* (Nicosia: Nicocles, 1985) and Stavros Panteli, *A New History of Cyprus from the earliest Times to the Present Day* (London: East-West Pub., 1984).

[68] On Archbishop Makarios see Stanley Mayes, *Cyprus and Makarios* (London: Putnam, 1960) and by the same author, *Makarios: A Biography* (London: Macmillan, 1981). On Grivas see Wilfred Byford-Jones, *Grivas and the Story of EOKA* (London: R. Hale, 1959).

[69] These figures are given in Taki Theodoracopulos, *The Greek Upheaval: Kings, Demagogues and Bayonets* (London: Stacey International, 1976), p. 24.

[70] On the events of July, 1974 see Theodoracopulos, *Greek Upheaval*, pp. 35-90; Mayes, *A Biography*, pp. 242-252; Zenon Stavrinides, *The Cyprus Conflict: National Identity and Statehood* (Wakefield: the author, 1975), pp. 85-91; Joseph S. Joseph, *Cyprus: Ethnic Conflict and International Concern* (New York: P. Lang, 1985), pp. 103-115 and many others. On a Turkish view of the conflict see: Rauf R. Denktash, *The Cyprus Triangle* (London: Allen and Unwin, 1982) and Sabahattin Ismail, *20 July Peace Operation: Reasons-Development and Consequences* (Istanbul: Kasta, 1989).

[71] The problems of present day Albania are discussed in Francis Trix, "The Resurfacing of Islam in Albania," in *East European Quarterly*, Vol. 28, No. 4 (Winter, 1994) and Miranda Vickers, *The Albanians: A Modern History* (London: I.B. Tauris, 1995).

X

Religion, Nationalism and Politics in East-Central Europe*

During the last four years the conflict in Bosnia-Hercegovina gave many newspaper readers and television watchers the impression that at the end of the 20th century Europe was, once again, the scene of a religious war pitting Orthodox Serbs, Catholic Croats and Muslims against each other. This interpretation of the tragic events involved is as mistaken as is the explanation that the conflict is simply the last manifestation of centuries old ethnic hatreds. These hatreds are at most 80-90 years old — a problem not analyzed in these pages — but the religious interpretation offers a good entry into the exploration of the inter-relatedness of religion, nationalism and politics in East-Central Europe.

Religion, any religion, is an attempt by groups of human beings to understand their relationship with the supernatural or even natural manifestations for which they could not produce an explanation. The various explanations/solutions to the problems these relationships presented had to be *true*, even in the metaphysical sense, otherwise they were not the sought-for solutions. These truths had to be codified and explained, producing theologies, and protected from misinterpretations (heresies) by the group of their guardians, the clergies. What resulted were rather sophisticated theories preached by the high churches, which the majority of the so-called faithful did not truly understand, and enforced by powerful organizations, the various churches. It was these organizations and their powers which the various communist governments feared much more as competitors to their organization and power than the teachings which they considered the opiates of the masses. Giving to Caesar what was Caesar's and following the Ten Commandments would only have helped these regimes. This is a clear connection between religion, or rather organized institutions, churches, and politics. It is also important to realize that the majority of the adherents of the various creeds did not understand most of the complicated theological arguments involved, but produced their own, often superstitious versions of belief, known as folk religions. Consequently, two types of "religions" played their parts in history.

The same was true of Marxism called Communism in the Soviet Union and from 1945 to 1989 in East-Central Europe. Its theology — Marxism-Leninism-Stalinism-etc. — could be and was debated and discussed by the movements' intellectuals and the state's political elites, but for the masses it remained incomprehensible and was replaced by folk communism.

Nobody is born a member of a nation. Individuals discover that they are French, American, Russian, etc. when their elders, schools, media, etc. teach them what they are. Nations are the politicized and state bound forms of ethnic groups whose members belong to them as a result of a consciously made (or learned) decision on the part of each of them. Nationalism is the institutionalized form of a nation's *truth* just as theology plays this part for a religious community. In this case the role of the clergy is played by the intellectual/economic/political elite of the nation who preach their version of nationalism. To what extent the masses believe these teachings is difficult to measure or establish, but given the growing influence of the media since the invention of printing it is certainly more and more pervasive.

Finally, turning to the third society activating force mentioned in the title of this paper, I define politics for the remainder of this essay as the method, system and/or tool which segments of a national or international elite use to maximize and retain power in the public sphere in which they operate.

All through history human beings needed more than simply means of survival to live a satisfactory life. Life has to have meaning, a purpose, a justification, a goal or an ideal, something that deserves supreme loyalty. Religion satisfied this need everywhere in Europe – and elsewhere on our globe – for a long time. It is still playing this role for some individuals, but not for the great majority of people. In Europe, East-Central Europe included, religion as the focus of supreme loyalty was replaced by personal loyalty (feudalism), culminating in the monarchical state. Louis XIV was arrogant, but told the truth when he uttered his famous words: "l'état c'est moi." In the 18th century the Enlightenment moved loyalty away from the monarchs to the nation state and made nationalism the dominant ideology which it remained to the present day.

Did religion lose all its influence and importance? When did it cease to be the major consideration dictating political action in East-Central Europe? These are the first questions which must be faced and answered. Religion, as defined by the various organized high churches has, indeed, lost practically all of its influence in the east-central part of the old world. Yet, in another sense it is still with us. Western Christianity — both Roman Catholic and Protestant, — Eastern Christianity in its various national forms, Islam and Judaism denote markedly *different world views* with serious consequences to the present day. Judaism can be disregarded with great regrets, because the Holocaust has eliminated it for all important purposes from playing any part in the ideological life of East-Central Europe.

Western Christianity lived its own life ever since the Holy Roman Emperor, Henry IV, had to go to Canossa in 1077. With the exception of the Anglican, since then no western church was a state church subject to the political domination of the state. This allowed the clergies of these churches to play independent political roles. In the Orthodox world each church is a national church and is, therefore, identified by the population with the government. Lenin understood this correctly when he allowed the restoring of the Russian patriarchate.[1] This very important difference already indicates that the followers of the Western and Eastern churches have drastically different world views. These differences are enhanced by the fact that beginning with the voyages of discovery culminating with Columbus's trip to our continent and ending with the great economic, technological and economic changes of the 18th-20th centuries, all major developments that shape today's world occurred in the lands of Western Christianity. These changes drastically altered the world view of the people who were part of the "western world" including Slovenes, Czechs, Slovaks, Croats, Poles and Magyars whose development was dictated – to a considerable extent – by the Holy Roman and later the Habsburg and Hohenzollern empires. While these changes occurred during the last two-three centuries in these East-Central European lands, the Orthodox world stagnated due to the conservatism and orthodoxy of the Russian and Ottoman Empires. That Islam represents a third and very different world view does not need much explanation. Consequently, religious labels, like those we use for the conflict in Bosnia-Hercegovina, are still valid, although not strictly religious; they indicate three different world views and approaches to life and problem solving. In this sense, the lasting influence of religion is still very important.

As already indicated, I believe that people always needed something which inspired them and to which they could owe supreme and primary loyalty. Before the second half of the question: when did religion cease to play a central role in Eastern Europe, can be answered, a caveat is required. The tendency of all kinds of analysts is to blame most of Europe's, especially of East-Central Europe's problems on nationalism. This might be true of the present but was not of most events in the past into which even historians like to read back the causal explanations of the present. Patriotism, local or broader in the region to which it applied, is, indeed, as old as history, but nationalism in its modern form dates from the eighteenth century and is tied closely to the birth of modern democracy and the concept of the nation-state which is unimaginable without democracy.

Having made this point it is possible to turn to the question of when did religion cease to be the primary force shaping decision making in East-Central Europe. The Reformation is a good test case although nothing really new can be added to what is well known already. Luther and the other reformers were certainly motivated by their deep religious convictions, but in most cases this was not motivating the various princes who followed their teachings. They were not nationalists, not even patriots, but representatives of the monarchical principle in its absolutist form and enjoyed weakening the ties that bound them to the Holy Roman Emperor. Their motivation was political. They also enjoyed getting rid of papal taxes, an added economic motivation. Convincing different answers are possible, but that the questions can be asked already indicates that the religious fervor that motivated the Byzantine akritoi, the Western Christian crusader or the Muslim gazi was gone by the early sixteenth century in Europe.[2]

This becomes even clearer when developments in East-Central Europe are considered. To what extent were the Czech Taborites, the second generation Hussites, motivated by religious zeal or by the social revolutionary aspect of their master's teachings? Looking back at the Czech lands after the Habsburgs successfully introduced the Counter-reformation after 1620, we find that the least religious of European societies developed in Bohemia-Moravia, often explained by the statement that the inhabitants of these provinces became Protestant Catholics who cared more about social than religious problems. This attitude changed after nationalism appeared rather late in these regions, when the Germans and Czechs began to court the Jews to increase their numbers in the national struggle that separated them, and Catholicism and Lutheranism became indicators of Czechness and Germanness.

Hungary is an even more interesting example. In this country, or rather that part of it not under Ottoman rule, the Reformation was at first successful and then the Counter-reformation made serious gains. Here too the Habsburgs were important roughly in what is today Slovakia and western Hungary, but even in Transylvania, independent from 1526 to 1690, the upper nobility, the ruling element, exclusively Hungarian returned to Catholicism rather quickly. It was this upper nobility that proclaimed religious equality in 1564, and the Hungarians are very proud of this sign of their early toleration and liberalism. They also point out that the rulers of Transylvania, who often fought the Habsburgs, always fought for religious freedom and equality in Habsburg-held Hungary.

Was true religious feeling behind this remarkable behavior? I am certain that it was not. The toleration of religions in Transylvania was never extended to the Orthodox, the creed of the Romanian peasantry, and Francis David, the father of Unitarianism, was jailed when he wanted further reform. Transylvania's rulers had to accept Calvinism favored by some important Hungarian nobles, Unitarianism accepted by the Székelys and the Lutheranism of the German speaking urban population if they wanted to keep their country in business. Clearly a political necessity dictated religious policy. When they defended Protestantism in Habsburg Hungary, they fought for the estate-based rights of the nobility that gave Hungary a special position in the Habsburg realm. Another political factor expressed on occasion in terms of religion.[3]

Poland presents an interesting case. In this country nationalism in its modern form and belief that Polishness is closely tied to Catholicism developed simultaneously. This is clearly illustrated by the last of Poland's many pre-partition confederations, that of Bar (1768-72) whose fate inspired Rousseau's *Considérations sur le Gouvernement de la Pologne* which, in turn inspired the first truly modern, liberal constitution in East-Central Europe, the Polish of 1791. The most influential leader of this Confederation, which aimed to save Poland's independence, was a bishop, J. Krasicki and its armed forces were *The Order of the Knights of the Holy Cross*. Yet, the commander of this force was the truly westernized liberal József Pulaski known also from American history.[4] The explanation for this interesting phenomenon is not too difficult to find. Poland needed new ideas and methods to save herself from the growing power and steady encroachment of her neighbors, Russia and Prussia. This opened the country to new, western inspired ideas, including nationalism, while the Lutheranism of Prussia and the Orthodoxy of Russia, both ready not only to conquer, but also to proselytize, made Catholicism a mark of opposition to their efforts. It is important to remember that Lutheranism in Prussia and Orthodoxy in Russia were state religions, the faiths of the enemies who had to be opposed on the military, political and spiritual levels.

The Balkans present a different picture because there the dominant world views were first Orthodoxy and then, for 500 years, Islam and Orthodoxy. Islam, and consequently the Ottoman Empire, recognized only one criterion to differentiate between people – religion. Muslims had privileges and rights, but also obligations that the majority of the people living in the Ottoman Empire's European provinces, the Orthodox, did not have. It is not clear why in Albania, Bosnia and Macedonia some people converted to Islam. Was it religious conviction or something else? I am convinced that for the majority of those who converted within a relatively few short years politics and economics played a major role because it was their new religion that gave them the political and economic advantages they sought. I believe that this was the case, first of all, because in the Balkans the Ottomans did not proselytize, because they needed the extra taxes paid by the non-Muslim masses. Secondly because it is very unlikely that masses suddenly see the same new light especially when nobody tries to turn it on.

Be it as it may, there was a sharp difference between Muslim and non-Muslim in the Balkans. Serious revolts began to threaten Ottoman mastery in the region in the early nineteenth century. It is not likely that religion was their primary motivating force. When the Bulgarian monk on Mt. Athos, Father Paisii, published his work which today's Bulgarians consider the clarion call that reawakened their identity, he did not attack Islam or defend Orthodoxy although he was a clergyman. In 1762 he brought out his *History of the Slavo-Bulgarians*. He was not an early modern nationalist. He was ethnically conscious, but lacked the western world view which created nationalism. Nor were the various Robin Hood types who appeared in the Balkans and are today considered early national freedom fighters by Bulgarian, Serb and Greek nationalists.[5] They were local patriots interested only in their immediate environment, conscious of the linguistic and religious differences that separated them from those, by now very corrupt office holders, who oppressed them mainly in numerous economic ways. When these misdeeds became in-tolerable they rose up. Any religious or political, let alone nationalistic motivation was either accidental or incidental. It is wrong to impute to them motivations with which they could not be and were not familiar.

Religion played an important political role in the Balkans for two reasons. The first of these was the basic incompatibility of the Ottoman approach to differentiating between people according to creed and the tradition of their various Orthodox subjects to see in national churches the proof of independent states. This created tension between the Greeks, to whom the Ottomans entrusted the affairs of the Orthodox millet, and the various Slavs of the Balkans and the Romanians. Out of this traditional equality of national churches emerged what became known as the Macedonian question.[6] It began on February 26, 1870 when the sultan Abdül-Aziz issued a firman establishing the Bulgarian Exarchate. He created a national church giving in to the pressure exerted by the Russian ambassador, count Nicholas P. Ignatiev, who belonged to the Asiatic department of the Russian Ministry of Foreign Affairs, its most imperialist section, trying to establish a foothold for his country in the Balkans. Not only was this new church established for political reasons, but the area – vaguely Macedonia – in which the sultan allowed free selection of church membership according to local wishes became the battleground of all Balkan nations, leading to the two Balkan wars of 1912 and 1913. This 45 year struggle is a good example of what the German scholar Emanuel Turczynski called *Konfessions-Nationalität*. Just as the Macedonian question is still with us in a new guise, so is *Konfessions-Nationalität*. For Turczynski it denoted the stage in historical development in which the national church-state identification descended from the political realm of the elites to the popular level, under the influence of modern nationalism, creating a new identification of nation with church membership on a somewhat vague purely folk religious, emotional level. This concept, once again in a new garb, is still useful in dealing with problems of the present.[7]

It was not only in the Balkans that church membership – not religiosity necessarily – played a political role. When in their part of partitioned Poland the Russians moved the last remaining Catholic seminary to St. Petersburg they tried to create a Catholic clergy that, while Polish, accepted the state as master of their church just as the Russian Orthodox clergy did. The existence of parochial schools is another good example. In Hungary, prior to World War I, the Orthodox had their school systems based on national divisions. The Catholic school-system was run by a unified, Hungarian dominated church. This difference was crucial. Romanian and Serb nationalism flourished while that of the Slovaks was weak, if it was even that. This is a clear indication, once again, of the political significance of what were in theory simply religion based institutions.

The nineteenth century, especially its second half, was dominated by nationalist feelings, propaganda and politics. Roman Dmowski and Józef Piłsudki disagreed on almost everything when they planned a future independent Poland, but both were nationalists who paid relatively little attention to religion. They did not have to: by then Catholicism was a firmly accepted component of Polishness. Orthodox and Uniates worked together in the Romanian movement of Transylvania. The situation among the southern Slavs is more interesting. That their national problem had numerous forms was clearly shown by Ivo Banac.[8] The Greater Serbia ideology dated by most scholars from 1844 when the Serb Prime Minister, Ilije Garašanin, published his *Načertanije* (Outline) is considered basic, and many people see in today's policy pursued by Slobodan Milošević a revival of this program. This document clearly rejected the Orthodox traditional approach and even rejected common Slavness.

Garašanin was a Serb nationalist. Yet, his ideas were based on the work of a Moravian Pan-Slav, Fratišek Zach, in the employ of a Pole, count Adam Czartoryski. Zach was a follower of the Czech historian, František Palacký, and wanted to move the Serbs away from Russia and Orthodoxy, turn them into a Slavic force in the Balkans capable to help Poland's rebirth. It was from his writings that Garašanin derived his ideas for a Great Serb Balkan state. That his view included all of Bosnia-Hercegovina and even parts of Croatia-Slavonia in his Serbia – just as Milošević's does today – was clearly shown by Charles Jelavich.[9] Given the events of the last few years, it is interesting to note that both of these men believed that Bosnia had to become part of Greater Serbia because otherwise "the Serbs would be split up into small provincial principalities...[who] would rival and envy each other."[10] This does not mean that religious prejudice has disappeared from Serbia. In a letter written on September 17, 1915 by the English scholar-publicist, R.W. Seton-Watson, to the Prince Regent of Serbia discussing post-war plans, he warned that a return to the Greater Serbia idea would be a mistake and that only a true Yugoslavia could bring peace to the region. While, wrote Seton-Watson to Prince Alexander, the advocates of Greater Serbia dream of an Orthodox state, a true Yugoslavia had to be based on "the idea that religion is only a private affair of the citizens, and that a Catholic is as good a citizen as...an Orthodox."[11]

The other approach to the Southern Slav question, the Croat based Yugoslav movement, was no better. It too claimed all of Bosnia, etc. as Croat territory, just as the Serbs claimed it for their own. After all, the leading light of this movement was a very western world view man, who – although a Catholic bishop – in 1870 opposed the proclamation of Papal Infallibility, bishop Josip J. Strossmayer. He declared that religion was secondary and that in a united southern Slav state he could live with a Karadjordjević ruler. Yet, we have the famous incident of his meeting with the Emperor-King, Franz Joseph. When the ruler questioned his willingness to work with the "enemy," the bishop explained that his love of Serbia and his toleration of Orthodoxy was proportional to the Hungarian oppression in Croatia. Once again, we have religion and politics closely involved with each other.

The First World War destroyed more than simply three empires; it destroyed most of Europe's order and, more importantly, its well established values. The years that separated the two great conflicts are often called the long armistice, and Prof. Ivan Berend labeled them the critical decades in the title of a first rate book.[12] Religion played practically no role anywhere during these twenty years and even nationalism – as practised and defined up to then – went into decline. In East-Central Europe the old form of nationalism continued to live in liberated Poland where the end of the partitions was considered the victory of nationalistic policy. Elsewhere in the area it was replaced by status quo and populistic revisionist politics which used nationalistic slogans and symbols but were basically political power plays on the fringe, disregarding the true power structure that destroyed both camps.

The true power structure was based on three new *isms*: Fascism, National Socialism and Bolshevism. Obviously, none of these were religious, and Bolshevism was openly anti-nationalistic. In my view Fascism and National Socialism were as anti-nationalistic as was Bolshevism. They used, as the status quo and revisionist camps did before, nationalistic symbols and slogans, but the nation, its well being and future did not really matter anymore. Fascism deified the state, National Socialism the race, two new deities the nation was supposed to serve. This became clear at the end of World War II when Hitler ordered Speer to destroy Germany because the Germans did not live up to what was expected of them and, therefore, did not deserve to survive. The imitators in East-Central Europe of these new, short-lived ideologies were no different from their idols whom they aped.

Even anti-Semitism, unfortunately well established for decades, changed its nature and became much more tragic. It ceased to be religious or even political in its motivation and became racial and bestial. It is high time that the people of East-Central Europe realize this, accept responsibility for the role they played in the Holocaust and stop blaming the Germans for what happened on their soil. The persecution of Serbs by the Ustaša Croat state during the Second World War is the best example of this new racially based world view. Serbs could avoid genocide if they converted from Orthodoxy to Catholicism. Although some Catholic clergymen were involved in this shameful practice of forced conversion, the motive was not religious, but a racially based, and therefore new, form of nationalism. The change of religion signified in the eyes of the Ustaši a change of national loyalty. This was a new way of looking at what Turczynski called *Konfessions-Nationalität*: *Konfession* simply became the obviously visible mark of *Nationalität*.

The forty-five years of communist rule that followed the Second World War everywhere in Eastern Europe were anti-religious and anti-national. It preached brotherhood and cooperation based on a common ideology enforced by Moscow, called Communism, but nothing short of imitative Stalinism. It lost ground everywhere gradually beginning with Stalin's death, the Hungarian revolution of 1956, the Prague spring of

1968, etc., culminating in the events of 1989. All this is well known. That communist policy failed to eradicate national antagonism, anti-Semitism and added new problems to these for the people living in East-Central Europe became obvious after the events of 1989-90. Tito, the man credited with inventing national Communism, tried to make this basic contradiction in ideologies work when he remodeled Yugoslavia – the well known Titoist solution to the Yugoslav problem – but that died with him. What is of interest is Tito's historical sense. When he created a Macedonian component in his federative state, he realized that no Orthodox state is truly that until it has its own national church and created one of these too.

The disappearance of Communism brought with it the re-appearance of nationalism. This nationalism has very little in common with its earlier manifestations not only in East-Central, but everywhere in Europe. It is worthwhile to spend a few minutes on the wider, European scene before returning to that part of the continent covered by these pages.

The disappearance of Communism brought with it the dis-appearance of anti-Communism as well. Anti-Communism was the ideology that animated the so-called West during the years of the Cold War. If the collapse of both of these ideologies left a spiritual vacuum in Europe and brought about the return of nationalism, why is this nationalism new and not what it had been before 1945?

The answer is simple: 1990 differed drastically from 1939. In the latter year Europe had five great powers – Great Britain, France, Germany, Italy and the Soviet Union – today it has none. In 1939 Europe was divided by numerous pacts including the Entente, the Little Entente, the Comintern, the Axis, the Balkan Pact, or what was left of them. Today only NATO and the European Community are left and these do not divide as the earlier pacts did, but act as a magnet for all those states who are not yet members. The levels of urbanization, industrialization, mass education and cultural homogenization brought on by the mass media are drastically different, especially in East-Central Europe, from what they were in 1939. Nationalism had to adjust to these changes if it wanted to fill the ideological vacuum Europe faced after 1989. This is exactly what happened. The new ideology took three major forms which some scholars have already labeled Nostalgic, State-of-Siege and Defensive National-isms.

As the label indicates, Nostalgic Nationalism is looking back to the days of old glory. Before the Second World War, Mussolini and Hitler foreshadowed this development. The first was ready to create a second Roman Empire while the second created a Third Reich. After 1945 the first manifestation of Nostalgic Nationalism was Gaullism. France had been defeated, was liberated by Anglo-Saxon powers, was admitted into the council of the great only by their sufferance. This was intolerable to Charles de Gaulle who had to prove that la Grande Nation still existed, had to be considered one of great powers and be treated accordingly. Therefore, he did not join NATO, created his own nuclear force and hung onto colonies much longer than the other ex-colonial powers did. France has a gaullist president again. He objects to multilingualism in spite of the European trend to the contrary. Not everybody in France was or is a gaullist, but today's France is the creation of what de Gaulle produced during the first post-war years. That Great Britain's and other western states' nationalisms also have nostalgic elements could easily be shown, but would take too much space. What is important to note is that while in the west of Europe Nostalgic Nationalism is a dominant type, it is not that in East-Central Europe in spite of the memories of the Lands of St. Steven's Crown, of two Bulgarian empires or the realm of Stepan Dušan. These are memories, but do not dictate policy. Even Solzhenitsyn, the most famous nostalgic nationalist, has been labeled "irrelevant" in Russia.

Defensive nationalism is the most common variety in today's Europe. Its essence was clearly and simply expressed by one of the banners used by Polish students during one of their numerous demonstrations in 1956. It read: "we will exchange our ideology for a better geographic location." What else could be more important for a country situated between Germany and – in 1956 – the Soviet Union? Today Russia objects to her neighbors joining NATO because, looking back at her past, she knows that most attacks threatening her came from the west. Just like Nostalgic Nationalism, Defensive Nationalism also rests on fear based on historical precedents. No nation wants to disappear. Fear of being absorbed triggers such national movements as those of the Flemish, Basque, Provençal, etc. They are Roman Catholics just as are the bigger nations whose domination they fear. This makes no difference. They will be satisfied with iron clad guarantees of their survival, but they will not strive for independence – as they would have in the pre-1939 world – because they realize that the economic and social consequences of such a move would be counterproductive.

The nationalism of all nations in East-Central Europe is at least defensive if not more drastic. All of them want to join the European Union not only for economic reasons, but also – possibly mainly – because they are afraid of revived German power and the potential of an equal revival in Russia. Furthermore, these nations are also as afraid of each other as they are of their big neighbors. Membership in the European

Union would protect them from themselves also. Everything else is secondary as far as determining policy is concerned. The change of the position in society of the Polish Roman Catholic Church shows this clearly. This church was the most important oppositional force during the years of communist rule because it was the only organized force that was anti-communist. Today the political role and power on the public stage of this church is minimal. There is no ideology it can oppose in the name of the nation and has, therefore, become irrelevant in a country that was considered more homogeneous and religiously conservative than any other in the old world. During the years when the Communists ruled Poland the Catholic Church in that country reverted to its defensive nationalistic role which it had learned to play very well during the long years of the partition period.

Another good example of Defensive Nationalism that emerged early in history is that of the Hungarians. They were on the defensive ever since Herder predicted that sooner or later they would disappear in the surrounding Slav sea. The Magyars also produced the earliest example of transition from Defensive to State-of-Siege Nationalism in the last thirty years of the 19th century. Faced with the growing nationalism of its South Slav, Slovak and Romanian citizens, the Hungarian government felt besieged on all sides and went on the counterattack. After all, offense is the best defense as any strategist knows. The result was an aggressive, jingoistic, militant form of nationalism typical of the State-of-Siege variety.

Today's Hungarian nationalism is a good example of the defensive kind. Both the first post-communist government, that of Antall, and that of Horn that followed it, gave up revisionism, being realistic enough to know that it is not a viable policy. But both listed highly among the duties they had to perform the defense of Hungarians and their rights beyond the borders of Hungary. It is an excellent example of today's Defensive Nationalism.

One of the countries the Hungarian governments watch is Slovakia. It is difficult to place Slovak nationalism into any category. The Slovaks have become fully independent for the first time in their history only a few years ago, and the dominant feature of their nationalism is euphoria. Are their exaggerated anti-minority measures simply part of this euphoria and will they be moderated when this feeling calms down, or are these measures signs of at least Defensive Nationalism if not worse? No answer to this question is possible today.

The Orthodox churches never played a political role similar to that of the Catholic in Poland and the Lutheran in East Germany. They were national churches, dependent on the state even in communist days, considered as a branch of the government by the politically conscious segment of the population.

The mention of the Orthodox Church brings me to the Balkans. When Bulgaria persecuted its Turkish minority, but not its equally Muslim Pomaks, during the closing years of the Zhivkov regime, the purpose was certainly not religious. Just as during the war time conversion of Serbs in Croatia was supposed to indicate the acceptance of a new national loyalty, so the acceptance of a new name played the same role in Bulgaria. Today, the Bulgarian Muslims – Pomaks included – have their own political party which has the second largest representation in Parliament. Today's government is not communist and could consider religious threats, but this is not the case. The enemies of this party demand its dissolution because ethnically based parties are not supposed to exist according to the country's constitution. Therefore, the argument goes something like this: a Turkish party is illegal. Fear of Turkey transformed even the Pomaks into Turks. Another good example of Defensive Nationalism.

The disintegration of Yugoslavia is the most tragic and interesting example of conflicting nationalisms which were defensive at the outset, but turned into something even more dangerous as the fight in Bosnia-Hercegovina developed. When Communism collapsed in Yugoslavia, nationalism could not take its place because Yugoslavism or Yugoslav nationalism was practically nonexistent. The component parts of the federations had to go their own way. In the case of the Serbs, Croats, Slovenes and even Macedonians this was a fairly clear matter, the fightings in Slovenia and Croatia notwithstanding. Bosnia-Hercegovina was a different case.

What was the future of this region once the federation broke up? According to the Serbs, it had to stay in what was left of Yugoslavia because they were not willing to become a minority population – a typical case of defensiveness based on fear – in a state not of their own. This solution was unacceptable to both Croats and Muslims who feared the same minority position in a new, smaller and much more lopsided in its ethnic composition Serbian Yugoslavia. The media in Western Europe and even more in the U.S.A. made a great deal out of the fact that the Serbs are Orthodox, the Croats Catholics and the Muslims are just Muslims. In short, a religious war in Europe in the 1990s! These barbarians take us back to the Stone or at least to the Middle Ages! Yet nothing could be further from the truth. I have been working with Bosnian Muslims for forty years and can testify that they had nothing in common with fundamental Islam or even with the moderate version of something like Kemalist Turkey's. Their world view was not that of their Christian fellow Bosnians. This was something Tito recognized when, in February 1968, he recognized a Muslim nationality. If the Bosnian Muslims will ever become good Muslims then they will do this under the influence of the last four years' civil war. Yet I doubt it. More and more they call themselves simply Bosnians and have even began to use for themselves the term Turcini – invented during the years of Austro-Hungarian rule – meaning Muslim Southern Slavs, that gives them their own ethnic identity different from that of the Turks who they call Turkusi.

These Bosnians, as well as some of their Serb and Croatian co-inhabitants, simply wanted to remain Bosnians, a typical case of Defensive Nationalism. This had no chance of succeeding without the prolonged struggle we have witnessed for over four years. Whoever is master of Dalmatia, Austria-Hungary in the last century and Croatia today, must control Bosnia-Hercegovina otherwise Dalmatia is indefensible. Defensive Nationalism is at work again. Mr. Franjo Tudjman, President of Croatia, has never tried to hide this fact. The Serbs had more in mind than simply defending their Serbness. The revival of the Greater Serbia ideal going back at least to Garašanin, the dream of gaining an outlet to the sea, combined with the well known Serb national persecution complex, well expressed in this contemporary form by the 1986 Memorandum of the Serb Academy of Sciences and Arts, took them beyond Defensive Nationalism. Persecuted, exploited, unjustly treated, always the ones who paid the piper, besieged on all sides, the Serbs believed that they had no alternative but to fight. Here is a good example of a state-of-siege nationalism in action. Unfortunately, the Serb variety of State-of-Siege Nationalism went beyond the features this type usually has. It is not only intolerant, aggressive, jingoistic, but it also reverted to the Nazi and Soviet practices of concentration camps and mass executions, and invented a new term, ethnic cleansing, for mass deportations. Religious labels in the Bosnian tragedy denote no creeds, no beliefs that belonging to a denomination secures a happy afterlife. These labels are simply pseudonyms standing for two Defensive and one State-of-Siege Nationalism and their conflict. This is the modern, contemporary version of *Konfessions-Nationalität*.

Serb nationalism is not the only one that can be placed into the State-of-Siege category. Romania presents another case. This feeling was very well expressed by one of the leading present day politicians in Bucharest, Mr. Vadim Tudor. When writing the Program of his party, the Greater Romanian Party, he pointed out that on every one of her borders Romania faced hostile or potentially hostile neighbors ready to take advantage of the disloyal disposition of her minorities.[13] Furthermore, on two of her borders, the Yugoslav and the Moldovan, the political situation was critical threatening regional peace. Romania was under siege, according to Mr. Tudor, and had to be ready to defend herself.

Greece presents a third example of Stage-of-Siege nationalism. According to her numerous vocal political elites and practically unregulated media, Greece is surrounded by hostile states: Albania, Turkey, and now Macedonia. The danger these three neighbors represent to the future of Greece is blown out of all proportion by everybody expressing an opinion which is often based more on nightmares, speculations, pure inventions than on facts. There is no doubt that serious problems exist in Turkish-Greek relations, but even these are not threatening the existence of Hellas. The stage-of-siege mentality becomes clear when one looks at what the Greeks consider the Macedonian danger. This has nothing to do with the name Macedonia or the sixteen point star in that country's flag. I was told repeatedly during my visit to Greece in 1993 that while present day Macedonia did not represent any danger for Greece, that country could become the nucleus of a large Slav state that would, indeed, threaten Greece. This argument is patently absurd. Macedonia has no chance of expanding at the expense of Serbia or Bulgaria, or becoming a large Slav state. Just the contrary is true. Her existence guarantees that the just mentioned two states will not become large Slav states on Greece's northern border. Yet my Greek discussion partners did not wish to see it this way. That Greece was surrounded and had to defend herself was the axiomatic truth for them.

There are other nations in East-Central Europe whose nationalisms have not been mentioned. They have features similar to those already presented. Dealing with them would not add much, if anything, to my arguments. What needs discussion is a purely political issue that operates in the region today and does not receive proper attention.

The United Nations and NATO have been involved, rather ineffectively, in the Balkans for the last few years. At the beginning of October 1995, the American envoy, Mr. Richard C. Holbrooke, managed to negotiate a cease-fire in Bosnia-Hercegovina and peace negotiations began. These negotiations ended in November with Milošević, Tudjman and Izetbegović agreeing to a peace treaty to be signed on December 16 in Paris. Some crucial actors on the Bosnian scene were not present in Dayton and subsequently objected to the meeting's results. Even if they are subsequently forced to go along, can any solution be called peace when those involved are dissatisfied and bitter enough to have the so-called peace *enforced* – this is the never used but correct term – by thousands of foreign troops? The answer is an obvious no. What is taking place has its precedents. It is nothing new to see politics on the international scene opt for "success" by adopting short range opportunistic solutions that practically guarantee new conflicts. The great powers, led by Austria-Hungary, made this mistake in Berlin in 1878, setting the stage for the Serb-Bulgarian war of 1885 and the two Balkan Wars. The great powers, this time the Entente, made the same mistake in London in 1913 when they drew the borders of Albania, a country they were considering a potential satellite of Vienna, narrowly enough to create the Kosovo problem that is with us to the present day. Now the only remaining great power, the United States, is about to make the same mistake in settling for a short range solution of the Bosnian problem.

Is there a way out of this seemingly endless series of confrontations, be they religious, political or national in their origin? For this to happen we need two developments to occur. The so-called West must take advantage of the East-Central European states' desire to join the European Community and must stop settling for stopgap solutions when facing crises. The first of these conditions that could bring an end to the endemic problems in East-Central Europe seems to be understood in the various Western capitals, who demand not only economic reform, but also a meaningful and correct settlement of minority-ethnic problems before they open their doors to those who knock at them. As for the second condition, enforcement of agreements, the direction in which the search for a solution in Bosnia-Hercegovina moves makes me pessimistic. It would be supremely ironic if the various East-Central Europeans would find ways to solve some of their problems, but would not reach a lasting peace due to the action of those who forced them into their much needed reforms.

Notes

*This paper was originally written as a lecture delivered in November 1995 at the University of California at Los Angeles.

1 - Donald W. Treadgold, *Twentieth Century Russia* (Westview Press; Boulder-San Francisco-Oxford; 8th ed., 1995), p. 121.

2 - On the interaction of these three types of "soldiers of religion" see: Speros Vryonis, Jr., *The Decline of Medieval Hellenism in Asia Minor and the Process of Islamization from the Eleventh through Fifteen*

Century (University of California Press; Berkeley-Los Angeles-London, 1871).

3 - Peter F. Sugar, Péter Hanák, Tibor Frank (eds.), *A History of Hungary* (Indiana University Press; Bloomington-Indianapolis, 1990), Chapters VIII & IX.

4 - W.F. Reddaway, J.H. Penson, O. Halecki, R. Dyboski (eds.), *The Cambridge History of Poland (1697-1935)* (The Cambridge University Press, Cambridge, 1951), Chapters VIII & IX.

5 - Charles and Barbara Jelavich, *The Establishment of the Balkan National States, 1804-1920*; Vol. VIII of *A History of East-Central Europe* – Peter F. Sugar and Donald W. Treadgold (eds.), (University of Washington Press; Seattle-London, 1977).

6 - Fikret Adanir, *Die Makedonische Frage. Ihre Entstehung und Entwicklung bis 1908* (Franz Steiner Verlag; Wiesbaden, 1979); Duncan M. Perry, *The Politics of Terror. The Macedonian Revolutionary Movements, 1893-1903* (Duke University Press; Durham-London, 1988); Mihailo Apostolski et al (eds.), *La Macédoine et les macédoniens dans le passé* (Institut de l'histoire nationale; Skopje, 1970).

7 - Emanuel Turczynski, *Von der Aufklärung zum Frühliberalismus*. Vol. 81 *Südosteuropaische Arbeiten* (R. Oldenburg; München, 1985).

8 - Ivo Banac, *The National Question in Yugoslavia. Origins, History, Politics* (Cornell University Press; Ithaca-London, 1984).

9 - Charles Jelavich, *South Slav Nationalisms. Textbooks and Yugoslav Union Before 1914* (Ohio State University Press; Columbus, 1990).

10 - Banac, p. 84.

11 - English translation by Dennison Rusinow in Peter F. Sugar (ed.), *Eastern European Nationalism in the 20th Century* (The American University Press; Lanham, Md – London, 1995), pp. 305-9.

12 - Ivan T. Berend, *Válságos évtizedek* [Critical decades] (Gondolat; Budapest, 1982).

13 - English translation by James P. Niessen in Peter F. Sugar (ed.), *Eastern European Nationalism*, pp. 277-9.

XI

EASTERN EUROPEAN NATIONALISM IN THE 20TH CENTURY

Let me begin by stressing once again something I have emphasized repeatedly in the past: when I speak of nationalism, I refer to a modern phenomenon roughly 250 years old that differs significantly from patriotism or any other sentiment that might make human beings prefer a certain region or a given group of people. As any other doctrine, nationalism also had a specific origin and history and changed, in accordance with local circumstances, as it travelled from its region of inception, all over the world.

As practically all doctrines, ideals, institutions, behaviors, and socio-economic practices that dominate the world today, nationalism was also born in a narrowly defined region of Western Europe west of the Rhine and north of the Pyrenées. It moved almost unchanged northward, but took on different forms moving to the south and even into the western provinces of the then Holy Roman Empire. In the eastern regions of this collection of states and in the lands east and south of it, nationalism took on new forms and meanings, It is these eastern lands we will survey today. I know that they differ considerably from each other, but also believe that their nationalisms in the present century contain enough similarities to permit discussing them as a specific variety of this dominant ideology.

* * *

In the Summer of 1964 a conference was held in Belgrade to commemorate the outbreak of the First World War. On July 28, the day on which the first shots of the war were fired on this city from the opposite bank of the Sava river, the chairman of the conference, the chairman of Belgrade University's History Department, invited a few people to a special dinner. We were picked, he told us, because he could relax in our company and speak with-

XI

out watching every word he uttered. After a few drinks, one in our company turned to him, Dr. Vaso Cubrilovic, the last living conspirator involved in the murder of the Archduke Franz Ferdinand, and asked him: After fifty years, how do you feel about what happened in Sarajevo in 1914? Our host's answer surprised me. He said: we destroyed a beautiful world that was lost forever due to the war that followed. The more I thought about his answer the more I realized that he was both right and wrong.

He was right because pre-1914 Europe, then the tone-giver of the entire globe, was a much more civilized, gentile and humanitarian place than it was after 1918 and what any place on earth is today. When the Russian Tsar sent people into exile into Siberia he did not assign them to specific gulags; no group of humans, not even the Gypsies, were considered subhuman by anybody; Richard Wagner was one of the best known anti-Semites of his days, but entrusted the world premier of Parsifal to a Jewish conductor, Hermann Levi; Marxists of all kind were consideret slightly or more seriously deficient when they were discussed in "good society" or "responsible political circles," but men like Jean Jaures or Karl Renner, among others, received the respect due to leading political thinkers of their respective countries. Civilized behavior was still considered a mark of distinction even in Cubrilovic's Belgrade. His country was certainly backward and primitive compared even to Central, let alone Western Europe at the time, but compared to what it is today it was the model of civilization. The world to which these few remarks refer had, indeed, disappeared forever with the First World War.

Yet, Cubrilovic's remark forgot one important fact. The word whose disappearance he regretted, was condemned to pass into history because people like himself in 1914 acted everywhere more and more in conformity with their rabid nationalistic beliefs. Sooner or later, these would have brought on a catastrophe like the one Princip's shots set into motion and the outcome would have been the same-war, increased inhumanity, economic crises, social dislocations and the end of the world which was the product of the incredibly dynamic 19th century. One of the major factors that make me believe that this tragedy was inevitable is the nature of the nationalism, East European nationalism, that motivated millions of young people and some of their elders as well by the beginning of our century. What was the nature of this nationalism, why was it so dangerous?

The most important feature that the followers of nationalistic ideologies in Eastern Europe have in common is the equating of nation, with state and geographic area. This was not the case in the lands where nationalism originated. The Bretons knew who they were and where Brittany's borders were, but this did not prevent the overwhelming majority of them to be good French citizens. Scots resented and still resent being called Englishmen, but this did not prevent them from serving Great Britain loyally at home and abroad. Numerous additional examples could be given to show that ethnic identity or geography did not stand in the way of loyalty to a state larger than what these primary identifier delimited. Outside of Europe and in that area of this continent covered in these pages this was not the case once nationalism became an important ideology and motivator. What explains this difference? It resulted from a long historical development of which the emergence of nationalism was an integral part.

With the voyages of discovery not only did the economic center of Europe shift from the shores of the Mediterranean to those of the Atlantic, but the socio-economic balance of the lands that profited from this change was also gradually transformed. This is well known. Let me mention quickly only the most salient aspects of this change. Cities grew, and the urban based economies rapidly outdistanced those of the countryside. Royalty, delighted with everthing that weakened the power of the obstreperous nobility, increased the rights and privileges of the urban population whose taxes supported and often increased the power of the central authorities and of the state. Population growth was also an important feature of developments in western Europe. By the late 17th and early 18th centuries the weakened rural economies could no longer supply the cities and towns with all their needs. This fact determined the developments in the eastern part of the continent. As supplying the west with agricultural products became good business, the landowning estates established neoserfdom, continued to dominate the various national economies and politicis and prevented the exodus from their lands and, consequently, the growth of cities and urban economies.[1] In the west the third estate became the richest, best educated and state supporting element, while in the east the first and especially the second estates prolonged their medieval dominance with tragic results of which the disappearance of Poland was the most drastic.

This basic difference in historical developments explains why nationalism was born in the west and why its eastern variant differed and still differs considerably from the one we find in the lands of its origin.

During the period which historians call the Age of Enlightenment the western urban population was finally ready to challenge what was left of the outdated and dysfunctional privileges of the first two estates. This the bourgeoisie could have done by demanding that it be given the same rights the clergy and nobility enjoyed, but this would have alienated both, its old protector, royalty, and something new, the emerging lower urban and rural classes.

XI

The old estate structure was based on hereditary privileges. The new class structure developed out of the new economic order which was just shortly sketched. It was based not on birth rights, but on a steadily developing and changing socio-economic reality. This was something the new middle class understood. It had to maintain a decent working relationship with the other classes. All of them had to be included in a new order. The all-encompassing unit in the name of which the abolition of the old order was demanded was the nation. If it coincided with the majority ethnic group living in a given state it could claim the right to run this state. The justification for all these changes was a new ideology, nationalism.

It should also be noted that this new ideology did not stand by itself. It was part and parcel of a larger package, born at the same time and for the same reasons. This included political democracy, a thorough revision of legal codes stressing equality before the law, and by the middle of the 19th century the gradual expansion of the right to vote drastically changing the membership of the various legislative bodies making further socio-economic changes possible. All these changes were supposed to serve the nation irrespective of who its members were. *This national identity rested not on ethnic belonging, but loyal citizenship.*

For this development the following preconditions had to exist: a well organized state within well established borders; a population used to identify with this state; a gradual replacement of the estate structure by the class structure; a numerically, financially and intellectually dominant urban element ready, willing and able to challenge successfully the existing order in the name of the "nation" that was justified to run the state. These preconditions existed in the west, but were totally absent in the east. When, together with many other features copied from the west, the concept and practice of nationalism made its entry into Eastern Europe, it had to and it did take different forms.

In the east no future nation had a state in the western sense. The Hungarians came closest, but even they were not truly masters of their own house. The Poles were in the process of losing their state, something that had happened to the Bohemians in the seventeenth century and to the people of the Balkans even earlier. The economies were, everywhere, pre-capitalist and the means of transforming them were not available and would have involved the giving up of privileges by the few who were in position to work for change. It appeared easier to these early eastern nationalists to fight for a state than to shape a nation in areas that were almost always multi-ethnic. As a result nationalists everywhere did what Andrew C. Janos so aptly wrote about the Hungarians -they devised a "new formula that assigned historical primacy to the state over the nation, arguing that the state was not so much a product as a producer of national sentiment."² In other words, these people decided that the state is the instrument which they can use to weld its inhabitants into a unified nation. Once this approach was accepted, the next question that needed an answer was: where are the borders of any given state? That everbody claimed the maximum possible based either on historical or ethnic grounds and that these claims overlapped those of other burgeoning nationalists goes without saying. What was born was the deadly equating of nation-state-area that was and still is the curse of Eastern European nationalism. This is what moved Gavrilo Princip, Vaso Cubrilovic and their companions in 1914. Bosnia-Hercegovina was considered by them to be part of Serbia, and the Serbs had the right to acquire it. If this sounds like the recent arguments advanced by Slobodan Milosevic and his companions it only proves that Eastern European nationalism entered fully formed into the present century and has not changed to the present day.

The history of the people living in East-Central and South-eastern Europe in the present century falls clearly into four distinct sub-periods. The first of these covers the few years preceding the First World War. Then come the twenty years separating this war from the second global conflict. The third and longest is the period during which these people lived under the various satraps of Stalin and his successors. Finally, we have the decade that followed the fall of communism. In a volume which I edited recently,³ my colleagues and I analyzed the nationalisms of the various people of the region comparing their manifestations in these four periods. We found that while the spokesmen of the different nations adjusted their vocabulary in accordance with the political reality at any given time, their messages differed very little. It is my contention that this was so because the basic identification of nation-state-area remained the basis of their thinking. I will now try to justify this contention by looking at some manifestations of nationalism moving from historical period to historical period.

By 1900 four different national concepts clashed in the Balkans. The Greek Megale (Great) Idea using both historical and ethnic arguments hoped for the expansion of Greece in extreme cases to the very borders of the old Byzantine Empire. That this claim was based on the state-nation-area argument and that it clashed with the dreams of her neighbors should be obvious. The Bulgars hoped to regain for their state the borders of the Peace Treaty of San Stefano (1878). While this request also disregarded numerous ethnic and other problems, it had the advantage that it referred to clearly defined borders. This could not be said of the Greater Serbia idea. This would be state was to include Macedonia, Kosovo, Vojvodina, Bosnia-Hercegovina and a good part of Croatia-Slavonia which was not inhabited, the argument went, by Croats, but by western Serbs. Not only could this huge state not be created without preventing the realization of the Bulgarian or Greek plans, but it also came into conflict with the Croats' demand of a Triune Kingdom - inside or outside the Habsburg domain - that included not only parts of Vojvodina, but also Bosnia-Hercegovina inhabited, in accordance with this view, by a people called Mountain Croats. The problem created by these conflicting nationalisms is very well presented by Charles Jelavich.[4]

The results of the irreconcilable nation-state-area concepts were not only the well known Balkan Wars of 1912 and 1913 and the Greek invasion of Asia Minor at the end of the First World War, but also two assasinations organized by the same people of whom Col. Dragutin Dimitrijevic, better known as Apis, is the best known. He and his co-conspirators were responsible for the murder in 1903 of the Serb king, Alexander Obrenovic, who was too pro-Austrian for their liking and who opposed Serb propaganda in Bosnia-Hercegovina. It was the same group of people who trained Princip and friends and organized the killing of Archduke Franz Ferdinand in Sarajevo in 1914. The reasons for these acts is well documented. Apis and his colleagues were determined to create Greater Serbia.[5]

Moving north of the Danube-Sava line a seemingly greater variety of nationalisms can be detected. The Greater Romania dream did not differ much from the expansionist dreams existing in the Balkans proper, but added to them one interesting feature. While the nation-state territory equating existed here too, Romanians were the first who were ready to exclude from the nation people - mainly Jews - they did not like by denying them citizenship.

In neighboring Hungary just the opposite could be observed. Ever since Hungarians were free to deal with the internal affairs of their country within borders they considered the correct ones, the problem they had to solve was the identity of a nation to complete the nationalist tripod. Magyars were not a majority in Hungary. Therefore, they welcomed anybody - including Jews - who were ready and willing to declare themselves Magyars. The number of those who did this voluntarily was not as great as the Magyars would have liked. Unlike Romanians, they granted citizenship and equality before the law to everybody, but when it came to acknowledging the existence of minorities and the group rights of these people the Magyar attitude had become extremely negative by 1900. These people were considered to be "Magyars speaking other languages" and it was important to magyarize them linguistically. The rightly criticized laws, known as the Lex Apponyi and Lex Kossuth dealing with education and railroad regulations respectively, are the best examples of this attempt.[6]

Clearly, both the Romanians and Magyars followed a policy that wanted to create states over well defined regions in which only their nation lived. - There is very little that must be noted when dealing with Western Slavs prior to 1914. The goals of the Czechs and Slovaks were not yet clearly defined. In the case of the Poles historians have noted sharp disagreements between various factions all of which hoped to reestablish the independence of their country. It is my contention that these divisions while real concerned details but not the essence: the desire to create a Poland in her proper borders inhabited by Poles. After all, when we analyze the famous dispute between Józef Pilsudski and Roman Dmowski, we find that they disagreed about the best borders and the "Polishness" of potential inhabitants of the country they wanted to create: state, region and nation had to coincide in the views of both men. When trying to sell socialism to her countrymen, even Rosa Luxemburg argued that a socio-economic revolution was the only means to end political oppression and lead to Poland's rebirth.[7] The equating of nation-state-territory was as strong north of the two border rivers as it was south of them.

Before the post-World War I years can be presented, a few sentences must be devoted to another idea - or ideal - that came from the west, just as nationalism did. This is the concept of the self-determination of nations and their right to live in their own nation-states. By 1914 most western European states ruled colonial empires. Obviously, it was not in the lands where nationalism was born that this new concept made its appearance. It had to come from the only great power that was openly multiethnic, even multi-racial, yet was convinced that all of its inhabitants were loyal citizens, the United States of America. At the end of the first World War our country was the dominant tone-giver of the victorious alliance. While the more experienced and ruthless diplomats of the Entente powers drastically subverted President Woodrow Wilson's ideas during the peace negotiations in Paris, they had to and did accept his insistence on the validity of these new concepts, especially when they helped in achieving what they wanted: the dissolution of the empires they had fought for the last four years. These losers were now declared unacceptable because they were multi-national and denied self-determination to the majority of the "nations" living within their borders. The new European order was to rest on the "democratic" guidelines which became known as "Wilsonianism." Of course, the victorious states were, in one sense at least, also multi-national, but, just as the United States, they did insist on loyal citizenship and not on ethnic conformity. Citizens form a political, but not an ethnic nation. This was the result of a historic development, existed before Wilson's ideas made their appearance and did conform to the nation-state idea. The political nation was not part of the nation-state-territory equation and had little to do with it. This was not the case in Eastern Europe, not even in Germany where being a Pole in Posen was anything, but a pleasure. The western concept worked for a short time only in

XI

Bohemia before Czechs and Germans went their own ways many years before 1918.

The Paris peace makers destroyed the "multi-national" eastern empires (Russia destroyed herself, but the Soviet Union remained multi-national), and created in their place "national states" in conformity with the right of self-determination. The tragedy was that these new national states were as multi-ethnic as had been those they replaced with the exception of the two greatest losers of the war, Hungary and Bulgaria. As a matter of fact, two nations had to be created - the Yugoslav and the Czechoslovak - to justify the existence of their states on the basis of Wilsonianism. It proved to be easy to create states and impossible to create nations. What made the matter worse was that the so called "successor states" formulated their policies continuing to equate nation-state-territory. Under these circumstances the nation-state idea proved to be inapplicable to Eastern Europe and turned into a total failure. The documents my colleagues and I published in the already mentioned volume clearly show how the various Southern Slav nations could not be welded into Yugoslavs and the Czechs and Slovaks into Czechoslovaks because the governments in Prague and Belgrade tried to run national states while their population was multi-national.

The 1920s were the first decade in many centuries during which the people of Eastern Europe were free of the domination of states or nations situated in other parts of the continent. This very fact should have alerted them to the realization that they had a rare chance to settle their own affairs free of foreign interference and to establish a regional order that will prevent outsiders to restore their influence if not dominance in the region. This they failed to do. The reasons of this failure are easy to see.

Everybody who has ever discussed this failure begins by pointing out that the states of the region belonged to two camps in the inter-war years. The status-quo states, the victors of the passed conflict, and the revisionists, the losers who demanded that the unjust peace treaties be rectified. This is perfectly true, but we must look beyond this obvious problem. Victors and some of the vanquished were multi-national states owing their existence to the assumption that they were national states whose inhabitants were members of a nation ready to support this state. This was not the case. In Poland not only the Ukrainians had their ethnically based political parties, but so had even the Jews, many of whom considered themselves to be members of an ethnic minority. For most Poles who were philosophically Dmowski's followers this proved that Poland was in danger because viewed from the nation-state-territory identity point-of-view a large segment of the country's inhabitants did not fit into the Polish nation-state. This "problem" took precendence over everything else. It could not be solved, and Poland gave up in all but form a parliamentary form of government and ended up with a military dictatorship.

The problems of the Kingdom of Serbs, Croats and Slovenes are too well known to demand much attention. What is interesting is that this state was admittedly trinational. In fact it was much more than that. Yet the goal was to transform it into a nation-state in which the nation-state-territory identity was realized. This is what King Alexander's dictatorship was supposed to achieve, but the renaming of the state Yugoslavia did not create a unified nation and, therefore, made its very existence questionable, even unjustified, in the eyes of those who created it to give the Southern Slavs = Yugoslavs a nation-state. This made it "justified" in the eyes of most Greeks and Bulgarians to continue dreaming of expansion into Macedonia. These two states felt, in spite of some minorities of their own, that they came close to being nation-states in the true sense of the word. After all, they had been the partners of Mustafa Kemal in a massive population exchange that forced people living in these two states and Turkey to change their domiciles in 1924 and 25. These exchanges involved 53,000 Bulgarians, 30,000 Turks and 1 1/2 million Greeks.[8] Although the term had not yet been coined, these exchanges are the first examples of forced "ethnic cleansing" undertaken to turn the idea of nation-state-territory into reality.

Even Czechoslovakia that remained "democratic" until Hitler destroyed it in 1938-39 faced the same problem. The country's so called "peculiar political institution", the Petka, the quasi permanent alliance of five political parties (Agrarian, National Democrat, Social Democrat, National Socialist and Populist) that were the core of all governments had only Czech leaders and relatively few Slovak members. The Slovak National Party joined this group in the govrenment only once.[9] The ill famed hyphen question was constantly in the public eye. It was important because without an unhyphenated Czechoslovak nation the fiction of a nation-state could not be maintained. The example of Czechoslovakia proves that not even democratic government can overcome the problems presented by a multi-national nation-state holding fast to the equating of nation-state-territory.

Being insecure of their very existence because of the contradiction between the theory and reality on which their sovereignty was based, faced by the economic dislocation caused by the war and the news borders and distrustful of their neighbors, the states of East-Central and Southeastern Europe became increasingly more and more fearful. In foreign affairs this manifested itself in searching for financial, political and even military support from the west - in the 1920s mainly from France or Italy. What is more important,

XI

when nationalism is analyzed, is a crucial further development of this ideology.

What emerged in the 1920s was a new form of extreme right wing politics. Of course, it was not without historical roots. Political anti-semitism was nothing new in Europe anywhere and the concept of race was also well known by the end of the war. Dmowski was clearly a racist as were such diverse people as the Grossdeutsch advocates in Austria, Nicolae Iorga in Romania and Eleutherios Venizelos in Greece. What was new was the creation of new ideologies based on these and othere similar building blocks. Once again, this is well known. What needs stressing is the fact that eastern Europeans did not have to wait for Mussolini and Hitler to learn what fascism in its various forms were and say a few words about timing. Alexandru C. Cuza formulated his ideas independently as did the Croat Frankovci. Gyula Gömbös stated proudly that Hungary's "Szeged Idea" was formulated before anything similar saw the light anywhere else in Europe.[10] These new pseudo-forms of nationalism made their appearance when they did for very good reasons: the war made violence an acceptable method of expression, old methods of government believed to be responsible for war were discredited as was left wing radicalism after its defeat everywhere but in Russia where - so people believed - it could not last long, etc. etc. To these factors should be added the fear of neighbours just mentioned and the problem of nation-states without nations or nations who were convinced that their state was deprived of its just territory. What was needed under the circumstances, the propagators of the new approach to politics believed, were professional nationalists whose reliability to the cause - whatever it was supposed to be - was unquestionable because it could not be anything else given their origin which was now defined in racial term.[11] The victories of Mussolini and Hitler only strengthened the position of the Eastern European extremists. What they did not realize was that they were in fact destroying the nation-state-territory which they hoped to serve better than anybody ever did before.

While the extreme nationalists were still only a vocal minority when the Great Depression hit their countries very hard, they had influenced their governments considerably pushing them more and more in the direction which they considered to be the correct one. When only Germany appeared to be able to help them to overcome the economic difficulties created by the Depression, the chance of independent policy making which existed in the 20s disappeared. When, with the exception of the Czechs (but not the Slovaks), the extremist politicians became more and more dominant and finally reached positions of government because ideological and economic interests appeared to coincide, that is in the 1930s, the situation in Eastern Europe acquired a new and highly destabilizing feature: competition for the favors of the master of the "new order". The old beliefs in nation-state-territory were voiced more and more clearly and loudly by the super nationalist leaderships, but their contradictory claims and demands were now submitted to the same arbitrator, Adolf Hitler, who had no interest in what these clients' interests were, but had only his own goals (not even Germany's) in mind. This dependence on an impossible overlord lead to the redrawing of borders, the introductions of nefarious laws, economic exploitation, and finally forced war on the people of East-Central and Southeastern Europe. This summarizes the 30s shortly, but completely. This is why I stated that the various extreme right politicians were bad nationalists, and their actions did not help, but destroyed the states and people they claimed to lead to unprecedented greatness.

The war had numerous consequences. As far as changes in nationalism are concerned, these included the heightening of some already existing hostilities and, more importantly, some significant ethnic transformations. These included the holocaust, the changes created by the refugées, the voluntary and forced recruitment of Eastern Europe's German minorities into the Nazi military and, at the end of the conflict, the next act of "ethnic cleansing" in the form of the mass expulsion of unwanted ethnic groups from the various states. While in some states this resulted in lowering the percentage of minorities in the population, it nowhere eliminated nationalism. The communists, who soon came to power (Greece excepted), condemned this ideology as the bourgeois tool that served to keep the lower classes subservient to the states ruled by the upper and middle classes. It was labeled a major error and was declared by fiat non-existent in the new peoples' democracies. Yet, it remained not only a strong sentiment, but became honored even more as the alternative to Soviet domination and communist rule.

Even before Stalin's death signs of the survival of nationalism were evident. The various "purge trials" eliminated the so-called "home communists" who, within the parties, represented national approaches to the new order. When Tito, after his break with Moscow, decided to solve Yugoslavia's problem, his solution was the exact opposite of what King Alexandar had tried in 1929. This ruler's approach - as the name change of the c ountry clearly indicated - was directed against the contradictory nationalisms of the various people living in his state trying to replace these by a common new one. The "Titoist solution," as it became known, was based not only on the recognition of existing national feelings, but went further and recognized even the existence of a Muslim nation in Bosnia-Hercegovina in 1968. Not only the fact that Tito's Yugoslavia remained communists even without the Soviets' help, but also this approach to the problems of a multi-national state produced an alternative to orthodox communism, national communism. This explains

XI

why "Titoism" became as popular as it did in the other states that had, supposedly, realized how incorrect nationalism was.

After Stalin's death in 1953, two political trends emerged in East-Central and Southeastern Europe: de-Stalinization and "domestic Stalinism." The first of these, once again, needs no detailed explanation. Its best known manifestations were the Hungarian Revolution of 1956 and the Czechoslovak attempt to introduce "socialism with a human face" in 1968. That both of these contained strong elements of nationalism both as motivators and goals is well known. What is more interesting is that in the states in which Stalinist bosses continued to run the show, in Enver Hoxha's Albania and in the Romania of both Gherogr̃e Gheorghiu-Dej and Nicolae Caeusescu, extreme nationalism justified everything these regimes undertook.

While the events in these two countries are the best known and the easiest to illustrate, nationally based problems continued to exist everywhere including Yugoslavia. Once again, this is well known. While during my numerous visits to that country most people with whom I came in touch tried to talk and behave as "Yugoslavs" and "Titoists," there were always the moments when their real sentiments came to the fore. I will never forget sitting in a side-walk café in Belgrade on a magnificent summer day waiting for the motorcade of Tito and King Olaf V of Norway to roll down the avenue. Beside me sat a young man who looked miserable. I asked him what was wrong. He answered: I am a Croat and all these happy people around us are Serbs! Remarks like these, with the needed local variations, I heard everywhere in the region.

The anti-Semitic aspect of nationalism also remained constant although it became "official" only in Poland, in the country that invented "anti-Semitism without Jews", where in 1967 Mieczyslaw Moczar managed to force the Gomulka regime into a major "anti-Zionist" campaign and the dismissal of the few Jews in party or government positions. I will use two incidents from my life to show again what one learned when the locals forgot that a foreigner was around. In Romania a colleague warned me to be careful when dealing with another historian because "after all, he is Jew." In Hungary, having a good time in a little night club, again with colleagues, we were singing with the music. One of them, watching one of his collaborators, remarked: Is it not disgusting to watch a Jew trying to behave like a Hungarian? I have more stories like these and so has everybody else who visited Eastern Europe regularly since 1945. Some of these stories deal with anti-semitism, others illustrate old national prejudices and some show the hatred Soviet dictation and communist rule had engendered. What they have in common is the sharp line separating the we from the they and stress that the we are right and the they are wrong when the two come into conflict. In other words, they prove that in spite of the proclaimed "socialist brotherhood" no feelings have changed.

In spite of its undiminished strength everywhere, the role of nationalism varied greatly from state-to-state during the long years of communist rule in Eastern Europe. Not just in Romania and Albania, but also in Bulgaria it was used to bolster the position of the regime and justify its action. By the way, this is true of nationalism also in non-communist Greece and Turkey during the same years. In Yugoslavia it justified the "Titoist solution" to that country's perennial problem, but it was also the cause of this problem and, once Tito and his prestige disappeared, the reason for its disintegration. While Alexander Dubcek's reform attempts were frustrated by the Soviets, his short months at the helm of the country produced some changes in Czech-Slovak relations and at least temporarily eased the national issues separating the two people. In Hungary and especially in Poland, nationalism helped considerably to ease the burden imposed on the population by the economic and political aspects of communist rule. No regime could ignore it; they either tried to use it or they had to make concessions to it. Nationalism remained a constant in all political equations. The question that must be asked is: was it the same nationalism that had existed prior to 1945? Was it still based on the equating of nation-state-territory and did it still believe that nation-states are the answer for East-central and Southeastern Europe? The answer to this double question is supplied by the events since 1989.

In spite of its strenght everywhere, it was not nationalism that brought about the drastic changes of 1989. Just as true and large scale de-Stalinization began not really with Stalin's death, but with Nikita Khruschëv's famous "secret speech" at the 20th Party Congress in February 1956, so too events in the Soviet Union made possible changes in the other communist states of Europe. This time is was Mikhail Gorbachëv's program including prestroika and glasnost that forced changes in Eastern Europe. Just as in the Soviet Union, these changes made the continued rule of the various parties impossible. Yet, the change was really not that sudden although the events of 1989 created this impression worldwide. Developments began roughly when Gorbachëv came to power in 1985 if not earlier and unfolded gradually just as the Soviet leader's activities produced gradual transformations in his country. These step-by-step moves away from what was left of orthodoxy and the parties' monopoly of power are interesting, but fall outside the topic of nationalism. As is well known, the famous year began when the Hungarian govrenment destroyed the fortifications on its border with Austria and permitted East Germans to use this newly cleared road to the west. It ended with the execution of the Ceasescus in December of this year.

Miklós Németh who made the crucial decisions in Hungary and Ion Iliescu who replaced Ceasescu as head of state in Romania were communists of long standing as were all other men - with the exception of the Bosnian Alija Izetbegovic - who took over their countries' leaderships either as presidents or prime ministers. This should not surprise anybody. After all, the number of non-communists who had political and/or administrative experience was minimal, and these few individuals were not in the strategic positions in which the by now ex-communists were. What is remarkable is how quickly and thoroughly these new-old leaders became vocal and fierce nationalists. This is true of those people also who now entered the political stage for the first time. Remarkable as the conversion to or the loudly voiced nationalism of these indivuduals was, it was not surprising. The leaders' statements in this respect simply mirrored the feelings of the population at large. Nationalism was the defense when people resisted communist indoctrination, it reminded them of a past that was non-communist and included independence, and, most importantly, it was a ready made, available and easily understood ideology.

People everywhere always need something in which they can believe, that justifies their activities and gives meaning to life beyond simply living for the sake of making ends meet. Religion played this role word-wide for centuries, but roughly at the same time when nationalism made its appearance, sometime in the late 17th and early 18th centuries, when religion began to lose its hold on the minds of many people, the age of ideology dawned. Nationalism was one of the strongest of these new secular religions. For nearly half a century the people of Eastern Europe were asked to make sacrifices and obey their govrenments blindly in the name of another ideology that promised to create paradise on earth. This harping on ideology as the justification for everything reinforced the already existing need of people to have something in which they could believe. This need remained even after the ideology that reinforced it failed. It meant that something else had to take its place. Nationalism was at hand, ready made, time tested, and clearly right because communism had labeled it wrong. The question is: did the old nationalism reemerge or did it take on new forms?

Statistics offer the first answer to this question. The place of the Soviet Union was taken by eleven independent states -twelve if the Chechens gain independence - in Europe since 1989. In the region covered by this paper we now have forteen states while in 1989 we had nine. What better proof is needed to illustrate the equating of nation-state-territory? Is this splintering process over? Will the Ingush fight Chechens as the Ossetians did Georgians? Will Ukraine split into two states? Will the Kosovo Albanians resume their fight? Questions like these cannot be answered, but the continued equating of nation-state-territory make them legitimate questions. Statements made by

Vladimir Meciar, the Prime Minister of Slovakia or by Gheorghe Funar, the Major of Cluj do not differ in spirit and intent from Slobodan Milosevic's classic equating of nation-state-territory the essence of which was: every Serb has the right to live in Serbia and Serbia is everywhere where Serbs live. Much less rabid and hostile was the remark of the first post-communist Hungarian Prime Minister, József Antall who, in May of 1990, stated that in principle he was the P. M. of fifteen million Hungarians. Although sharply criticized for this remark, he repeated it in August 1992 in his speech opening the Third World Congress of Hungarians. At both occasions, Antall was careful in rejecting the notion of revisionism, if you wish at least the territory part of the equating definition, but he still maintained the right of the state to speak for every member of the nation irrespective of where they lived. That his statements were not well received in the states in which four million of his fifteen live goes without saying. Reading the Greek press makes it quite clear that the Greek-Turk controversy in the Aegean is really not an economic issue which the western experts assume and which would make sense, but something that goes even beyond the equating of nation-state-territory - although it is that too - but a defense of European civilization against Asiatic barbarism! The indications are quite clear - at least they are to me - that the nationalism that became the dominant ideology after 1989 in East-Central and Southeastern Europe is the same that it had been prior to 1945. At the same time, it is also obvious that it is better controlled by the authorities than it had been any other time in the 20th century. Dealing with this aspect of it is the last topic that needs mentioning.

The disintegration of the Soviet Union, the end of the Cold War and the resulting drastic change in the economic and political realities in Europe left the by now fourteen East European states desperately needing some larger forces guaranteeing their existence, something the Soviet Union did for most of them prior to 1989. They realized that the growing power of Germany - the country that dominated them in the 1930s and during World War II - could present a danger for them and that in a few years time a reborn Russia could do the same. Their economies also needed help desperately. The answer to these economic needs and national insecurities was obvious: join the European Economic Community and NATO. These organizations would not only help solving their problems, but would also protect them from the possible difficulties their own reemerging nationalisms could potentially create. The members of these western European organizations were not willing to admit new members whose instutitions and philosophies contradicted those which they were building with hard work since 1945. They demanded drastic changes from the would be new members which could only be met if the eastern nationalisms were transformed. Willingly and/or unwillingly the governments of the eastern European states had to control the manifestations of their people's nationalism. Except in the lands that were once Yugoslavia, they were fairly successful in doing this. Yet, this is not the end of the story. What is controlled is not yet eliminated. What is not eliminated can reassert itself. Before eastern European nationalism in the form in which it existed in the twentieth century will become part of history not only will it be necessary to have governmets take international obligations - mostly imposed on them - seriously and enforce them scrupulously, but they will also have to change their attitudes and then educate the populations accordingly. It was during the First World War that R. W. Seton-Watson pointed out to the then Prince-Regent of Serbia, Alexandar, in a letter dated September 17, 1915 that "a Catholic as Catholic is as good a citizen as a Protestant or Orthodox."[12] Translated into ethnic terms, citizenship had nothing to do with ethnic (Croat-Catholic and Serb-Orthodox) identity. Now, some eighty years later, this lesson is the first that must be learned by everbody in Eastern Europe. The nation-state idea is not applicable in a multi-national region, but states with people of different ethnic origins can securely exist if they demand loyal citizenship and not ethnic-linguistic conformity. Once the rights of every individual as a human being and of every ethnic group as such is recognized and safeguarded it will not be necessary any more to equate the state with a given territory. Thus by giving up the nation-state ideal, the nation-state-territory equating as a basis of nationalism can also be dropped.

Will these drastic changes ever occur? Even if the western alliances carefully supervise the manner in which eastern European governments satisfy the obligations they accepted; even if these governments will honestly and consistently work at inculcating the needs for human and group rights into the numerically most numerous ethnic segments of their citizenry; even if Europe as a whole will have the required time to allow the gradual elimination of the glaring economic, political and ideological differences that now exists between the different regions of the continent; even if all these preconditions for change would exist - and hopefully they will - it will take at least two generations before the type of nationalism that dominated eastern Europe in our century will disappear. It is too firmly embedded in the culture, literature, history and public attitude of all nations of the region to change, let alone disappear, rapidly even if it is in the best interest of everbody.

Notes

1. On Neoserfdom and related issues see the series of articles in *Slavic Review*, XXXIV/2 (June, 1975).
2. Andrew C. Janos, *The Politics of Backwardness in Hungary, 1825-1945* (Princeton; Princeton University Press, 1982), p. 69.

3. Peter F. Sugar (ed.), *Eastern European Nationalism in the 20th Century* (Washington, D.C.; The American University Press, 1995).
4. Charles Jelavich, *South Slav Nationalism* (Columbus, Ohio; Ohio State University Press, 1990). See also Ivo Banac, *The National Question in Yugoslavia. Origins, History, Politics* (Ithaca and London; Cornell University Press, 1984).
5. The only study I found in a western language dealing with Apis is Milos Bogicevic, *Le Colonel Dragutin Dimitrijevic* (Paris, 1928). For a short introduction to this man in English see: Joachim Remak, *Sarajevo. The Story of a Political Murder* (New York; Criterion Books, 1959), pp. 49-57.
6. The Lex Apponyi made it very difficult to use any language but Hungarian in the schools. The Lex Kossuth excluded from employment on the railroad anybody who could not perform his duties speaking Hungarian while dealing with the public in any form. This created problems everywhere, but especially in Croatia.
7. Aleksander Gieysztor, Stefan Kieniewicz, et al (eds.), *A History of Poland* (Warszawa; Polish Scientific Publisher, 1968), p. 571.
8. Leften Stavrianos, *The Balkans Since 1453* (New York-Chicago; Holt, Rinehart and Winston, 1966), p. 590.
9. Victor S. Mamatey and Radomir Luza (eds.), *A History, of the Czechoslovak Republic, 1918-1948* (Princeton; Princeton University Press, 1973), p. 108.
10. Thomas L. Sakmyster, *Hungary, the Great Powers and the Danubian Crisis, 1936-1939* (Athens; The University of Georgia Press, 1980), p. 16.
11. Peter F. Sugar (ed.), *Native Fascism in the Successor States* (Santa Barbara; ABC-Clio, 1971) discusses this problem state-by-state.
12. *Eastern European Nationalism in the 20th Century*, p. 308.

INDEX

In preparing this index I have omitted expressions which occur almost on every page (e.g. nation, government, country) except when modifiers are involved (e.g. Nation-building). Publishers do not always include accents, etc. in what they print. In this index I have used them for names even if they do not appear on the following pages.

The names of cities appear in the index only when they refer to events that occurred there. If they are used as synonyms for governments that resided in them the reference appears under the heading of the country involved (e.g. Budapest under Hungary).

The following abbreviations are used in this index: A–Austrian; Al–Albanian; AH–(Austro-Hungarian); B–Bulgarian; Bo–Bosnian; C–Croatian; Cz–Czech; CzS–Czechoslovak; G–Greek; H–Hungarian; P–Polish; R–Romanian; S–Serbian; Sl–Slovak; Sv–Slovene; Y–Yugoslav; l–language. Foreign words and titles of works are in italic.

Abdülaziz, Sultan: IX 25; X 6
Absolutism: III 67; IV 12; VI 5, 7; VII 19
Act of Union (1698): III 7; IV 12; VI 5, 7; VII 19; VIII 49
Adamantios, Koraës: IX 10
Adamović, Gherasim: IX 11
Additional Convention: V 76, 78
Adriatic Sea: IV 14; V 69, 74, 76, 80; IX 20, 35
Aegean Islands: IX 8
Aegean Sea: IX 38, 40–4l; XI 361
A Felvidék: IV 29
Agrarians: II 4; VII 21
Agrarian Party (CzS): XI 355
Akritoi: X 4
Albania: III 12; V 74, 77, 80; VI 18; VIII 56; IX 7–8, 20, 23, 28, 37, 41; X 5, 15–16; XI 358–9
Albanians: III 12; VIII 11, 27–37, 42; XI 360
Albanian League: IX 28
Albert, Archduke: V 68, 70, 75, 79
Albrecht, Archduke: VII 24
Alexander I, Tsar: II 5; IX 15
Alexander II, Tsar: V 70, 73, 76
Alexander I, King (Y): VI 14; VII 16, 25; X 8; XI 355, 357, 362
 assassination of: IX 31; XI 352
America: I 75; VI 5; IX 33; *see also* USA
Ancestry: II 3, 8–9
Andrássy, Count Gyula, Jr: IV 36

Andrássy, Count Gyula, Sr: IV 20–21, 23; V 66–9, 71–80; VI 11; IX 22
Anschluss: IV 26
Antall, József: X 12; XI 361
Anti-
 Bolshevism: VII 22
 British feeling: IX 39
 Catholicism: VIII 51–2
 Church: VIII 43–4
 Clericalism: VIII 43–4
 Communists: X 10, 12
 Fascists: VII 16
 Germans: IV 27
 Habsburg: VIII 54
 Hungarian: IV 26
 Internationalists: VII 16
 Italian: IV 14, 27
 Marxists: VII 22
 minority: X 12
 Polishness: VIII 51–2
 Religionists: VIII 43, 50; X 9
 Russians: V 77
 Semitism: IX 23; X 9–10; XI 348, 356, 358
  without Jews: XI 358
 Slavs: IV 17, 26
 Slovaks: VIII 55
 State: VIII 26
 Turk: IX 38
 Zionists: Xl 358
Antonescu, Ion: VII 17, 26
Apis: *see* Dimitrijević

INDEX

Apponyi School Law: IV 38
Aristocracy: II 11; IV 13, 45–6; VIII 51; *see also* Nobility
Armies: *see also* Military
   Austro-Hungarian: IV 13, 31; IX 28
   Greek: IX 24, 38
   Nazi: XI 357
   Ottoman: VIII 57; IX 28
   Serb: IX 30
   Soviet: III 11
   Yugoslav: IX 34
Army Bill (AH)
   of 1890: IV 31
   of 1905: IV 36
Arrow Cross Party (H): VII 18
Asker: IX 9
Aspaturian, Vernon: II 2–3, 10, 19
Astra; IX 13, 19
Atheists: VIII 42
Atlantic Sea: XI 349
August Wilhelm, Prince: VII 24
Ausgleich: IV 11, 14, 17, 20–21, 23, 26, 29, 31, 36, 38, 44; V 67, 81; IX 20, 22
Austria: IV 3–6, 9, 11–8, 20–24, 26–9, 32–3, 35–40, 42–3, 44, 46; V 11; VII 18, 26; VIII 52–3, 57; IX 11, 21; XI 359
Austrians: IV 8; VIII 52
Austria-Hungary: I 76; IV 1–5, 7, 9–11, 15, 19–21, 25–8, 31, 34–40, 42–4, 46; V 66–77, 79–81, VI 11, VII 19; VIII 57; IX 12, 19, 21, 23, 28–30; X 14, 16; XI 356
Austro-
   Germans: VII 14
   Marxists: II 14
   Slavists: IX 21–2
Austro-Prussian War: IX 19
Autarky: IV 21; VII 21
Authoritarianism: II 14; VI 3–7, 10–11,13–15, 17–21; VII 17, 19
   definition of: VI 1–3
Authority: IV 5, 12, 20; VI 3–4; VII 14
Autocracy: II 5; VI 3, 5–6, 10–11, 13, 17–18
Autonomous region: III 11
Axis: X 10
Âyans: IX 8, 13

Bach Period: IX 19
Badeni, Count Kasimir: IV 32, 34
Baky, László: VII 25
'Balkan conditions': V 75
Balkan League: II 13
Balkan Pact: X 10

Balkan Peninsula/Balkans: III 11; IV 39; V 66–77, 79–81; VI 8, 10, 13; VIII 52, 56; IX 7–8, 10–14, 23, 26, 28, 33, 37–8, 41–2; X 5–8, 13, 15; XI 350–52; *see also* Europe, Southeastern
   partition of: V 68
Balkan Range: IX 26
Balkan Wars: IV 42; IX 24–6, 28; X 7, 16
Banac, Ivo: IX 18; X 7
Banat: IX 23
Bánffy, Baron Dezső: IV 34, 41
Bánffy, Count György: IX 11
Ballhausplatz: V 60, 70, 73, 75, 78, 80
Banovina: IX 31
Banus: IV 31, 36, 38; IX 12, 19–20
Barițiu Gheorge: IV 18, 31
Basarab: V 80
Bavarians: I 71, 76; IX 17
Beck, Max V. von: IV 34
Beck-Rzikowski, Count Friedrich: V 68–9, 75
Behschnitt, Wolf D.: IX 18
Belcredi, Count Richard: IV 19
Belgrade: IX 25, 35; XI 347–8, 354
   Pashalik of: IX 13
Belief: I 82; II 2, 8; IV 8; VII 20
Beneš, Eduard: VII 24
Benkovski, Georgi: IX 25
Beran, József: VIII 54
Berend, Iván: X 8
Berlin
   Congress of: V 66–7, 72, 80–81; IX 24, 26, 28; X 16
   Memorandum: V 72
   Protocol of: V 66
Berlinger, Enrico: VI 20
Bernolak, Anton: VIII 55
Bessarabia: III 12; V 74, 76, 80; IX 23, 41
Bethlen, Count István: VI 14; VII 24
Bismarck, Prince Otto: IV 5; V 68, 72, 75, 79, 81; VIII 43–4, 51
Bittó, István: IV 28
Blacks (American); I 75; II 9
Bobović, Mirko: IX 19
Bodin, Jean: VI 9
Bohemia: IV 8, 17, 25, 33; V 73; X 4; XI 354
Bohemians: XI 350
Bolsheviks: VIII 49
Bolshevism: I 77; III 4, 7; VII 14, 22; VIII 44; X 9
Borders: I 73, 76, 80–81; II 10; III 14; IV 8, 14; V 76–9; VII 13, 18; VIII 46; IX 15, 26, 35; X 12, 15–16; XI 350–53, 355, 357
Bosnia: V 68, 71, 83; VIII 56; IX 37; X 5

Bosnians: V 23
Bosnia-Hercegovina: V 69, 71–80; VIII 57;
  IX 8, 23, 30, 33–6, 42; X 1, 3, 8, 13–15;
  XI 351–2, 357
  annexation of: IV 38; V 69; IX 23
Bosnian nationality: IX 23
Böszörményi, Zoltán: VII 26
Botev, Hristo: IX 25
Bourgeoisie: I 79; III 3–4; VI 11; VII 23;
  XI 349; *see also* Class, middle
Boyars (R): IX 9–10
Boycotts (political): IV 16, 19, 23, 25–6
Brass, Paul: II 2
Brațianu, Ion: VI 11, 14
Bretons: I 71; XI 348
Brzezinski, Zbigniew: VII 14
Bucharest: II 8; III 14; IV 34; V 71, 77;
  IX 10, 25
Budapest
  Convention: V 76
Bukovina: III 6; IV 34, 39; IX 23
Bulgaria: III 12; V 71–4, 76–7, 80; VI 14;
  VII 13, 18, 21; VIII 48, 50, 56; IX 24–8,
  37–8, 40; X 13, 15; XI 354, 359
Bulgarians: II 8; III 5, 8; V 72; VIII 47, 49;
  IX 8–9, 11, 21, 25–7; X 6; XI 351,
  355
Bulgarian Central Committee: IX 25
Bureaucracy: II 6, 13; VI 4–19, 21; VII 19–20,
  22, 27
Byzantium: VII 46–7; XI 351

Calvinism: X 5
Canada: I 73, 75, 78–9; III 9
Canossa: VIII 43; X 3
Cantons: I 79–80
Capital: II 12; VI 90
Capitalism: VI 2, 4–5, 7
Capodistrias, Agostino: IX 10
Carillo, Santiago: VI 20
Carol II, King (R): VII 16
Carpathians: I 75; IV 34
Carsten, Francis L.: VII 15
Caste: I 74; IV 1
Ceaușescu, Nicolae: IX 41; XI 358–60
Center Party (G): VIII 44
Centralization: I 77, 83; III 13–14; IV 3–5,
  15–17, 20, 43; V 8, 11; VII 14; VIII 53;
  IX 19
Century
  sixteenth: X 4
  seventeenth: XI 349–50, 360
  eighteenth: I 76–7; II 5, 10, 12; III 2;
    IV 7; VI 5; VIII 52, IX 8–9, X 2–3;
    XI 349, 360

  nineteenth: I 72; II 6, 10; III 2, 12; IV 1, 7;
    V 66; VI 10–11, 13; VII 19; VIII 43,
    56; IX 7, 10–12, 20; X 5–7, 12;
    XI 348, 350
  twentieth: I 72; X 3, XI 347, 351
Cernojević, Arsenije: IX 9
Četniks: IX 31–3
Charles I, Charlemagne: VII 46; IX 12
Charles VI, Holy Roman Emperor: II 6
'Charter 77': VI 2
Christian Socialist Party (A): IV 26–7, 32;
  VIII 43
Churches (institution): IV 30; VII 19–20;
  VIII 44–6, 48, 50–2, 54–9; IX 9, 11, 17;
  X 1–3, 7
Church, Slavonic: VIII 48; IX 9
Çiftlik: IX 8
Cisleithania: IV 46
Citizens: II 12, 14; IV 6, 11; V1 5–7, 12; X 8;
  XI 349, 353
Citizenship: I 77, 79; XI 350, 352–3, 362
Class: IV 1, 6; VI 4; VII 14
  conflict: II 14; III 4
  distinction: II 2
  lower: IV 27, 29; VI 15–6; VII 15; IX 349,
    357
  middle: I 68; II 11–12; III 3–5, 8; IV 6, 25;
    VI 9–10; VII 15, 17–18, 23; IX 16;
    XI 350, 357; *see also* Bourgeoisie
  ruling: III 3; VI 6
  structure: XI 350
  upper: II 11; VII 15, 18; IX 10; XI 357
  working: I 68; III 3, 8; VI 10
Clergy: II 11, 14; III 5; IV 27, 30, 41;
  VIII 43–4, 47–9, 50–51, 53, 56;
  IX 9–11, 14, 16, 21, 26–7, 32; X 1, 3, 7,
  9; XI 349
Cluj: II 8; VIII 53; XI 361; *see also* Kolozsvár
Coalition
  Croato-Serb: IV 37–8; IX 21
  Hungarian: IV 36–7
Codreanu, Corneliu Z.: IV 16; VII 16, 20
Cold War: X 10; XI 361
Collective leadership: VI 18
Colonialism: I 73, 80; IX 39; XI 353
Columbus, Christopher: X 3
Comintern: X 10
Common ministries (AH): IV 4; IX 23
Communications: II 3, 7, 9; VI 10, 13; VII 13
  means of: I 29
Communism: III 12; VI 3; VIII 43–4, 46, 49;
  IX 33, 35, 38; X 1, 9
  disintegration of: X 10; XI 351, 359
  in one State: III 12; V 18
  National: III 1, 11–12, 15; VI 18–21; X 10

(Communism continued)
  role of: VI 18
  'with a Human Face': VI 18, 20–21
Communist
  domination: VI 17
  government: VIII 51; X 1
  idoctrination: XI 360
  parties: VI 17–8, 20; VII 22; VIII 42–5, 53; IX 33
  period: VIII 52
  policy: X 10
  power: VIII 55
  regimes: VIII 43, 35; IX 38
  rule: VIII 46; IX 7, 41; X 9, 12; XI 357–9
  society: VIII 42
  State: VIII 42
  supremacy: IX 7
  take-over: VIII 49
Communists: III 10; VI 16; VII 21; VIII 42–3, 49–50; XI 357
Concentration camps: X 14
Concordia: IV 14
Confederation of Bar: X 5
Connor, Walker: I 80; II 2–3
Conservatism: II 7; VII 21–2; X 3
Conservatives: IV 15–16, 21, 25–6
Considération sur le gouvernment de la Pologne: X 5
Constantine I, the Great: VIII 40
Constantinople: *see also* Istanbul
  conference at: V 74–6
  Patriarch of: VIII 48–9; IX 8–9, 14, 17, 25
Constitution: III 8–9; VII 2, 14
  Polish, of 1791: X 5
Constitutional Party (H): IV 36
Conversion: IX 32
Çorbaci: IX 25
Corfu Agreement: IX 29–30
Council of Nicaea: VIII 26
Counter-Reformation: VIII 50, 53–4; X 4
County: IX 5, 20, 22, 30
  Government of: IX 4
Crete: V 73; IX 24–5
Crisis of 1905 (H): IV 36
Croatia: IV 4, 13, 20, 28, 31, 36–8, 41–2; V 73, 75; VIII 52, 57; IX 11–12, 18–21, 30–31; 33–7
Croatia-Slavonia: IV 9; IX 12, 19; X 8; XI 351
Croats: I 71, 73; III 6, 14; IV 9, 14, 16, 24, 28, 31, 36–9, 42; VIII 47, 51–3, 55, 57; IX 11–12, 18–19, 21–2, 29–32, 34–36; X 1, 3, 8, 13–14; XI 352
Croatian Party of the Pure Right: IV 31, 36
Croatian Party of the Right: IV 14, 27, 36

Croatian Peasant Party: IV 36; VII 20; IX 21, 31
Croatism: VIII 52
Croato-Serb:
  Coalition: IV 37–8; IX 21
  controversy: VIII 52
Crown Council (AH): IV 5; V 68
Čubrilović, Vaso: XI 358, 351
Culture: I 69, 76–7; XI 362
Curia(e): IV 5, 16, 28, 32
Customs: I 71, 82; VI 7; VIII 47; IX 29
Cuza, Alexandru C.: XI 356
Cvetković, Dragiša: IX 31
Cypriots: IX 39
Cypriot Turkish Republic: IX 40
Cyprus: IX 28, 39–41
Czartoryski, Count Adam: X 8
Czechs: III 5; IV 7, 9, 11, 15, 17, 20–21, 26–7, 32, 35, 40, 46; X 3–4; XI 353–4, 356
Czech (l): IV 2, 5
Czech Club: IV 39
Czech Lands: IV 25; VII 18; VIII 54; X 4; *see also* Bohemia, Moravia
Czech-Slovak relations: XI 354
'Czechness': X 4
Czechoslovak nation: XI 354
Czechoslovakia: I 7, 73, 79; II 13; III 8, 12, 15; IV 20; VII 18, 21, 25; VIII 54; XI 454–5

Daco-Roman Theory: IX 10
Dahis: IX 13–14
Dalmatia: IV 9, 27, 33, 36–7; V 69, 71, 73; IX 12; X 14
Danube: V 77; IX 20, 26
Danube-Sava Line: V 70; VI 13; XI 352
Danubian Federation: III 8
Dardanelles: V 79
Dávid, Ferenc: X 5
Dayton Agreement: X 15
Daxner, Štefan: IV 18
Deák, Ferenc: IV 19–20, 22–4
Declaration of the Rights of Men and Citizens: III 3
Debrecen: VIII 54
Decentralization: IV 21; IX 33
DeGaulle, Charles: I 73; X 11
Delegations (AH): I 67
Deligiannes, Theodore: IX 24
Democracy: III 3, 8–9; VI 2–5, 7, 20–21; VII 15, 24; IX 33; X 3–4; XI 350
Demos: IX 15
Denktaş, Rauf: IX 39
Despots
  enlightened: I 68

Destabilization: XI 358–9
Deutsch, Karl W.: I 69
Dictatorship: I 81; II 13; III 9; VI 3, 16;
    VII 1, 22, 24
  military: XI 355
  royal: XI 355
Diets: II 9; IV 15
  Austrian: IV 20
  Bohemian: IV 21
  Hungarian: IV 17–18, 20; IX 19
  Provincial: IV 21
  Transylvanian: IV 18–19, 23
Dillehay, Ronald, C.: VI 1
Dimitrijević, Dragutin: XI 352
Dimitrov, Georgi: VI 17; IX 27
Diószegi, István: V 77, 81
Djakovo: VIII 51
Djilas, Milovan: II 6; VI 19
DMKE: IV 30
Dmovski, Roman: III 8; VI 14; X 7; XI 353–4, 356
Doda, Trajan: IV 31
Doctrine: IV 4; VI 20; XI 347
Dogma: I 68; II 8; VII 20; VIII 43, 47–8
Dollfuss, Engelbert: VII 16
'Domestic Stalinism': XI 358
Don Pacifico Affair: IX 24
Drina (river): IX 20, 35
Dual Monarch: *see* Austria-Hungary
Dubček Alexander: XI 359
Dunajewski, Julian: IV 25
Dušan, Stepan: X 11

East Germany: X 12; XI 359
Eastern Question: V 72
Eastern Rumelia: V 78; IX 26
Economy: I 77; II 6, 10, 12; III 8, 14; IV 21;
    V 69; VI 2, 6, 9, 14; VII 13, 18, 21;
    IX 322; X 6; XI 349–50, 355, 357, 361
Edirne: V 77, 79
Education: III 4; VII 20; VIII 23; X 10;
    XI 352; *see also* Schools
Elites: IV 2, 5; VII 22, 28–30; X 2, 7, 15
Emergency Ordinance Paragraph: IV 17
EMKE: IV 30
Engels, Friedrich: VIII 42
England: I 72, 75–6, 80; IV 4; VI 6; VII 27;
    see also Great Britain
English (l): III 4
Enlightenment: I 67, 76; VI 6; IX 10, 12; X 2;
    XI 349
Enloe, Cynthia H.: II 2
Entente: X 10, 16; XI 353
Enosis: IX 24, 29
EOKA: IX 59

Eötvös, Baron József: IV 20, 22–3; IX 22
Equating nation with state and area: XI 351–7, 359–62
Estates: IV 5; VIII 53; XI 349–50
  structure of: XI 350
Esztergom: VIII 50
Ethnarch: II 2
Ethnic
  belonging: XI 350
  category: II 2
  conformity: XI 353, 362
  feeling: II 2
  groups: I 74, 79–80; II 1–2; IV 1, 6; XI 350, 357, 362
  hatred: X 1
  identity: I 2; II 9–10; IX 36; X 1; XI 349
  nation: XI 353
  transformation: XI 357
  units: I 79
'Ethnic cleansing': IX 34–5, 37, 41; X 14;
    XI 355, 357
Ethnogenesis: I 75; II 2
Ethnonationalism: I 80; II 3–5, 10–14; III 13
Eugen, Prince of Savoy: IX 37
Europe: I 67, 75; III 2; V 68–9, 71, 78–80;
    VI 1, 5; VII 14; VIII 46, 50; IX 7–8, 13,
    37; X 1–4, 8, 10–11, 13; XI 348–9, 356, 360–62
  Central: III 8; IV 10; VI 8, 13; VII 24–5,
    28; IX 12; XI 348
  East-Central: I 67; X 1–4, 9–11, 15–16;
    XI 351, 355–9
  Eastern: I 68; II 1, 3–5, 8–11; III 1–2, 4–5,
    10–15; IV 10; VI 1, 3, 6, 11, 13–21;
    VI 14–21, 24–30; VIII 42–3, 45–6, 56;
    X 3, 9; XI 350–51, 357–61
  Southeastern: II 6; III 8; V 70, 73, 77;
    IX 8; XI 351, 355; *see also* Balkan
    Peninsula
  Western: III 2–3, 9; IV 43; VI 4, 6–8, 21;
    VII 15, 24–5, 28; IX 33; X 13;
    XI 347–9, 353
Eurocommunism: III 13; VI 20–21
European
  Community: X 10, 16; XI 361
  Union: X 11–12
Evgenios, Patriarch: IX 14
Exarchate: IX 25–6; X 6

Faith: VIII 43, 48, 56; X 5
Family: I 74; III 2
Fascism: I 77; VI 13, 15; VII 15, 17–19, 24–5;
    VIII 15; X 9; XI 356
  Clerico: VII 166
  definition of: VII 14

(Fascism continued)
  feature of: VII 14
  Monarcho: VII 16
Fascists: VII 16–30; IX 32
February Patent: IV 5, 15–16
Federalism: I 79; IV 12; X 13
Federalization: IV 15, 21, 41
Fejérváry, Baron Géza: IV 36–7, 40
Fellner, Fritz: VI 11
FEMKE: IV 30
Festetics, Count Sándor: VII 24
Feudalism: I 76; IV 4; VI 2, 4–5, 7, 12; X 2
Feuerbach, Ludwig A.: VIII 42
Filipović, Ivan: IX 19
Firman: IX 25–6; X 6
Fishman, Joshua A.: II 2; 8–9, 11
Fiume Resolution: IV 7, 37
Folk
  communism: X 2
  lore: II 9, 11
  religion: II 8–9; VIII 43–4, 55; X 1, 7
Foreign office, British: V 78
France: I 70, 76; IV 4, 21; V 69; VI 5–6, 12–13; X 10–11; XI 355
Francis I, Emperor: IV 4
Franco-Prussian War: I 70
Franchise: *see* Suffrage
Frank, Josip: IV 36–7; IX 20
Frankovci: XI 356
Franz Ferdinand, Archduke: IV 36–7; IX 21
  assassination of: IX 24; XI 348, 352
Franz Joseph, Emperor: IV 7, 16–19, 21, 31–2, 36–7, 41, 43–4; V 68, 70, 73, 75, 78; X 8
Frashëri, Naum: IX 28
Frashëri, Sami: IX 28
Freedom: I 74–5; VI 3–5; IX 9
  of speech: IV 28
French (l): III 4
French: VII 13
French National Assembly: III 3
Friedjung Trial: IV 38
Friedrich, Carl: VII 14
Fromm, Erich: VI 9
Funar, Gheorghe: XI 361

Gaj, Ljudevit: IX 18–19
Gajda, Rudolf: VII 24
Galicia: III 6; IV 9, 13, 18, 21, 27, 33–4; VIII 52
Garašanin, Ilija: III 8; IX 18, 21; X 7–8, 14
Gaullism: X 11
Gazi: X 4
Gellner, Ernest: I 68; II 2, 7, 10, 14; III 2–4, 10

Georgios (George) I, King (G): IX 24
German (l): I 71; III 4; IV 13, 25, 27, 46
Germans: I 70; IV 8–9, 11–12, 16–17, 20–21, 25–6, 33–4, 46; IX 20, 31, 34, 36; X 4, 9; XI 356
  Bohemian: IV 8
German Confederation: IV 12
Germanness: X 4
Germany: I 68, 73; III 70; IV 5, 14, 26, 34; V 70, 73, 75; VI 12, 14; VII 13–14, 18, 25, 27; X 97–110; XI 353, 356–7, 361
  East: X 12
Gerrymandering: IV 17, 28
Gesamtmonarchie: I 76
Gheg: IX 27
Gheorgiu-Dej, Gheorghe: XI 358
Giskra, Carl: IV 17
Glasnost: XI 359
Gleichschaltung: VIII 45
Gniezno: VIII 50
Goga, Octavian: VI 16; VIII 50
Gołuchowski, Count Agenor, Sr: IV 13
Gömbös, Gyula: VII 26; XI 356
Gomulka, Władysław: XI 358
Gorbachëv, Mikhail: XI 359
Gorchakov, Prince Alexander M.: V 71–2, 76, 78–9; XI 10–11
Gottwald, Klemens: VI 7
Grabski, Władysław: IV 15
Great Britain: I 72, 76, 78–9; III 7; V 79; VII 24; IX 39; X 10–11; XI 349; *see also* England
Great Depression: VI 15; VII 22, 27–8; XI 356
Great Germany: IV 12, 21, 32
Great Hungary: IX 22
Great Moravian Empire: IV 7
Great Powers: V 66, 71–2, 74, 79; IX 24, 26, 28; X 11, 15; XI 353
Greater Croatia: IV 1
Greater Romania: IV 42; IX 22; XI 352
Greater Romanian Party: X 14
Greater Serbia: IX 18, 21–2, 29, 35; X 7–8, 14; XI 351–2
Greece: I 75; III 5; VIII 48; IX 8, 15, 25, 28, 37–41; X 15; XI 351, 356–7
  Colonels' Regime in: IX 39
Greek (l): I 68; IX 9, 17, 19
Greeks: I 75; III 5; VIII 48; IX 9–11, 14–15, 19, 38–9, 41; X 6; XI 355
Greek-Ottoman War (1897): IX 24; XI 352
Greek-Turk Controversy: XI 361
Greg, Edward: IV 17
Gregorios, patriarch: IX 14
Grivas, Georgios-Digonis: IX 39

INDEX

Grossdeutsch: IV 11, 38; XI 356
Gypsies: XI 348

Habits: I 74, 82; VI 17; VII 20; IX 29
Habsburgs: II 5; III 6–7; IV 1–2, 5, 7, 11, 14, 32, 44; VI 1; IX 11; X 4
Habsburg Empire (domain, lands, monarchy): II 5–6; III 6–7; IV 2–3, 6, 12–5, 36, 39, 40; V 69, 71; VI 1, 6–8; VIII 49, 51–4; IX 11–12, 18, 28; X 3, 5; XI 352
Habsburgstreue: IV 6, 32, 43
Hajduks: III 5; IX 9
Hantsch, Hugo: IV 39
Haumont, Emile: IX 29
Hegel, George W.F.: VI 9
Helsinki Agreement: VI 21
Henlein, Konrad: VII 25
Henry IV, Emperor: VIII 43; X 3
Hercegovina: V 66, 68, 71, 74; *see also* Bosnia-Hercegovina
Herder, Johann G. von: II 11; III 6; X 12
Heretics: VIII 55; X 1
History of the Slavo-Bulgarians: X 6
Hitler, Adolf: VI 15–16; VII 16–17, 24, 26–8; X 9–10; XI 355–7
Hlas: IV 35
Hlinka, Andrej: IV 35, 41; VI 14; VIII 55
Hobbes, Thomas: VI 19
Hoçabaşi: IX 14, 25
Hodža, Milan: IV 35
Hofer, Tamás: II 2, 9
Hohenwart, Count Sigismund: IV 15, 21, 23–4
Hohenzollern
   Dynasty: III 6
   Empire: X 3
Holbrooke, Richard C.: X 15
Holocaust: X 3, 9; XI 357
Home communists: XI 357
Horn, Gyula: X 12
Horthy, Miklós: VII 16, 25
Hospodars: IX 7, 10
Hoxha, Enver: XI 358
Hungarian (l): IX 19
Hungarians: I 71, 75; III 5–6, 8, 14; IV 17; V 15; VIII 49; IX 12, 41; X 12; XI 350, 352, 361; *see also* Magyars
Hungary: II 8; III 8–9, 13–15; IV 4–6, 8, 11, 13, 15–19, 22–4, 26–7, 29–35, 37–8, 40, 42–3, 45; VI 14, 16; VII 13, 18, 20–22, 24, 26; VIII 49–50, 52–4, 57; IX 11–12, 19–22, 41; X 4–5, 7, 12; XI 352, 354, 356, 358–9
Huns: VIII 46
Huntington, Samuel: VI 1
Hussites: VII 54; X 4

'Hyphen question': XI 355

Iași: IX 10
Ideology: I 68, 70–71; II 11–12, 14; III 1, 5, 7, 9, 13, 15; IV 1, 12, 42–3; VI 10, 14–16, 18–20; VII 15, 20; VIII 46, 52, 58; IX 8, 11, 14, 16, 32; X 2, 9–10, 12; XI 347–50, 353, 356, 360
Ignatiev, Count Nicholas P.: V 79; X 6
Iliescu, Ion: IX 41; X 359
Illiteracy: II 12; VIII 55; IX 8
Illyrians: IX 18
Illyrian province: IX 12
Illyrianist movement: IX 18
Ioannides, Demetrios: IX 40
Immunities: VI 17
Imrédy, Béla: VI 15–16
IMRO: IX 17
Independence: IV 24, 27; VIII 54; IX 22, 30; XI 360
Independent Party (H): IV 23, 31, 36
Industrialization: II 3; III 4, 8; VI 9; X 10
Industry: II 12; V 69; VI 10; VII 18
Inflation: VII 13
Integration: IV 3
Intelligentsia: III 4–5; IV 27, 30; VII 30; X 2
Internationalism: III 11; VIII 50
Intolerance: VIII 43
Ionia: IX 38
Iorga, Nicolae: XI 356
Ipek: *see* Peć
Ireland: I 72
Irish (people): I 76
'Iron Ring': IV 21, 25–6, 32
Irredentism: IX 23–4
Irredentists: IV 14
Islam: I 75; VIII 56; IX 8, 23; X 2–3, 5–6
   fundamentalist: X 13
'Isms': I 68; X 9
Istanbul: II 8; IX 7–8, 10; *see also* Constantinople
   Conference: IX 24
Istoria raznyh slavenskih: IX 11
Istria: IV 36
Italians: IV 9, 14, 16, 21, 26–7, 33–4, 38; VII 13; IX 31; 36
Italy: V 14, 16, 14, 26–7; VIII 46; X 10; XI 355
Ivan Assen III (B): VIII 47
Iványi-Grünwald, Béla: IV 29
Izetbegović, Alije: IX 33; X 15; XI 360
Izmir: IX 38

Jakoljević, Marko: IX 29
Janos, Andrew: VI 4, 9, 15; XI 350

Janissaries: IX 13
Jaures, Jean: XI 348
Jelačić, Baron Josip: IX 19
Jelavich, Charles: X 8; XI 352
Jews: III 10; IV 14; VII 27, 29; VIII 56; IX 8, 32; X 4; XI 3, 358
  emancipation of: VIII 52
Jingoism: III 8; IX 24; X 12, 14
Joseph II, Emperor: II 5; IV 4, 13; VI 1, 6; IX 11
Jowitt, Kenneth: VI 5, 7
Judaism: IX 8; X 2–3

Kádár, János: III 13
Kaisertreue: II 5; IV 4, 31–2, 44; IX 20, 22
Kállay, Benjamin: VIII 57; IX 23
Kálmán, King (H): IX 11
Karadjordjević family: IX 30; X 8
Karadžić, Radovan: IX 36
Karadžić, Vuk: IX 18
Kars: V 80
Kazan: II 7
Kedourie, Elie: III 2
Khlepts: IX 19
Khrushchev, Nikita A.: VI 18; XI 359
Khuen-Héderváry, Count Károly: IV 31, 36, 41; IX 20
Kingdom of Serbs, Croats and Slovenes: VII 18; VIII 53, IX 29
Kirscht, John P.: IX 13
Knez(es): IX 13
Kohn, Hans: IV 1–2, 43
Kollár, Jan: VIII 58
Kolozsvár: IV 18; *see also* Cluj
Kombi: IX 28
Konfessions Nationalität: IX 13, 32, 35; X 7, 9, 14
Korošeć, Anton: IX 30
Kossova: III 12; IX 37, 41; X 16; XI 351, 360
Kossuth, Ferenc: IV 36
Kossuth, Lajos: III 8; IV 31; IX 19
Krajina: IX 34–5
Kramař, Karl: IV 40
Kraków: IV 25
Krasicki, Ignacy: X 5
Kremlin: III 11; VI 21
Kristóffy, József: IV 37
Kroměříž (Kremsier): IV 12–13
Küçük, Fazil: IX 39
Kukuljević, Ivan: IX 19
Kulturkampf: VIII 43, 51
Kun, Béla: III 9; VI 14
Kvaternik, Eugen: IX 14; IX 20

Lackó, Miklós: VII 11

Laibach Conference: IX 15
Lands of the Crown of St Steven: IV 23; VIII 52; IX 19; X 11
Language: I 69–70, 74–5, 82; II 2–4, 8–9, 11; III 5; IV 15, 17, 31, 33, 42; VI 11; IX 34
  barrier: IV 6
  official: IV 13
  ordinances: IV 24
  public: IV 13
  reform: II 10; III 5, 8
Latin: IX 19
Latin America: I 72, 74
Leaders: VI 2–3, 15–16; VII 20–21; VIII 42; IX 7
League
  of Nations: VII 12
  of Prizren: IX 27
Legends: I 74; II 9
Legitimacy: VI 18–19; VIII 58
Leitha (river): IV 16–17, 28
Lenin, Vladimir I.: III 3; VI 17; X 3
Leo I, the Great, Pope: VIII 46
Leo III, Pope: VIII 46
Levi, Hermann: IX 348
Levski, Vasil: IX 25
Lex Apponyi: XI 352
Lex Kossuth: XI 352
Liberal Party (H): IV 23, 29
Liberal Party (R): IX 22
Liberalism: III 3, 7; IV 6, 14, 21, 25; VI 7, 10; VIII 52; IX 19; X 4
Lim region: III 3
Linz Program: IV 26
Literacy: II 12; VI 10
Literature: II 2–3; VI 13; XI 362
Little Entente: II 13; X 10
Ljotić, Dimitrije: VII 25
Localism: I 64; IV 1
Locke, John: VI 9
London
  Conference (1913): X 16
  'Long Armistice': VII 13, 17, 30; X 8
Lónyai, Count Menyhért: IV 15, 23
Louis I, the Great, King (H): VIII 49
Louis XIV: VI 53; X 2
Loyalty: I 68–9, 71, 73–4, 76, 81; II 5–6; III 1; IV 32, 37, 44; VI 6; VII 21; VIII 44–5; IX 11, 13, 28; X 2–3, 9, 13; XI 349
  acquired: I 69
  natural: I 69
Luther, Martin: X 4
Lutheranism: VIII 51, 55; IX 16; X 4–5, 12
Luxemburg, Rosa: XI 353
Lyssarides, Vassos: IX 40

INDEX

Macedonia: II 9; III 12; V 77; VIII 49–50, 56; IX 25–7, 33, 37; X 5–7, 13, 15; XI 351, 355
Macedonian Question: IX 25–7; X 6, 13
Maček, Vladko: VII 16; IX 31
Machiavelli, Nicolo: VI 9
Machtergreifung: VII 16, 24, 28
Macronationalism: IV 3, 12, 44, 46
Magyar (l): IV 29
Magyars: IV 8, 11, 13, 16–17, 20–21, 23, 25, 30, 34–5, 37, 39, 41, 45–6; IX 16, 19–20, 36; X 3, 12; XI 352; *see also* Hungarians
Magyarization: IV 8, 29, 30, 35, 41–2; XI 352
Magyarones: IX 20
Majorities: IV 17; VI 6; IX 7; XI 350, 353
Makarios III, Archbishop Mouskos, Mikhail K.: IX 39–41
Málnási, Ödön: VII 22–3
Maniu, Juliu: IV 42; IX 22
Marchais, George: VI 20
Mare sober: IX 11
Maria Theresa, Empress: II 5–6; IV 3, 43; VI 4, 6–7
Maritsa (river): V 77
Marseille: IX 31
Martalose: III 5; IX 9
Marx, Karl: VI 4; VII 42
Marxism: I 68; III 4, 12, 15; VI 4, 15, 19–20; VII 20; VIII 44; X 1
Marxism-Leninism: VI 18; VIII 44
Marxism-Leninism-Stalinism: X 1
Masaryk, Tomáš G.: IV 35, 40; VI 14
Mass
  mobilization: VI 15–16
  psychosis: IV 2
Matica Česka: IV 13
Matica Hrvatska: IV 13
Matica Slovenska: IV 13, 29
Matica Srbska: IV 13
Mavrocordatos, Alexander: IX 16
  family: IX 10
May, Arthur J.: IV 40
Mazzini, Giuseppe: VI 10
Mečiar, Vladimir: XI 361
Media: X 2, 10, 13, 15; *see also* Newspapers
Mediterranean: XI 349
Megale Idea: IX 15, 17, 24, 38; XI 351
Mehmed II, the Conqueror, Sultan: VIII 47
Memorandum of the Serb Academy of Arts and Sciences: X 14
Merchants: IX 10, 14, 25
Metaxas, Ioannis: VII 16–17
Metternich, Prince Klemens: IX 15
Micu, Ioan I.: IX 10
Middle Ages: IV 5; VI 5, 11; VIII 50

Miletić, Svetozar: IV 1, 29
Military: VII 19–20, 22; *see also* Army
  Frontier: IX 11
Mill, John S.: VI 9
Millet system: VIII 48; IX 8–9, 42; X 6
Milošević, Slobodan: IX 33–4, 36; X 7–8, 15, XI 351, 361
Mindszenty, József: II 8; VIII 54
Minorities: II 4–5; III 4, 10–11, 14; IV 1, 6, 8, 15–18, 45–6; XI 352, 354–5, 357
Mir: VII 19–20, 22
Mladić, Ratko: IX 36
Moczar, Mieczysław: XI 358
Modernity: II 10; VI 17
Modernization: II 3–5, 7, 13–14; III 8; IV 4; VI 2, 15
Modernizers: II 6–7; VI 9; VIII 55
Mohács (battle of): VIII 53
Moldavia: VIII 49; IX 17; *see also* Romania
Mollinary, Baron Anton: V 75
Montenegro: V 68, 71, 73–6, 78–80; IX 7, 28
Montenegrins: II 8; V 71, 74
Montenegrin Committee; IX 30
Moore, Clement H.: VI 51
Moravia: IV 33; X 4; *see also* Czech Lands, Czechoslovakia
Morea: IX 8, 15
Morlaks: IX 9
Moscow: III 11; VI 17, 21
Mount Athos: X 6
Multi-
  ethnicity: I 82; II 6; XI 350, 353–4
  lingualism: II 6; X 11
  nationality: I 82; III 8,12; IV 3; 46; V 81; VI 10; VII 18; XI 252–5, 357, 362
  racism: IX 353
  religious: II 6
Muslims: IV 8; VIII 47, 50, 55–7; IX 8–9, 17, 23, 27–9, 31, 35–8; X 1, 5–6, 13–14
  Hanafi: IX 37
  Hanbali: IX 37
  fundamentalist: IX 37
Muslim nationality: X 14; XI 357
Mustafa Kemal: IX 38; XI 355
Myths: II 2; III 6; VI 3, 18; VIII 54

Načertanije: III 8; IX 18; X 7
Nagodba: IV 9, 20, 23, 28, 37
Napoleon I: IX 12
Napoleonic Wars: IX 12
Národny Listy: IV 14
'Natio' (political nation): II 6–7; VI 12; VIII 49; IX 12; XI 353
Nation-building: I 71–2, 74, 79–80; II 7, 10; III 6–7, 13–14; XI 350, 354

Nation-state: X 2, 4; XI 353–6, 359, 362
'Natioethnicism': I 80, 82–3
National
   characteristics: I 71
   church: VIII 47–9, 50; IX 9, 17, 26–7; X 3;
      XI 357
   Communism: III 1, 11–12, 15, 18;
      VI 18–21; X 10; XI 357
   concept: XI 351
   conflict: III 4
   front: III 4
   group: IV 6
   identity: IX 36; XI 350
   income: VI 16
   insecurity: XI 261
   persecution complex: X 14
   Resistance: VIII 50–53
   Socialism: VI 16; X 9
National Democrats (CzS): XI 355
National Democrats (P): VII 23
National Youth Movement (C): IX 2
National Work Party (H): IV 41
Nationalism
   acquired: I 69; III 2
   arrested: I 68
   defensive: X 10–14
   definition of: I 67; III 2, 15; IV 1–2
   doctrine of: III 2
   natural: I 69
   nostalgic: X 10–11
   state-of-siege: X 10, 12, 15
Nationalismus bei Serben und Kroaten,
   1830–1914: IX 18
Nationality Law of 1868 (H): IV 5, 22
Németh, Miklós: XII 359
Neoabsolutism: IV 7, 12, 15–16; IX 19
Neo-serfdom: XI 349
New Ethnicity: III 13–14
'New Right': VII 16, 20, 22–3, 25–6, 28–9
Newspapers: IV 31; VII 28–30; IX 29: *see also* Media
Niš: IX 29
Nobility: II 7; III 3, 10; IV 28; VI 8;
   VIII 53–4; IX 12; X 4–6; XI 349; *see also* Aristocracy
Noli, Fan S.: IX 28
Nolte, Ernst: VII 15
Nová Škola: IV 18, 30
Novikov, Eugene: V 75–6

Obrenović, Alexander: IX 2
   murder of: XI 352
October Patent: IV 13, 15
Ohrid: II 12; IX 9
'Old Czechs': IV 17

'Old Right': VII 18, 20, 22–3, 25–6, 28–9
Organic work: II 3
Orthodoxy: II 5; IV 19; VIII 46, 52, 55;
   IX 8–9, 11, 16–18, 22–4, 32; X 3, 5–9, 13
Ost und West: IV 15
Österreichische Rundschau: IV 42
Otho, King (G): IX 17, 24, 28
Othonian System: IX 17
Ottomans: V 71–2, 74, 80; VI 6; VII 16;
   VIII 48–9, 56; IX 8–10, 16, 24, 26, 42;
   X 6; *see also* Turks
Ottoman Empire: II 5–6; III 6; IV 29; V 6–8,
   70–4, 77–80; VI 7; VIII 47, IX 7–8, 10,
   13, 23–5, 27; X 3, 5; *see also* Turkey
Ottoman
   rule: VIII 57; IX 7–8, 11, 13, 17, 23, 25, 39;
      X 4
   system: VIII 47; IX 14
Ottoman-Greek Yoke: VIII 48; IX 10
Ottoman-Russian War: V 74, 76, 78
Ottomanism: II 6

Padeş Manifesto: IX 16
Paisii, Father: X 6
Palacký, František: X 8
Pálffy, Count Fidél: VII 24
Palmer, Robert R.: I 68
Pangermanism: I 71; IV 26–7
Panslavism: I 71; III 6; IV 30
Panturanism: I 71
Paragraph 14: IV 17, 19, 24, 33, 40
Paris
   Treaty of 1856: V 79
   Treaty of 1919–20: XI 353–4
   Treaty of 1995: IX 42; X 15
Parliament: IV 5
Parsifal: XI 348
Partisans: IX 31
Party-state: VIII 45, 57
Pašic, Nikola: VII 11, 14; IX 22, 29
Passarowitz
   Peace of: IX 37
Passivism: IV 29, 30, 35, 37
Pasvanoğlu, Osman: IX 13
Patriarchate
   Bulgarian: VIII 47
   Russian: VIII 49; X 3
   Serb: VIII 47, IX 9
   of Constantinople: VIII 48–9; IX 8–9, 25
Patrimony
   Ethnic: I 74
Patriotism: I 69; II 2; IV 1; VII 21; IX 38;
   X 3; XI 347
   Local: X 6
Pavelić, Ante: VII 16, 25; IX 31

Peasants, peasantry: II 10–11, 13; III 6, 8, 10; VI 16; VII 14; VIII 43; IX 17, 19, 23; X 5
Peć: II 8; VIII 47
People: I 73; II 2, 5, 8, 11, 14; III 1, 4, 9, 11, 13–14; IV 1–3, 6–7, 12; VI 2–3, 15; VII 18; VIII 44, 54–6; IX 8, 10, 16–17; XI 347, 354, 357–60
People's Party (H): IV 36
Perestroika: XI 359
Personality cult: VI 17
Pest'budinske vedomosti: IV 14
Pesti-Napló: IV 19
'Petka': XI 355
Petrovich, Michael B.: II 3, 8
Phanariotes: IX 7, 9–10, 14, 16
Philhellenes: IX 15
Philiki Etairia: IX 15
Piasecki, Bolesław: VII 16
Piłsudski, Józef: III 8; VI 14; VII 16; X 7; XI 353
Pireus: IX 24
Plastiras, Nikolaos: VII 16
Plevna: V 77–8
Pluralism: VI 4–5, 7, 14, 20; VIII 18
Poland: II 3, 8; III 13, 15; V 1, 4, 7–8, VII 14, 18, 21, VIII 50, 52–3, 57; IX 34; X 5, 7–8, 12; XI 349, 535–5, 358–9
  Partitions of: III 8; VI 6; VIII 51–2; X 9
Poles: II 3; III 5–6, 8; IV 7, 9, 13, 17, 21, 25, 27, 32–3, 46, 67, 69; VII 20; VIII 51–2, 58; X 3; XI 350, 353
Polish Club: IV 39
Polishness: VIII 51–2; X 5, 7; XI 353
Polit, Michael: IV 29
Politics: X 6–7; XI 349, 356
  definition of: X 2
  extremist: IX 356
Political nation: *see* 'Natio'
Pomaks: X 13
Population: I 72; II 12–4; III 9, 13; IV 8, 30; V 69–70; VI 8, 19; VII 17, 20; VIII 45, 50, 53–4, 56–8; IX 8, 23; X 3, 13, 349–50, 357, 359–60
  exchange: IX 38; XI 355
  growth: XI 349
Populist Party (CzS): XI 355
Porte: *see* Ottoman Empire
Posen: XI 353
Pragmatic Sanction: II 6
Prague: I 71; III 6; IV 26, 32, 39; VII 26
  Spring: III 12–13; VI 2, 19–21; VIII 54; X 9
  University: IV 25
Primary Education Act, 1868 (H): IV 22

Premodernity: II 6
Principles: IV 1, 16, 29, 42; VIII 15
Priština: IX 28; X 2
Privileges: III 3, 7; IV 6, 8, 10, 16, 45–6; IX 11; X 5; XI 349
  hereditary: XI 350
Professional nationalists: XI 356
Pronunciament de la Blaj: IV 23
Propaganda: I 70–71; II 3; VI 13; VIII 50; IX 36, 41; X 7
Pro-Slavs: IV 17
Proselytizing: X 6
Protestantism: VIII 57; X 5
'Protestant Catholics': X 4
Protofascism: III 11
Protonationalism: VIII 56
Prussia: IV 16, 21; VI 7; VIII 51; X 5
Pseudonationalism: XI 356
Public opinion: V 67, 70; VI 18; VII 29; IX 7
Pułaski, Józef: X 5
Purge Trials: XI 359
Putnik, Mojsije: IX 10
Pyrenées: XI 347

Quebec: I 73–5, 78–9

Race: VII 19; IX 32; X 9; XI 356
Racial purity: VI 16
Racism: VI 16; VII 22, 24; VIII 46; X 9; XI 356
Racists: IX 32; XI 356
  Laws: XI 357
Račić, Puniša: IX 31
Rački, Franjo: IX 20–21
Radetzky, Count Joseph: V 69
Radić, Stjepan: IX 21, 31
Radical Party (S): IX 22
Radicalism: XI 356
Railroads: II 7; XI 352
  Service Act (H): IV 38
Rajić Iovan: IX 11
Rakovski, Georgi: IX 25
Rauch, Baron Paul: IV 38
Raya: IX 9
Realpolitik: III 7; V 68
Reform: IV 4, 6
  administrative: IV 21
  economic: VII 13, 15, 22
  electoral: IV 21, 27–8, 32–3, 40, 42
  land: III 9; VII 22, 28
  language: II 10; III 5, 8
  Ottoman: V 71–2
  school: III 9; IV 12
Reformation: II 67; VIII 50, 53–4; IX 12; X 4–5

Reformed (Calvinist) Church (H): VIII 54;
    IX 16
Reformers: II 11; X 4
Refugées: XI 357
Regat: I 70; VII 18
Reichsrat: IV 4, 16, 19, 25, 39–40
Reichstadt
    Agreement: V 73–6, 78
    resume of: I 70
Reichstag: IV 11, 21
Religion: I 67, 69, 74–5; II 8–9; III 3; VIII 42,
    45, 52, 56; IX 7–8, 13, 26, 28, 32; X 1–6,
    8; XI 360
Renaissance: IX 12
Renner, Karl: XI 348
Resolution Party (H): IV 27
Revisionism: III 8; VII 18; X 9, 12; XI 361
Revisionists: III 9; XI 354
Revolution
    French: IV 1; VI 1, 6; IX 10, 17
    Industrial: I 76; III 2
    Serb: IX 10, 13
    socio-economic: XI 353
    of 1848: III 5–7; IV 6, 8, 12–14, 31
    of 1956: VI 18; X 9; XI 358
Rezler, Julius: II 3
Rhigas, Pheraios: IX 10
Rhine: XI 347
Rhodope Range: IX 25
Rieger, František: IV 17
Rights: IV 12–13, 20, 23; X 5; XI 349
    birth: XI 350
    civil: I 82; III 3
    economic: III 3
    equal: III 3
    estate based: X 5
    group: XI 352, 362
    historic: IV 5, 23, 33
    individual: I 76
    local: IV 16–17
    minority: IX 36
    national: IX 36; XI 353
    political: III 3; IV 8, 28
    social: III 3
Roman Catholicism: II 5; IV 1, 20, 30,
    34; VIII 50–56; IX 11, 16, 18–19,
    21, 23, 27, 29, 35; X 2, 4–5, 7, 9,
    11–13
Roman, Petru: IX 41
Romania: I 70; III 12, 14; IV 42; V 70, 77,
    80; VI 16–17; VIII 20–21, 26; IX 41;
    X 14; XI 356, 358–60; *see also*
    Moldavia, Wallachia, Romanian
    Principalities
Romanian (1): IV 19

Romanians: I 71; II 8; III 5–6; IV 9, 13, 18,
    23, 29, 30–31, 37–9, 42; VIII 48–9, 55;
    IX 10–11, 16–17, 19–20, 22, 41; X 6–7,
    15; XI 352
Romanian National Party: IX 31, 34
Romanian Principalities: IX 7, 9–10, 15–17,
    19, 22
Romanian
    Cultural League: IV 34
    Memorandum of 1887: IV 31
    Petition of 1892: IV 34
Romanianism: VII 20
Romanov Empire: II 5; III 6–7
Rome: IV 34; VIII 46
Rousseau, Jean J.: III 6; VI 9; X 5
Rumelia: V 73–4, 77, 80; IX 8
Russia: I 75; II 5; III 7; IV 27, 30, 33; V 67–8,
    70–80; VI 7, 11, 14; VII 15; VIII 49, 51;
    IX 10; X 3, 5, 7–8, 11; XI 354, 356, 361;
    see also Soviet Union
Russians: I 75; II 5; V 75–6; IX 25–6
Russification: VIII 51
Rydz-Śmigly, Edward: VII 14

Sabor (C): IV 4–5, 20, 38; IX 20
Sabor (S): IX 10–11
Šafařik, Pavel J.: VIII 55
Şaguna, Andreiu: IV 18
Šandjak of Novi Pazar: V 74, 47; IX 23, 25
San Stefano: V 78
    Peace Treaty of: V 80; IX 26; XI 351
Sarajevo: IX 23, 36; XI 348, 352
Sava rive: XI 347; *see also* Danube-Sava
    Line
Sava (Saint): VIII 49
Saxons: VIII 49; IX 16
Schlamperei: II 6
Schmerling, Anton von: IV 16–17
Schönerer, George: VII 17
Schools: I 70; II 3; III 15; IV 13–14, 29–30,
    32, 42; VII 20, 29–30; VIII 55; IX 9–10;
    X 2; *see also* Education
    confessional: IV 38
    elementary: IV 22, 25, 29
    parochial: IX 22; X 7
Schwarzenberg, Prince Felix: IV 12
Scots: I 71–3, 76; XI 349
Scotland: I 72, 80
Secession: III 12; IV 24, 31
'Secret speech': VI 18; XI 359
Security: I 74, 78; III 14; VI 4–5
Self-
    awareness: III 4; VII 20, IX 14
    centeredness: IV 23
    defense: IX 13

(Self- continued)
  determination: I 70, 72, 76; III 14; IV 15; XI 353–4
  doubt: III 10
  government: II 6; III 7; IX 11, 20
  identification: I 69; II 5, 7–8, 11; VIII 50; IX 7–8, 13; IX 28, 32, 36
  image: VII 14–15; IX 11, 13
  interest: VI 5
  rule: IV 18
  satisfaction: III 10
Selim III: VI 1, 6–7; IX 7, 13
Semimodernity: II 5–6, 8, 10–11, 13–15; IV 9
Serbs: I 71; II 8; III 5–6, 8; IV 9, 13–14, 30–31, 36–9; V 71; VIII 47, 52–3, 57; IX 13–5, 19–22, 28–32, 34–7; X 1, 7–9, 13–14; XI 351–2, 361
  Precani: IX 10–11, 14
Serbia: IV 34, 37–8; V 6, 8; VI 71, 73–80; VII 20; VIII 48, 50; IX 8, 13, 19, 21, 25, 27–30, 33–5; X 8, 15; XI 351, 361
Serbness: X 14
Serbo-Bulgarian War: X 16
Serfs: III 6
Šešelj, Vojislav: IX 34, 36–7
Seton-Watson, Hugh: I 69, 74; II 12–13; III 3
Seton-Watson, R.W.: X 8; XI 362
Seyss-Inquart, Arthur: VII 16
Shafer, Boyd C.: III 2
Shipka Pass: V 77
Sibiu: II 8; IV 18–19, 23
Silesia: IV 33
Sima, Horia: VII 25
Simeon (Knyaz, B.): VIII 47
Sincere History of the Hungarian Nation: VII 22
Sinikoğlu, Haci-Mustafa: IX 13
Skrlec, Nicola: IX 12
Slavs: IV 7, 16–17, 38, 41; V 69–71, 74, 77, 79; VIII 47–9; IX 9, 17, 21, 23; X 6–7
Slav Congress of 1848: IV 13
Slavery: I 75; VI 2
Slavici, Roman: IV 31
Slavonia: IX 20, 34: *see also* Croatia-Slavonia
Slovaks: I 71; III 6, 12–14; IV 4, 11, 17–18, 23, 29–31, 35, 41; VI 20; VIII 55; IX 29; X 3–4, 7, 12; XI 353–4, 356
Slovakia: I 71; IV 29, 35–6; VII 18; VIII 534; X 12; XI 361
Slovak (l): IV 18
Slovak National Party: IV 31, 35; XI 355
Slovak People's Party: IV 35; VII 20, 25
Slovenes: I 71; III 14; IV 9, 11, 14, 27, 38–9; VIII 52; IX 11–12, 18, 21, 29, 31, 34–6; X 3, 13

Slovenia: IV 36, 46; VIII 52, 56; IX 12, 18, 30, 33; X 13
Slovene People's Party: IX 30
Smith, Anthony D.: III 2
Snyder, Louis L.: I 76
Social
  action: IV 6
  change: I 67
  class: IV; *see also* Class
  conditions: III 2
  dislocation: XI 348
  groups: I 67, 69; IV 6; IX 17
  institutions: VIII 55
  mobility: IV 6
  order: VI 5
  position: IV 45; VII 22
  problems: VII 13, 18, 21–2; X 4
  revolution: VII 22; VIII 54; X 4
  structure: VI 13; VII 18–19, 26
Social Democrats: VI 10
  Austrian: IV 38
  Czech: XI 355
Socialism: VI 4, 10; XI 353
  'with a human face': XI 358
Socialists: VII 21–2
Socialist Party
  Austrian: IV 25, 39
  Polish: IV 388
Society: I 68; II 4; III 4; IV 1; VI 2, 6, 18; VII 18, 20; VIII 42, 45; IX 23; X 2
  centralized: III 10
  civil: VI 2, 5–8, 13, 18, 20
  communist: VIII 42
  formation of: VI 3
  industrial: II 2, 10
  industrializing: II 3; III 2
  modern: VI 5
  political: VI 5
  preindustrial: II 2
  structure of: IV 4
  units of: I 78
  urban: II 10; III 2
Solidarity: II 6, 9; III 3, 15
Solidarity Movement: III 13; VIII 45
Solzhenitsyn, Aleksandr, I: X 11
Sovereignty: III 6, 9; IV 2; VII 21; IX 9; XI 355
  Popular: III 3; IV 1, 4
Soviet: IX 39
  dictation: XI 358
  domination: VIII 50; XI 357
  model: III 11
  republics: III 11
  Zone: III 11

14　INDEX

Soviet Union: I 68, 77; III 11–12, 15; VI 18, 20–21; VII 14, 21; X 1, 9–11; XI 354, 359–60; *see also* Russia
　disintegration of: XI 361
　politics of: VIII 57
Speer, Albert: X 9
Split: VIII 51
Sporazum: VII 26; IX 31
Srbi svi i Svuda: IX 18
Sremski Karlovci (Karlowatz): II 8; IV 13, 19; X 10, 22
　Archbishopric of: IV 19; VIII 49; IX 9
Srobar, Vavro: IV 35, 41
Staatsangehörigkeit: I 79
Stadler, Josip (Archbishop): VIII 53
Stalin, Josip V.: III 3, 11–12; VI 18; XI 351
　Death of: X 9; XI 357–9
Stalinism: X 9
Stambuliski, Alexandur: III 9; VI 14
Stambulov, Stefan: VI 11
Starčević, Ante: IV 14, 31; IX 20
State
　accepted: I 73, 77
　building: I 71–2, 80; III 8, 12–14; XI 354
　centralized: I 67–8; IV 1
　makers: I 81
　modern: I 68
　new: I 73, 77
　old established: I 73, 77
　popular: IV 1
　potential: I 80
　religion: X 5
　successor: IX 354
Status quo politics; X 9; XI 353
Stepinać, Alojzije (Archbishop): IX 32
Stojadinović, Milan: VI 15–16; VII 26
Štokavian: IX 18
Stokes, Gale: IX 36
Stříbrny, Jiří: VII 24
Strossmayer, Josip J. (Archbishop): VIII 52; IX 19–21; X 8
Štur, L'udevit: VIII 55
Subjects: VI 6–8; VIII 47; IX 11
Sudeten Germans: VII 25
Suffrage: II 12; IV 5, 21, 26; XI 350
　regulation: IV 23
　universal: IV 26; VI 14, 17, 30, 32–3, 37, 39
Supilo, Franjo: IV 37; IX 21, 29
Supplex libellus Valachorum: IX 16
Supranationalism: I 4
Sylvester Patent: IV 12
Symbols: I 74; II 2; 8–9; VII 20; VIII 52–5; IX 9; X 9
Szálasi Ferenc: VI 16; VII 16, 25

'Szeged Ideal': VII 20; XI 356
Székelys: VIII 49; IX 16; X 5
Széll, Kálmán: IV 35
Szlávy, József: IV 23

Taaffe, Count Edward: IV 21, 25–7, 31–2, 38
Taboos: I 74; II 9
Taborites: VIII 54, X 4
Tanzimat: II 5; VII 16
Teachers: VII 28–9
Technocrats: II 14; VI 15
Technology: I 77; VI 10
Tegetthof, Baron Wilhelm: V 69
Temesvár (Timişoara): IX 10–11
Ten Commandments: VIII 42; X 1
Theology: X 1–2
The Order of the Knights of the Holy Cross: X 5
Thessaly: V 74; IX 24
Third Reich: X 10
Third World: I 70, 79–80; II 10; III 1, 9
Three Emperors' League: V 70, 72, 74, 79
Three Faces of Fascism: VII 15
Thun-Hohenstein, Count Franz: IV 33
Thun-Hohenstein, Count Leo: IX 12
Timars: IX 8
Tiso, Józef: VII 26; VIII 55–6
Tito, Josip (Broz): III 11–12; VI 17–18; VIII 50, 57; IX 27, 32–4; X 10, 14; XI 359
Tito-Stalin break: VI 17; XI 357
Titoism: III 12; XI 358
Titoists: XI 358
Titoist Solution: XI 357, 359
Tisza (river): IV 42
Tisza, István: IV 36, 41–3, 45–6
Tisza, Kálmán: IV 23–5, 27–32, 34, 38
Tkalac, Imbro I.: IV 16, 19
Tosk: IX 27
Totalitarianism: VII 15–16, 22; VIII 44
　definition of: VII 14
Tradition: I 69–71, 74; II 4, 11; VIII 43, 47
Traditionalists: VI 8
Transylvania: I 71; II 7; III 7, 12, 14; IV 13, 18, 20, 23, 27, 30–31, 41; VII 18; VIII 49, 53–5; IX 10–11, 16–17, 19–20, 22–3, 41; X 4, 5, 7
Travnik: IX 23
Treadgold, Donald W.: VI 2
Treitschke, Heinrich von: VI 9
Trieste: IV 27
Trieste e l'Istria . . . : IV 14
Trikupis, Charilaos: IX 24
Triple Alliance: IX 23

Triune Kingdom: III 7; IV 14, 36–7; IX 12; XI 352
Trotsky, Leon: III 12; VI 18
Trumbić, Ante: IX 29–30, 35
Tudjman, Franjo: IX 34; X 1–5
Tudor, Corneliu V.: IX 14–15
Tuka, Vojtěch: VII 25–6
Tundza (river): V 77
Turanism: II 6
Turčiansky Sväti Martin: IV 18
Turcini: X 14
Turczynski, Emanuel: IX 14, 32; X 7, 9
Turks: III 5; VI 8; VIII 56; IX 9, 38–9, 41; X 13–14; XI 355; *see also* Ottomans
Turkey: V 68, 71, 75, 79–80; VII 14; IX 37–41; X 13–15; XI 355; *see also* Ottoman Empire
Turkism: II 6
Turkusi: X 14
Tweed, William: IX 17
Tyrol: IV 14, 21, 26–7, 33

Ujedinjenie ili Smirt: IX 24
Ukraine: III 7; IX 34; XI 360
Ukrainians: III 6; IV 9, 13, 27, 29, 33, 38–9
Ulema: VIII 56
Uniates: II 8; IV 42; VIII 49, 52, 55; IX 10–11, 16, 22; X 7
Unionist Party (C): IV 31
Unitarians: IX 16; X 5
Urbanization: II 4; III 8; X 10
USA: I 73, 75, 82; III 9; IX 28, 39–40; X 13, 16; XI 353; *see also* America
Uskoks: IX 9
USSR: *see* Soviet Union
Ustaša: VII 20, 25–6; VIII 53; IX 31, 34; X 9

Vaida-Vojvod, Alexandrŭ: IV 42; IX 22
Vajansk, Svetozár H.: IV 30
Vajda, Mihály: VI 3
Valenta, Jiří : VI 2
Valentinian III, Roman Emperor: VIII 46
Vatra: IV 28
Venizelos, Eleutherios: IX 25; XI 356
Vice Sheriff: IV 22
Vidovdan Constitution: IX 30
Vienna
  Congress of: VI 8
Villages: I 7; II 4; VI 16
Village explorers: III 10
Vladimirescu, Tudor: IX 15–16
  revolt of: IX 16
Vlora, Ismail K.: IX 28
Vojvodate: IX 11

Vojvodina: III 14; IV 13, 20, 30; IX 11, 19–20, 37; XI 351–3
Voltaire, François M.A.: VIII 43
Voyages of discovery: X 3; XI 349
Vucinich, Wayne S.: IX 14

Wagner, Richard: XI 348
Wales: I 73, 80
Wallachia: VIII 49; IX 17; *see also* Romanian principalities
Wars
  Anti Avar: IX 12
  Austro-Prussian: IV 19
  Balkan: IV 42; IX 24–6, 28, 38; X 7, 16
  Franco-Prussian: I 70
  Greek Independence: IX 14–15
  Greek-Ottoman: IX 24; XI 352
  Napoleonic: V 69
  Ottoman-Russian: V 74, 76, 78; IX 26
  Serbo-Bulgarian: X 16
  World War I: I 72, 74; II 14; III 8, 11; IV 11, 27, 34, 39; VII 13–15, 18, 28; VIII 54–5; IX 7, 12, 21, 26, 28–9, 31; XI 347–8, 351–3, 261–2
  World War II: I 67, 70, 77, 80, 82; III 1, 9, 14; VI 13, 16–17, 26; VIII 45, 49, 50, 53, 55; IX 27, 34, 29; X 9; XI 357
Warsaw: VIII 51
  Pact: III 15
WASP: I 82
Weber, Eugene: VII 16
Weber, Max: II 2; VII 18
Wekerle, Sándor: IV 32
Welsh: I 72, 76
Weltanschauung: VII 28; X 2
Westernization: II 5
Westernizers: VI 8–9
White Mountain (battle of): VIII 54
William II, Emperor (G): IV 5
Wilson, Woodrow: XI 353
Wilsonianism: IX 353–4
Windischgrätz, Prince Alfred: IV 32
Wohlgemut, Ludwig: IX 20
Woolf, S.J.: VII 15
Wyszyński, Stefan, Cardinal: VIII 57

Xenophobia: III 8

'Young Czechs': IV 17, 25–6, 32
Young Turks: IX 28
Ypsilantes, Alexandros: IX 10, 15–16
Yugoslav
  committee: IX 29
  idea: IV 7

(Yugoslav continued)
   movement: X 8
   nation: XI 354
Yugoslavs: XI 354, 358
Yugoslavia: I 71, 73, 79; III 8, 11–12, 14;
   VI 4; VII 26; VIII 50, 53, 56; IX 12, 21;
   IX 27–9, 31–3, 35–7; X 8; XI 355, 357–9
   disintegration of: VIII 52; IX 18, 20–21;
      XI 359
   royal dictatorship in: IX 31

Zach, Frantisek: X 8

Zadar
   Resolution: IV 7, 37
Zadruga: II 9
Zagreb
   trial: IV 38
Zastava: IV 14
Zeka, Haxhi Mulla: IX 28
Zhivkov, Todor: IX 38; X 13
Zichy, Count Aladár: IV 36
Zionists: IV 39
Žižkra: Jan: VIII 54–5
Zürich-London Agreement: IX 39